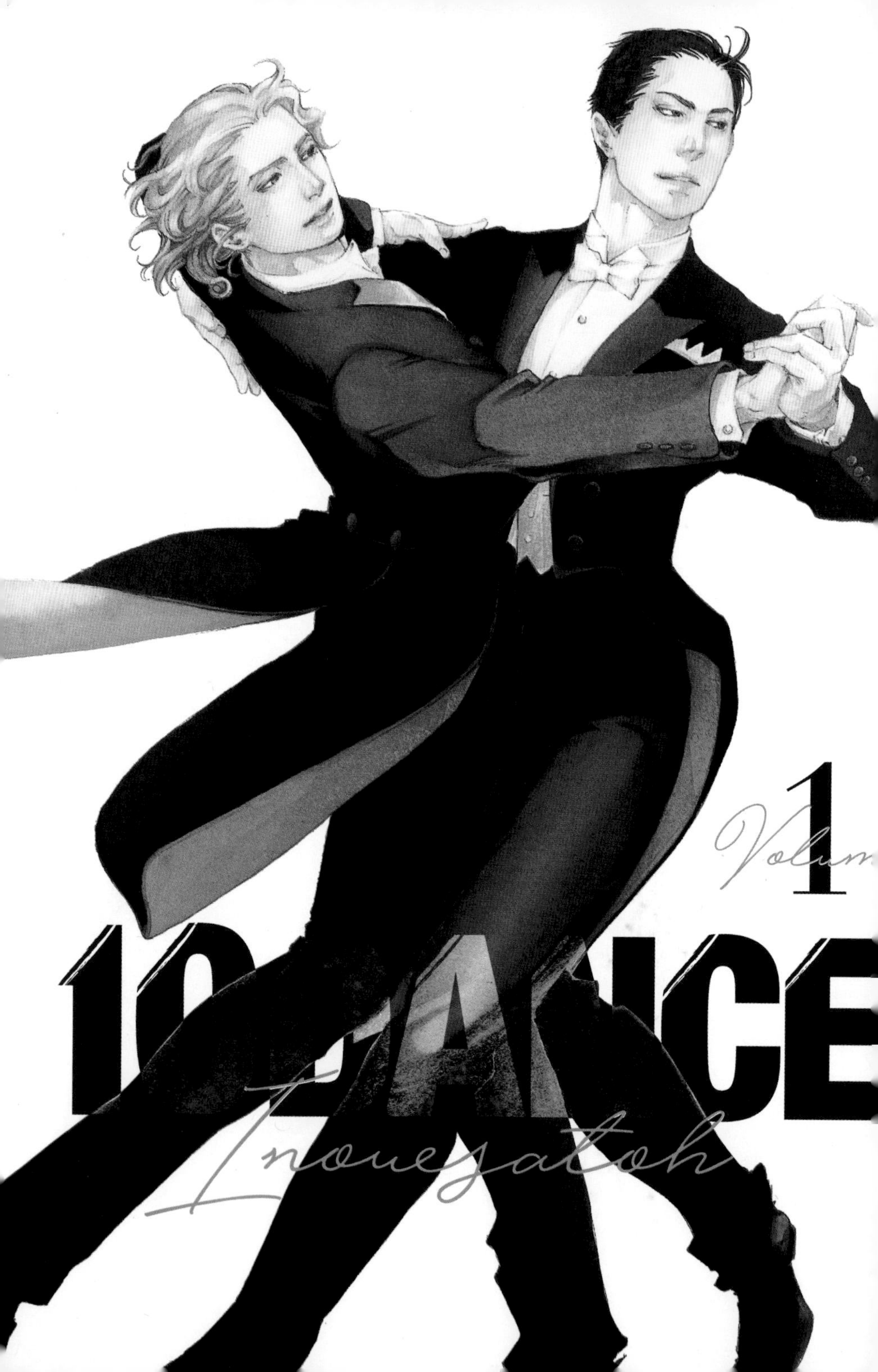

1
Volum
10DANCE
Inouesatoh

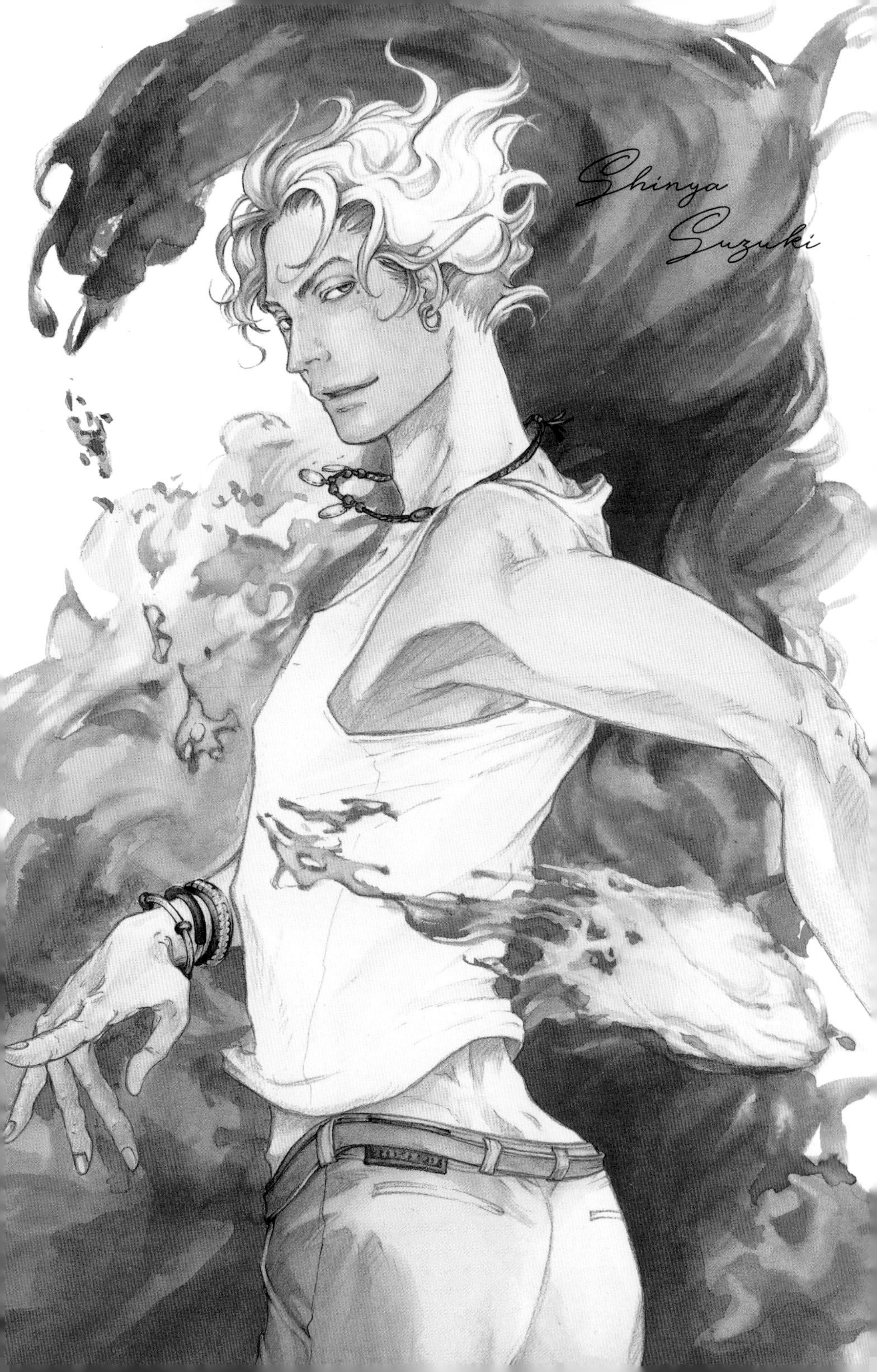
Shinya Suzuki

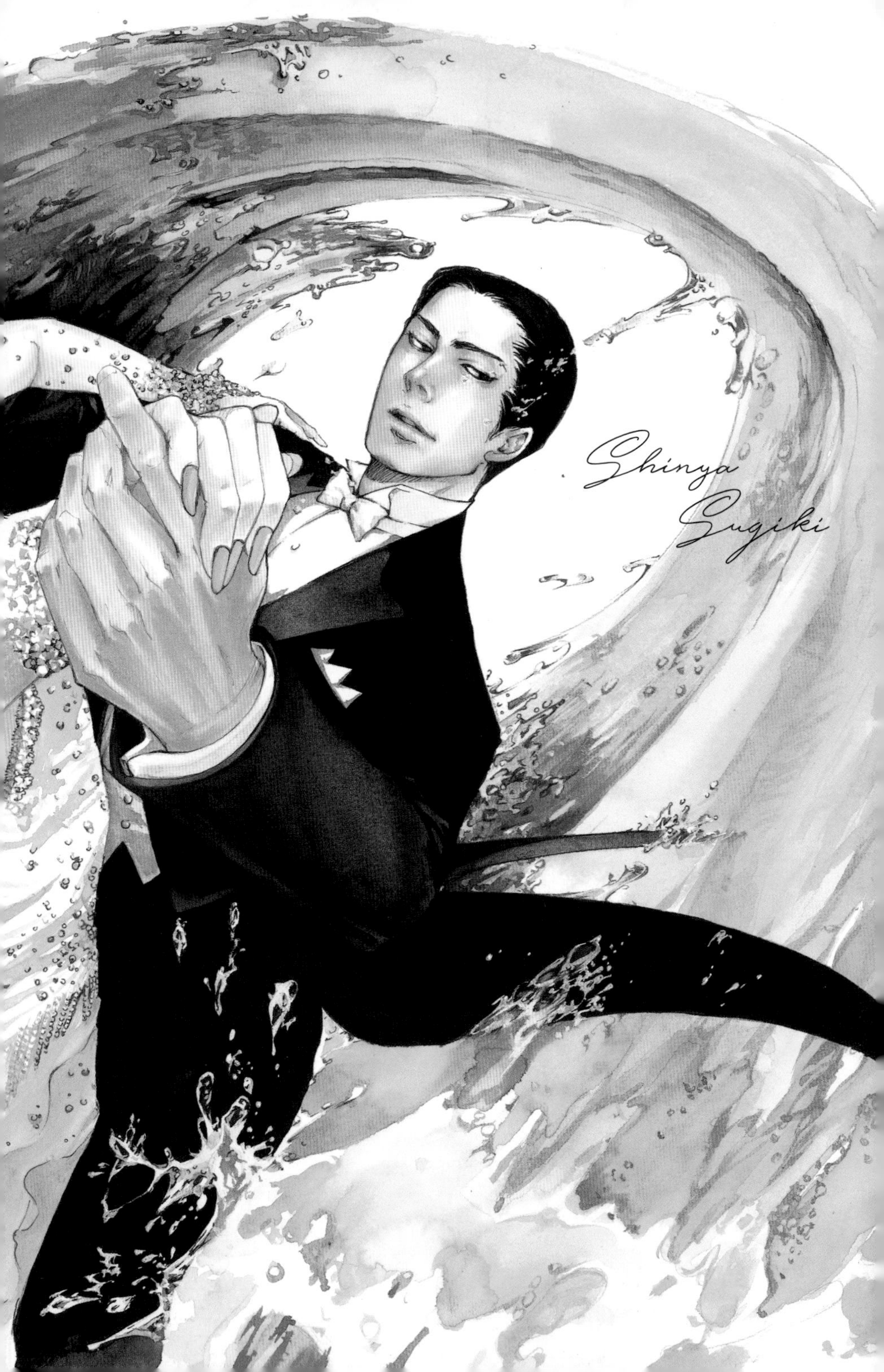
Shinya
Sugiki

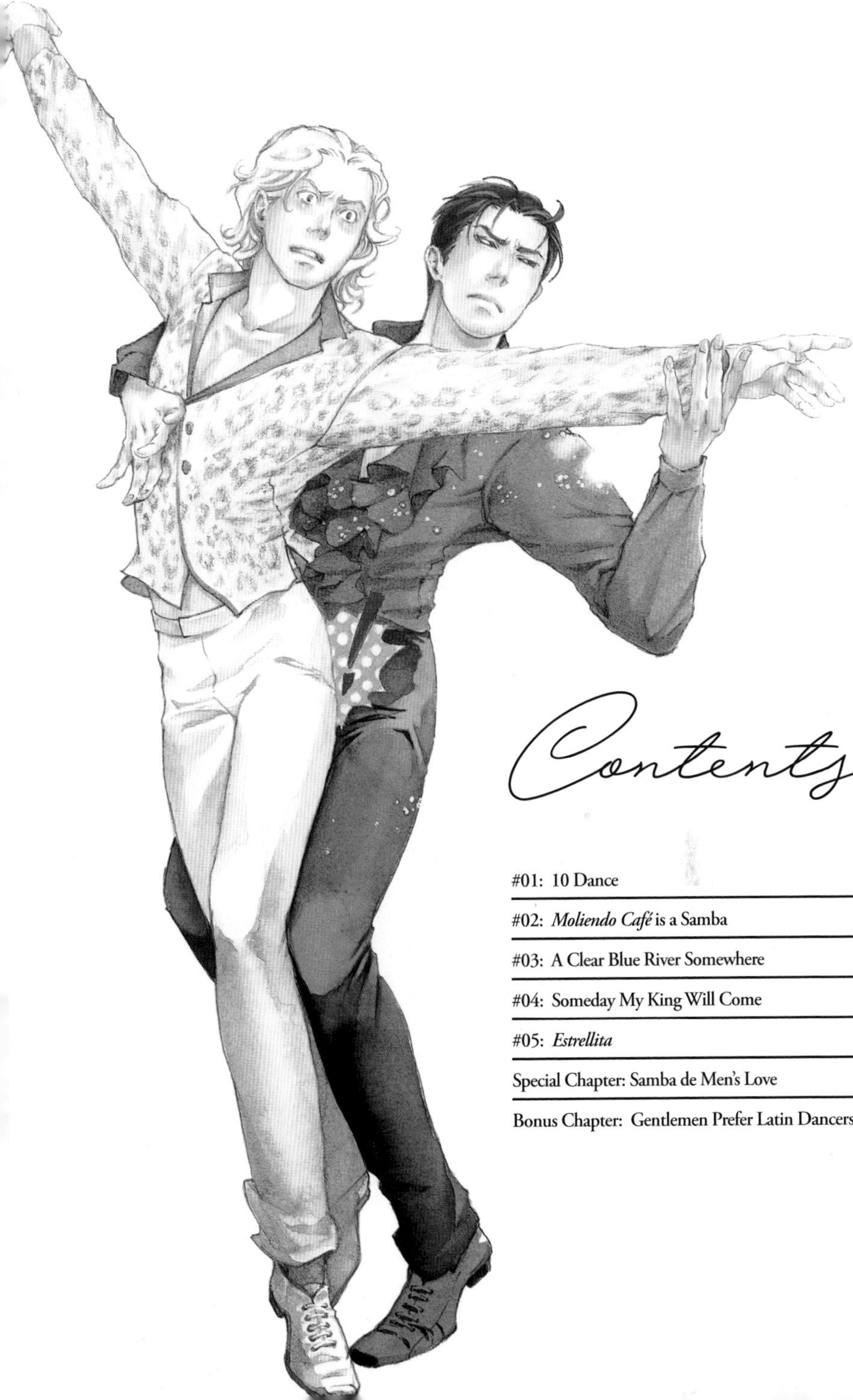

Contents

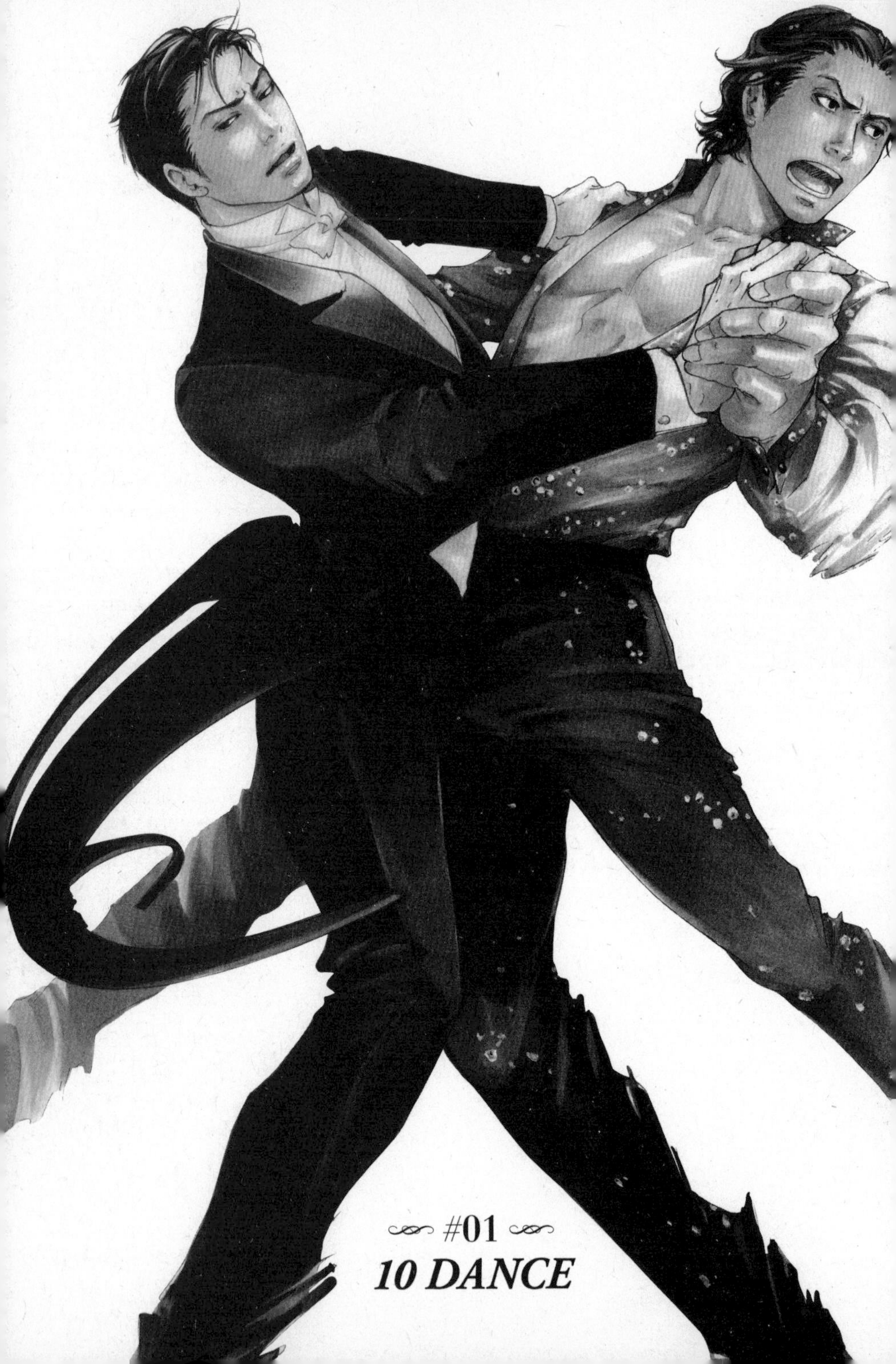

#01

10 DANCE

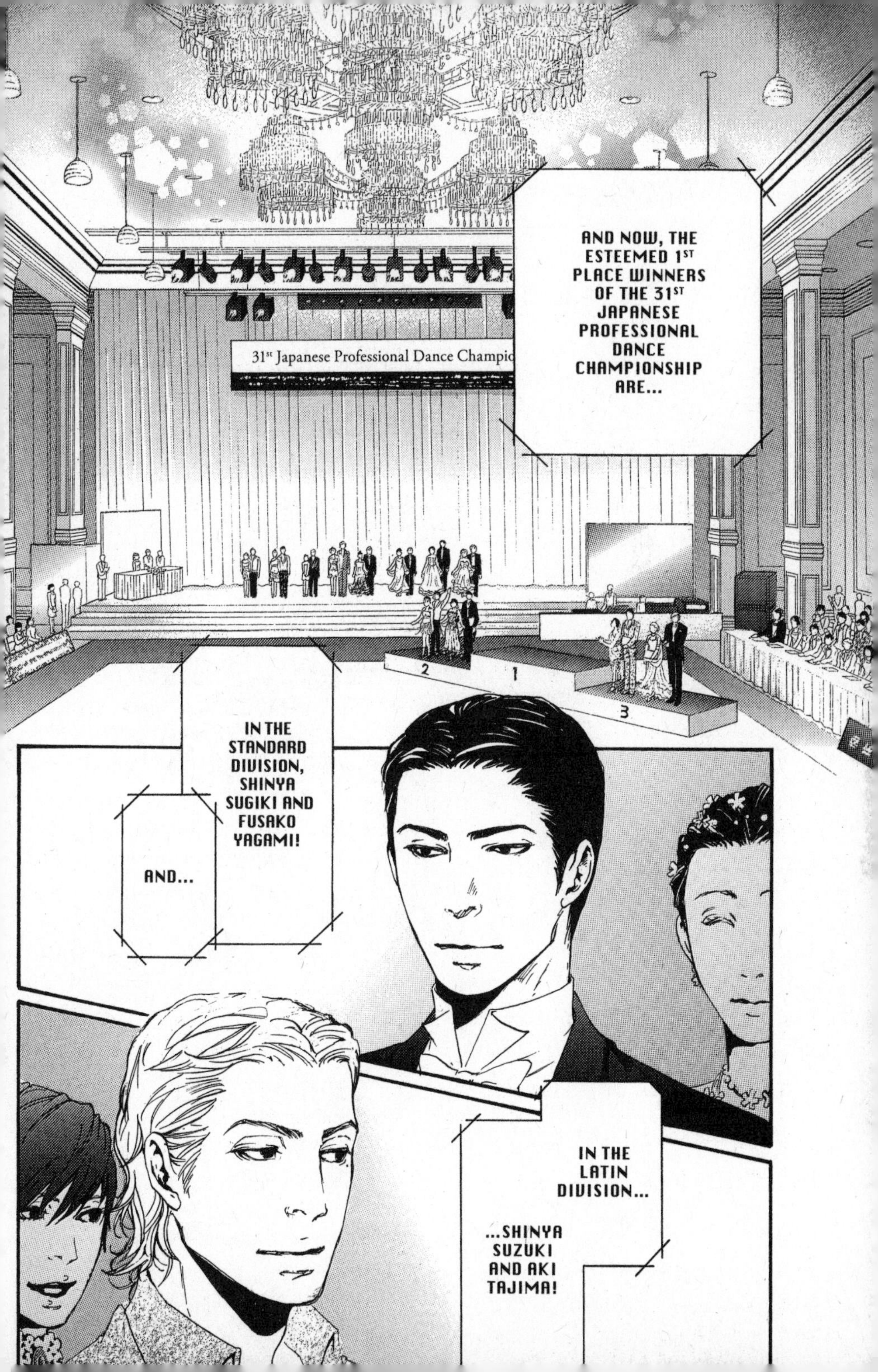
31st Japanese Professional Dance Champio
AND NOW, THE ESTEEMED 1ST PLACE WINNERS OF THE 31ST JAPANESE PROFESSIONAL DANCE CHAMPIONSHIP ARE...
2
1
3
IN THE STANDARD DIVISION, SHINYA SUGIKI AND FUSAKO YAGAMI!
AND...
IN THE LATIN DIVISION...
...SHINYA SUZUKI AND AKI TAJIMA!

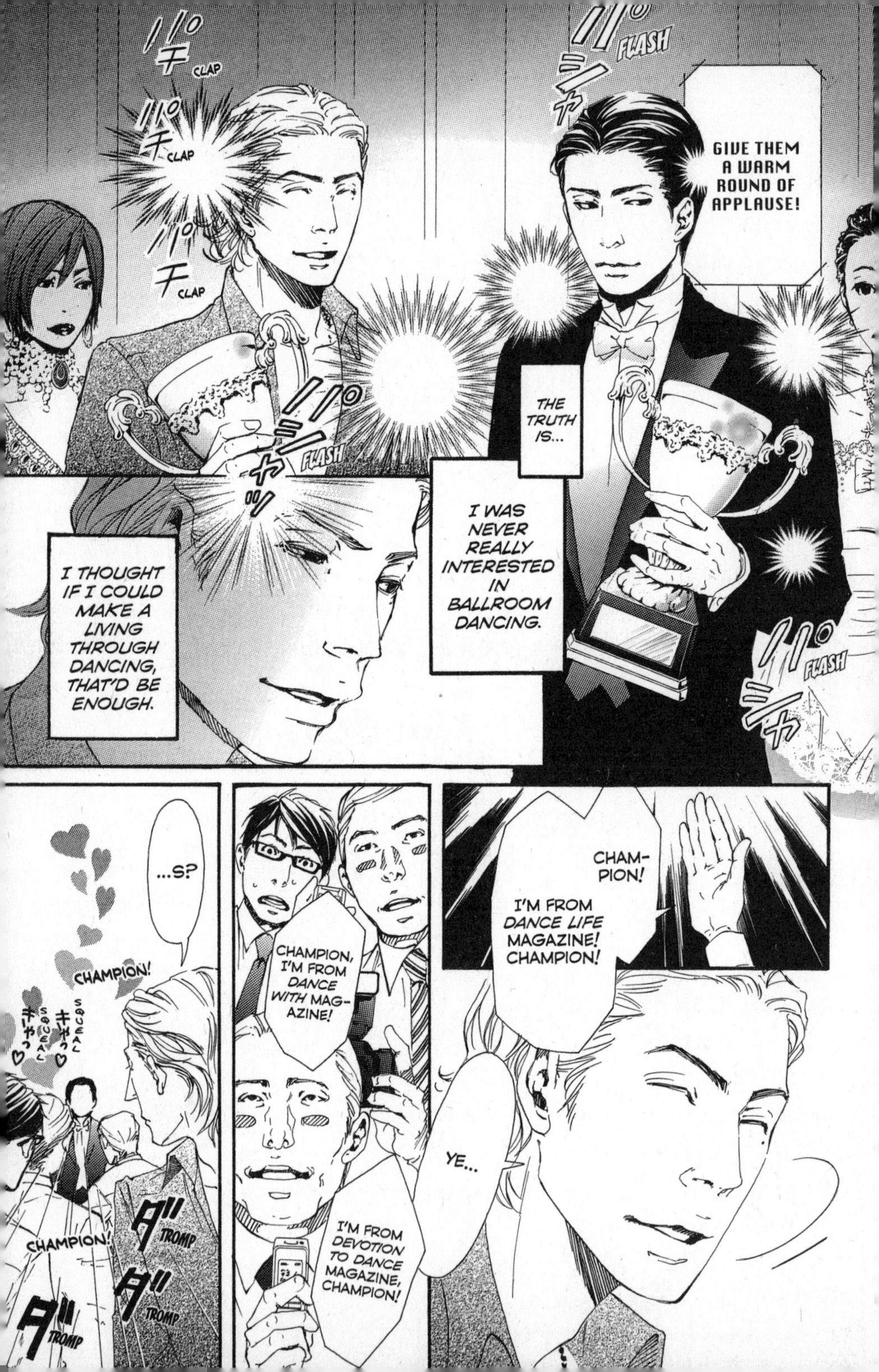

パシャ FLASH
GIVE THEM A WARM ROUND OF APPLAUSE!
パチ CLAP
パチ CLAP
パチ CLAP
パシャッ FLASH
THE TRUTH IS...
I WAS NEVER REALLY INTERESTED IN BALLROOM DANCING.
パシャ FLASH
I THOUGHT IF I COULD MAKE A LIVING THROUGH DANCING, THAT'D BE ENOUGH.
CHAMP-ION!
I'M FROM *DANCE LIFE* MAGAZINE! CHAMPION!
CHAMPION, I'M FROM *DANCE WITH* MAG-AZINE!
YE...
I'M FROM *DEVOTION TO DANCE* MAGAZINE, CHAMPION!
...S?
CHAMPION!
キャッ SQUEAL
キャッ SQUEAL
CHAMPION!
ダッ TROMP
ダッ TROMP
ダッ TROMP

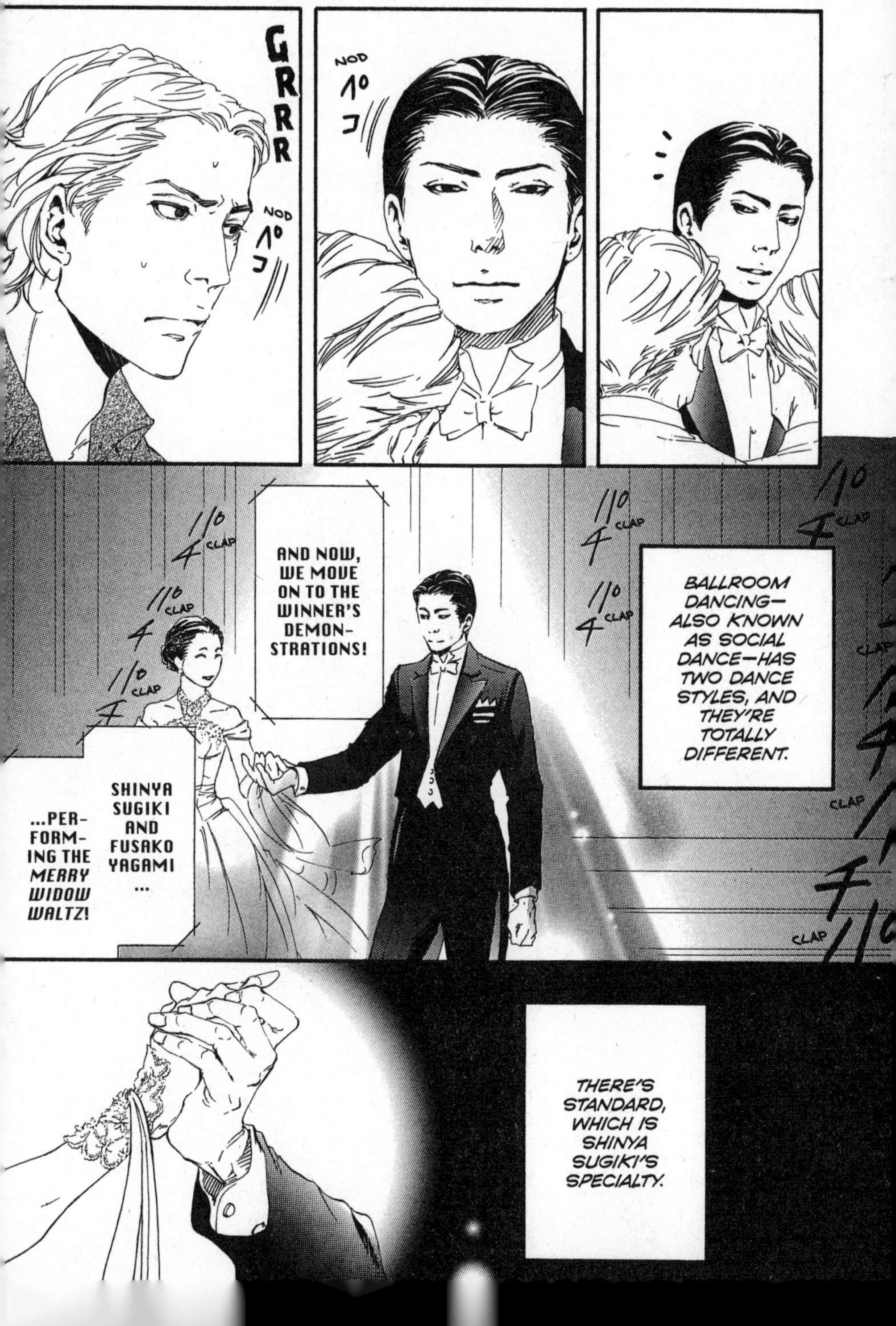
NOD
GRRR
NOD
BALLROOM DANCING—ALSO KNOWN AS SOCIAL DANCE—HAS TWO DANCE STYLES, AND THEY'RE TOTALLY DIFFERENT.
CLAP
CLAP
CLAP
CLAP
CLAP
CLAP
CLAP
CLAP
AND NOW, WE MOVE ON TO THE WINNER'S DEMON-STRATIONS!
SHINYA SUGIKI AND FUSAKO YAGAMI ...
...PER-FORM-ING THE *MERRY WIDOW WALTZ!*
THERE'S STANDARD, WHICH IS SHINYA SUGIKI'S SPECIALTY.

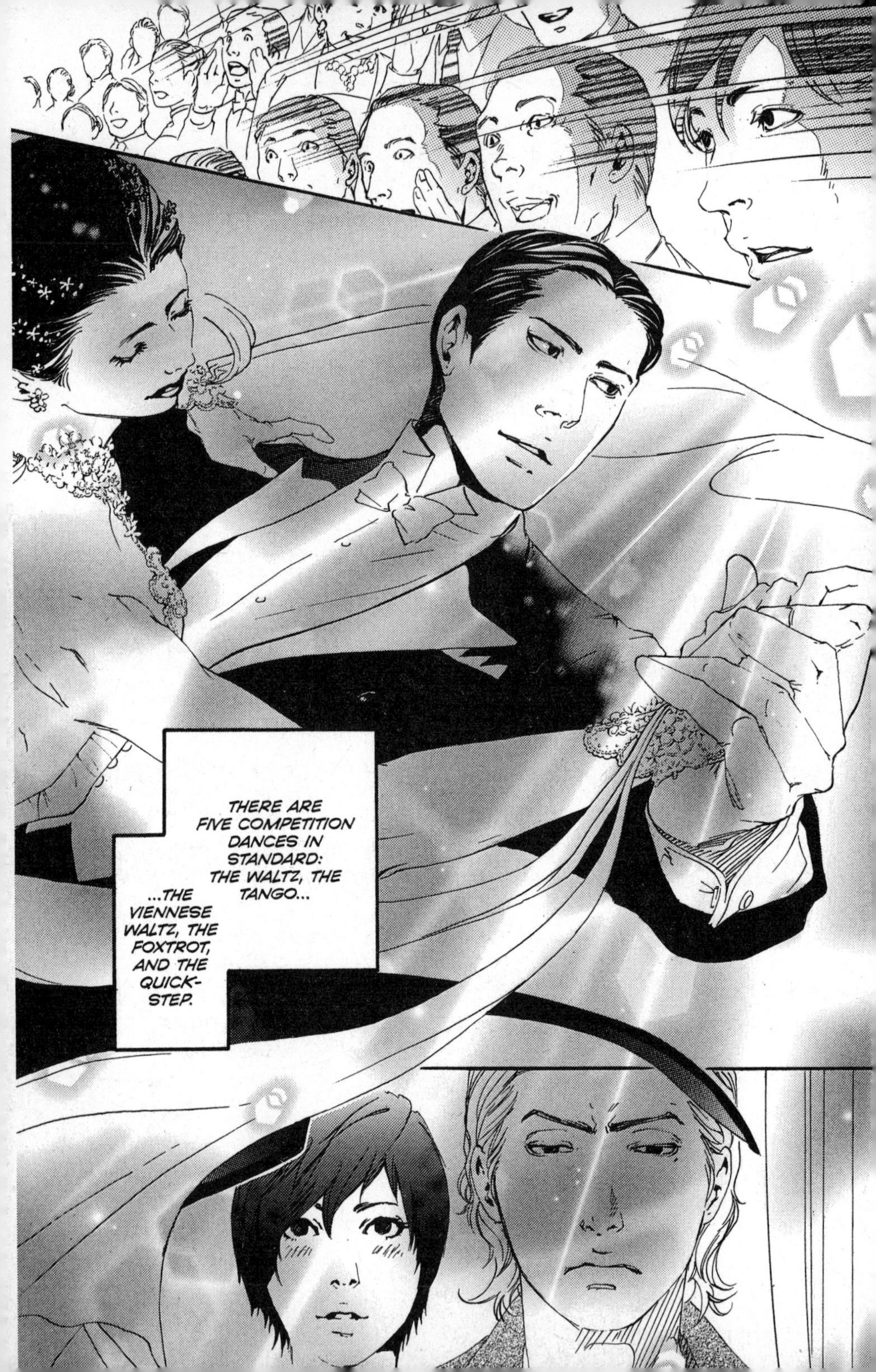
THERE ARE FIVE COMPETITION DANCES IN STANDARD: THE WALTZ, THE TANGO...
...THE VIENNESE WALTZ, THE FOXTROT, AND THE QUICK-STEP.

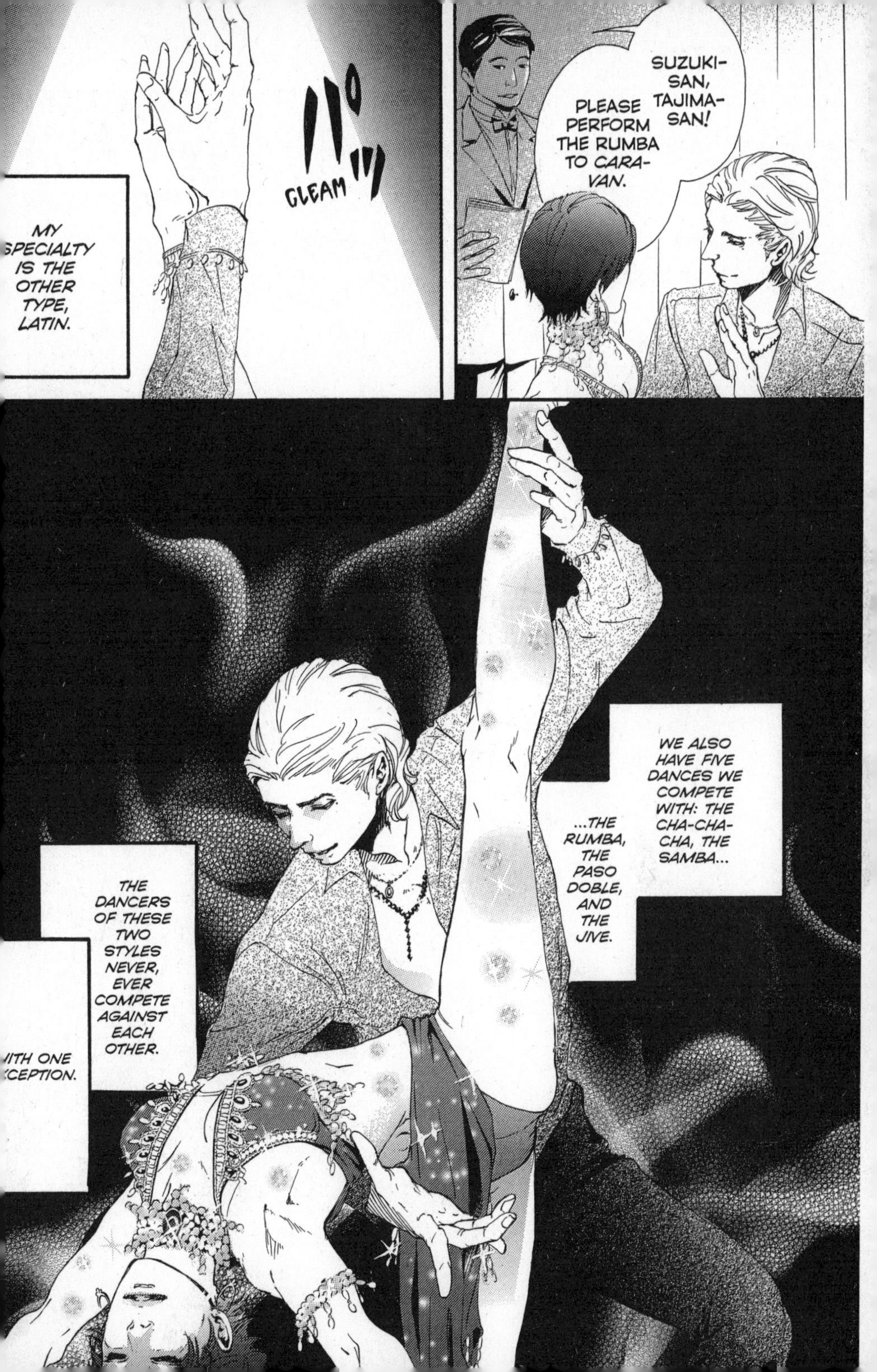

SUZUKI-SAN, TAJIMA-SAN!
PLEASE PERFORM THE RUMBA TO CARAVAN.
GLEAM
MY SPECIALTY IS THE OTHER TYPE, LATIN.
WE ALSO HAVE FIVE DANCES WE COMPETE WITH: THE CHA-CHA-CHA, THE SAMBA...
...THE RUMBA, THE PASO DOBLE, AND THE JIVE.
THE DANCERS OF THESE TWO STYLES NEVER, EVER COMPETE AGAINST EACH OTHER.
WITH ONE EXCEPTION.

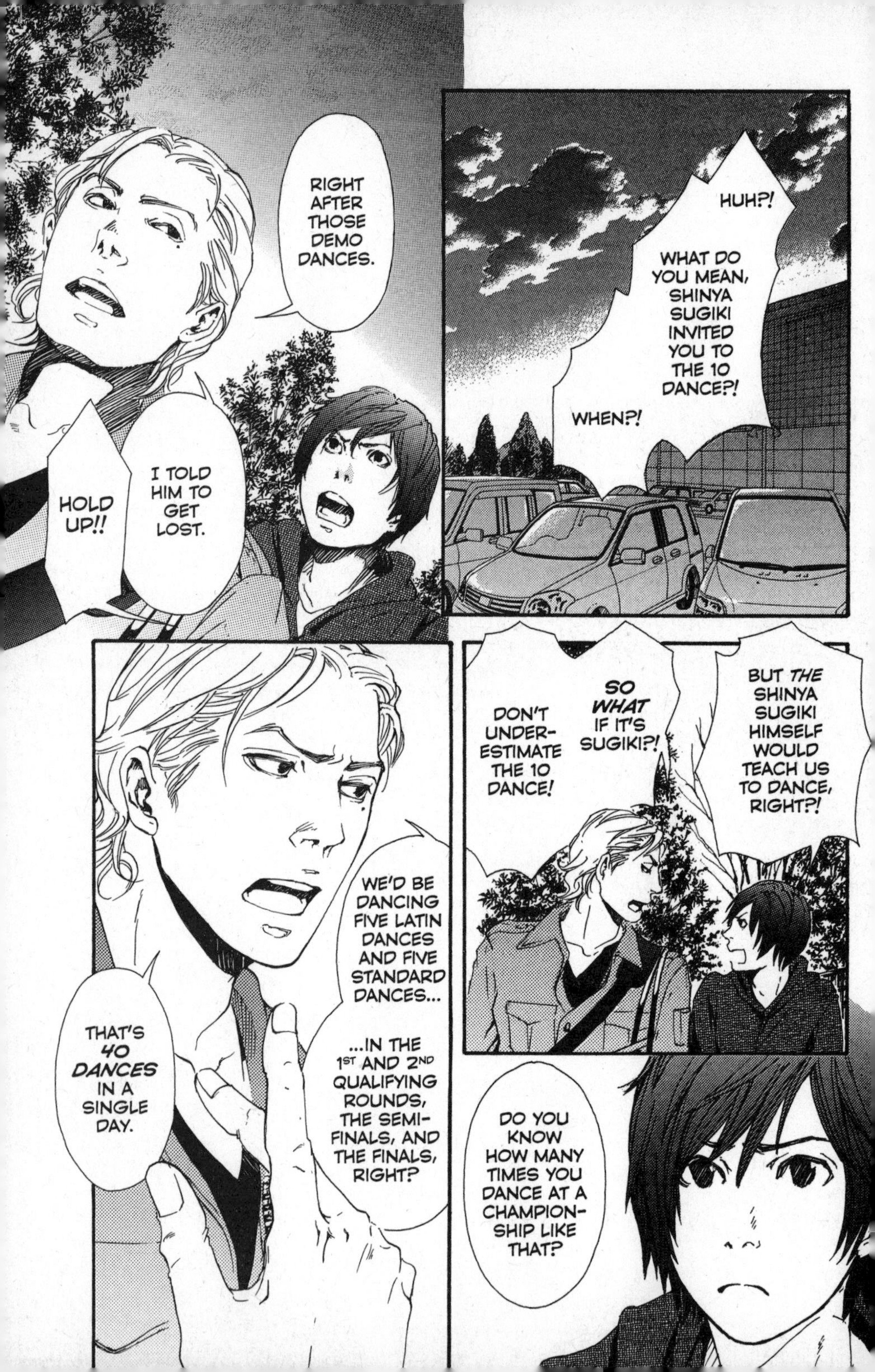
HUH?!
WHAT DO YOU MEAN, SHINYA SUGIKI INVITED YOU TO THE 10 DANCE?!
WHEN?!
RIGHT AFTER THOSE DEMO DANCES.
I TOLD HIM TO GET LOST.
HOLD UP!!
BUT *THE* SHINYA SUGIKI HIMSELF WOULD TEACH US TO DANCE, RIGHT?!
SO WHAT IF IT'S SUGIKI?!
DON'T UNDER-ESTIMATE THE 10 DANCE!
DO YOU KNOW HOW MANY TIMES YOU DANCE AT A CHAMPION-SHIP LIKE THAT?
WE'D BE DANCING FIVE LATIN DANCES AND FIVE STANDARD DANCES...
...IN THE 1ST AND 2ND QUALIFYING ROUNDS, THE SEMI-FINALS, AND THE FINALS, RIGHT?
THAT'S *40 DANCES* IN A SINGLE DAY.

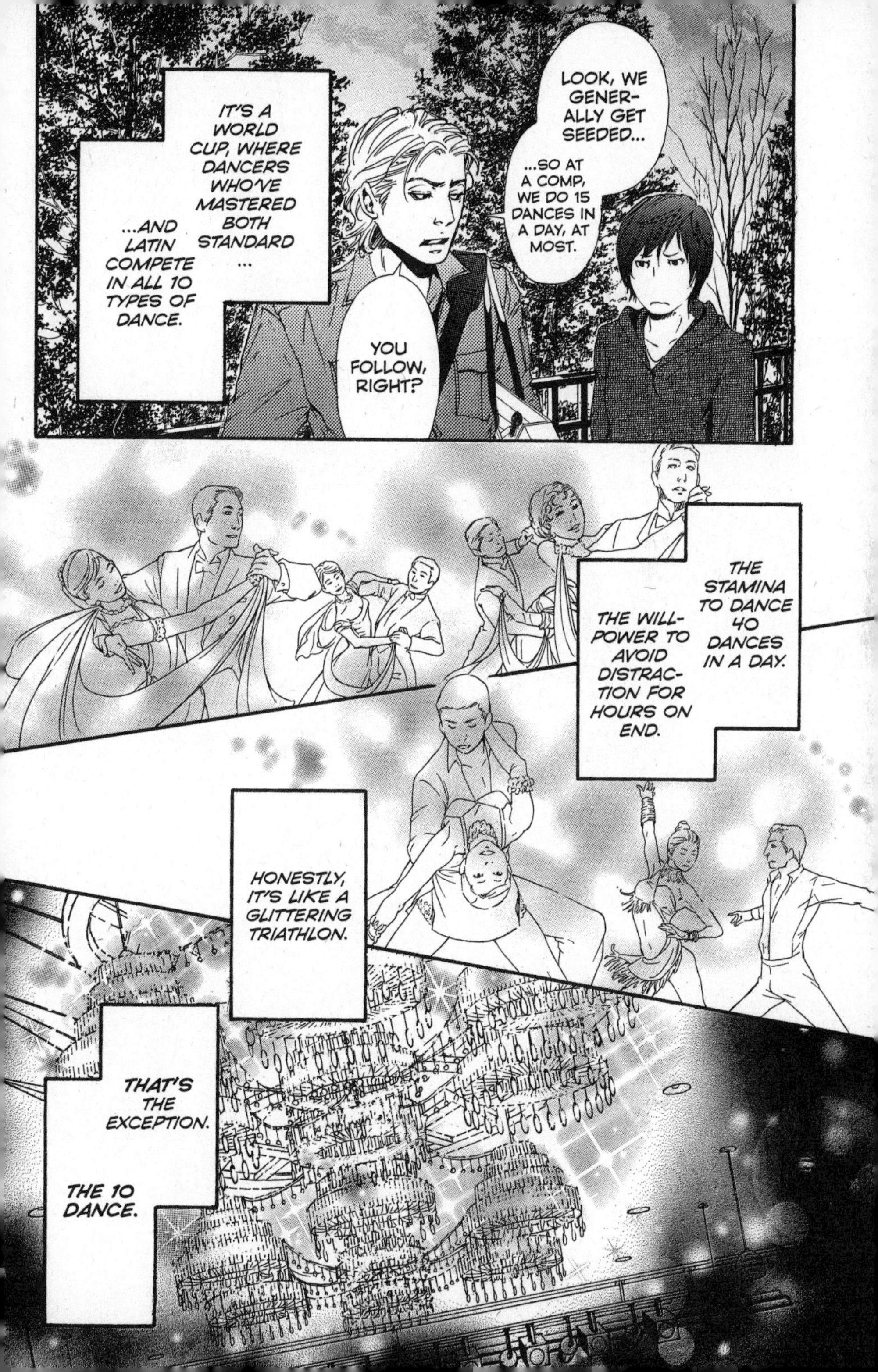
LOOK, WE GENER-ALLY GET SEEDED...
...SO AT A COMP, WE DO 15 DANCES IN A DAY, AT MOST.
YOU FOLLOW, RIGHT?
IT'S A WORLD CUP, WHERE DANCERS WHO'VE MASTERED BOTH STANDARD ...
...AND LATIN COMPETE IN ALL 10 TYPES OF DANCE.
THE STAMINA TO DANCE 40 DANCES IN A DAY.
THE WILL-POWER TO AVOID DISTRAC-TION FOR HOURS ON END.
HONESTLY, IT'S LIKE A GLITTERING TRIATHLON.
THAT'S THE EXCEPTION.
THE 10 DANCE.

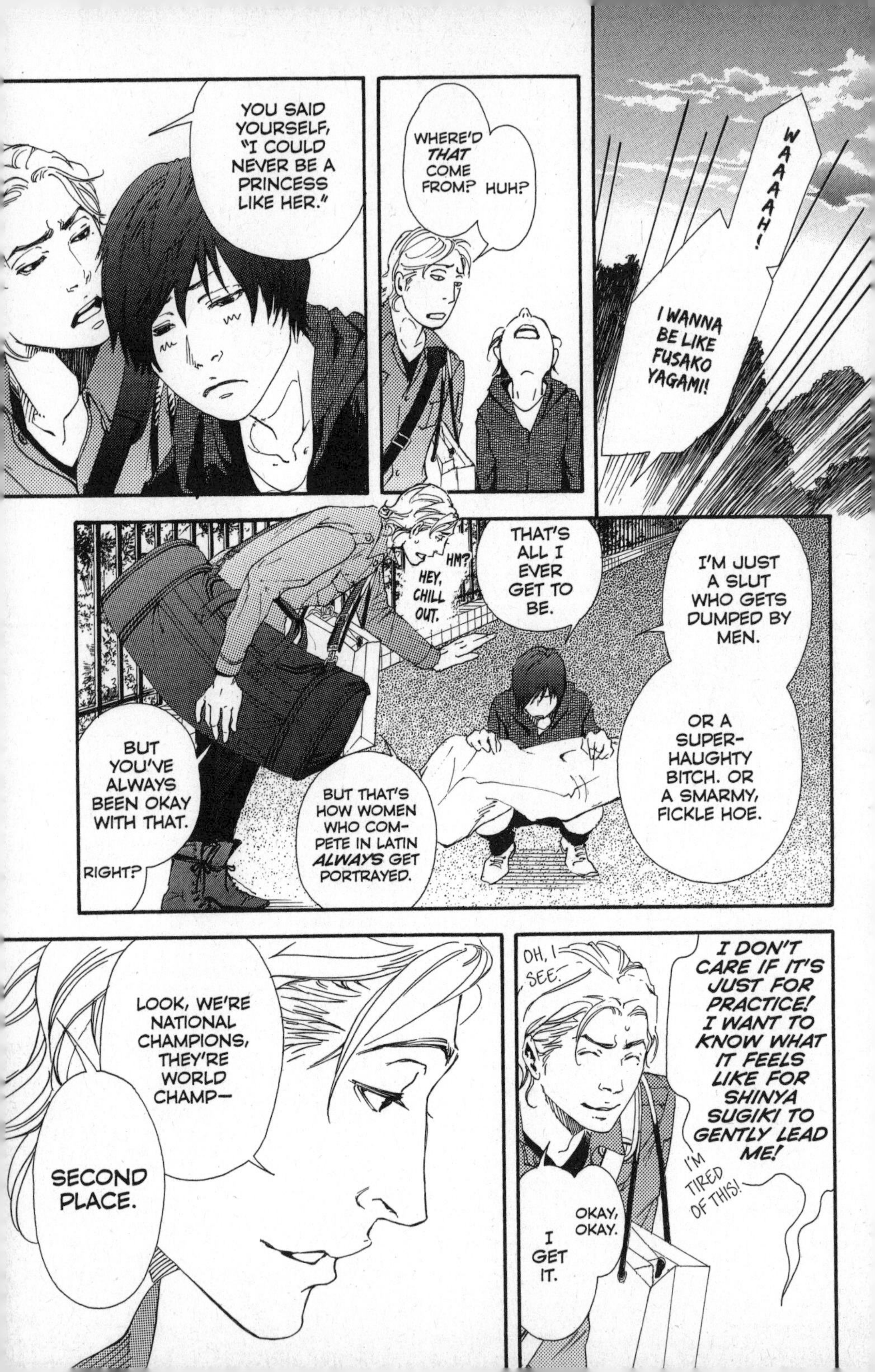
WAAAAAH!
I WANNA BE LIKE FUSAKO YAGAMI!
WHERE'D THAT COME FROM? HUH?
YOU SAID YOURSELF, "I COULD NEVER BE A PRINCESS LIKE HER."
I'M JUST A SLUT WHO GETS DUMPED BY MEN.
OR A SUPER-HAUGHTY BITCH. OR A SMARMY, FICKLE HOE.
THAT'S ALL I EVER GET TO BE.
HM?
HEY, CHILL OUT.
BUT THAT'S HOW WOMEN WHO COMPETE IN LATIN ALWAYS GET PORTRAYED.
BUT YOU'VE ALWAYS BEEN OKAY WITH THAT.
RIGHT?
I DON'T CARE IF IT'S JUST FOR PRACTICE! I WANT TO KNOW WHAT IT FEELS LIKE FOR SHINYA SUGIKI TO GENTLY LEAD ME!
I'M TIRED OF THIS!
OH, I SEE.
OKAY, OKAY.
I GET IT.
LOOK, WE'RE NATIONAL CHAMPIONS, THEY'RE WORLD CHAMP—
SECOND PLACE.

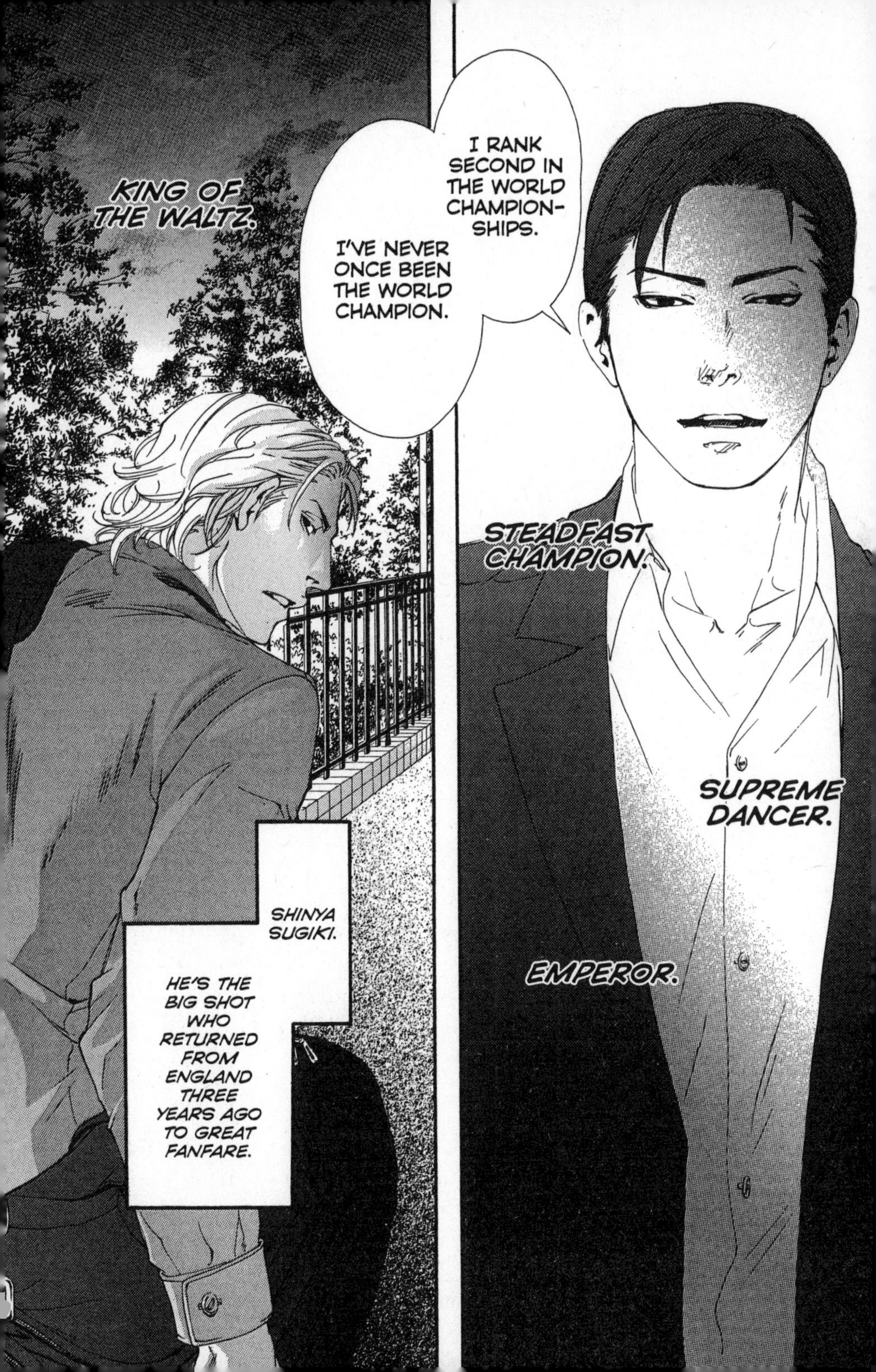
I RANK SECOND IN THE WORLD CHAMPIONSHIPS.
I'VE NEVER ONCE BEEN THE WORLD CHAMPION.
STEADFAST CHAMPION.
SUPREME DANCER.
EMPEROR.
KING OF THE WALTZ.
SHINYA SUGIKI.
HE'S THE BIG SHOT WHO RETURNED FROM ENGLAND THREE YEARS AGO TO GREAT FANFARE.

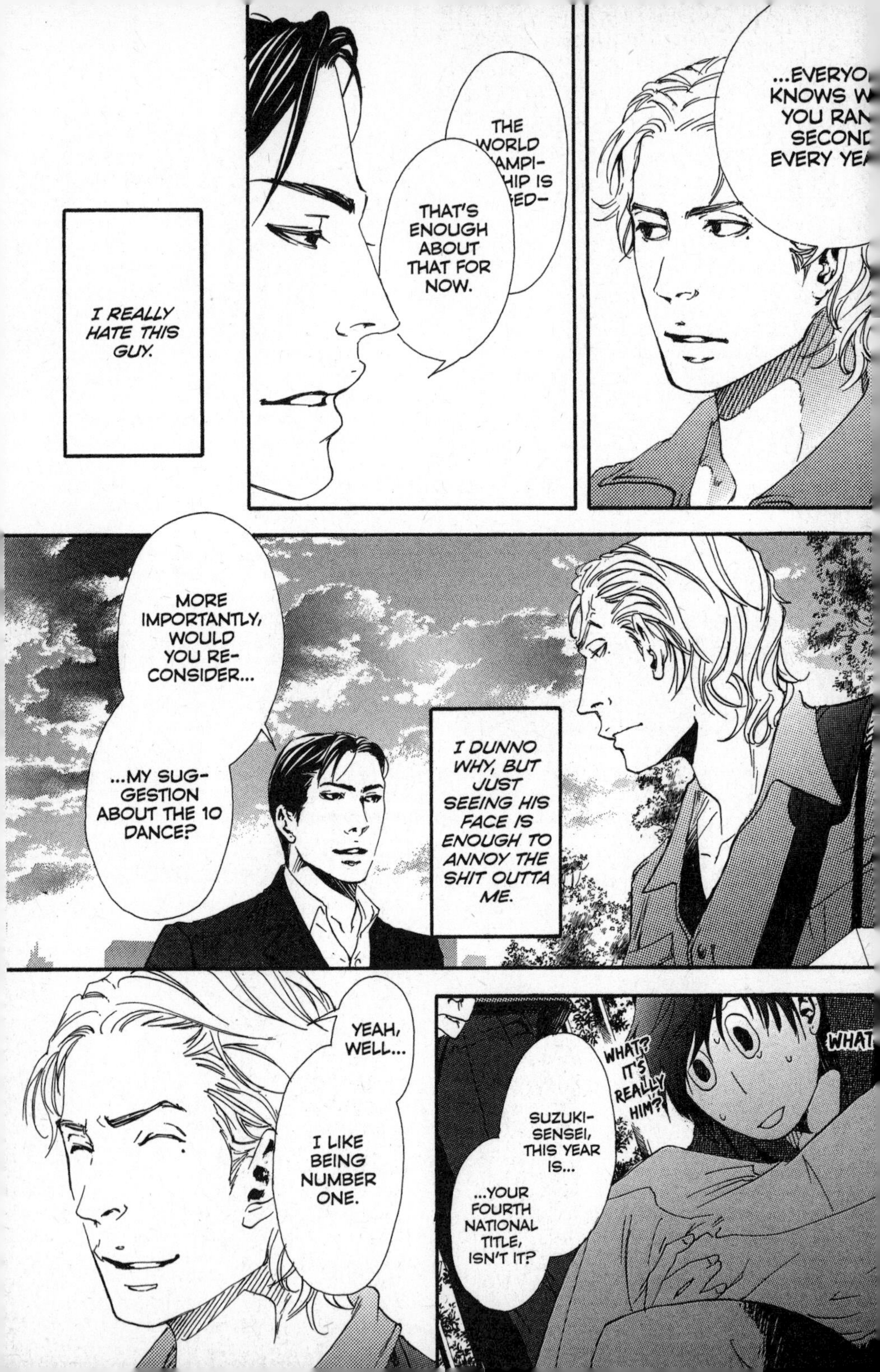
...EVERYO KNOWS W YOU RAN SECOND EVERY YEA
THE WORLD AMPI- HIP IS GED–
THAT'S ENOUGH ABOUT THAT FOR NOW.
I REALLY HATE THIS GUY.
MORE IMPORTANTLY, WOULD YOU RE-CONSIDER...
...MY SUG-GESTION ABOUT THE 10 DANCE?
I DUNNO WHY, BUT JUST SEEING HIS FACE IS ENOUGH TO ANNOY THE SHIT OUTTA ME.
WHAT
WHAT? IT'S REALLY HIM?
SUZUKI-SENSEI, THIS YEAR IS...
...YOUR FOURTH NATIONAL TITLE, ISN'T IT?
YEAH, WELL...
I LIKE BEING NUMBER ONE.

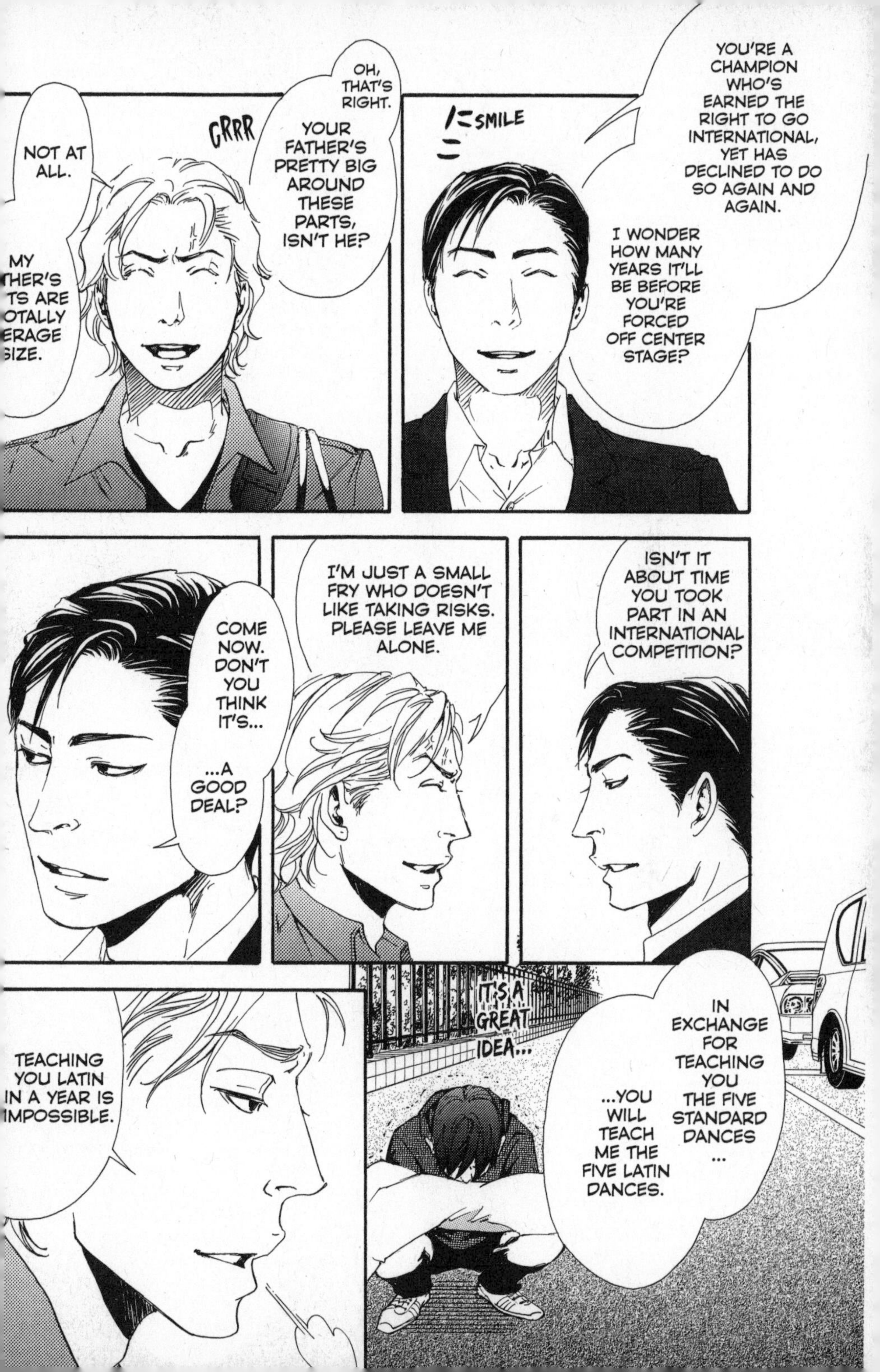
YOU'RE A CHAMPION WHO'S EARNED THE RIGHT TO GO INTERNATIONAL, YET HAS DECLINED TO DO SO AGAIN AND AGAIN.
I WONDER HOW MANY YEARS IT'LL BE BEFORE YOU'RE FORCED OFF CENTER STAGE?
SMILE
OH, THAT'S RIGHT.
YOUR FATHER'S PRETTY BIG AROUND THESE PARTS, ISN'T HE?
GRRR
NOT AT ALL.
MY
THER'S
TS ARE
OTALLY
ERAGE
SIZE.
ISN'T IT ABOUT TIME YOU TOOK PART IN AN INTERNATIONAL COMPETITION?
I'M JUST A SMALL FRY WHO DOESN'T LIKE TAKING RISKS. PLEASE LEAVE ME ALONE.
COME NOW. DON'T YOU THINK IT'S...
...A GOOD DEAL?
IN EXCHANGE FOR TEACHING YOU THE FIVE STANDARD DANCES ...
...YOU WILL TEACH ME THE FIVE LATIN DANCES.
IT'S A GREAT IDEA...
TEACHING YOU LATIN IN A YEAR IS IMPOSSIBLE.

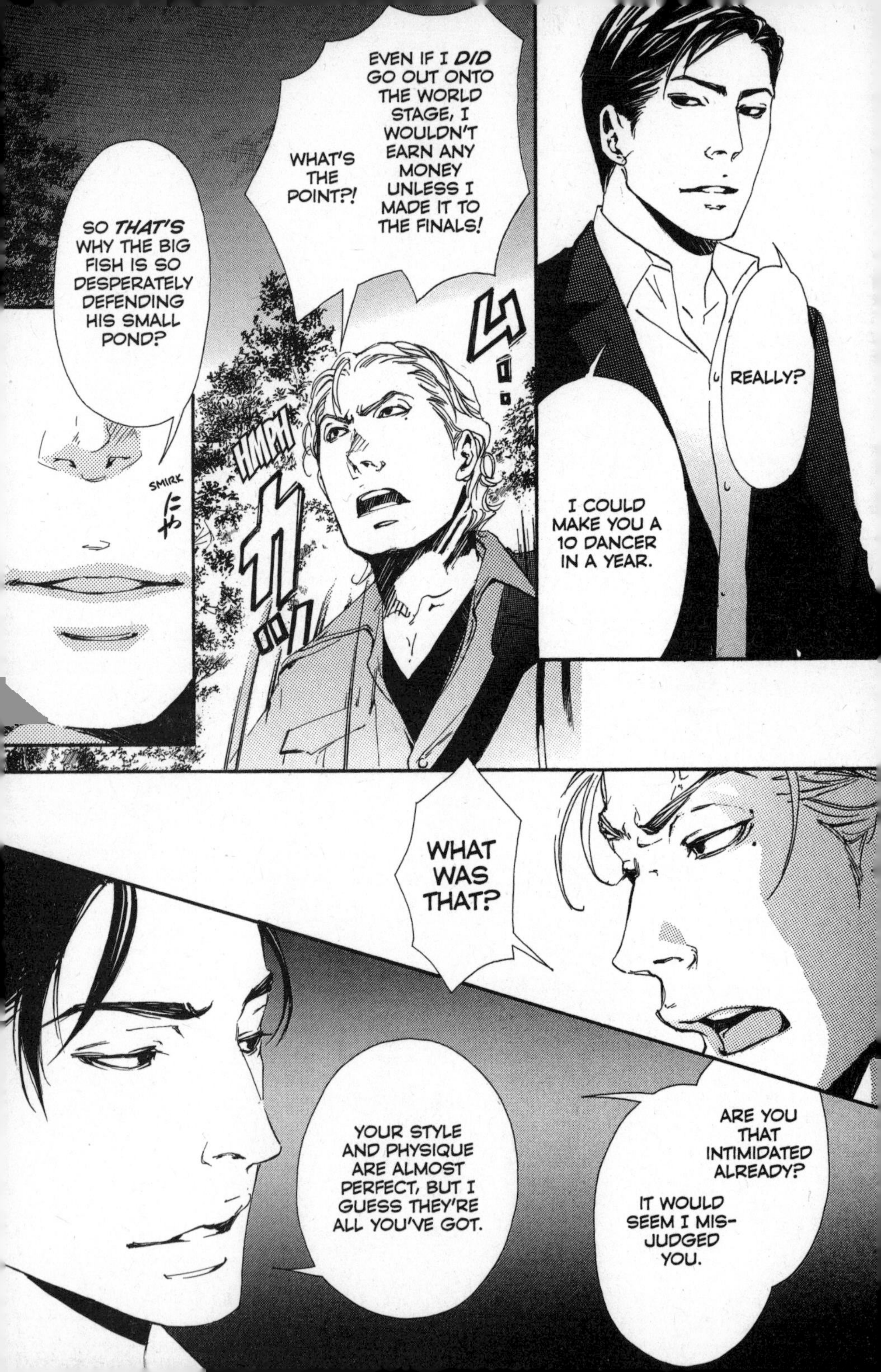
REALLY?
I COULD MAKE YOU A 10 DANCER IN A YEAR.
EVEN IF I *DID* GO OUT ONTO THE WORLD STAGE, I WOULDN'T EARN ANY MONEY UNLESS I MADE IT TO THE FINALS!
WHAT'S THE POINT?!
HMPH
SO *THAT'S* WHY THE BIG FISH IS SO DESPERATELY DEFENDING HIS SMALL POND?
SMIRK
にや
WHAT WAS THAT?
ARE YOU THAT INTIMIDATED ALREADY?
IT WOULD SEEM I MIS-JUDGED YOU.
YOUR STYLE AND PHYSIQUE ARE ALMOST PERFECT, BUT I GUESS THEY'RE ALL YOU'VE GOT.

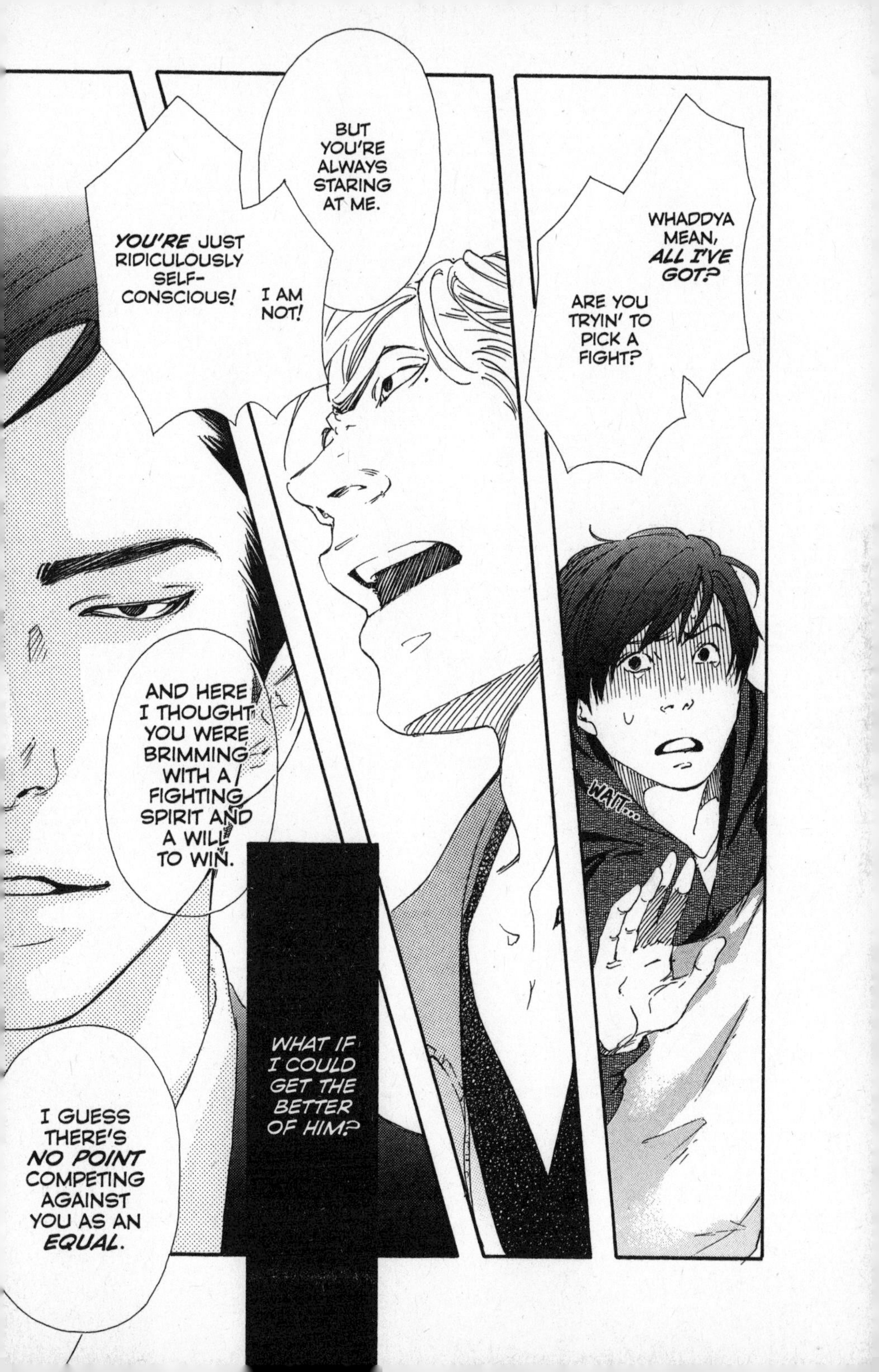
WHADDYA MEAN, ***ALL I'VE GOT?***
ARE YOU TRYIN' TO PICK A FIGHT?
WAIT...
BUT YOU'RE ALWAYS STARING AT ME.
I AM NOT!
YOU'RE JUST RIDICULOUSLY SELF-CONSCIOUS!
AND HERE I THOUGHT YOU WERE BRIMMING WITH A FIGHTING SPIRIT AND A WILL TO WIN.
WHAT IF I COULD GET THE BETTER OF HIM?
I GUESS THERE'S ***NO POINT*** COMPETING AGAINST YOU AS AN ***EQUAL***.

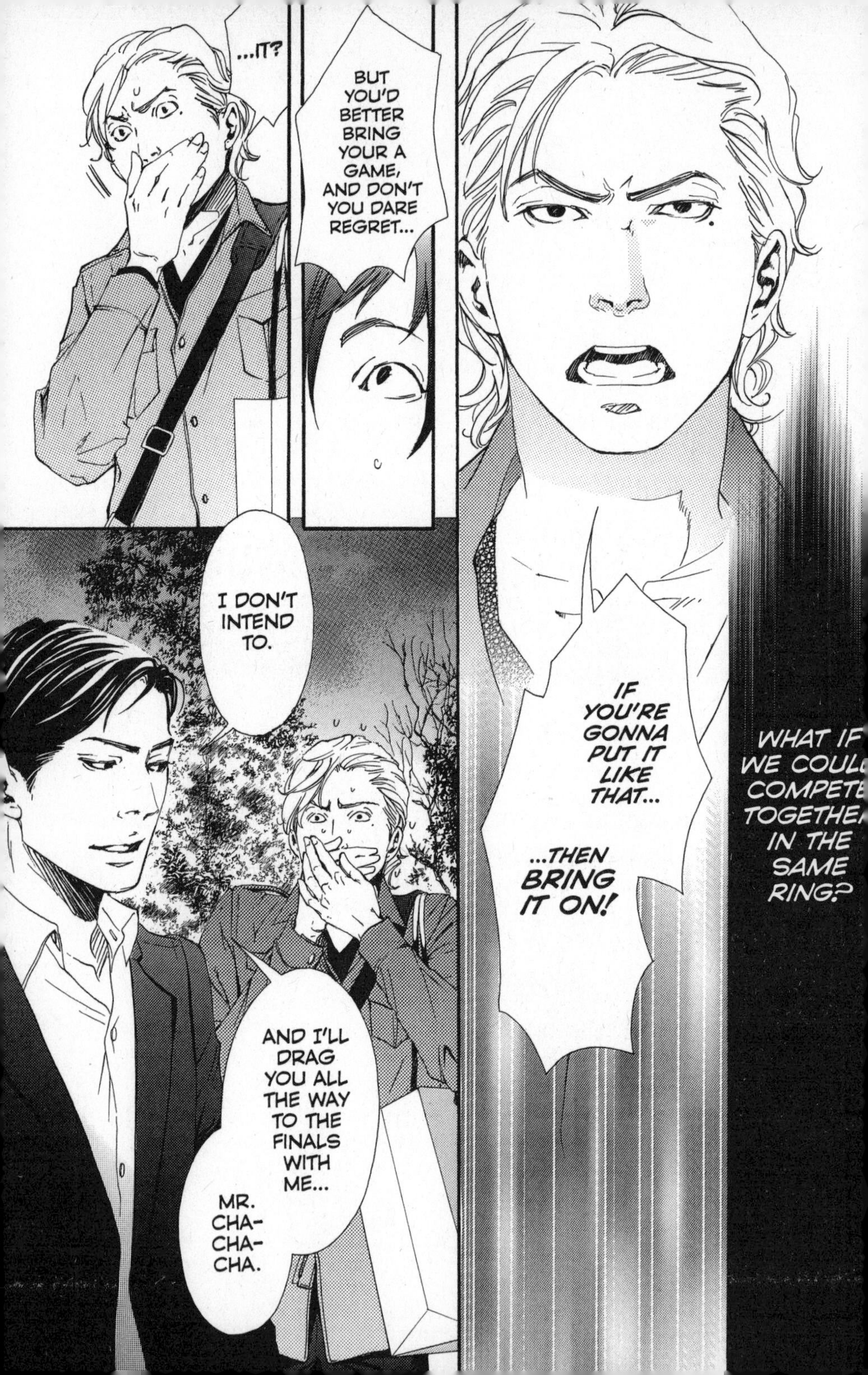
IF YOU'RE GONNA PUT IT LIKE THAT...
...THEN BRING IT ON!
WHAT IF WE COULD COMPETE TOGETHER IN THE SAME RING?
BUT YOU'D BETTER BRING YOUR A GAME, AND DON'T YOU DARE REGRET...
...IT?
I DON'T INTEND TO.
AND I'LL DRAG YOU ALL THE WAY TO THE FINALS WITH ME... MR. CHA-CHA-CHA.

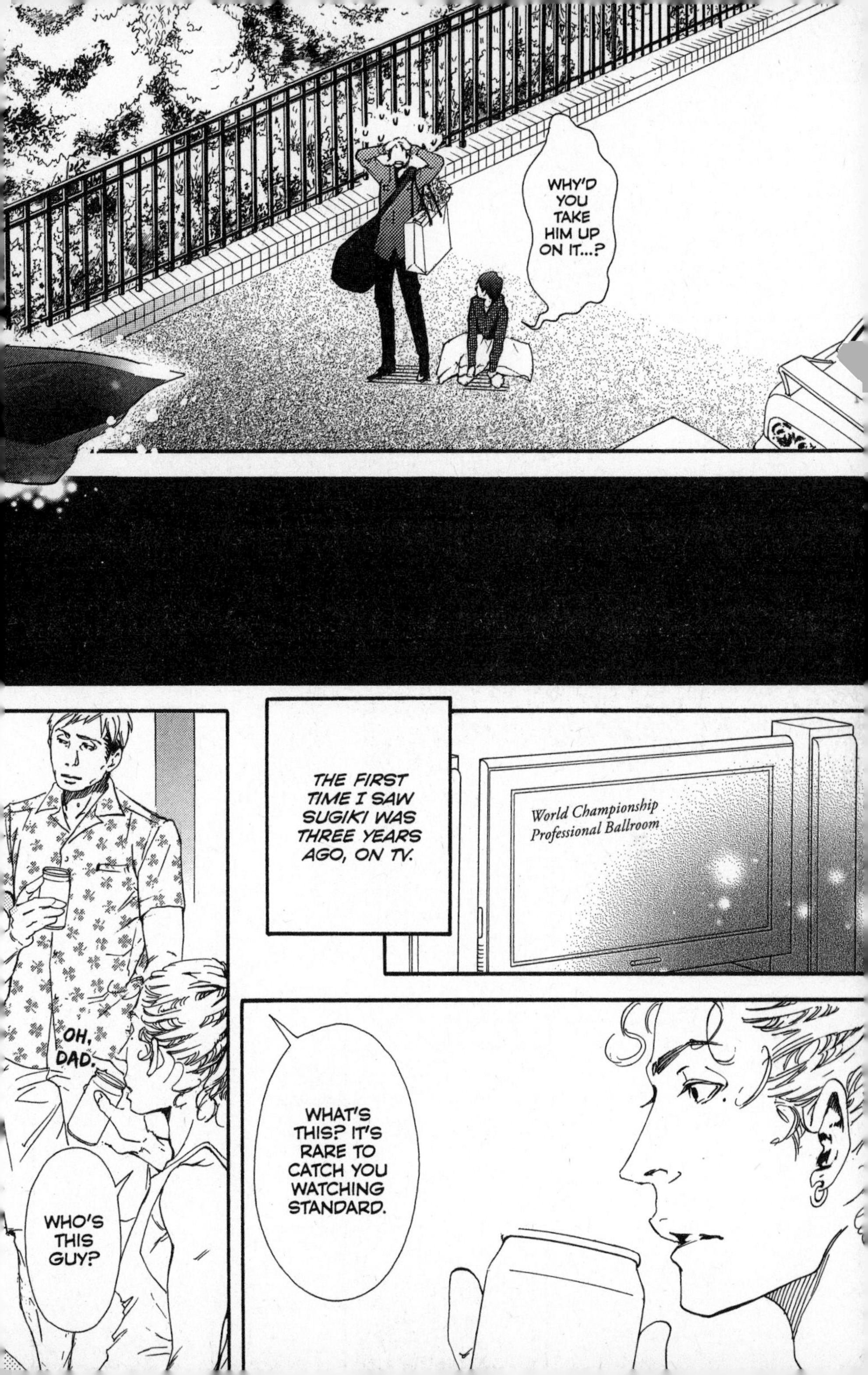
WHY'D YOU TAKE HIM UP ON IT...?
World Championship Professional Ballroom
THE FIRST TIME I SAW SUGIKI WAS THREE YEARS AGO, ON TV.
WHAT'S THIS? IT'S RARE TO CATCH YOU WATCHING STANDARD.
OH, DAD.
WHO'S THIS GUY?

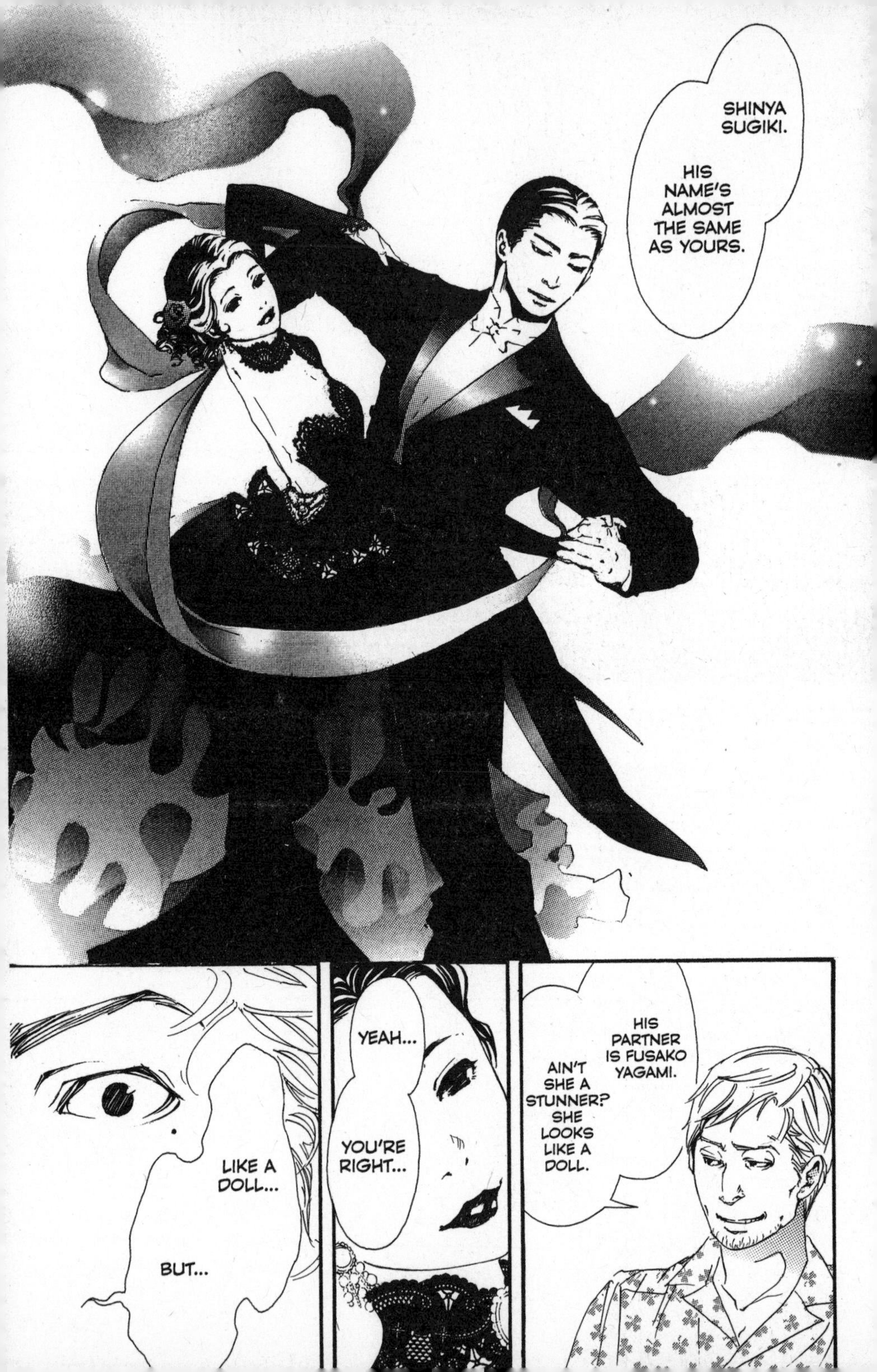
SHINYA SUGIKI.
HIS NAME'S ALMOST THE SAME AS YOURS.
HIS PARTNER IS FUSAKO YAGAMI.
AIN'T SHE A STUNNER? SHE LOOKS LIKE A DOLL.
YEAH...
YOU'RE RIGHT...
LIKE A DOLL...
BUT...

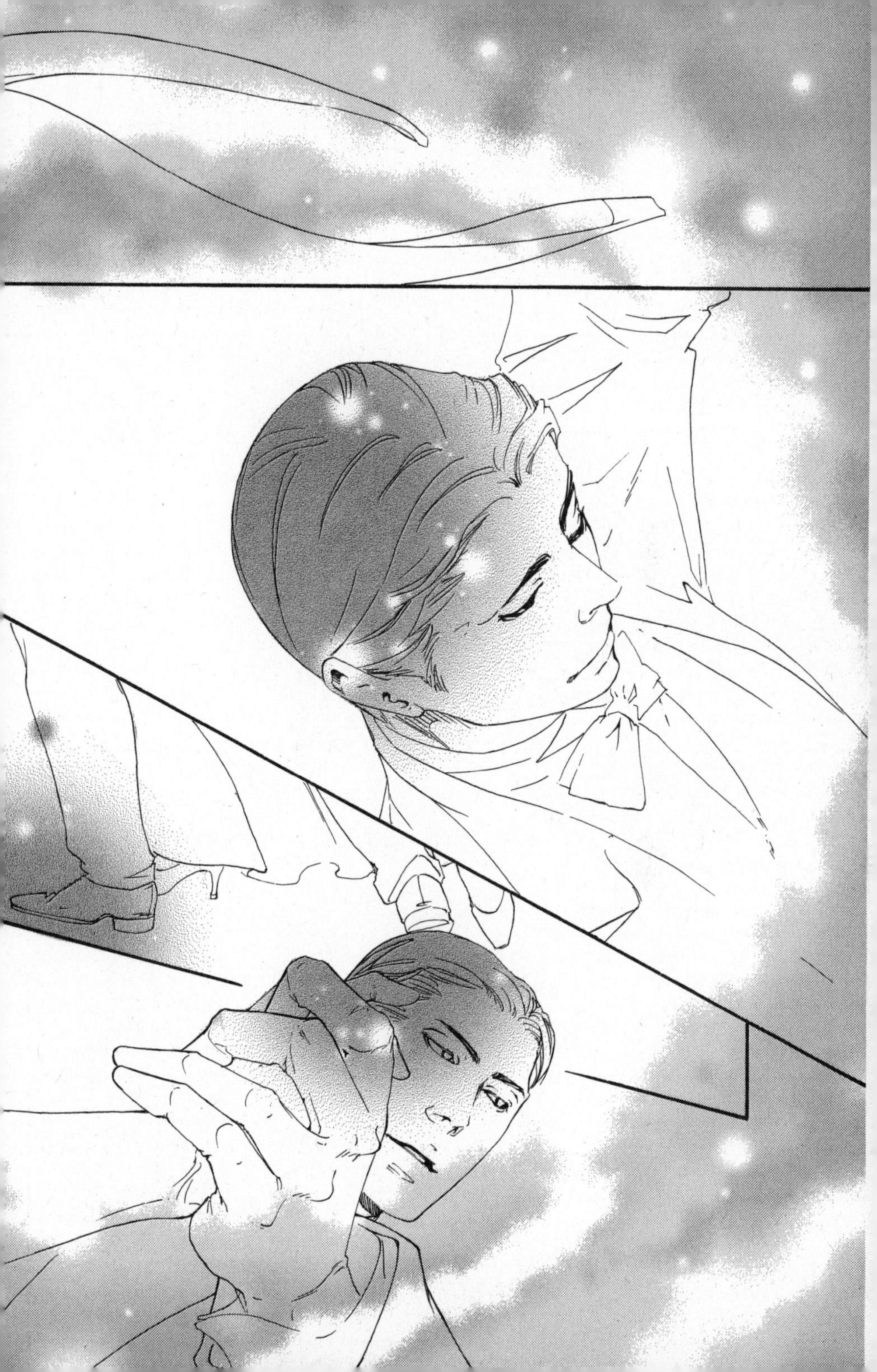

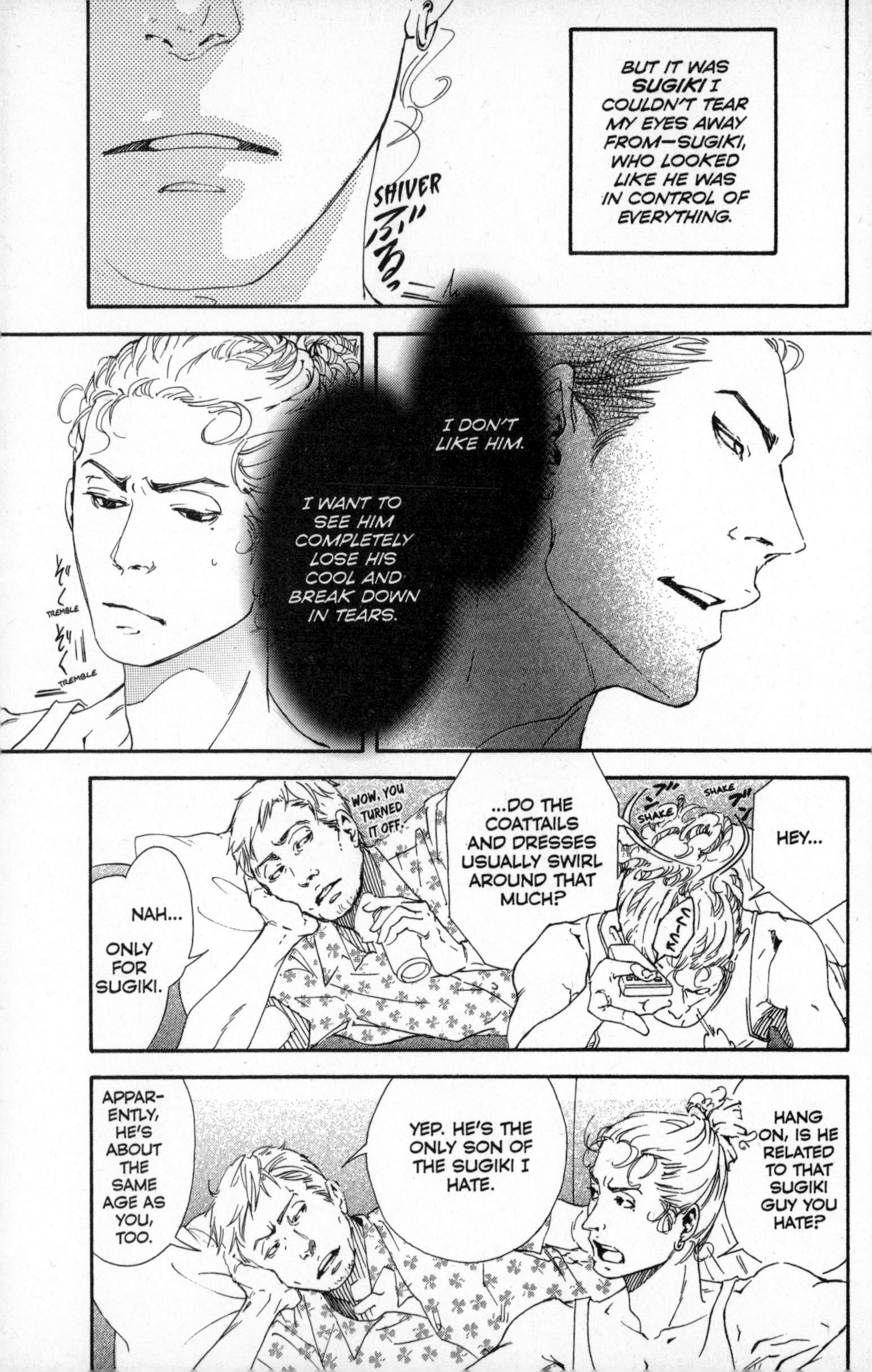
BUT IT WAS SUGIKI I COULDN'T TEAR MY EYES AWAY FROM—SUGIKI, WHO LOOKED LIKE HE WAS IN CONTROL OF EVERYTHING.
SHIVER
I DON'T LIKE HIM.
I WANT TO SEE HIM COMPLETELY LOSE HIS COOL AND BREAK DOWN IN TEARS.
TREMBLE
TREMBLE
HEY...
SHAKE
SHAKE
...DO THE COATTAILS AND DRESSES USUALLY SWIRL AROUND THAT MUCH?
WOW, YOU TURNED IT OFF.
NAH...
ONLY FOR SUGIKI.
HANG ON, IS HE RELATED TO THAT SUGIKI GUY YOU HATE?
YEP. HE'S THE ONLY SON OF THE SUGIKI I HATE.
APPARENTLY, HE'S ABOUT THE SAME AGE AS YOU, TOO.

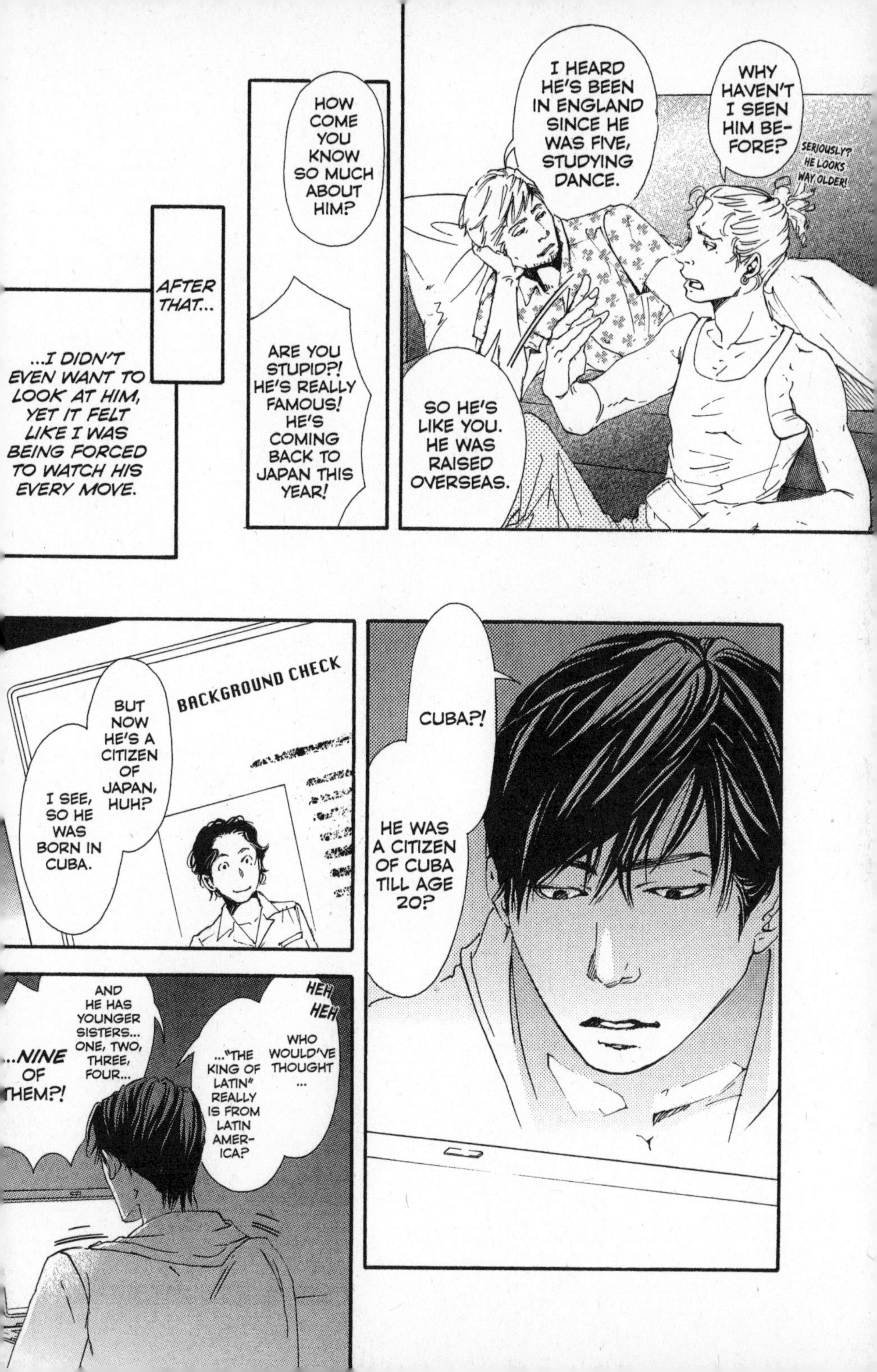

WHY HAVEN'T I SEEN HIM BE-FORE?
SERIOUSLY? HE LOOKS WAY OLDER!
I HEARD HE'S BEEN IN ENGLAND SINCE HE WAS FIVE, STUDYING DANCE.
SO HE'S LIKE YOU. HE WAS RAISED OVERSEAS.
HOW COME YOU KNOW SO MUCH ABOUT HIM?
ARE YOU STUPID?! HE'S REALLY FAMOUS! HE'S COMING BACK TO JAPAN THIS YEAR!
AFTER THAT...
...I DIDN'T EVEN WANT TO LOOK AT HIM, YET IT FELT LIKE I WAS BEING FORCED TO WATCH HIS EVERY MOVE.
CUBA?!
HE WAS A CITIZEN OF CUBA TILL AGE 20?
BACKGROUND CHECK
BUT NOW HE'S A CITIZEN OF JAPAN, HUH?
I SEE, SO HE WAS BORN IN CUBA.
HEH HEH
WHO WOULD'VE THOUGHT...
..."THE KING OF LATIN" REALLY IS FROM LATIN AMERI-CA?
AND HE HAS YOUNGER SISTERS... ONE, TWO, THREE, FOUR...
...NINE OF THEM?!

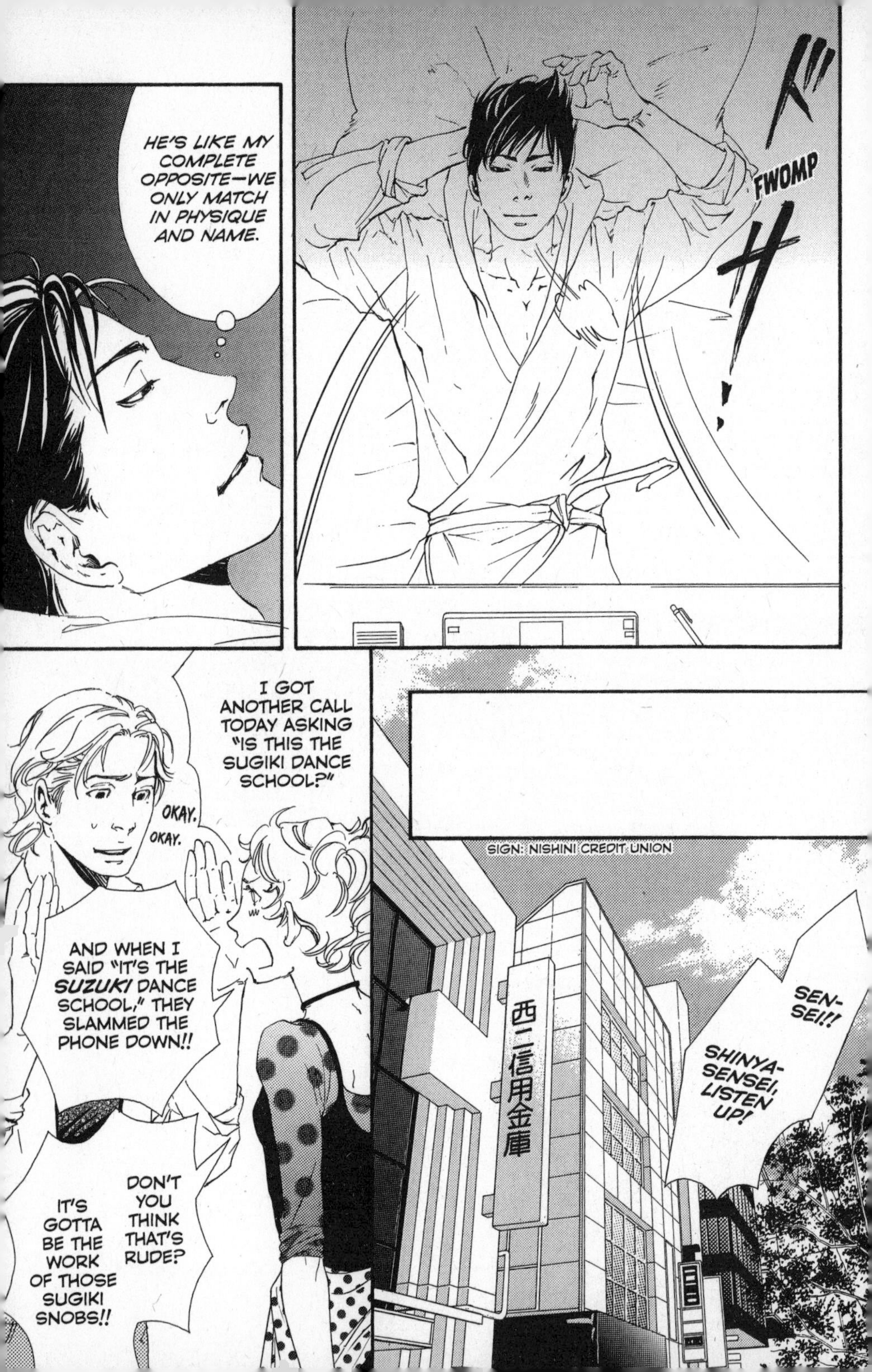
FWOMP
HE'S LIKE MY COMPLETE OPPOSITE—WE ONLY MATCH IN PHYSIQUE AND NAME.
SEN-SEI!!
SHINYA-SENSEI, LISTEN UP!
SIGN: NISHINI CREDIT UNION
西二信用金庫
I GOT ANOTHER CALL TODAY ASKING "IS THIS THE SUGIKI DANCE SCHOOL?"
OKAY. OKAY.
AND WHEN I SAID "IT'S THE *SUZUKI* DANCE SCHOOL," THEY SLAMMED THE PHONE DOWN!!
DON'T YOU THINK THAT'S RUDE?
IT'S GOTTA BE THE WORK OF THOSE SUGIKI SNOBS!!

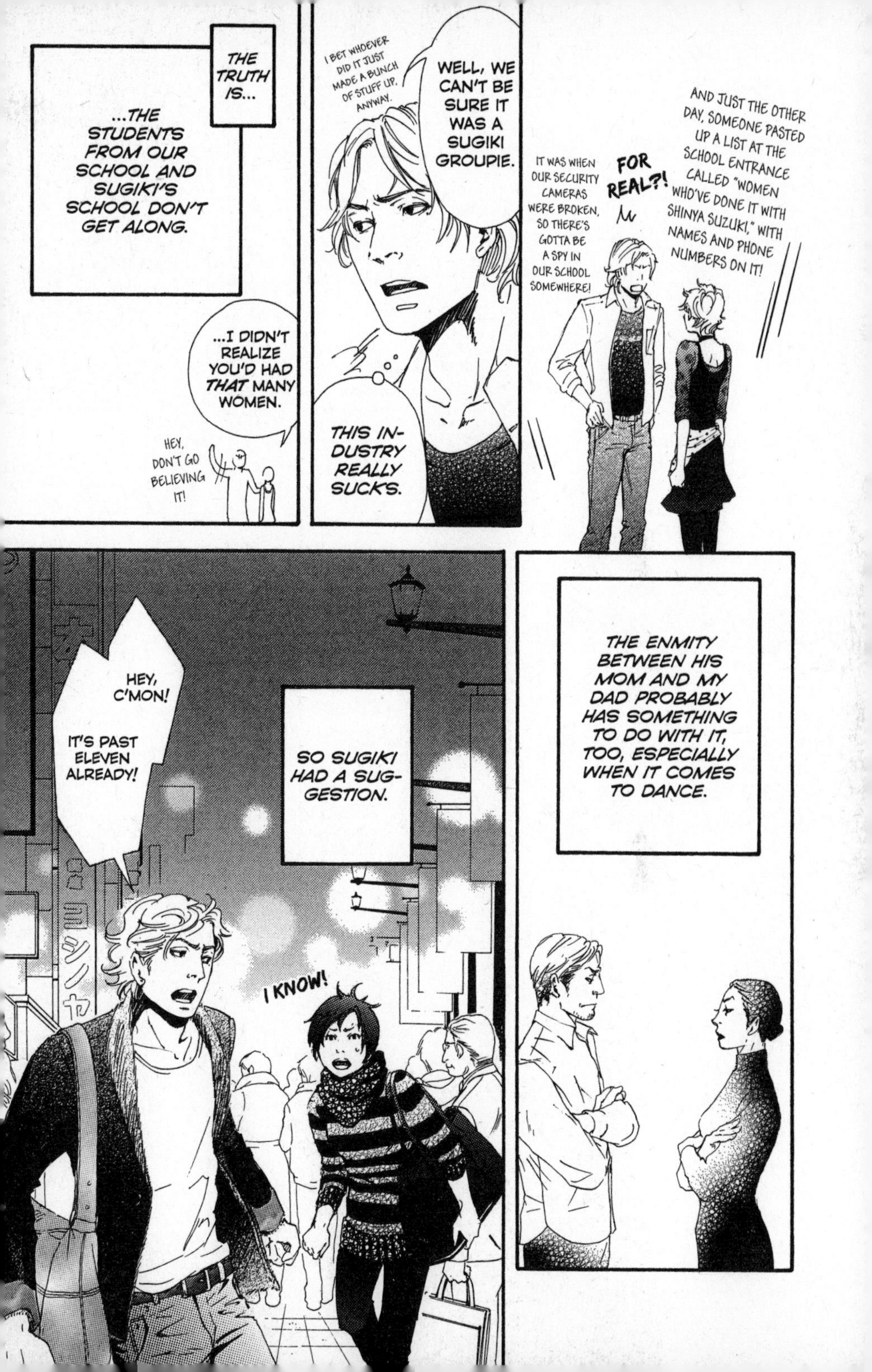
AND JUST THE OTHER DAY, SOMEONE PASTED UP A LIST AT THE SCHOOL ENTRANCE CALLED "WOMEN WHO'VE DONE IT WITH SHINYA SUZUKI," WITH NAMES AND PHONE NUMBERS ON IT!
FOR REAL?!
IT WAS WHEN OUR SECURITY CAMERAS WERE BROKEN, SO THERE'S GOTTA BE A SPY IN OUR SCHOOL SOMEWHERE!
WELL, WE CAN'T BE SURE IT WAS A SUGIKI GROUPIE.
I BET WHOEVER DID IT JUST MADE A BUNCH OF STUFF UP, ANYWAY.
THIS IN-DUSTRY REALLY SUCKS.
THE TRUTH IS...
...THE STUDENTS FROM OUR SCHOOL AND SUGIKI'S SCHOOL DON'T GET ALONG.
...I DIDN'T REALIZE YOU'D HAD THAT MANY WOMEN.
HEY, DON'T GO BELIEVING IT!
THE ENMITY BETWEEN HIS MOM AND MY DAD PROBABLY HAS SOMETHING TO DO WITH IT, TOO, ESPECIALLY WHEN IT COMES TO DANCE.
SO SUGIKI HAD A SUG-GESTION.
HEY, C'MON!
IT'S PAST ELEVEN ALREADY!
I KNOW!

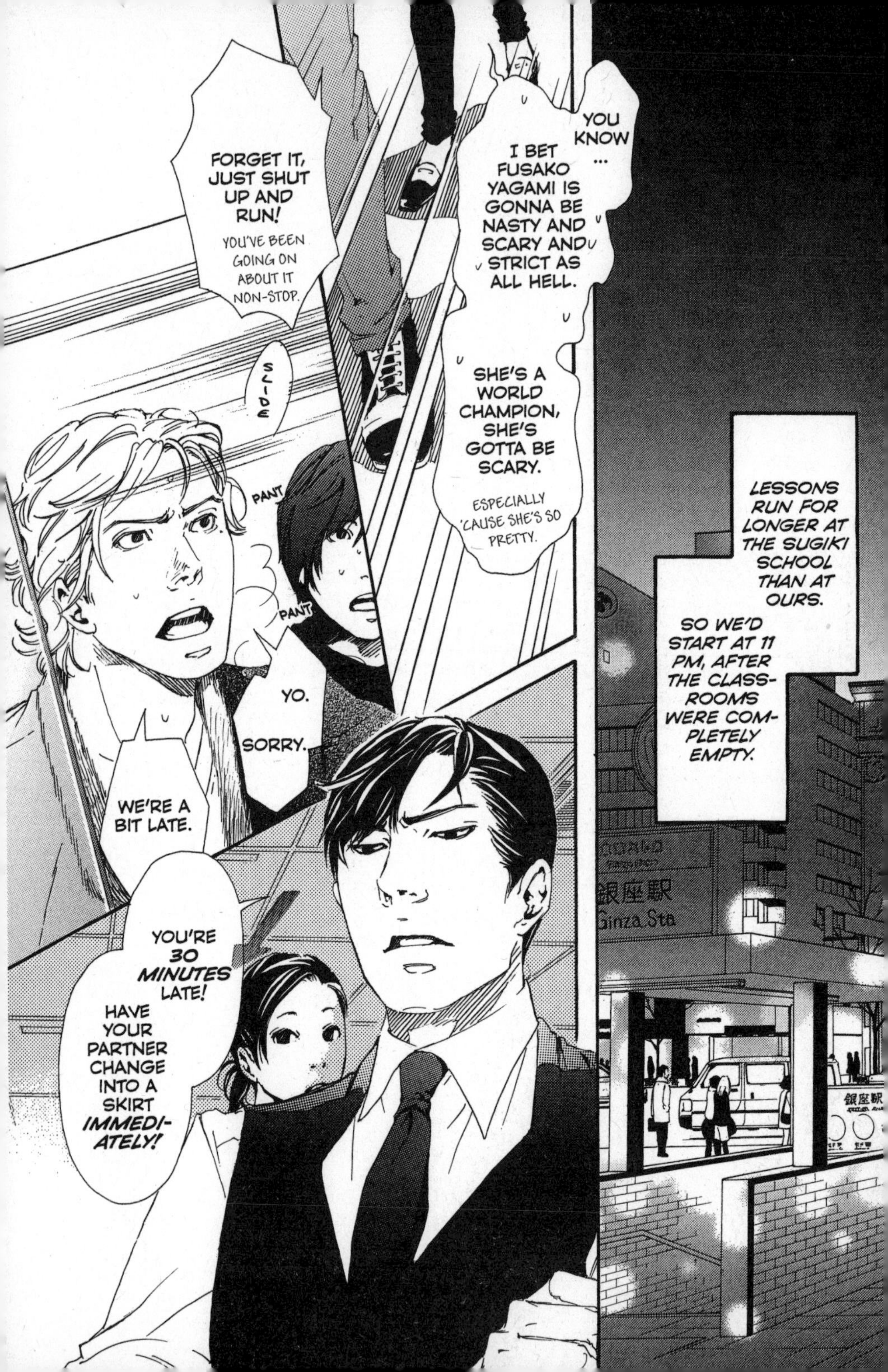
LESSONS RUN FOR LONGER AT THE SUGIKI SCHOOL THAN AT OURS.
SO WE'D START AT 11 PM, AFTER THE CLASSROOMS WERE COMPLETELY EMPTY.
銀座駅
Ginza Sta
銀座駅
YOU KNOW...
I BET FUSAKO YAGAMI IS GONNA BE NASTY AND SCARY AND STRICT AS ALL HELL.
SHE'S A WORLD CHAMPION, SHE'S GOTTA BE SCARY.
ESPECIALLY 'CAUSE SHE'S SO PRETTY.
FORGET IT, JUST SHUT UP AND RUN!
YOU'VE BEEN GOING ON ABOUT IT NON-STOP.
SLIDE
PANT
PANT
YO.
SORRY.
WE'RE A BIT LATE.
YOU'RE 30 MINUTES LATE!
HAVE YOUR PARTNER CHANGE INTO A SKIRT IMMEDIATELY!

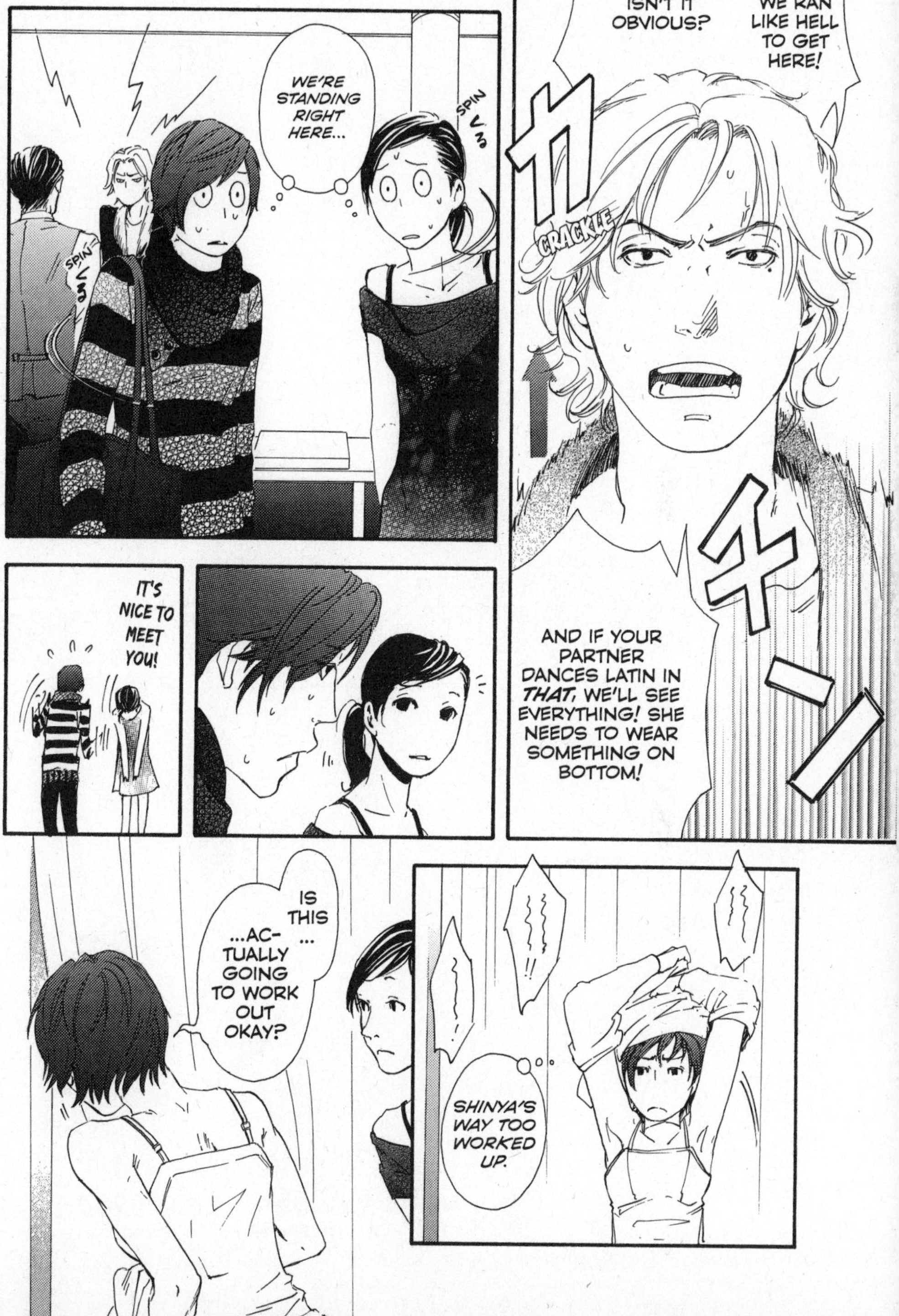

WE RAN LIKE HELL TO GET HERE!
ISN'T IT OBVIOUS?
CRACKLE
AND IF YOUR PARTNER DANCES LATIN IN *THAT*, WE'LL SEE EVERYTHING! SHE NEEDS TO WEAR SOMETHING ON BOTTOM!
SPIN
WE'RE STANDING RIGHT HERE...
SPIN
IT'S NICE TO MEET YOU!
SHINYA'S WAY TOO WORKED UP.
IS THIS ...ACTUALLY GOING TO WORK OUT OKAY?

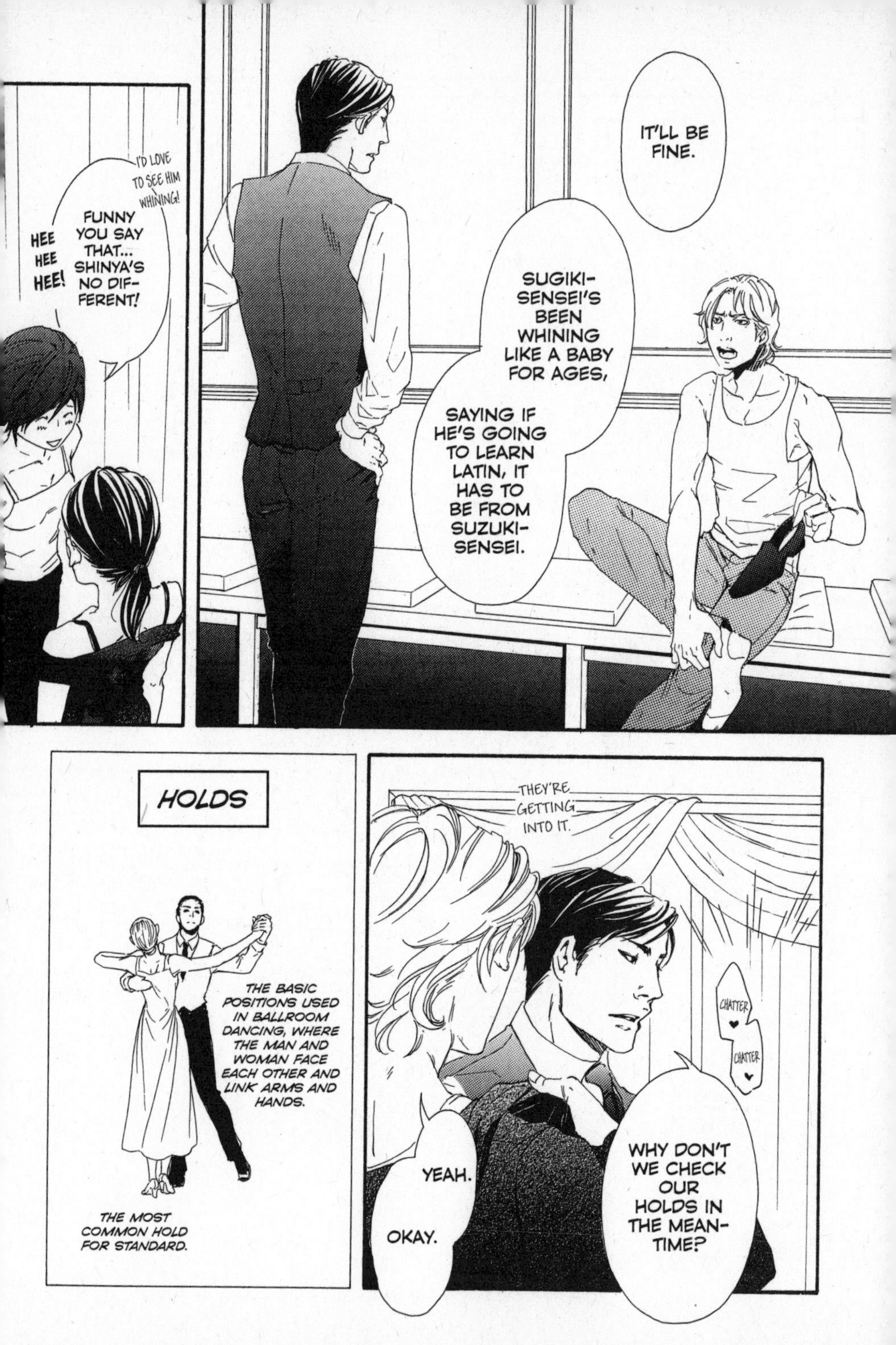

IT'LL BE FINE.
SUGIKI-SENSEI'S BEEN WHINING LIKE A BABY FOR AGES,
SAYING IF HE'S GOING TO LEARN LATIN, IT HAS TO BE FROM SUZUKI-SENSEI.
FUNNY YOU SAY THAT... SHINYA'S NO DIF-FERENT!
I'D LOVE TO SEE HIM WHINING!
HEE HEE HEE!
THEY'RE GETTING INTO IT.
CHATTER ♥
CHATTER ♥
WHY DON'T WE CHECK OUR HOLDS IN THE MEAN-TIME?
YEAH.
OKAY.
HOLDS
THE BASIC POSITIONS USED IN BALLROOM DANCING, WHERE THE MAN AND WOMAN FACE EACH OTHER AND LINK ARMS AND HANDS.
THE MOST COMMON HOLD FOR STANDARD.

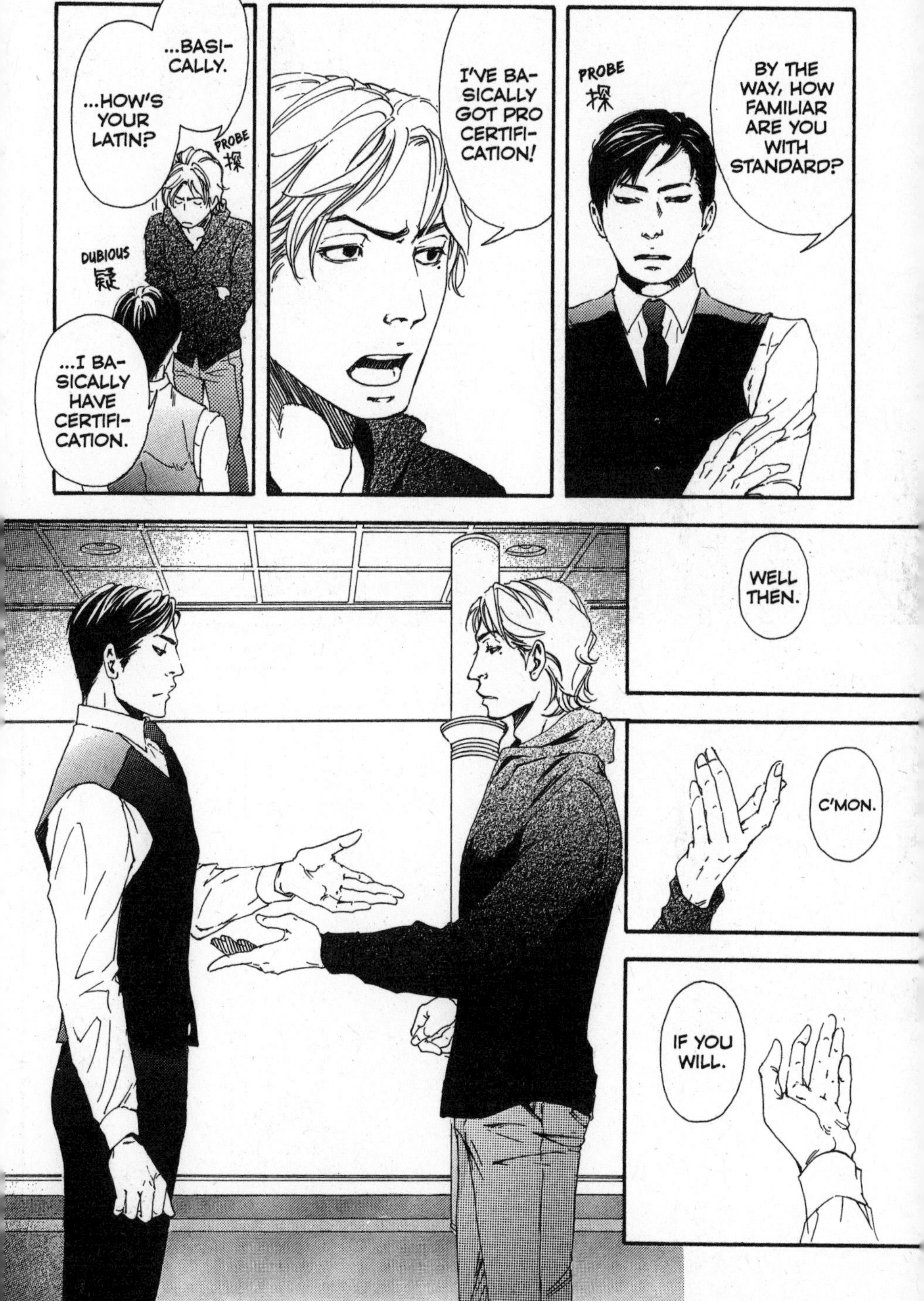
PROBE 探
BY THE WAY, HOW FAMILIAR ARE YOU WITH STANDARD?
I'VE BASICALLY GOT PRO CERTIFICATION!
...BASICALLY.
...HOW'S YOUR LATIN?
PROBE 探
DUBIOUS 疑
...I BASICALLY HAVE CERTIFICATION.
WELL THEN.
C'MON.
IF YOU WILL.

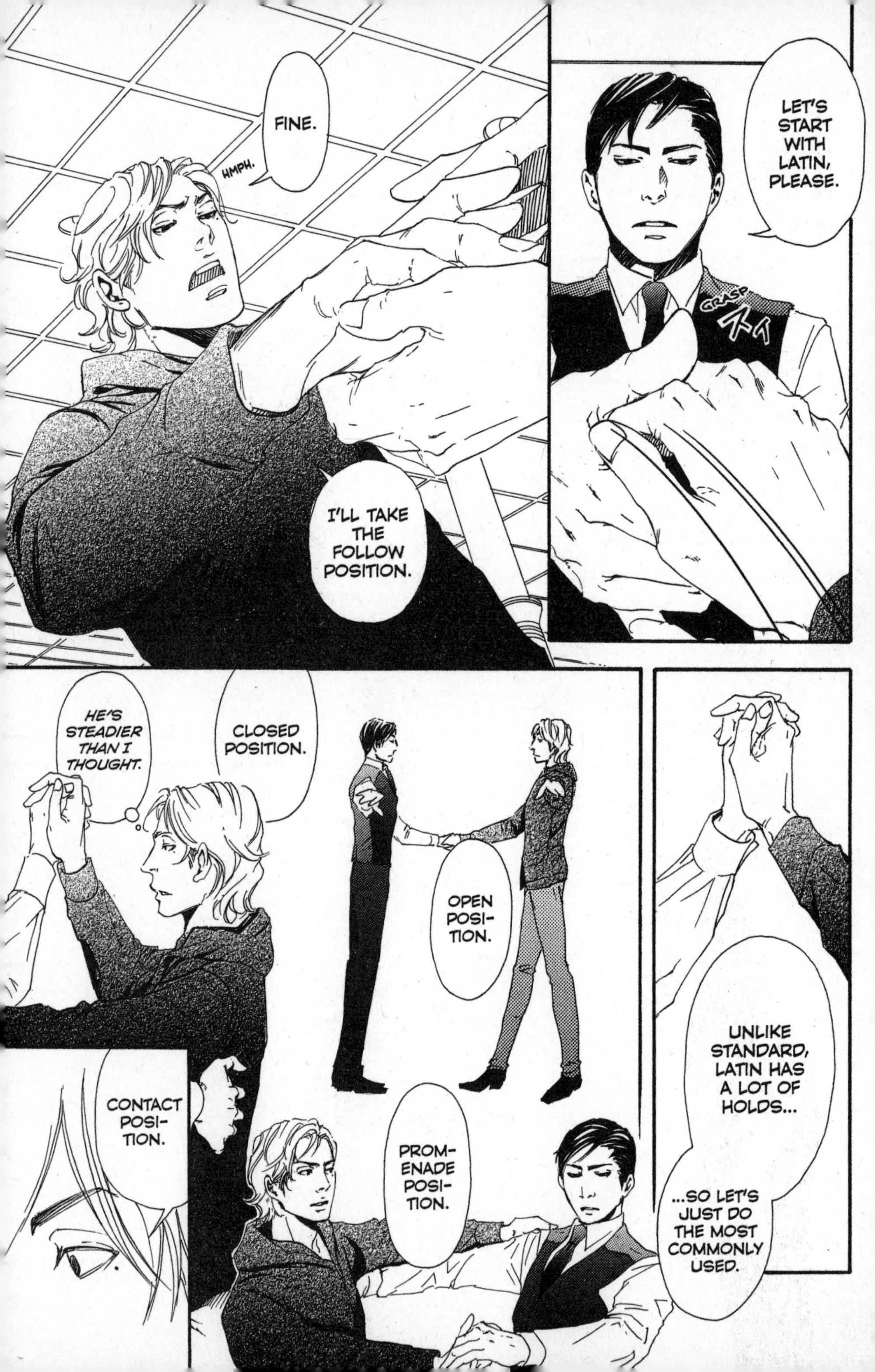
LET'S START WITH LATIN, PLEASE.
GRASP
スイ
FINE.
HMPH.
I'LL TAKE THE FOLLOW POSITION.
UNLIKE STANDARD, LATIN HAS A LOT OF HOLDS...
...SO LET'S JUST DO THE MOST COMMONLY USED.
CLOSED POSITION.
OPEN POSI-TION.
HE'S STEADIER THAN I THOUGHT.
PROM-ENADE POSI-TION.
CONTACT POSI-TION.

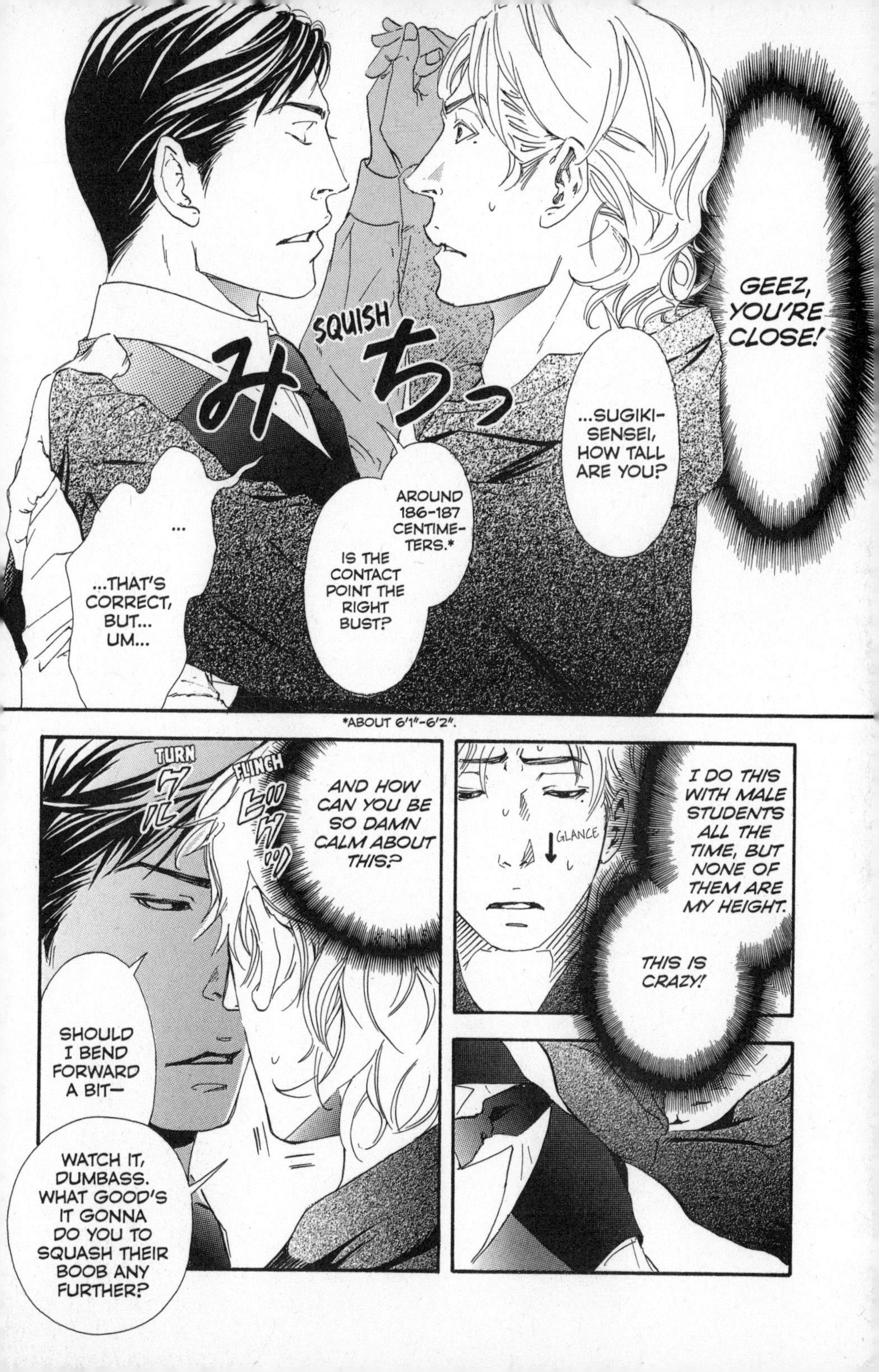
GEEZ, YOU'RE CLOSE!
...SUGIKI-SENSEI, HOW TALL ARE YOU?
SQUISH
みちっ
AROUND 186-187 CENTIMETERS.*
IS THE CONTACT POINT THE RIGHT BUST?
...
...THAT'S CORRECT, BUT... UM...
*ABOUT 6'1"-6'2".
I DO THIS WITH MALE STUDENTS ALL THE TIME, BUT NONE OF THEM ARE MY HEIGHT.
GLANCE
THIS IS CRAZY!
TURN
FLINCH
AND HOW CAN YOU BE SO DAMN CALM ABOUT THIS?
SHOULD I BEND FORWARD A BIT—
WATCH IT, DUMBASS. WHAT GOOD'S IT GONNA DO YOU TO SQUASH THEIR BOOB ANY FURTHER?

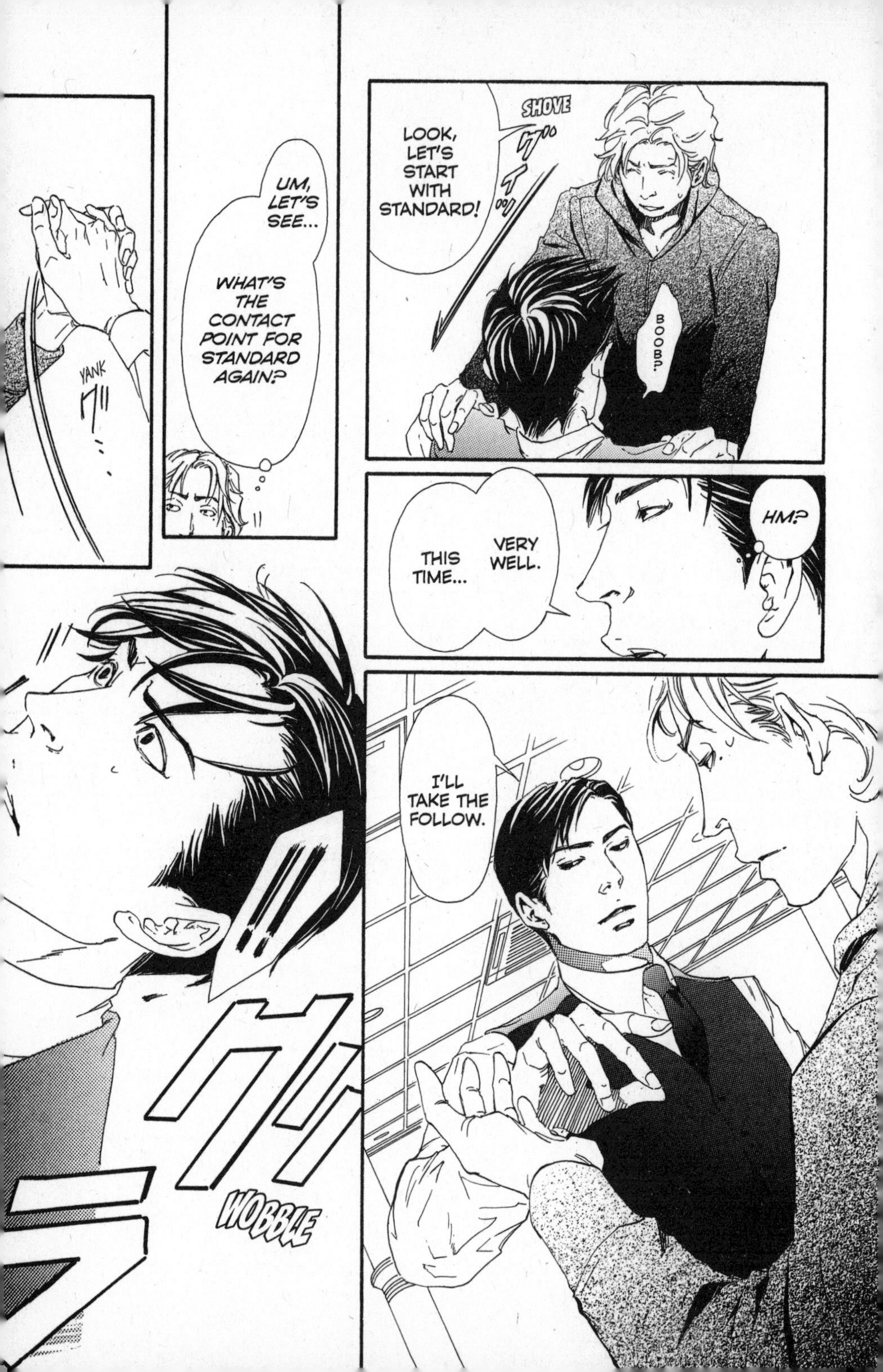
SHOVE
LOOK, LET'S START WITH STANDARD!
BOOB?
UM, LET'S SEE...
WHAT'S THE CONTACT POINT FOR STANDARD AGAIN?
YANK
HM?
VERY WELL.
THIS TIME...
I'LL TAKE THE FOLLOW.
WOBBLE

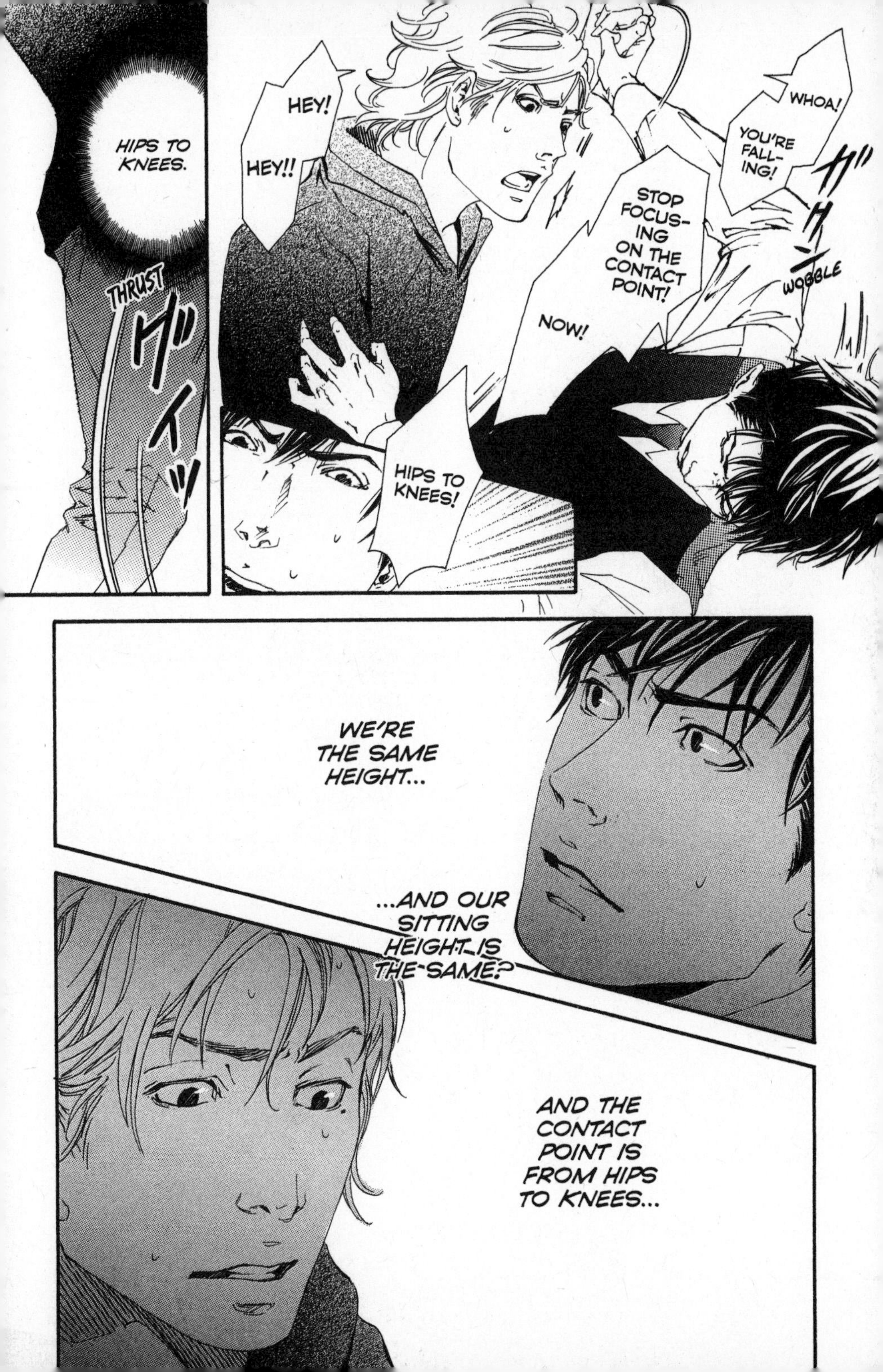
WHOA!
YOU'RE FALLING!
WOBBLE
STOP FOCUSING ON THE CONTACT POINT!
HEY!
HEY!!
NOW!
HIPS TO KNEES!
HIPS TO KNEES.
THRUST
WE'RE THE SAME HEIGHT...
...AND OUR SITTING HEIGHT IS THE SAME?
AND THE CONTACT POINT IS FROM HIPS TO KNEES...

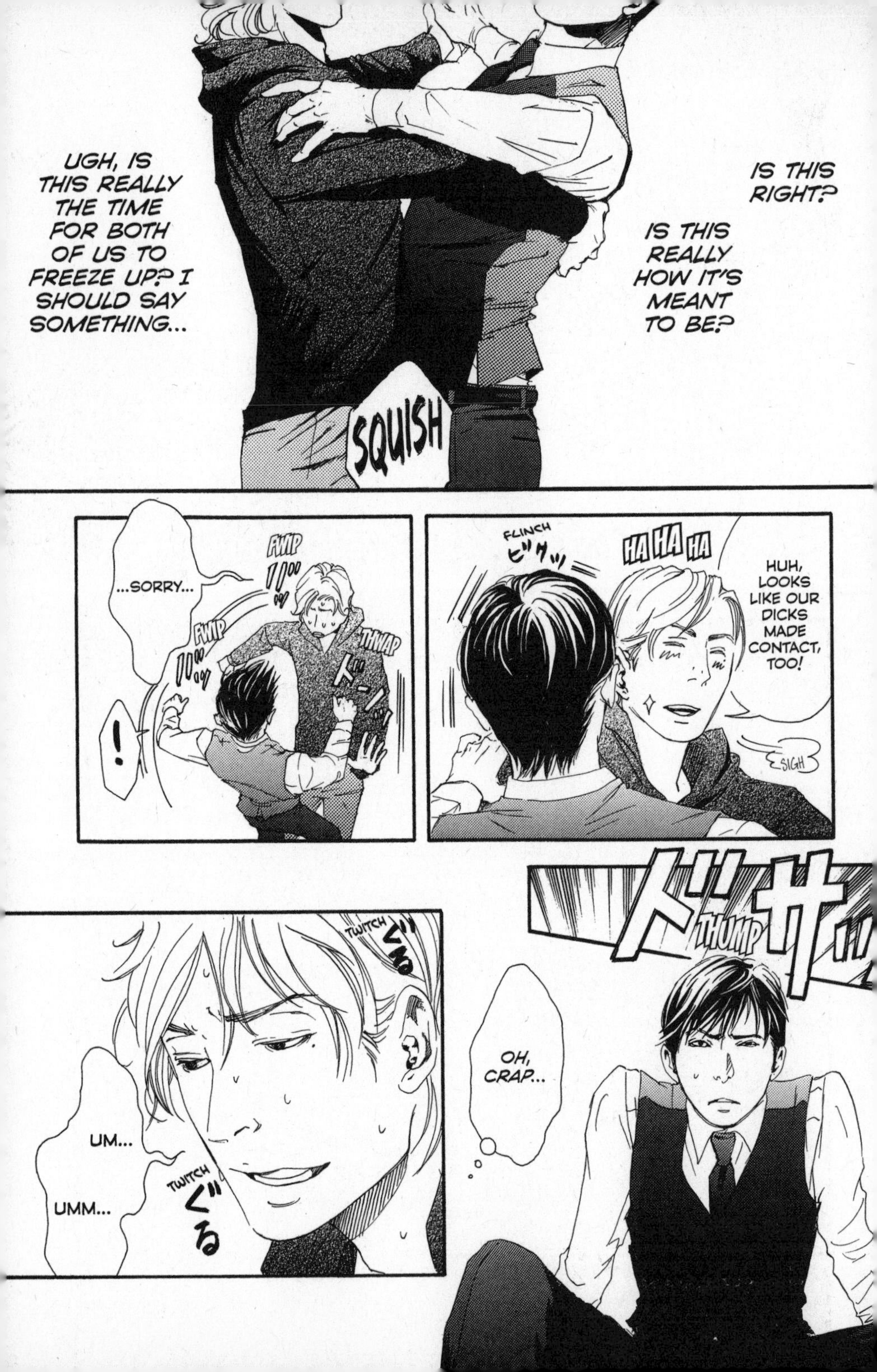
IS THIS RIGHT?
IS THIS REALLY HOW IT'S MEANT TO BE?
UGH, IS THIS REALLY THE TIME FOR BOTH OF US TO FREEZE UP? I SHOULD SAY SOMETHING...
SQUISH
FLINCH
HA HA HA
HUH, LOOKS LIKE OUR DICKS MADE CONTACT, TOO!
SIGH
FWIP
...SORRY...
FWIP
THWAP
!
THUMP
OH, CRAP...
TWITCH
UM...
UMM...
TWITCH

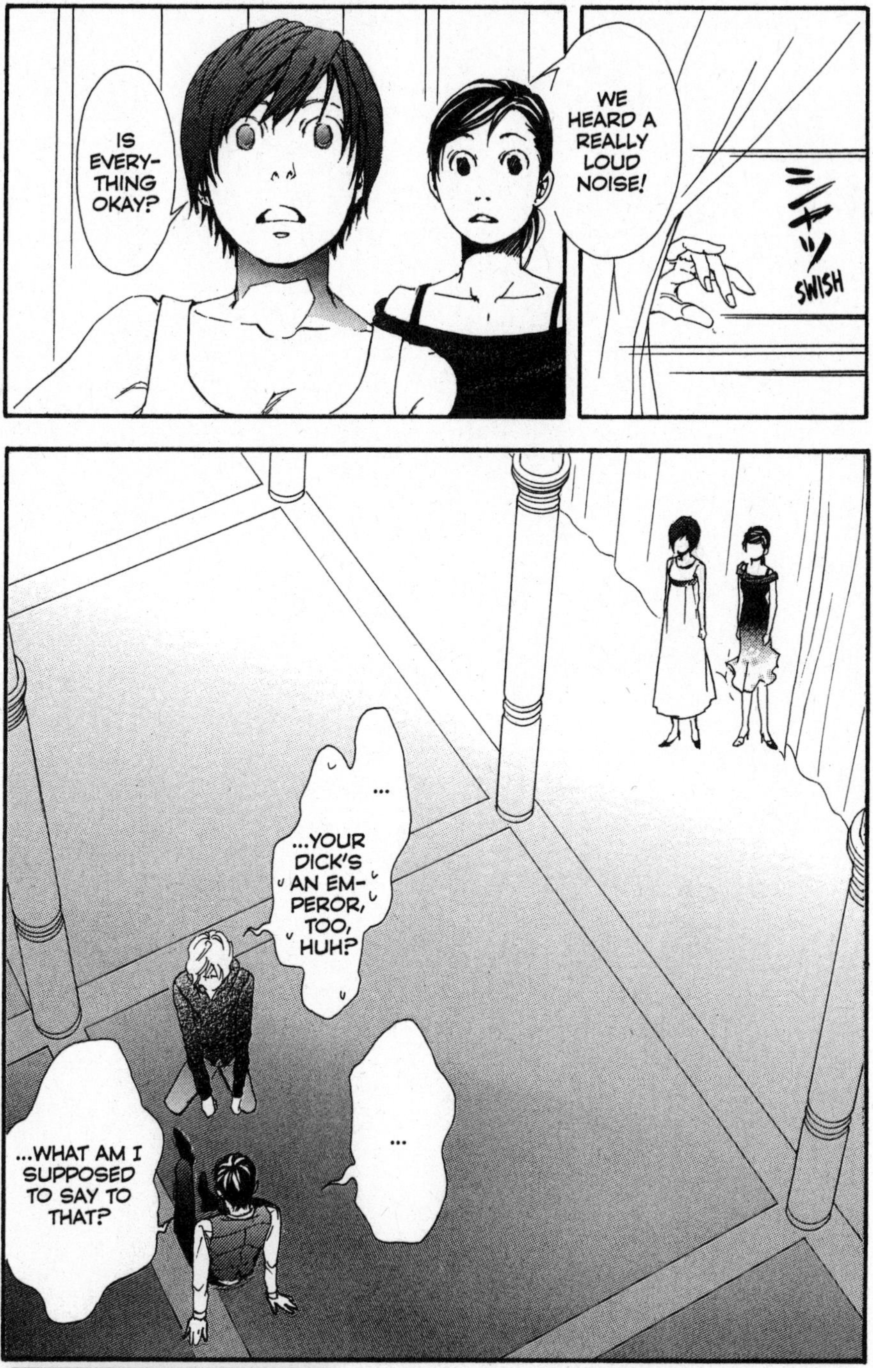
WE HEARD A REALLY LOUD NOISE!
シャッ
SWISH
IS EVERY-THING OKAY?
...
...YOUR DICK'S AN EMPEROR, TOO, HUH?
...
...WHAT AM I SUPPOSED TO SAY TO THAT?

END OF CHAPTER 1

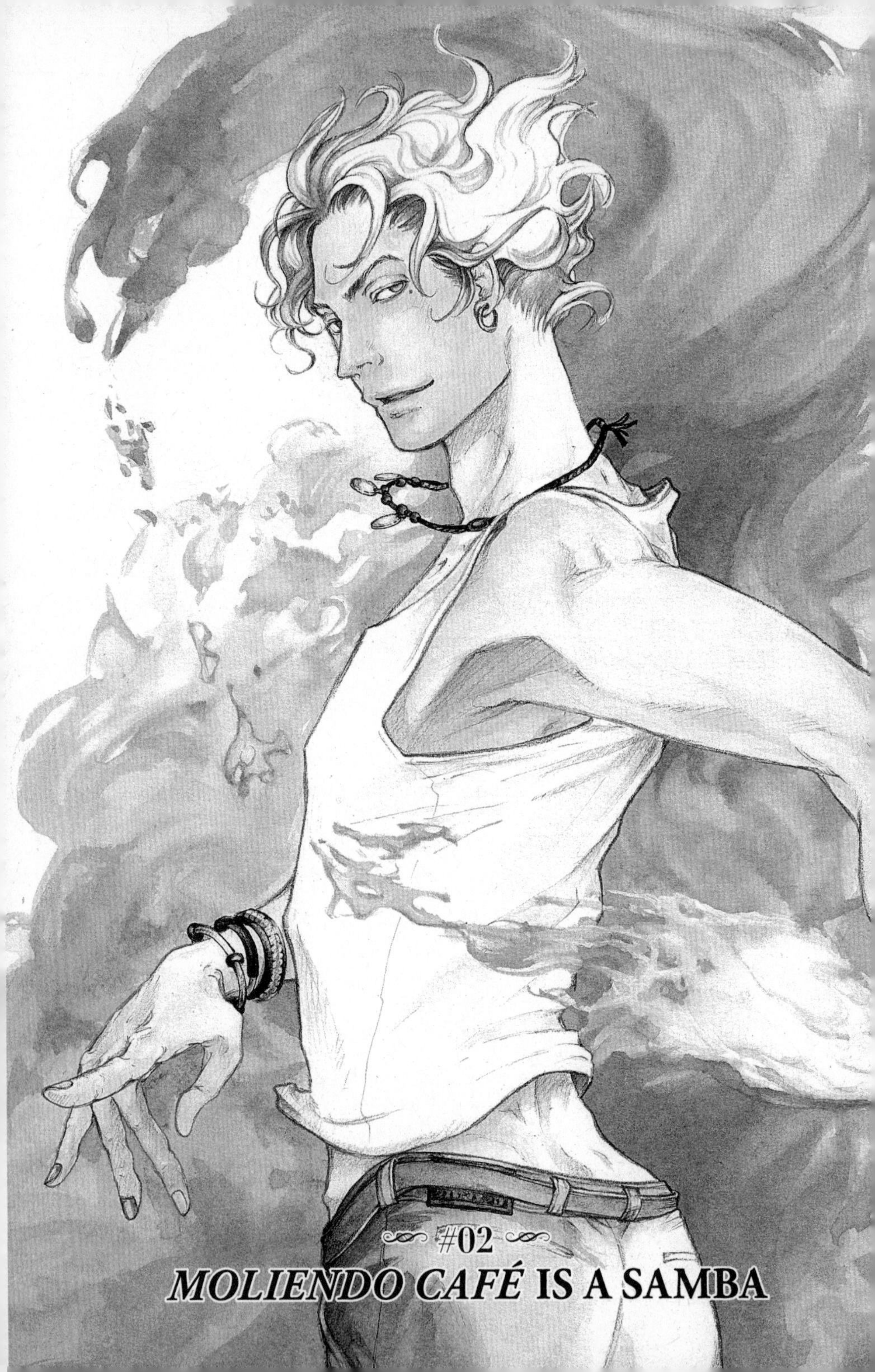

#02
MOLIENDO CAFÉ IS A SAMBA

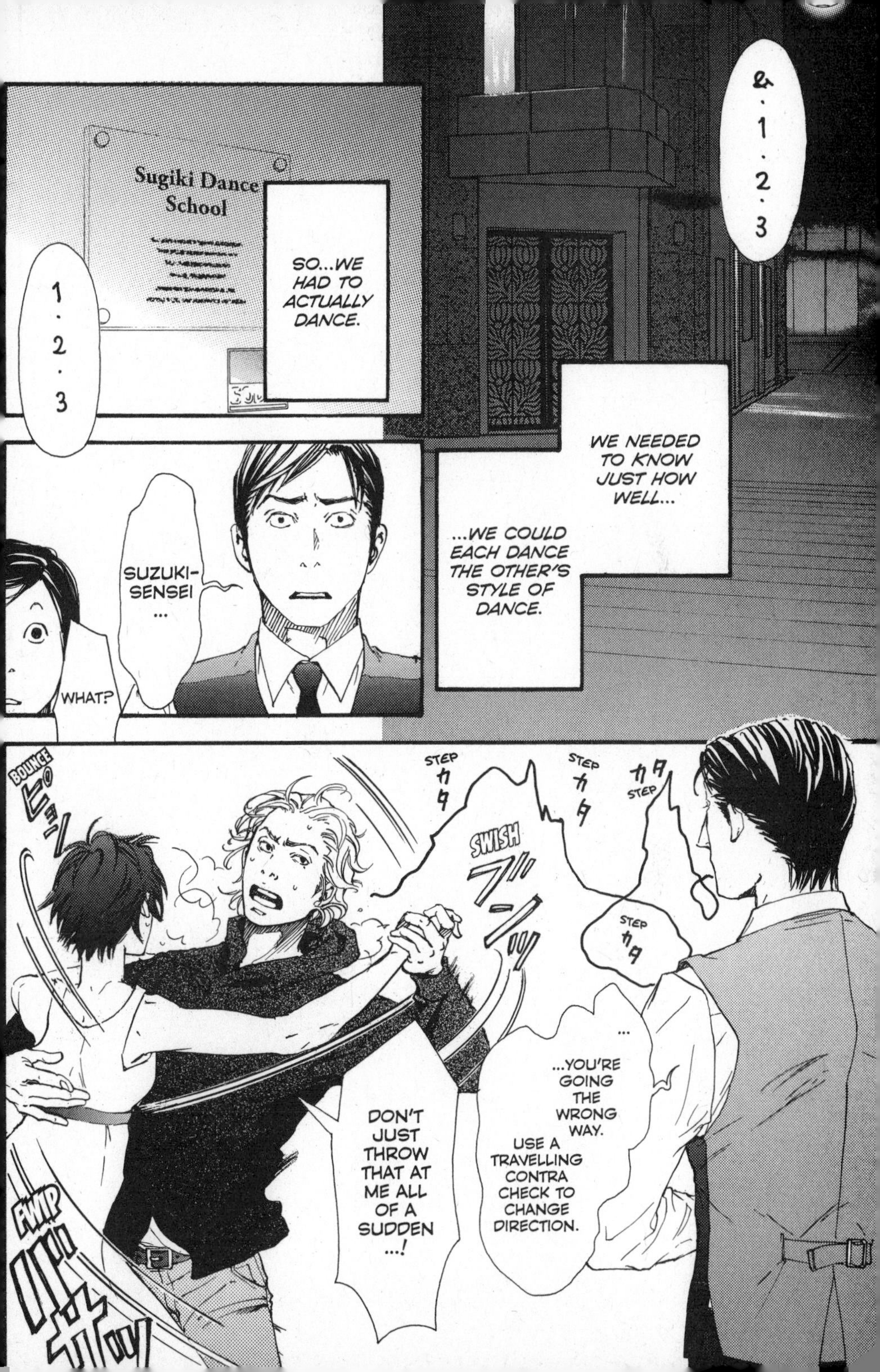
&·1·2·3
WE NEEDED TO KNOW JUST HOW WELL...
...WE COULD EACH DANCE THE OTHER'S STYLE OF DANCE.
Sugiki Dance School
SO...WE HAD TO ACTUALLY DANCE.
1·2·3
SUZUKI-SENSEI...
WHAT?
STEP カタ
STEP カタ
STEP カタ
SWISH
STEP カタ
...
...YOU'RE GOING THE WRONG WAY.
USE A TRAVELLING CONTRA CHECK TO CHANGE DIRECTION.
DON'T JUST THROW THAT AT ME ALL OF A SUDDEN...!
BOUNCE
FWIP

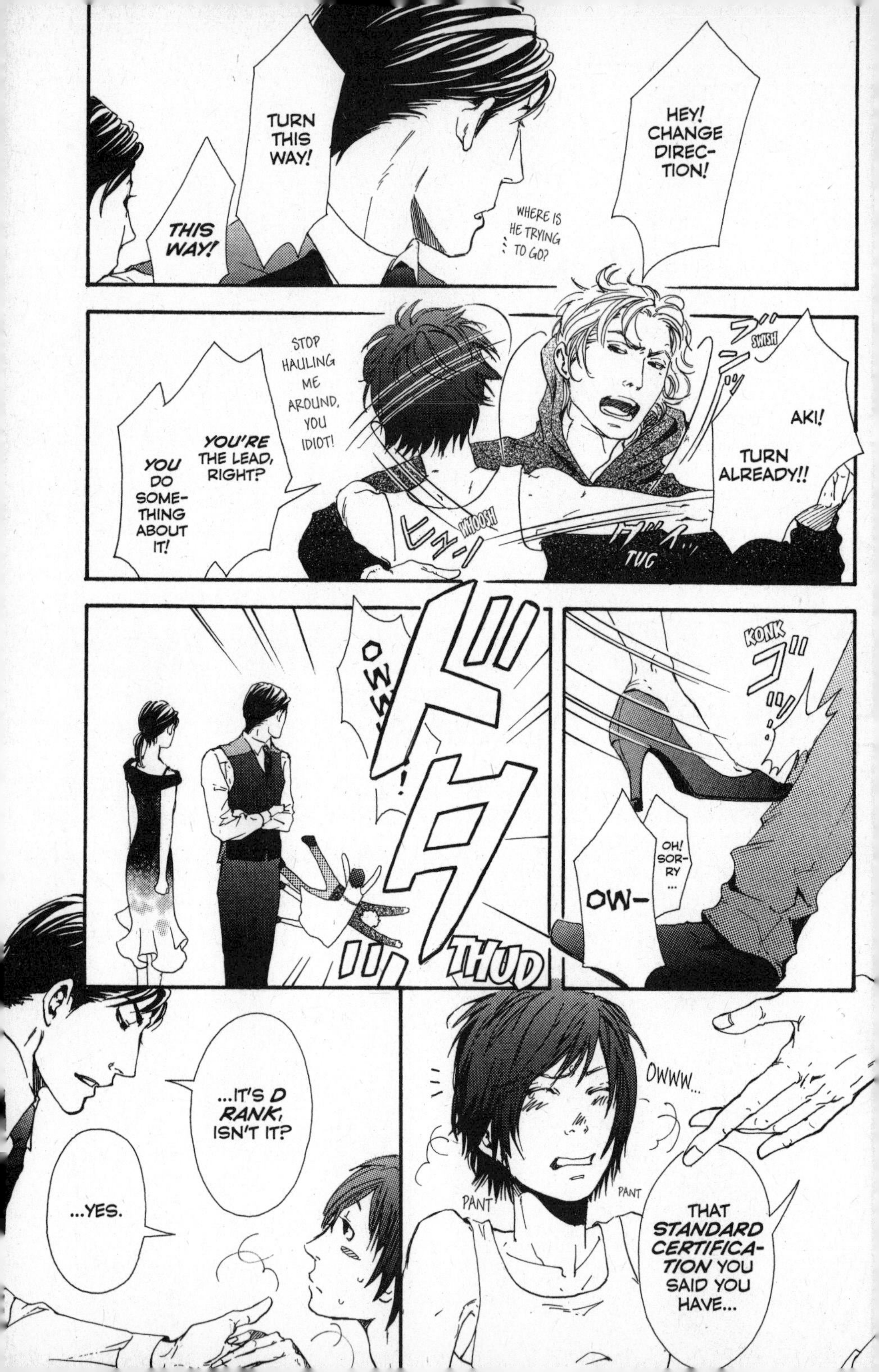
HEY! CHANGE DIREC-TION!
WHERE IS HE TRYING TO GO?
TURN THIS WAY!
THIS WAY!
AKI!
TURN ALREADY!!
SWISH
STOP HAULING ME AROUND, YOU IDIOT!
WHOOSH
TUG
YOU'RE THE LEAD, RIGHT?
YOU DO SOME-THING ABOUT IT!
KONK
OH! SOR-RY...
OW-
THUD
...IT'S D RANK, ISN'T IT?
...YES.
OWWW...
PANT
PANT
THAT STANDARD CERTIFICA-TION YOU SAID YOU HAVE...

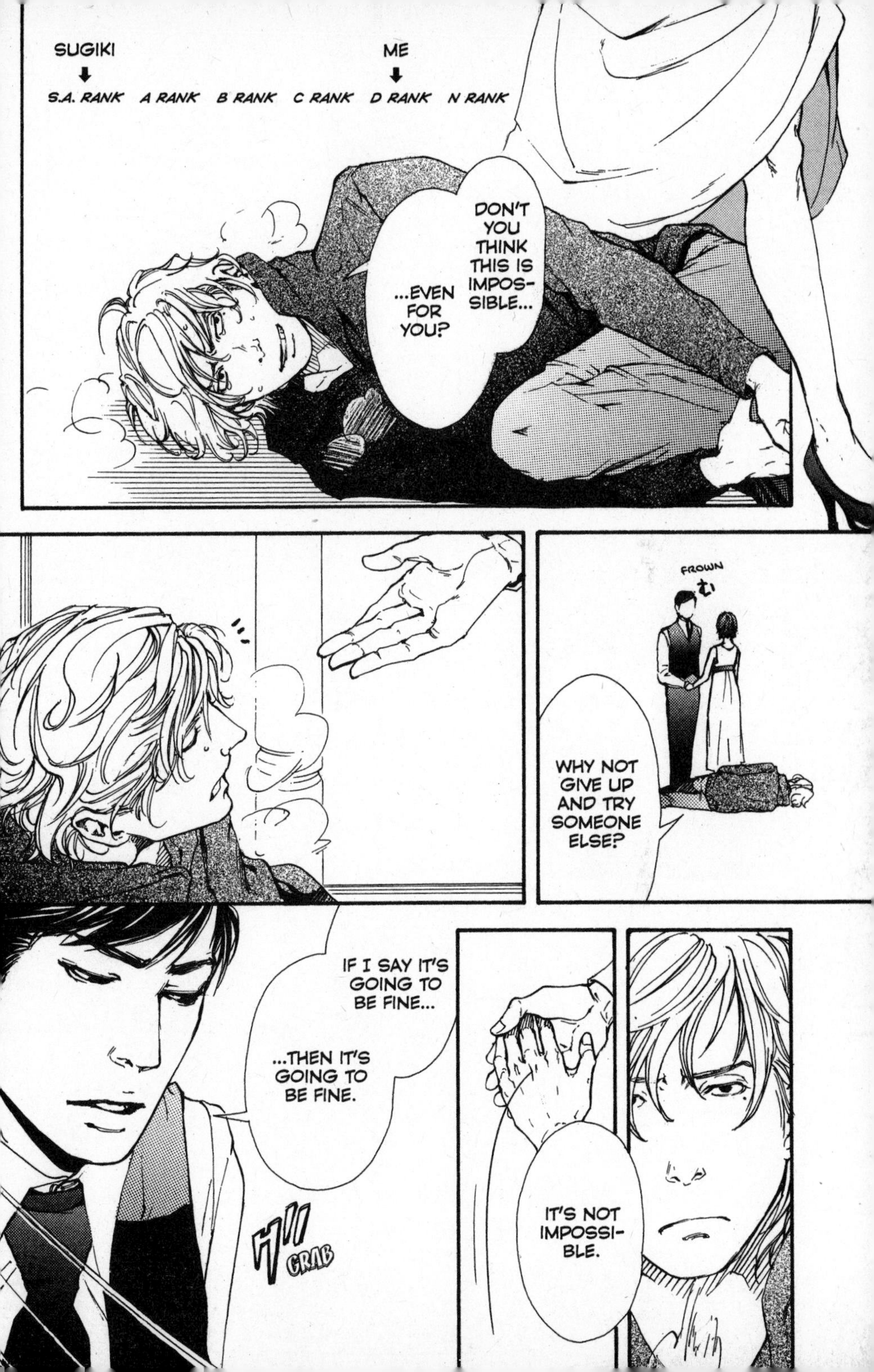
SUGIKI
ME
S.A. RANK
A RANK
B RANK
C RANK
D RANK
N RANK
DON'T YOU THINK THIS IS IMPOSSIBLE...
...EVEN FOR YOU?
FROWN
WHY NOT GIVE UP AND TRY SOMEONE ELSE?
IT'S NOT IMPOSSIBLE.
IF I SAY IT'S GOING TO BE FINE...
...THEN IT'S GOING TO BE FINE.
GRAB

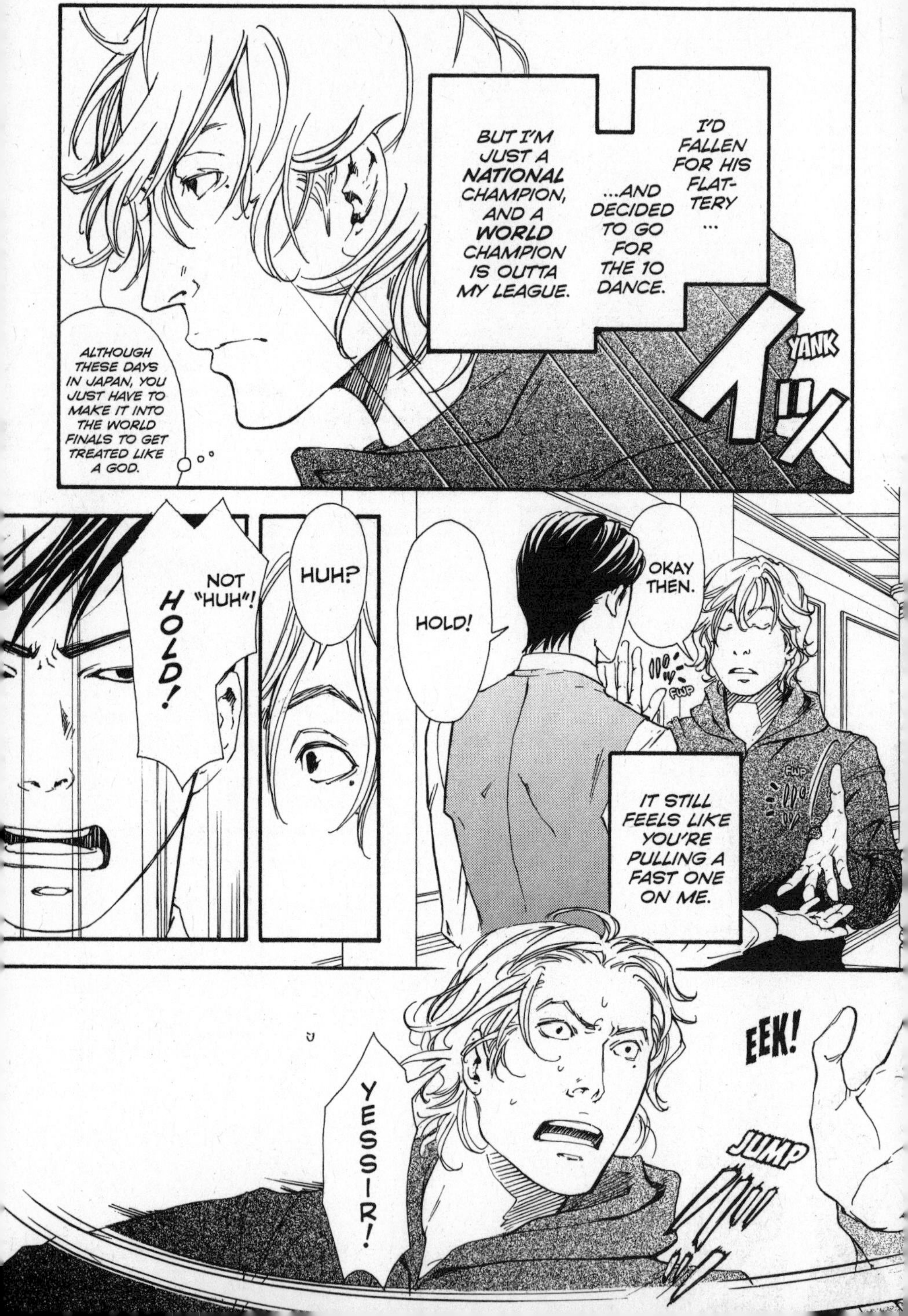
I'D FALLEN FOR HIS FLATTERY...
...AND DECIDED TO GO FOR THE 10 DANCE.
BUT I'M JUST A NATIONAL CHAMPION, AND A WORLD CHAMPION IS OUTTA MY LEAGUE.
YANK
ALTHOUGH THESE DAYS IN JAPAN, YOU JUST HAVE TO MAKE IT INTO THE WORLD FINALS TO GET TREATED LIKE A GOD.
OKAY THEN.
FWP
FWP
IT STILL FEELS LIKE YOU'RE PULLING A FAST ONE ON ME.
HOLD!
HUH?
NOT "HUH"!
HOLD!
EEK!
JUMP
YESSIR!

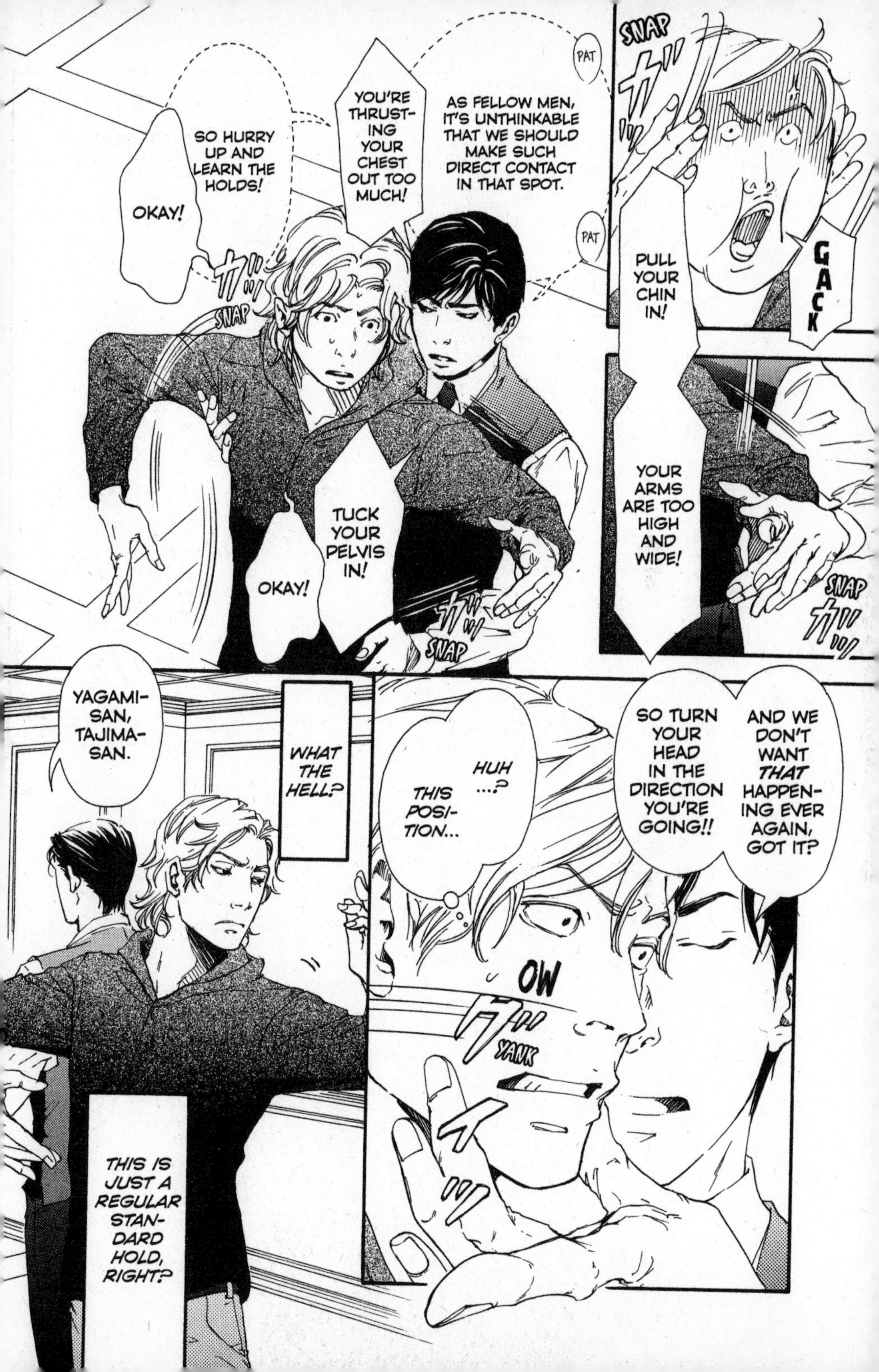
SNAP
GACK
PULL YOUR CHIN IN!
YOUR ARMS ARE TOO HIGH AND WIDE!
SNAP
PAT
AS FELLOW MEN, IT'S UNTHINKABLE THAT WE SHOULD MAKE SUCH DIRECT CONTACT IN THAT SPOT.
YOU'RE THRUST- ING YOUR CHEST OUT TOO MUCH!
SO HURRY UP AND LEARN THE HOLDS!
OKAY!
SNAP
PAT
TUCK YOUR PELVIS IN!
OKAY!
SNAP
AND WE DON'T WANT *THAT* HAPPEN- ING EVER AGAIN, GOT IT?
SO TURN YOUR HEAD IN THE DIRECTION YOU'RE GOING!!
HUH ...?
THIS POSI- TION...
OW
YANK
WHAT THE HELL?
YAGAMI- SAN, TAJIMA- SAN.
THIS IS JUST A REGULAR STAN- DARD HOLD, RIGHT?

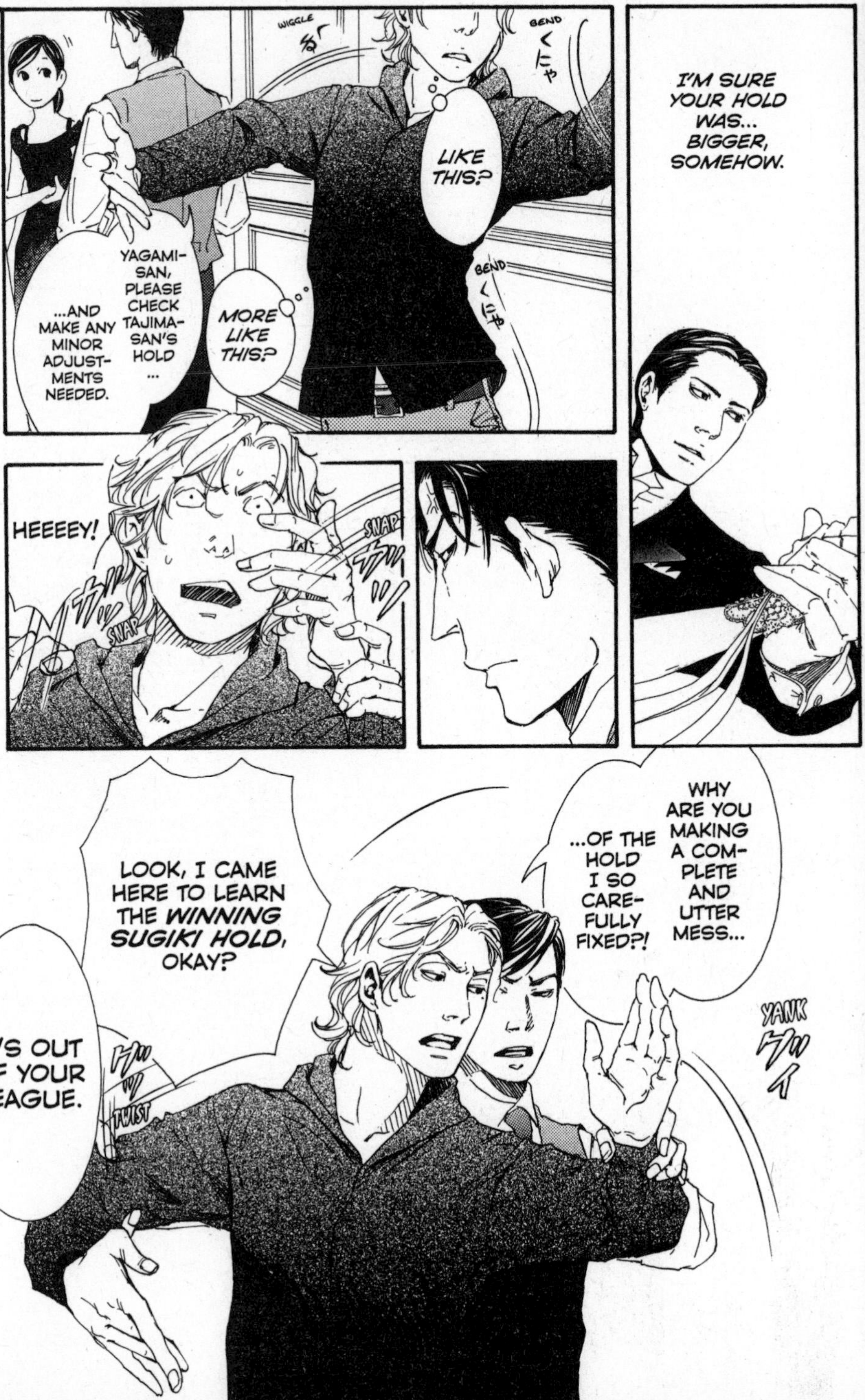

I'M SURE YOUR HOLD WAS... BIGGER, SOMEHOW.
BEND
WIGGLE
LIKE THIS?
BEND
MORE LIKE THIS?
YAGAMI-SAN, PLEASE CHECK TAJIMA-SAN'S HOLD ...
...AND MAKE ANY MINOR ADJUST-MENTS NEEDED.
SNAP
HEEEEY!
SNAP
YANK
WHY ARE YOU MAKING A COM-PLETE AND UTTER MESS...
...OF THE HOLD I SO CARE-FULLY FIXED?!
LOOK, I CAME HERE TO LEARN THE *WINNING SUGIKI HOLD*, OKAY?
TWIST
IT'S OUT OF YOUR LEAGUE.

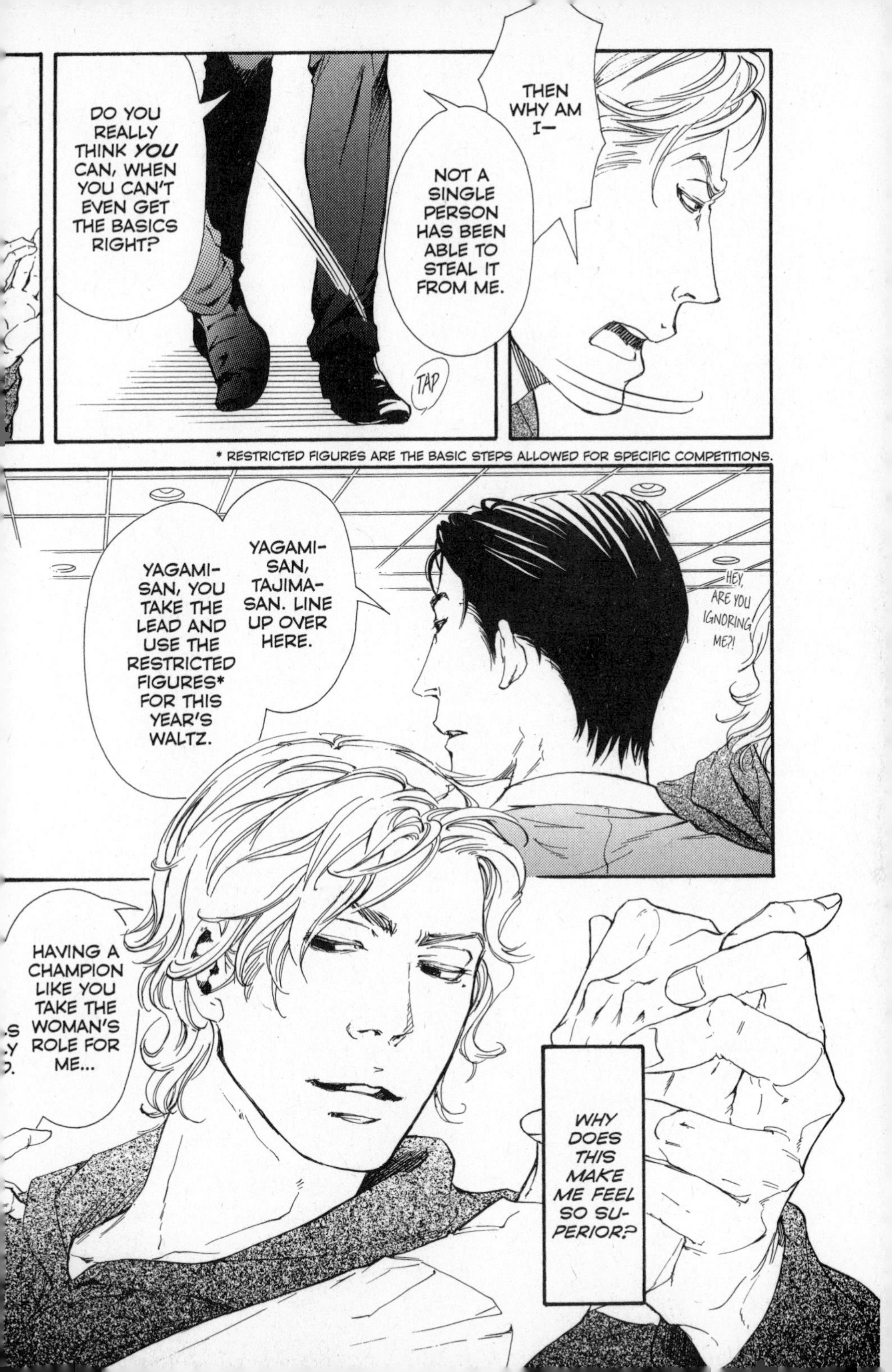
THEN WHY AM I—
NOT A SINGLE PERSON HAS BEEN ABLE TO STEAL IT FROM ME.
DO YOU REALLY THINK *YOU* CAN, WHEN YOU CAN'T EVEN GET THE BASICS RIGHT?
TAP
* RESTRICTED FIGURES ARE THE BASIC STEPS ALLOWED FOR SPECIFIC COMPETITIONS.
HEY, ARE YOU IGNORING ME?!
YAGAMI-SAN, TAJIMA-SAN. LINE UP OVER HERE.
YAGAMI-SAN, YOU TAKE THE LEAD AND USE THE RESTRICTED FIGURES* FOR THIS YEAR'S WALTZ.
WHY DOES THIS MAKE ME FEEL SO SU-PERIOR?
HAVING A CHAMPION LIKE YOU TAKE THE WOMAN'S ROLE FOR ME...

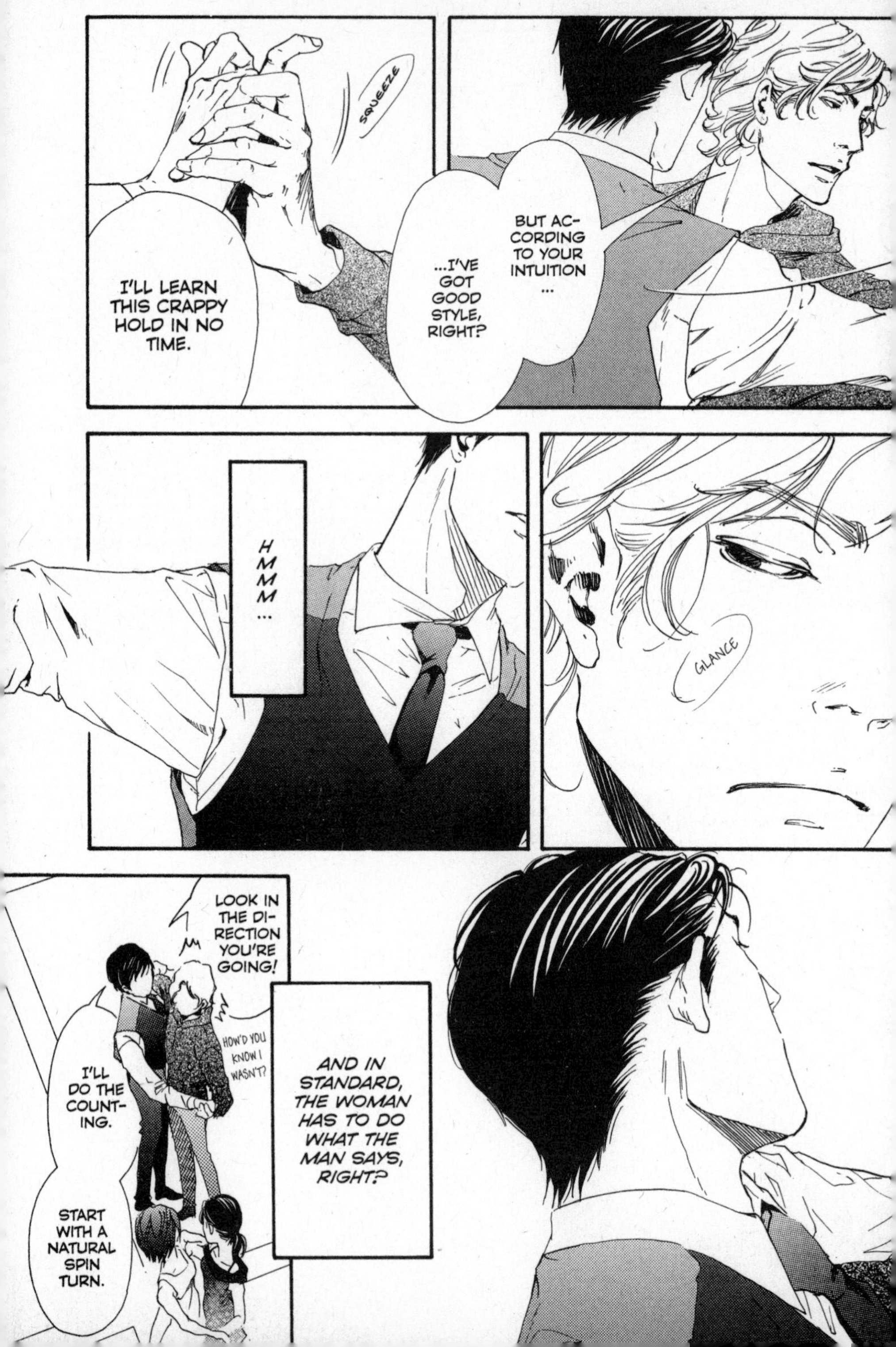
BUT ACCORDING TO YOUR INTUITION ...
...I'VE GOT GOOD STYLE, RIGHT?
SQUEEZE
I'LL LEARN THIS CRAPPY HOLD IN NO TIME.
GLANCE
HMMM...
AND IN STANDARD, THE WOMAN HAS TO DO WHAT THE MAN SAYS, RIGHT?
LOOK IN THE DIRECTION YOU'RE GOING!
HOW'D YOU KNOW I WASN'T?
I'LL DO THE COUNTING.
START WITH A NATURAL SPIN TURN.

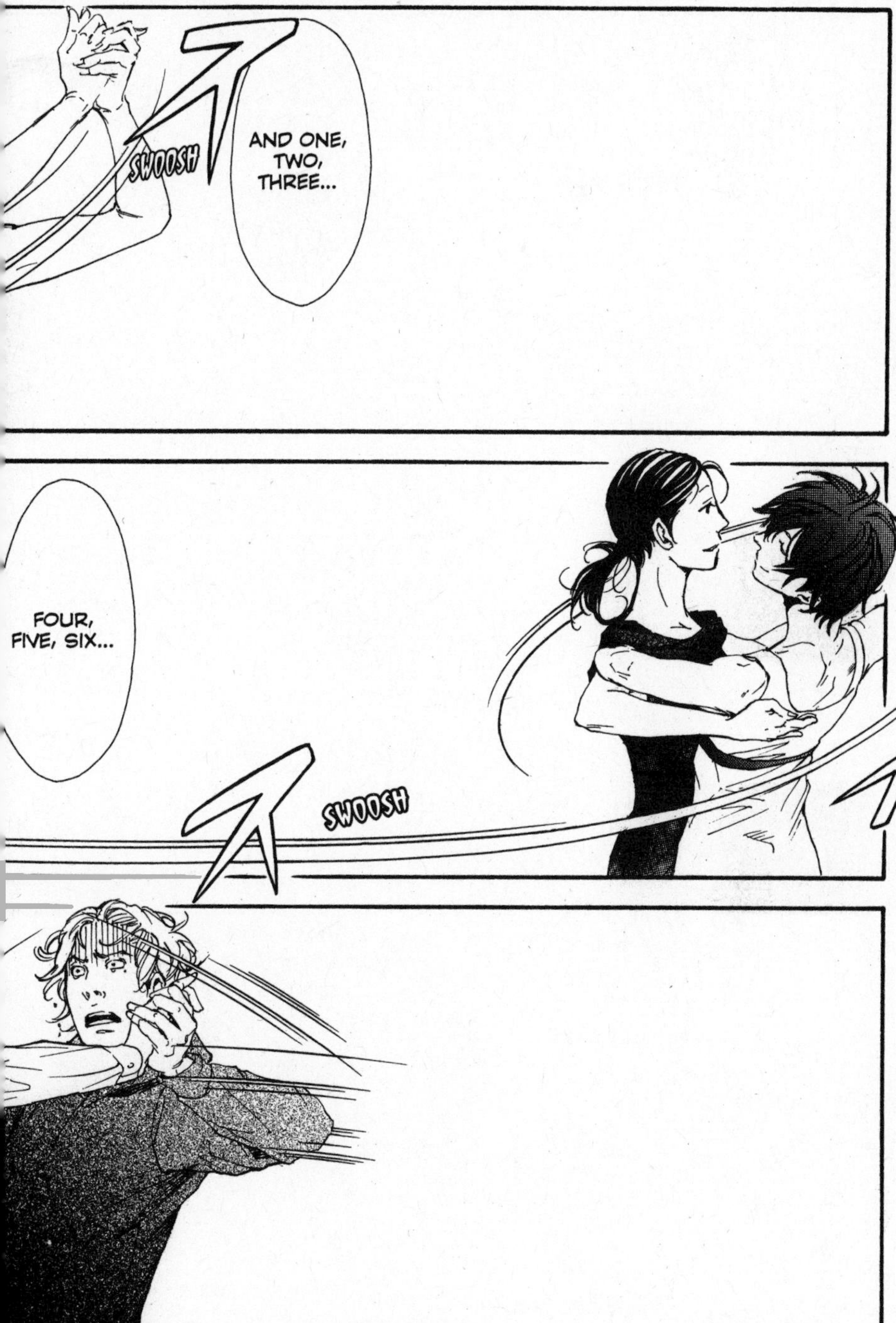
AND ONE, TWO, THREE...
SWOOSH
SWOOSH
FOUR, FIVE, SIX...

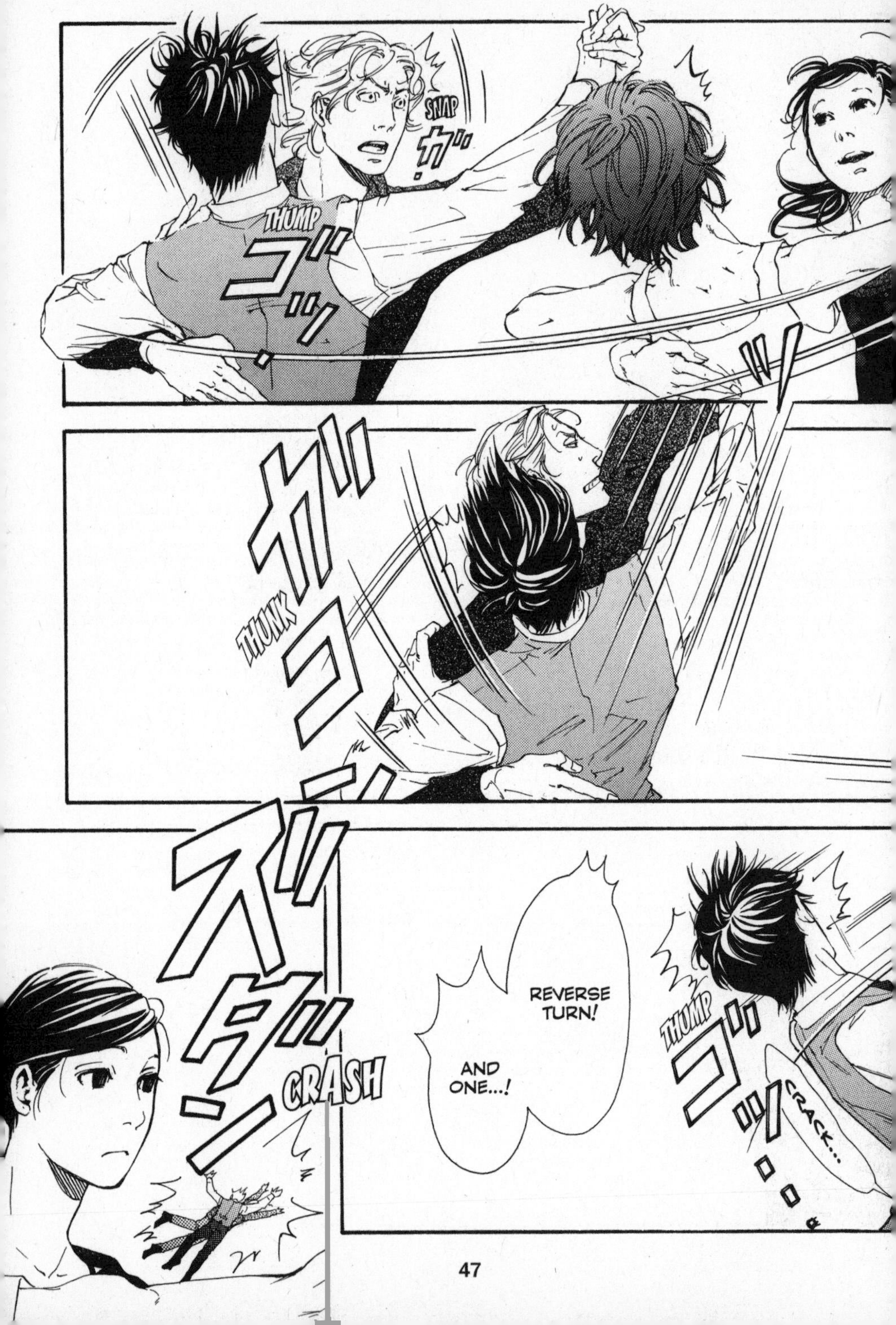
SNAP
ガッ
THUMP
ゴッ
THUNK
ガッ
THUMP
ゴッ
CRACK...
REVERSE TURN!
AND ONE...!
ズダーン
CRASH

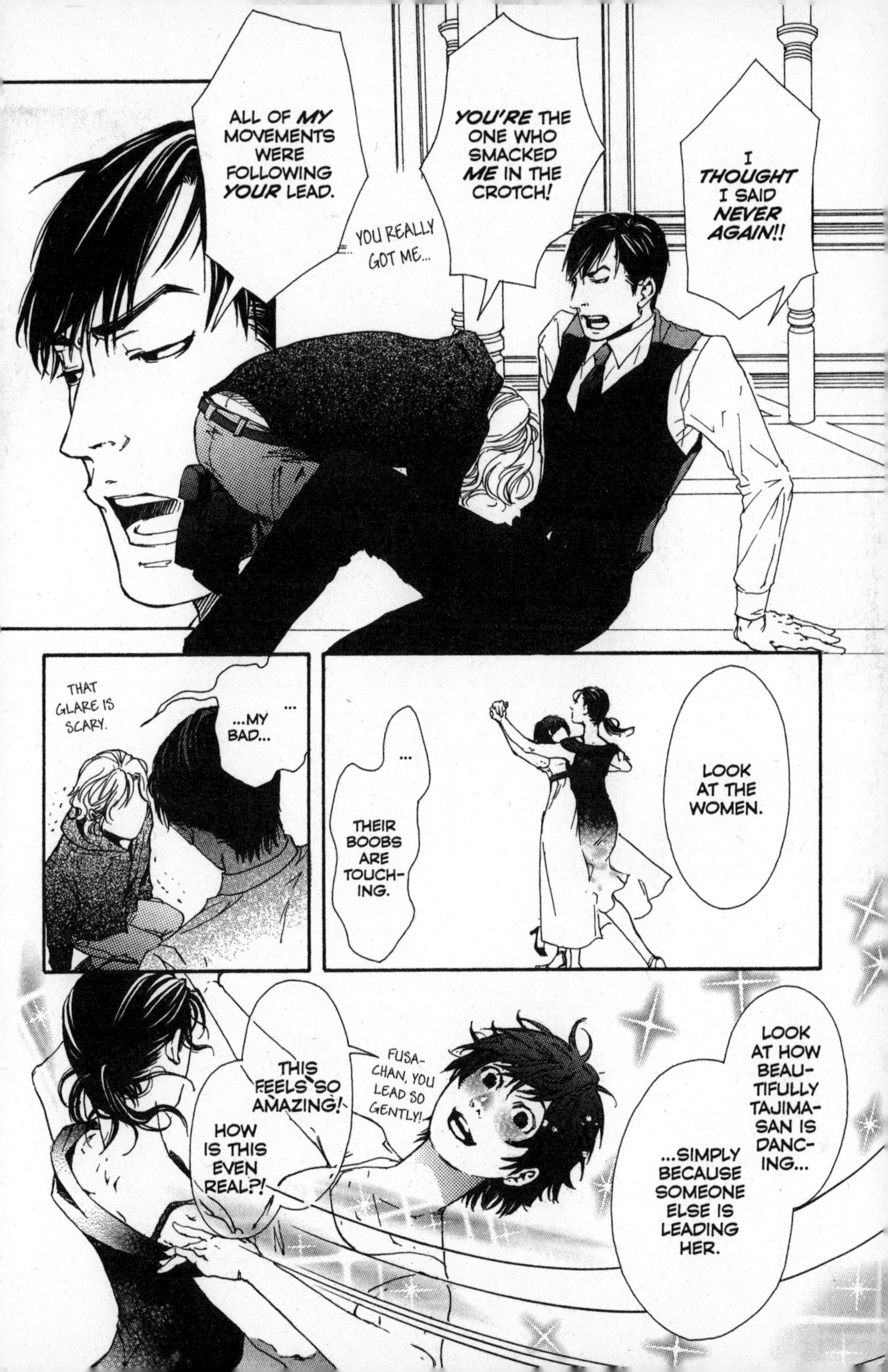
I THOUGHT I SAID NEVER AGAIN!!
YOU'RE THE ONE WHO SMACKED ME IN THE CROTCH!
...YOU REALLY GOT ME...
ALL OF MY MOVEMENTS WERE FOLLOWING YOUR LEAD.
LOOK AT THE WOMEN.
...
THEIR BOOBS ARE TOUCHING.
...
...MY BAD...
THAT GLARE IS SCARY.
LOOK AT HOW BEAUTIFULLY TAJIMA-SAN IS DANCING...
...SIMPLY BECAUSE SOMEONE ELSE IS LEADING HER.
FUSA-CHAN, YOU LEAD SO GENTLY!
THIS FEELS SO AMAZING!
HOW IS THIS EVEN REAL?!

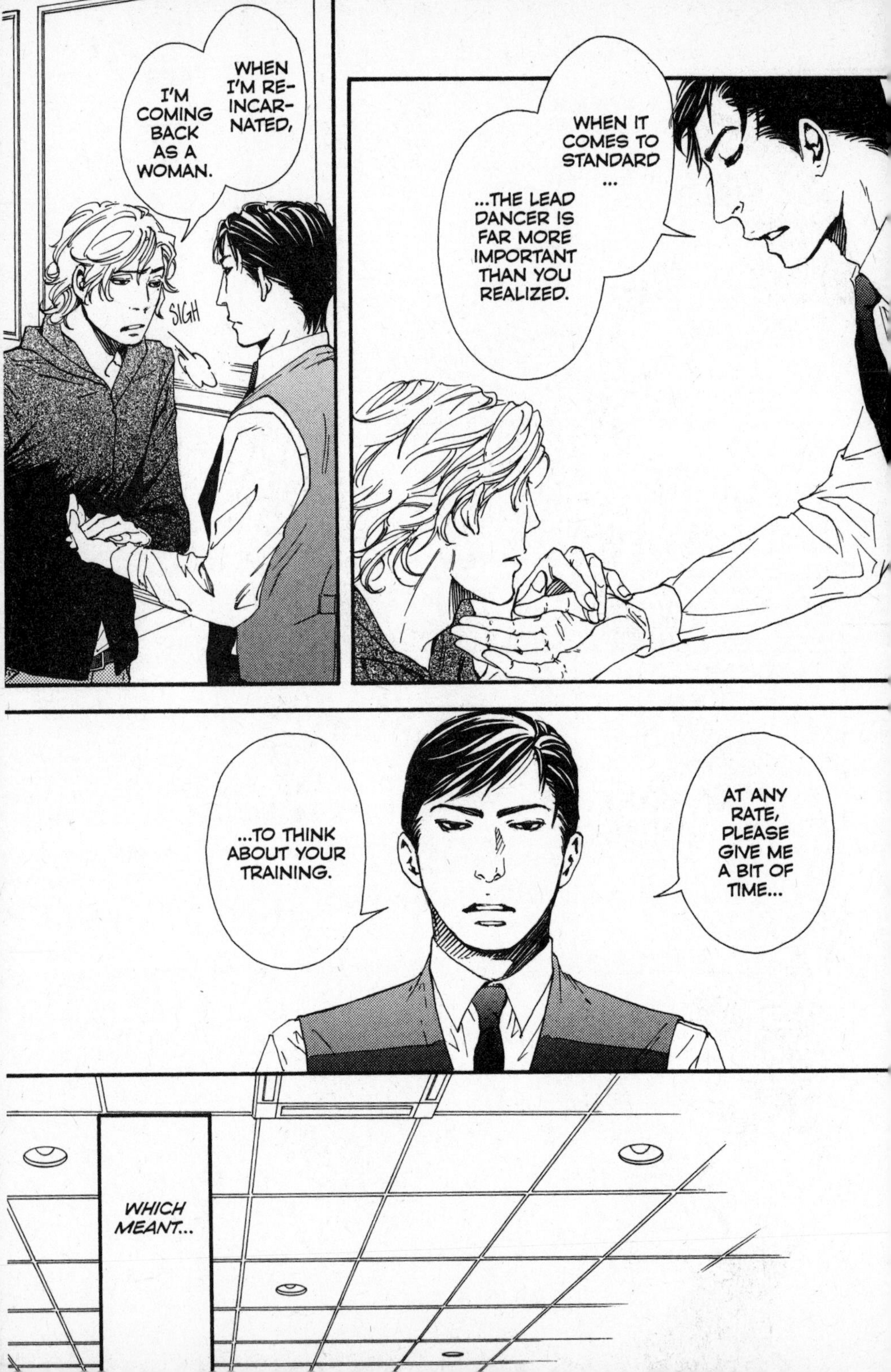
WHEN IT COMES TO STANDARD ...
...THE LEAD DANCER IS FAR MORE IMPORTANT THAN YOU REALIZED.
WHEN I'M RE-INCARNATED,
I'M COMING BACK AS A WOMAN.
SIGH
AT ANY RATE, PLEASE GIVE ME A BIT OF TIME...
...TO THINK ABOUT YOUR TRAINING.
WHICH MEANT...

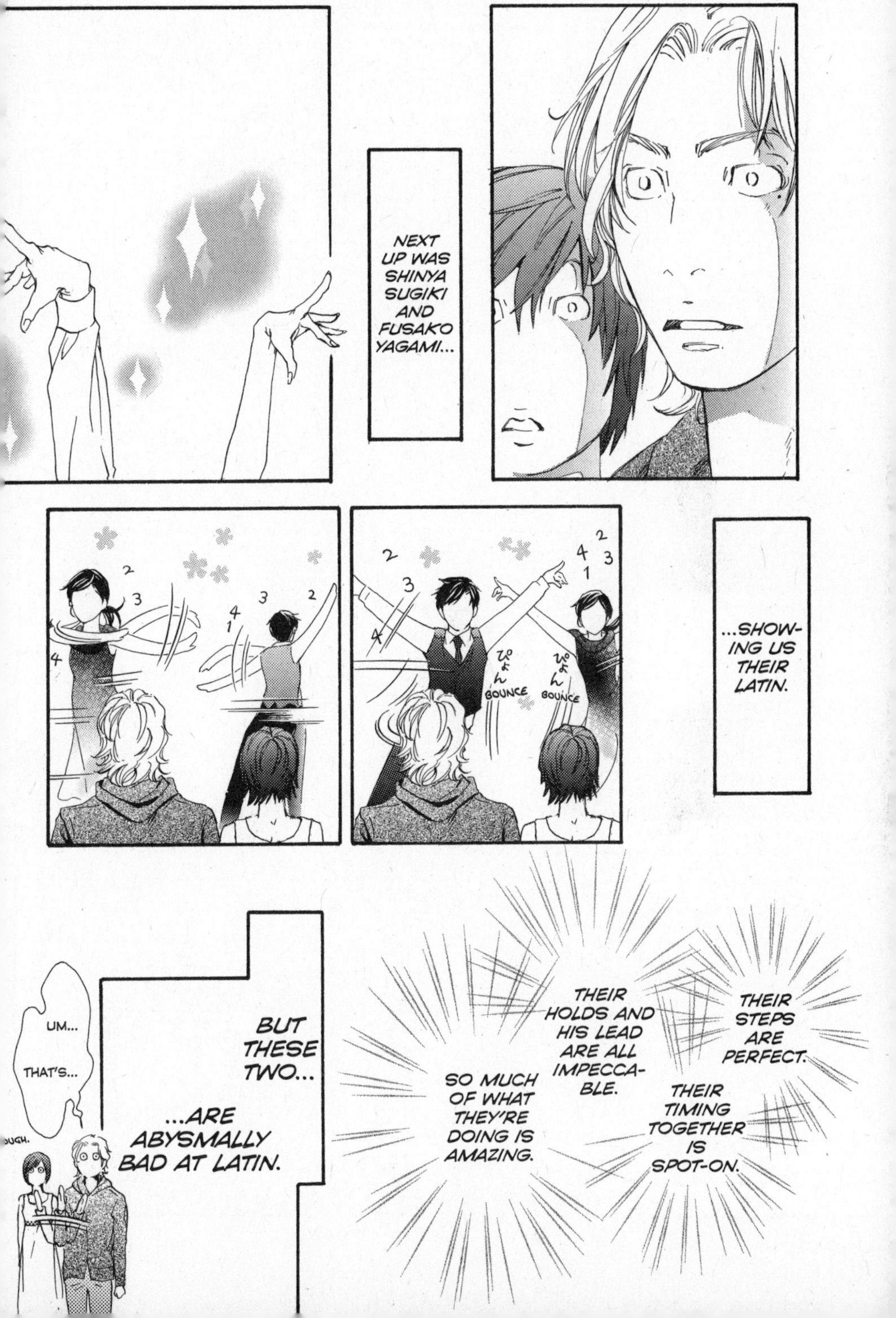
NEXT UP WAS SHINYA SUGIKI AND FUSAKO YAGAMI...
...SHOWING US THEIR LATIN.
ぴょん
BOUNCE
ぴょん
BOUNCE
THEIR STEPS ARE PERFECT.
THEIR HOLDS AND HIS LEAD ARE ALL IMPECCA-BLE.
THEIR TIMING TOGETHER IS SPOT-ON.
SO MUCH OF WHAT THEY'RE DOING IS AMAZING.
BUT THESE TWO...
...ARE ABYSMALLY BAD AT LATIN.
UM...
THAT'S...
UGH.

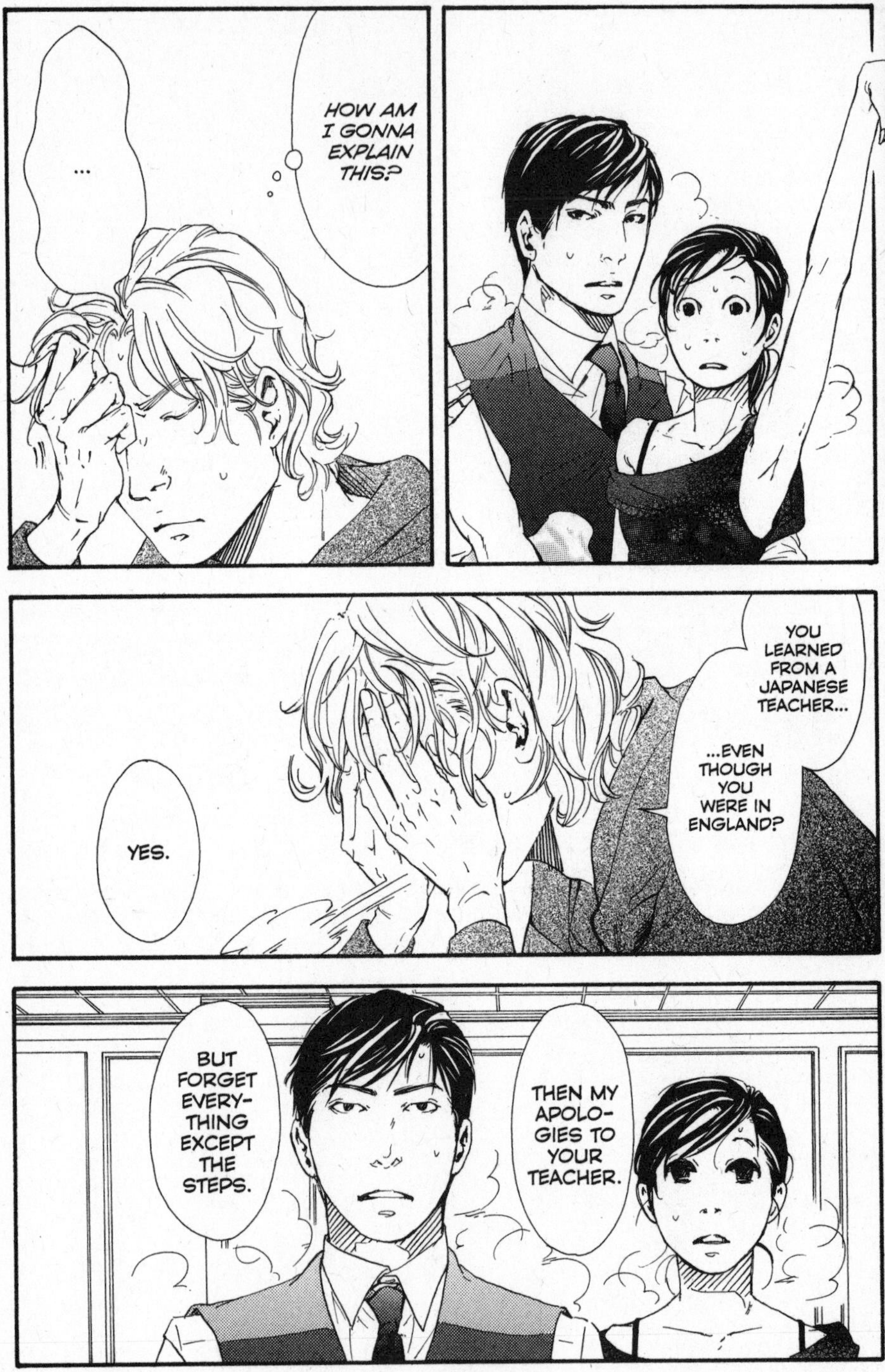
HOW AM I GONNA EXPLAIN THIS?
...
YOU LEARNED FROM A JAPANESE TEACHER...
...EVEN THOUGH YOU WERE IN ENGLAND?
YES.
THEN MY APOLOGIES TO YOUR TEACHER.
BUT FORGET EVERY-THING EXCEPT THE STEPS.

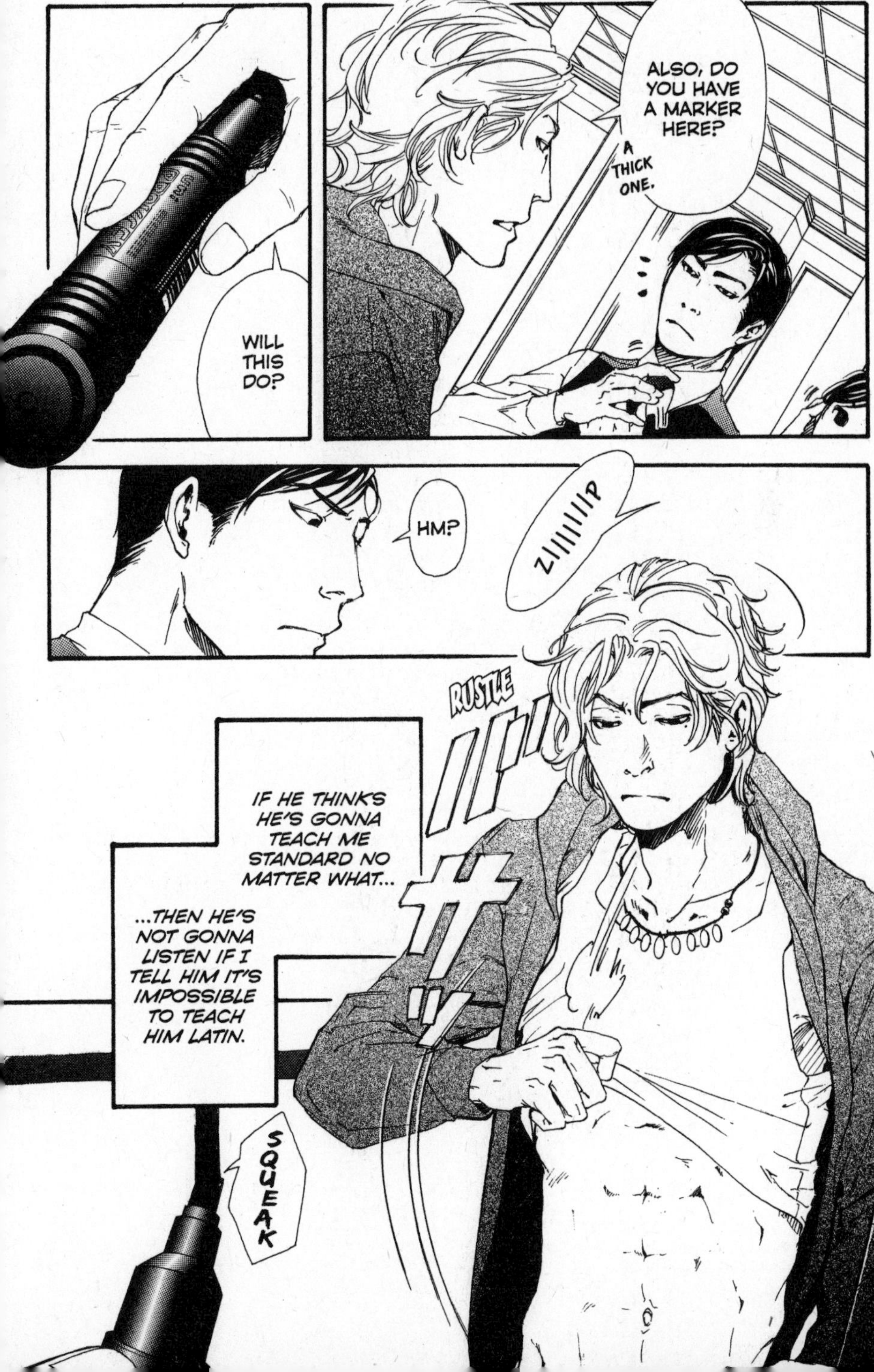
ALSO, DO YOU HAVE A MARKER HERE?
A THICK ONE.
WILL THIS DO?
ZIIIIIIP
HM?
RUSTLE
IF HE THINKS HE'S GONNA TEACH ME STANDARD NO MATTER WHAT...
...THEN HE'S NOT GONNA LISTEN IF I TELL HIM IT'S IMPOSSIBLE TO TEACH HIM LATIN.
SQUEAK

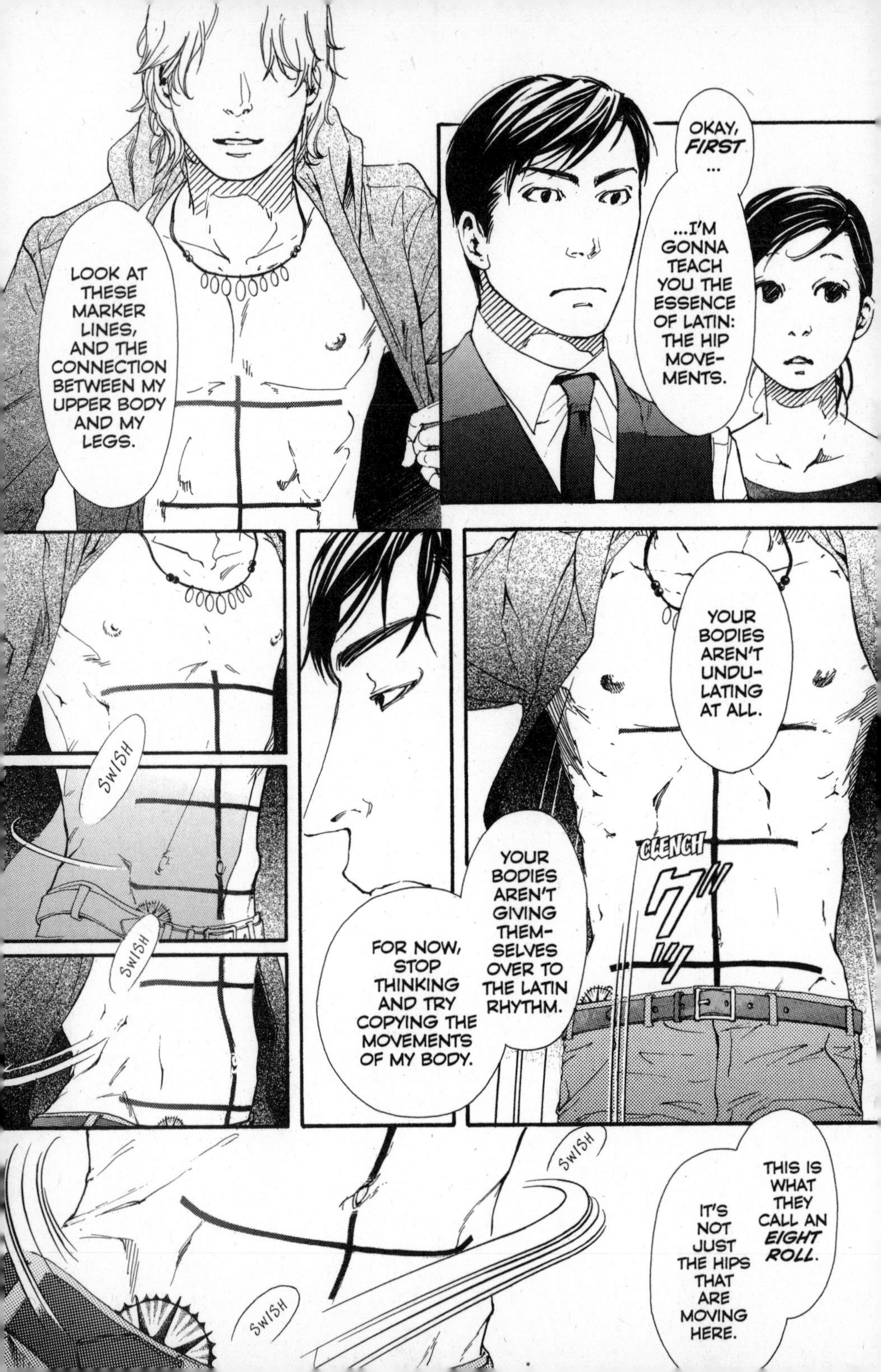
OKAY, *FIRST* ...
...I'M GONNA TEACH YOU THE ESSENCE OF LATIN: THE HIP MOVEMENTS.
LOOK AT THESE MARKER LINES, AND THE CONNECTION BETWEEN MY UPPER BODY AND MY LEGS.
YOUR BODIES AREN'T UNDULATING AT ALL.
CLENCH
YOUR BODIES AREN'T GIVING THEMSELVES OVER TO THE LATIN RHYTHM.
FOR NOW, STOP THINKING AND TRY COPYING THE MOVEMENTS OF MY BODY.
SWISH
SWISH
THIS IS WHAT THEY CALL AN *EIGHT ROLL*.
IT'S NOT JUST THE HIPS THAT ARE MOVING HERE.
SWISH
SWISH

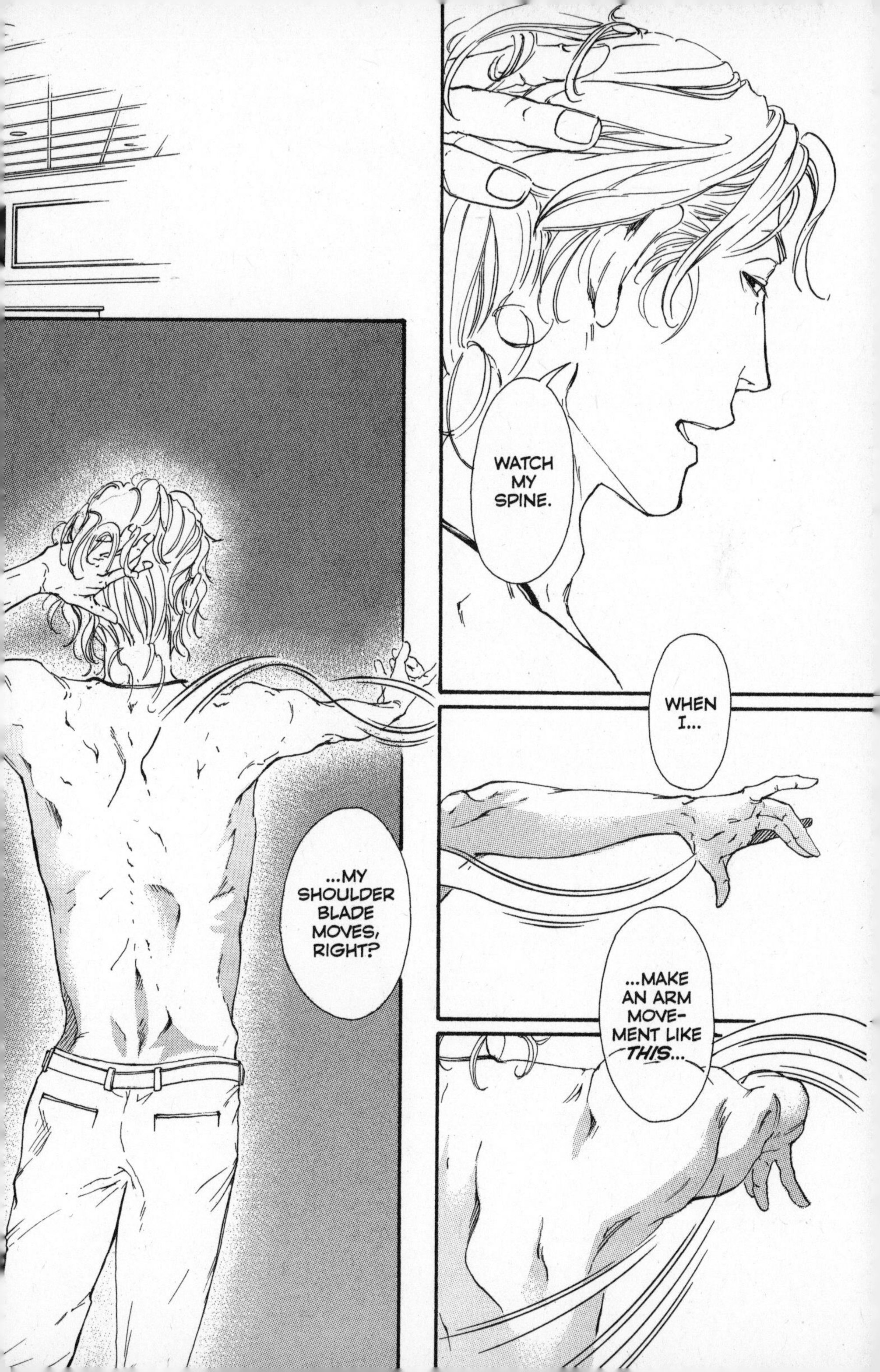
WATCH MY SPINE.
WHEN I...
...MAKE AN ARM MOVE-MENT LIKE *THIS*...
...MY SHOULDER BLADE MOVES, RIGHT?

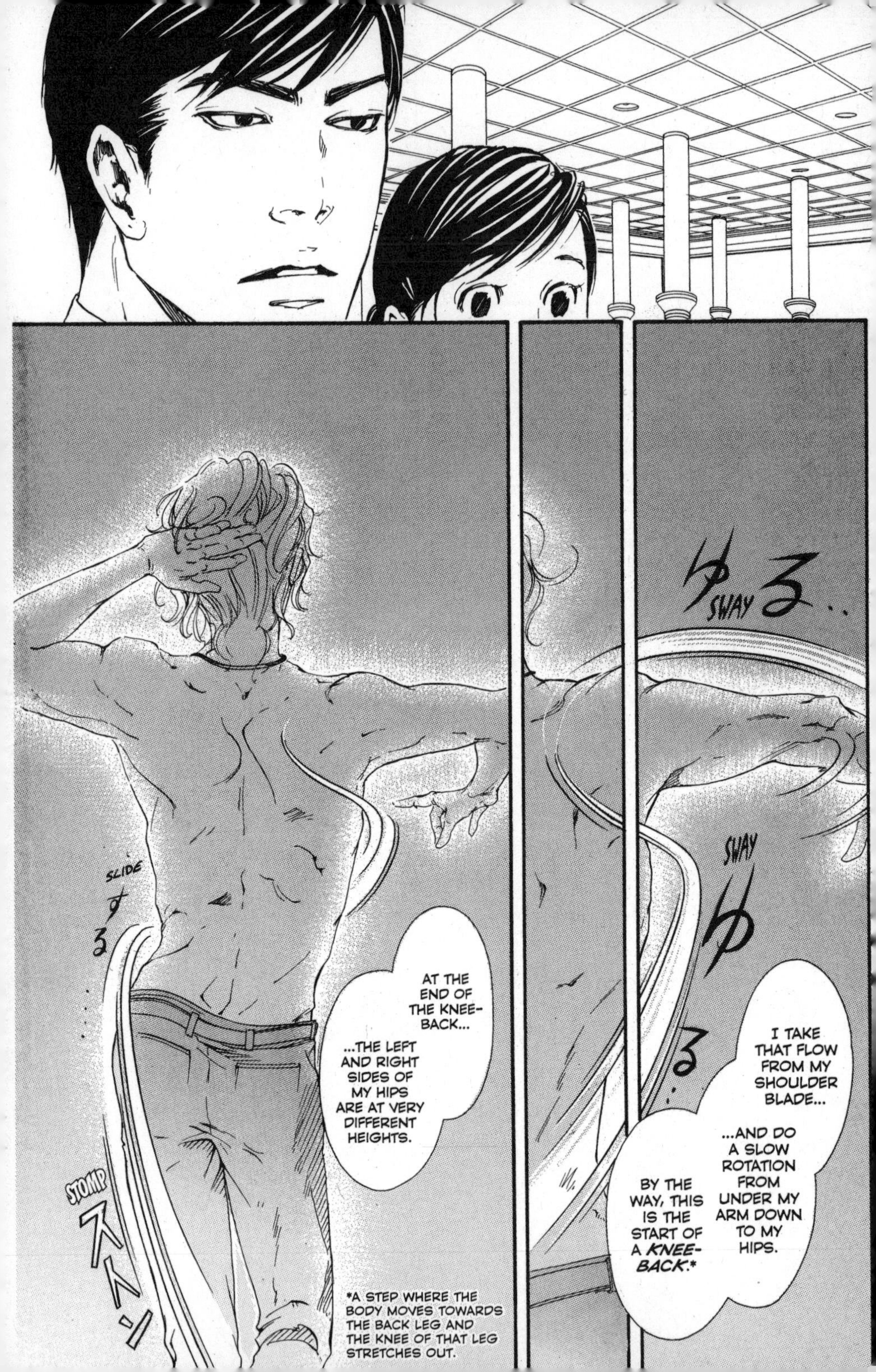
SWAY
SWAY
I TAKE THAT FLOW FROM MY SHOULDER BLADE...
...AND DO A SLOW ROTATION FROM UNDER MY ARM DOWN TO MY HIPS.
BY THE WAY, THIS IS THE START OF A ***KNEE-BACK.****
SLIDE
AT THE END OF THE KNEE-BACK...
...THE LEFT AND RIGHT SIDES OF MY HIPS ARE AT VERY DIFFERENT HEIGHTS.
STOMP
*A STEP WHERE THE BODY MOVES TOWARDS THE BACK LEG AND THE KNEE OF THAT LEG STRETCHES OUT.

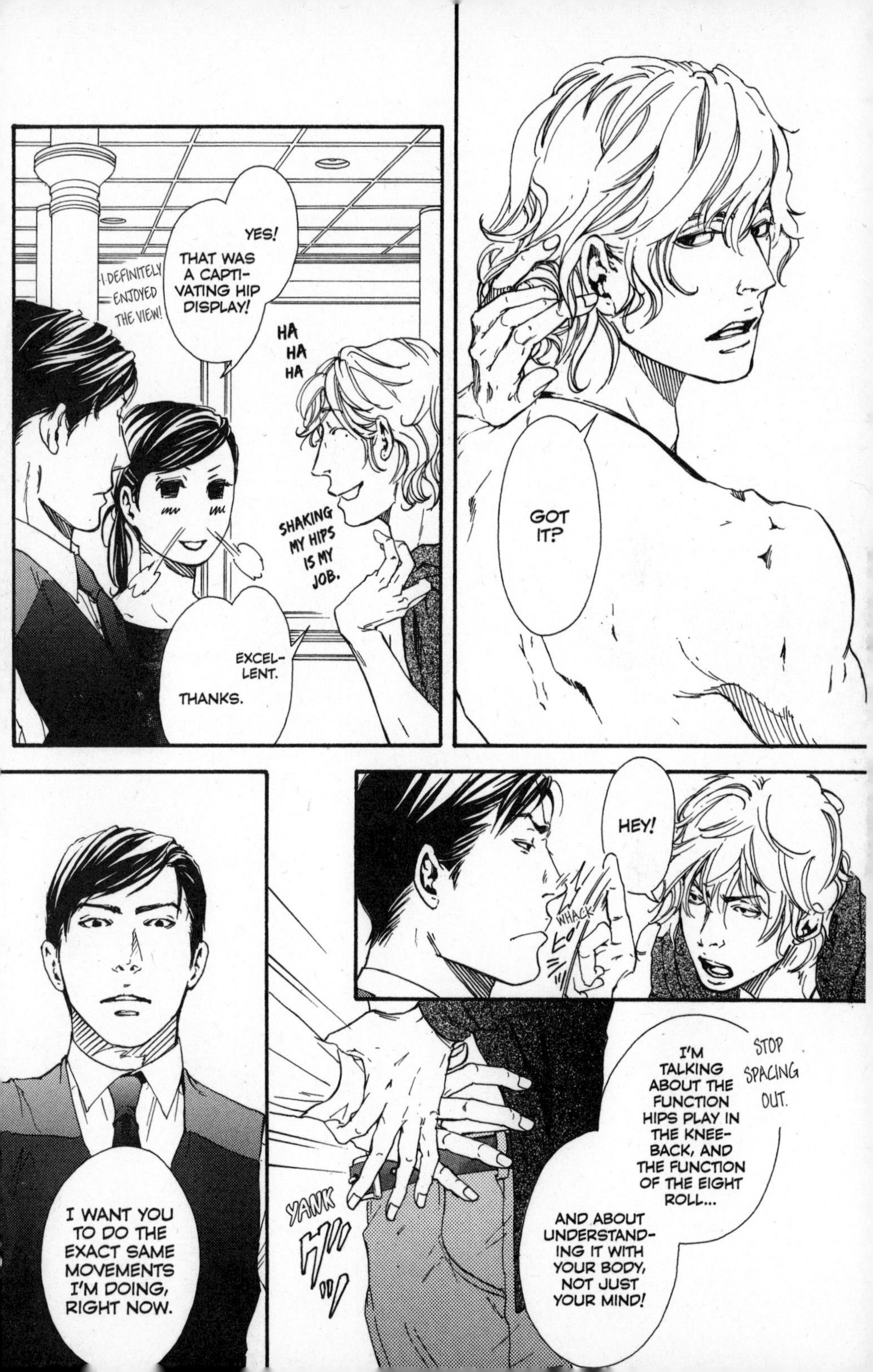
GOT IT?
YES!
THAT WAS A CAPTIVATING HIP DISPLAY!
I DEFINITELY ENJOYED THE VIEW!
HA HA HA
SHAKING MY HIPS IS MY JOB.
EXCEL-LENT.
THANKS.
HEY!
WHACK
YANK
STOP SPACING OUT.
I'M TALKING ABOUT THE FUNCTION HIPS PLAY IN THE KNEE-BACK, AND THE FUNCTION OF THE EIGHT ROLL...
AND ABOUT UNDERSTAND-ING IT WITH YOUR BODY, NOT JUST YOUR MIND!
I WANT YOU TO DO THE EXACT SAME MOVEMENTS I'M DOING, RIGHT NOW.

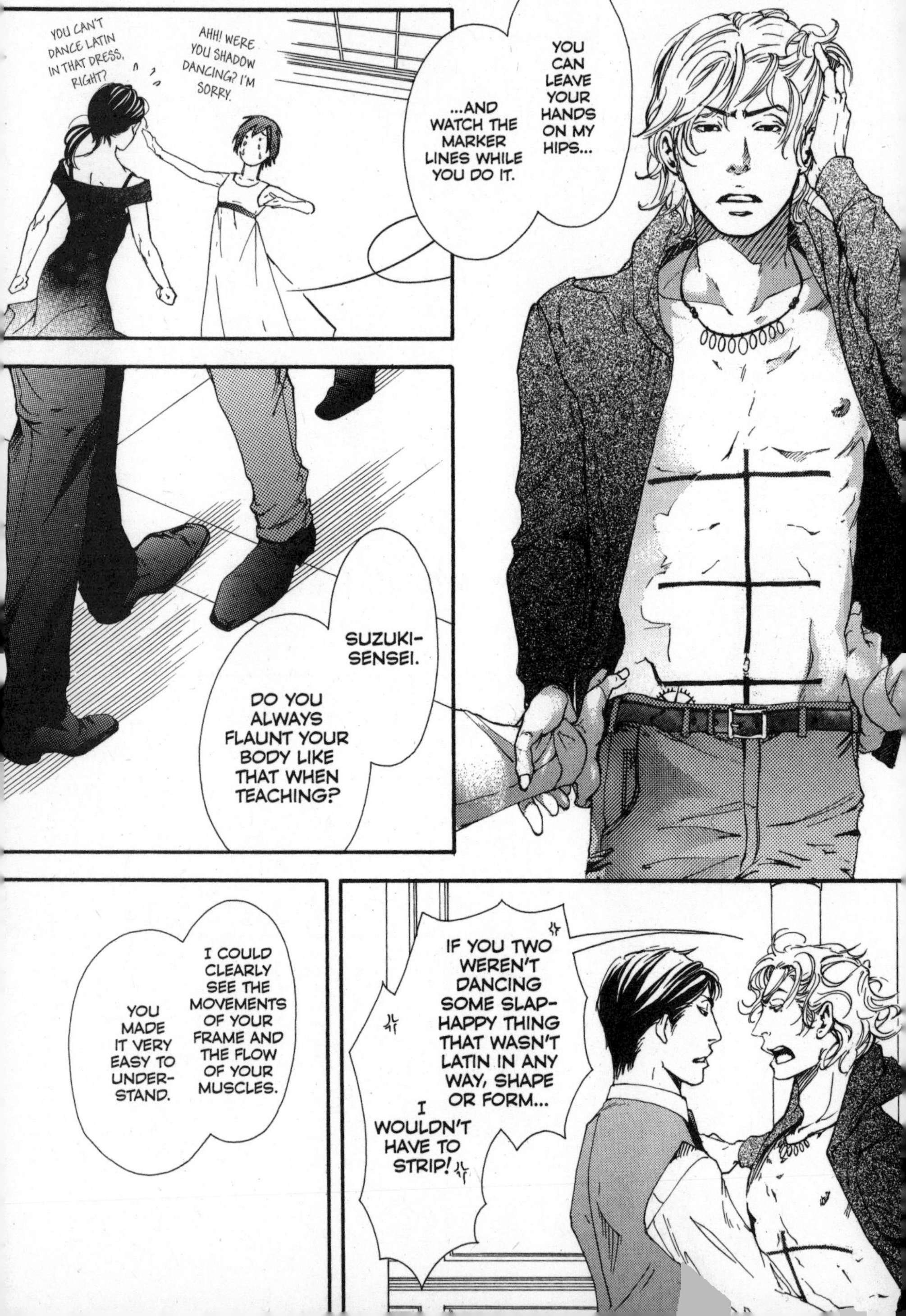
YOU CAN LEAVE YOUR HANDS ON MY HIPS...
...AND WATCH THE MARKER LINES WHILE YOU DO IT.
AHH! WERE YOU SHADOW DANCING? I'M SORRY.
YOU CAN'T DANCE LATIN IN THAT DRESS, RIGHT?
SUZUKI-SENSEI.
DO YOU ALWAYS FLAUNT YOUR BODY LIKE THAT WHEN TEACHING?
IF YOU TWO WEREN'T DANCING SOME SLAP-HAPPY THING THAT WASN'T LATIN IN ANY WAY, SHAPE OR FORM...
I WOULDN'T HAVE TO STRIP!
I COULD CLEARLY SEE THE MOVEMENTS OF YOUR FRAME AND THE FLOW OF YOUR MUSCLES.
YOU MADE IT VERY EASY TO UNDER-STAND.

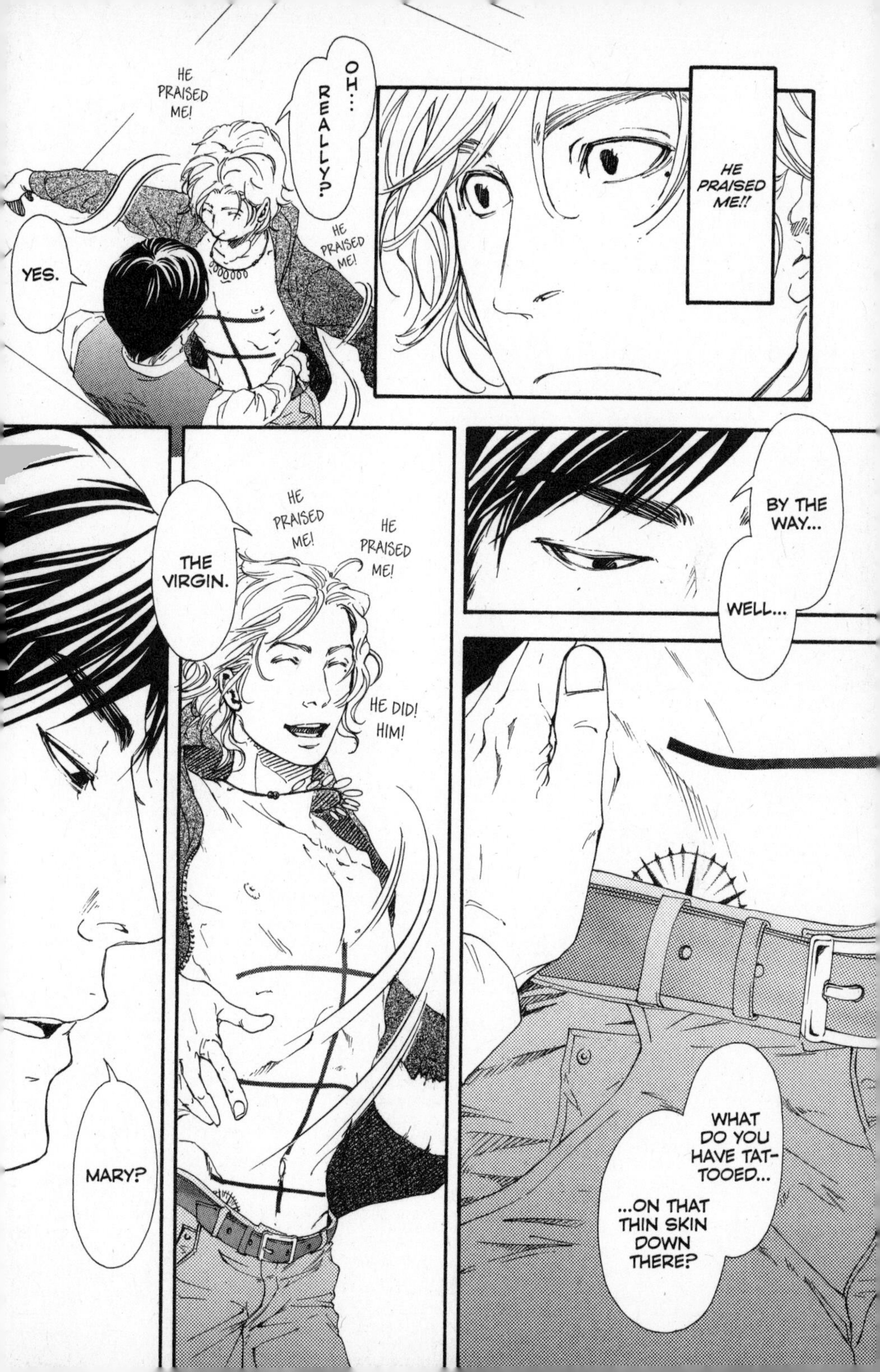
HE PRAISED ME!!
OH... REALLY?
HE PRAISED ME!
HE PRAISED ME!
YES.
BY THE WAY...
WELL...
WHAT DO YOU HAVE TAT-TOOED...
...ON THAT THIN SKIN DOWN THERE?
HE PRAISED ME!
HE PRAISED ME!
THE VIRGIN.
HE DID! HIM!
MARY?

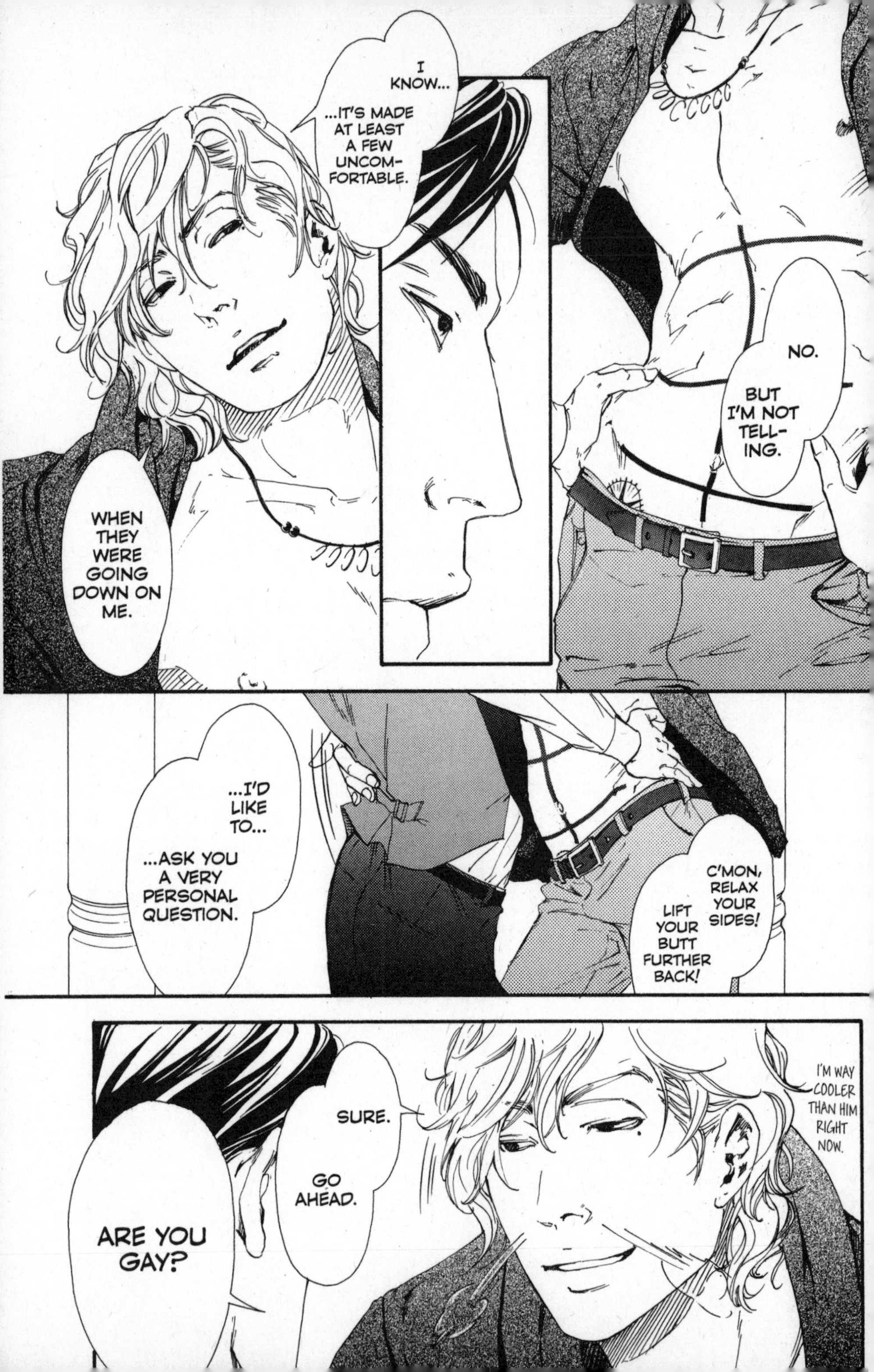
NO.
BUT I'M NOT TELLING.
I KNOW...
...IT'S MADE AT LEAST A FEW UNCOMFORTABLE.
WHEN THEY WERE GOING DOWN ON ME.
C'MON, RELAX YOUR SIDES!
LIFT YOUR BUTT FURTHER BACK!
...I'D LIKE TO...
...ASK YOU A VERY PERSONAL QUESTION.
I'M WAY COOLER THAN HIM RIGHT NOW.
SURE.
GO AHEAD.
ARE YOU GAY?

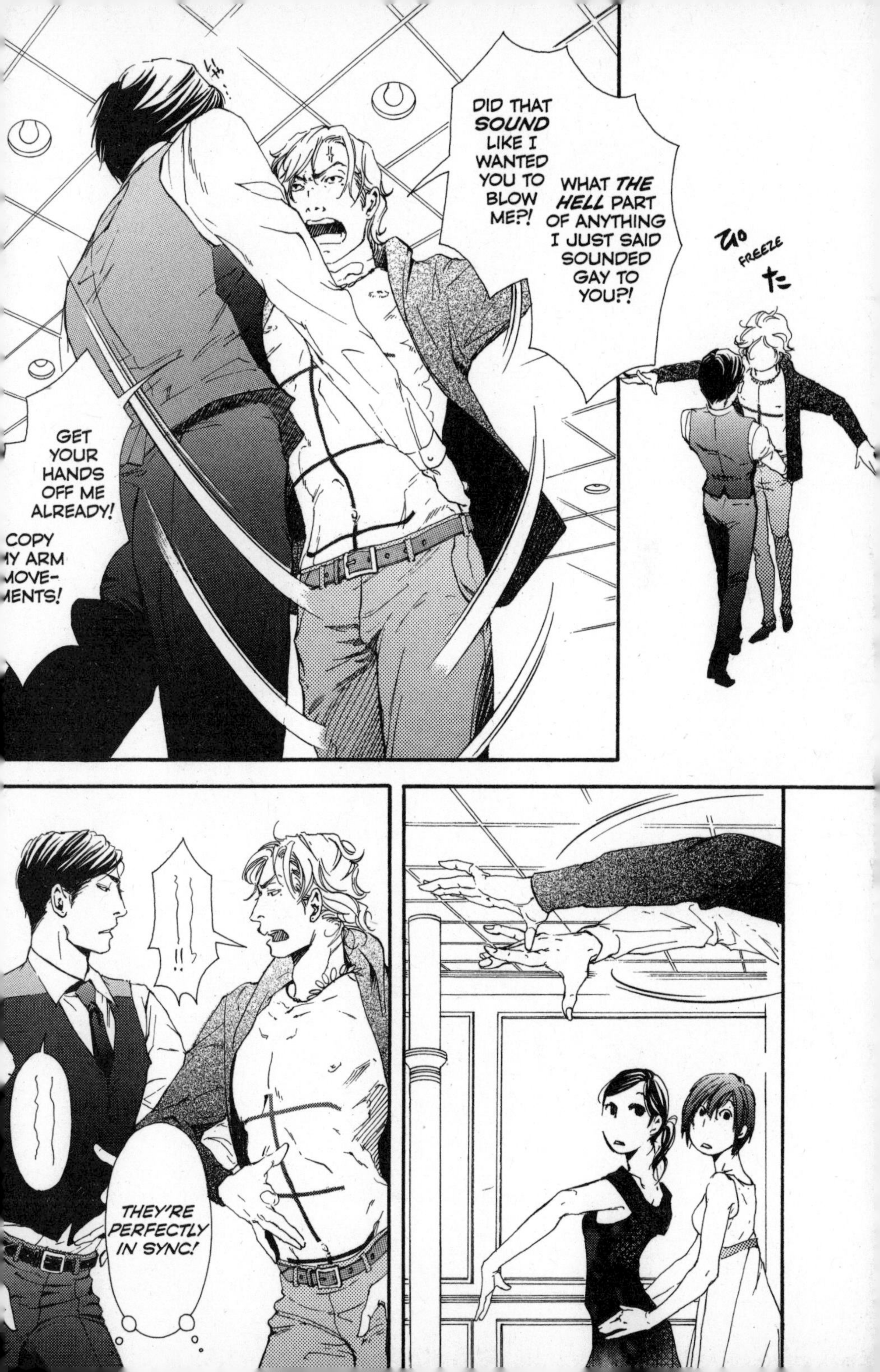
FREEZE
WHAT THE HELL PART OF ANYTHING I JUST SAID SOUNDED GAY TO YOU?!
DID THAT SOUND LIKE I WANTED YOU TO BLOW ME?!
GET YOUR HANDS OFF ME ALREADY!
COPY MY ARM MOVEMENTS!
!!
THEY'RE PERFECTLY IN SYNC!

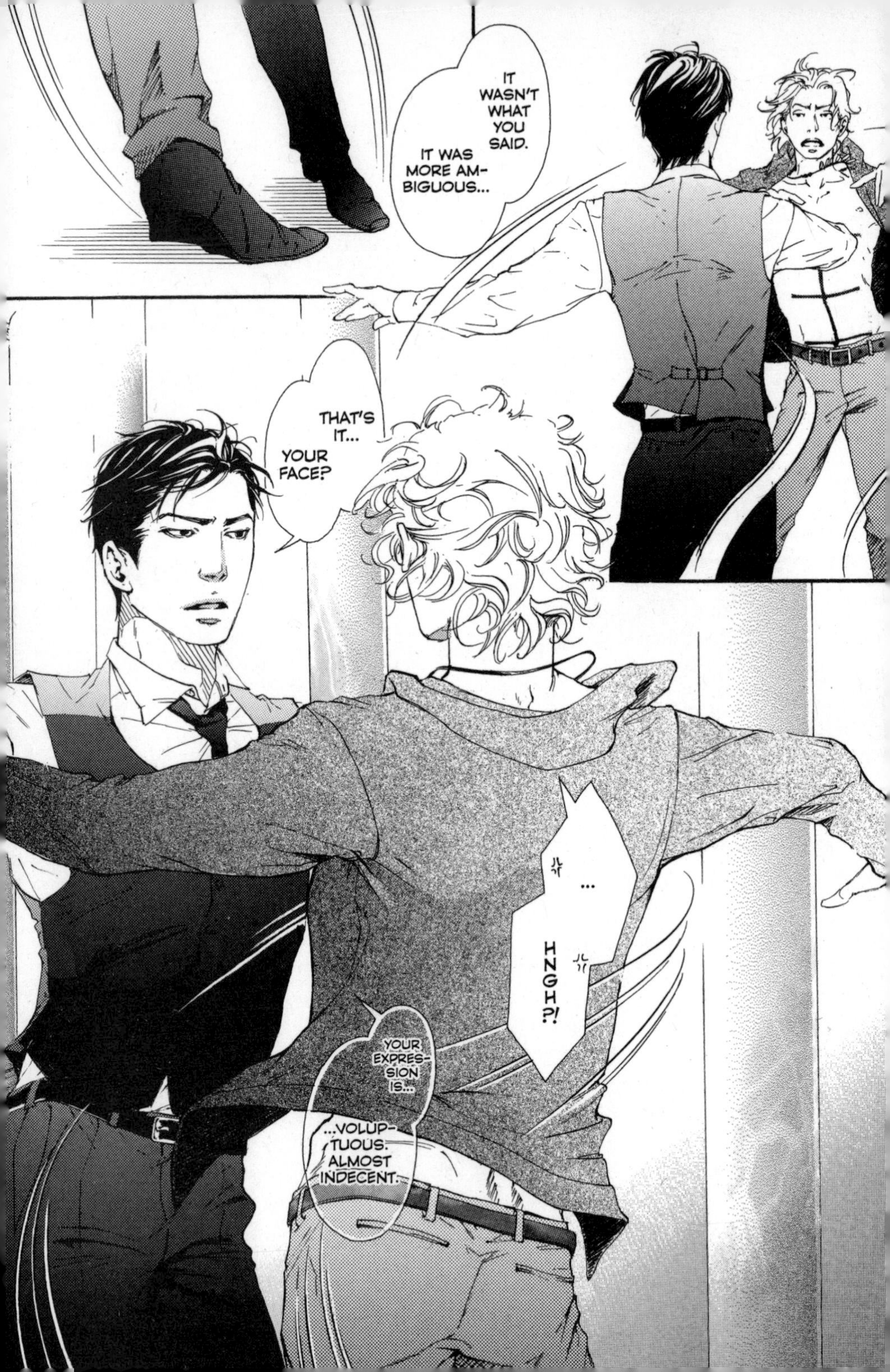
IT WASN'T WHAT YOU SAID. IT WAS MORE AM-BIGUOUS...
THAT'S IT... YOUR FACE?
... HNGH?!
YOUR EXPRES-SION IS... ...VOLUP-TUOUS. ALMOST INDECENT.

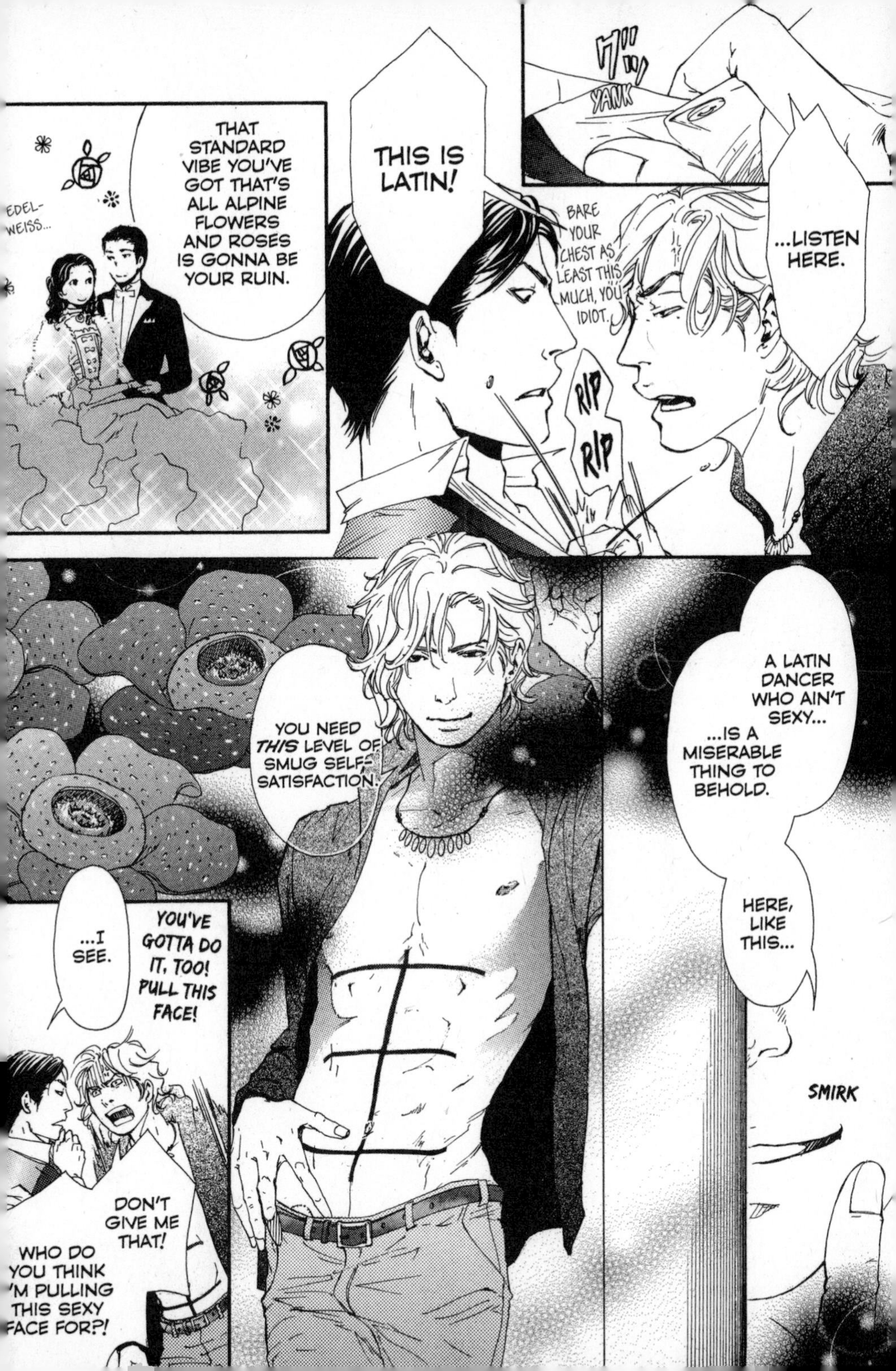
YANK
...LISTEN HERE.
BARE YOUR CHEST AS LEAST THIS MUCH, YOU IDIOT.
RIP
RIP
THIS IS LATIN!
THAT STANDARD VIBE YOU'VE GOT THAT'S ALL ALPINE FLOWERS AND ROSES IS GONNA BE YOUR RUIN.
EDEL-WEISS...
A LATIN DANCER WHO AIN'T SEXY...
...IS A MISERABLE THING TO BEHOLD.
HERE, LIKE THIS...
SMIRK
YOU NEED *THIS* LEVEL OF SMUG SELF-SATISFACTION.
YOU'VE GOTTA DO IT, TOO! PULL THIS FACE!
...I SEE.
DON'T GIVE ME THAT!
WHO DO YOU THINK I'M PULLING THIS SEXY FACE FOR?!

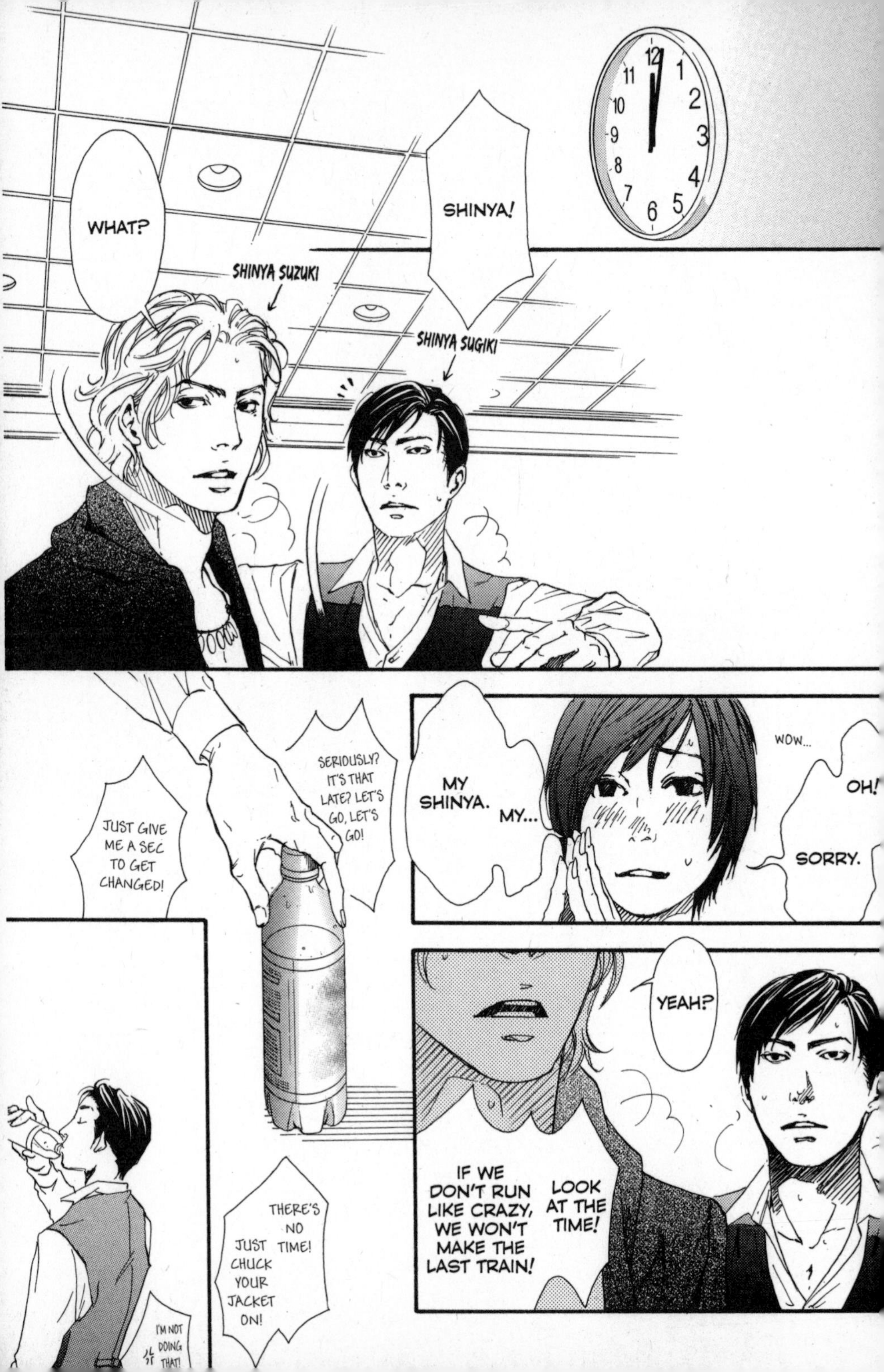
SHINYA!
WHAT?
SHINYA SUGIKI
SHINYA SUZUKI
WOW...
OH! SORRY.
MY... MY SHINYA.
SERIOUSLY? IT'S THAT LATE? LET'S GO, LET'S GO!
JUST GIVE ME A SEC TO GET CHANGED!
YEAH?
LOOK AT THE TIME!
IF WE DON'T RUN LIKE CRAZY, WE WON'T MAKE THE LAST TRAIN!
THERE'S NO TIME! JUST CHUCK YOUR JACKET ON!
I'M NOT DOING THAT!

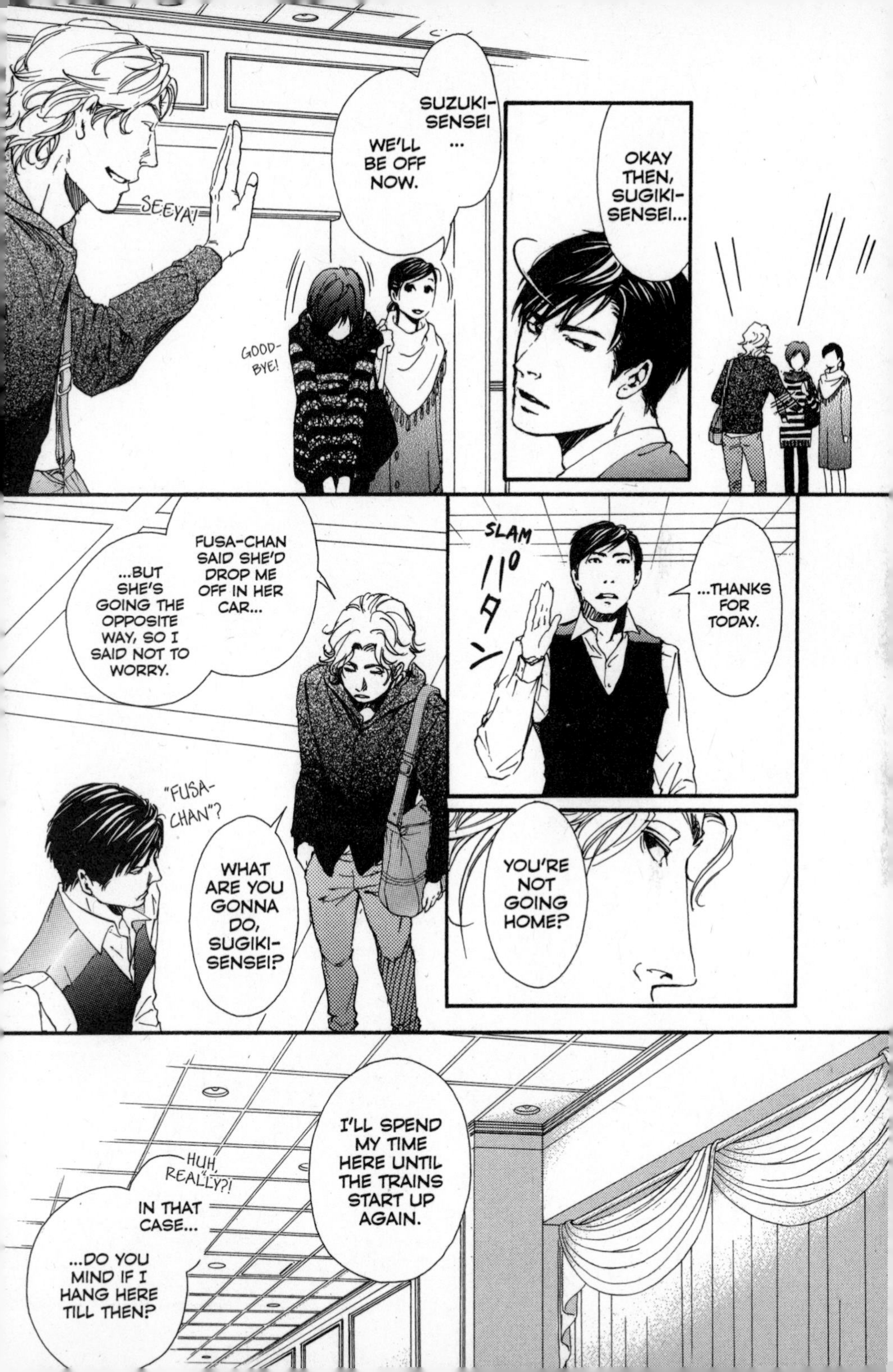
OKAY THEN, SUGIKI-SENSEI...
SUZUKI-SENSEI...
WE'LL BE OFF NOW.
SEE YA!
GOOD-BYE!
SLAM
バタン
...THANKS FOR TODAY.
YOU'RE NOT GOING HOME?
FUSA-CHAN SAID SHE'D DROP ME OFF IN HER CAR...
...BUT SHE'S GOING THE OPPOSITE WAY, SO I SAID NOT TO WORRY.
WHAT ARE YOU GONNA DO, SUGIKI-SENSEI?
"FUSA-CHAN"?
I'LL SPEND MY TIME HERE UNTIL THE TRAINS START UP AGAIN.
HUH, REALLY?!
IN THAT CASE...
...DO YOU MIND IF I HANG HERE TILL THEN?

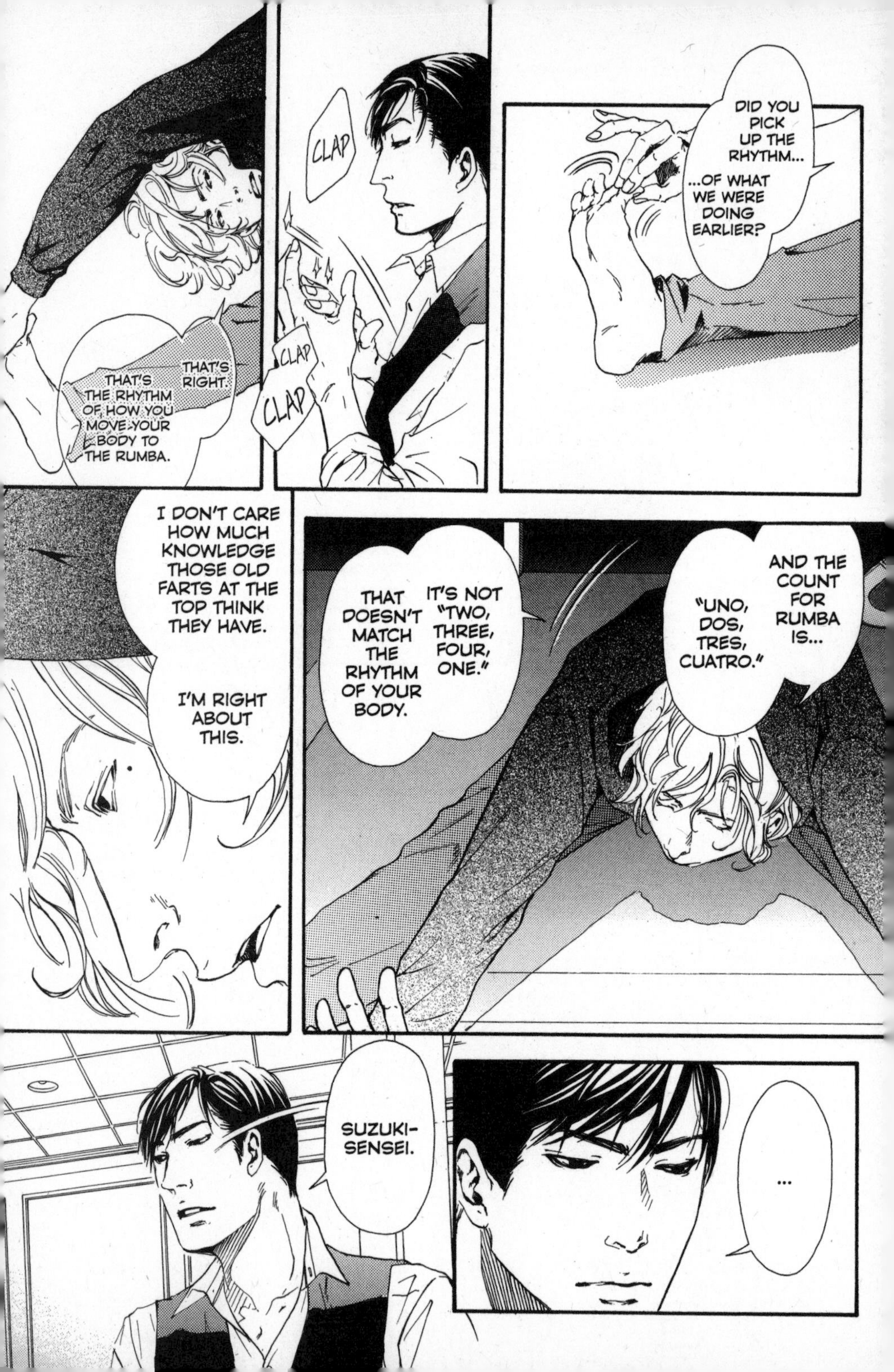
DID YOU PICK UP THE RHYTHM...
...OF WHAT WE WERE DOING EARLIER?
CLAP
CLAP
CLAP
THAT'S RIGHT.
THAT'S THE RHYTHM OF HOW YOU MOVE YOUR BODY TO THE RUMBA.
AND THE COUNT FOR RUMBA IS...
"UNO, DOS, TRES, CUATRO."
IT'S NOT "TWO, THREE, FOUR, ONE."
THAT DOESN'T MATCH THE RHYTHM OF YOUR BODY.
I DON'T CARE HOW MUCH KNOWLEDGE THOSE OLD FARTS AT THE TOP THINK THEY HAVE.
I'M RIGHT ABOUT THIS.
...
SUZUKI-SENSEI.

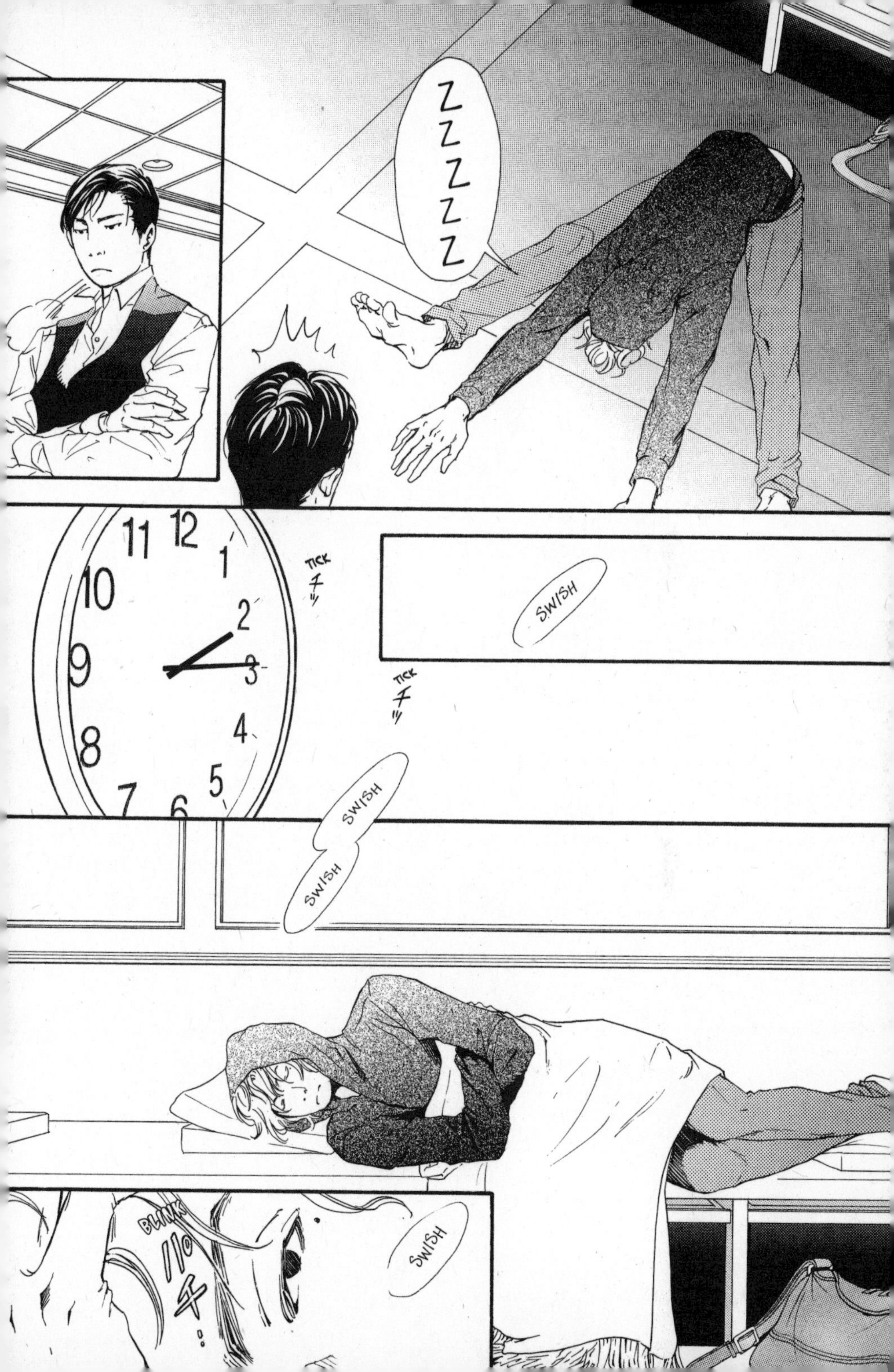
ZZZZZ
SWISH
TICK チッ
TICK チッ
SWISH
SWISH
SWISH
BLINK パチ

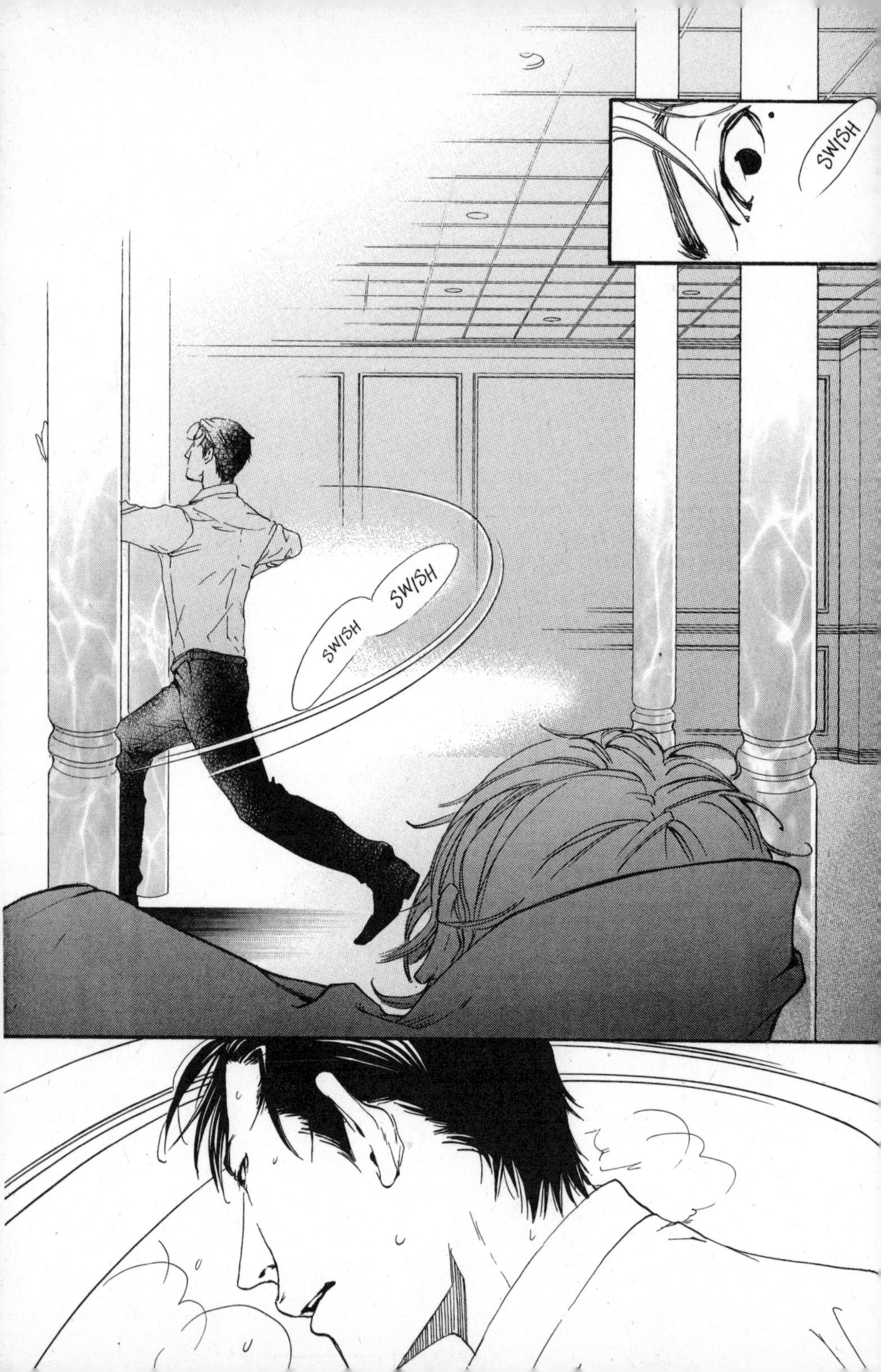
SWISH
SWISH SWISH

SLIDE

LIFT

SWOOSH

THEY'RE ALL BASIC STEPS.

YOU'RE A CHAMPION. WHY ARE YOU DOING THOSE NOW?

THOSE ARE BIG MOVE-MENTS.

SLOWER THAN YOU DO THEM AT COMPETI-TIONS.

BOTH OF THOSE THINGS PUSH YOUR MOVEMENTS TO THEIR LIMITS. IT'S ALMOST LIKE YOU'RE *TRYING* TO LOSE YOUR BALANCE.

...

DO YOU ALWAYS DO THAT?

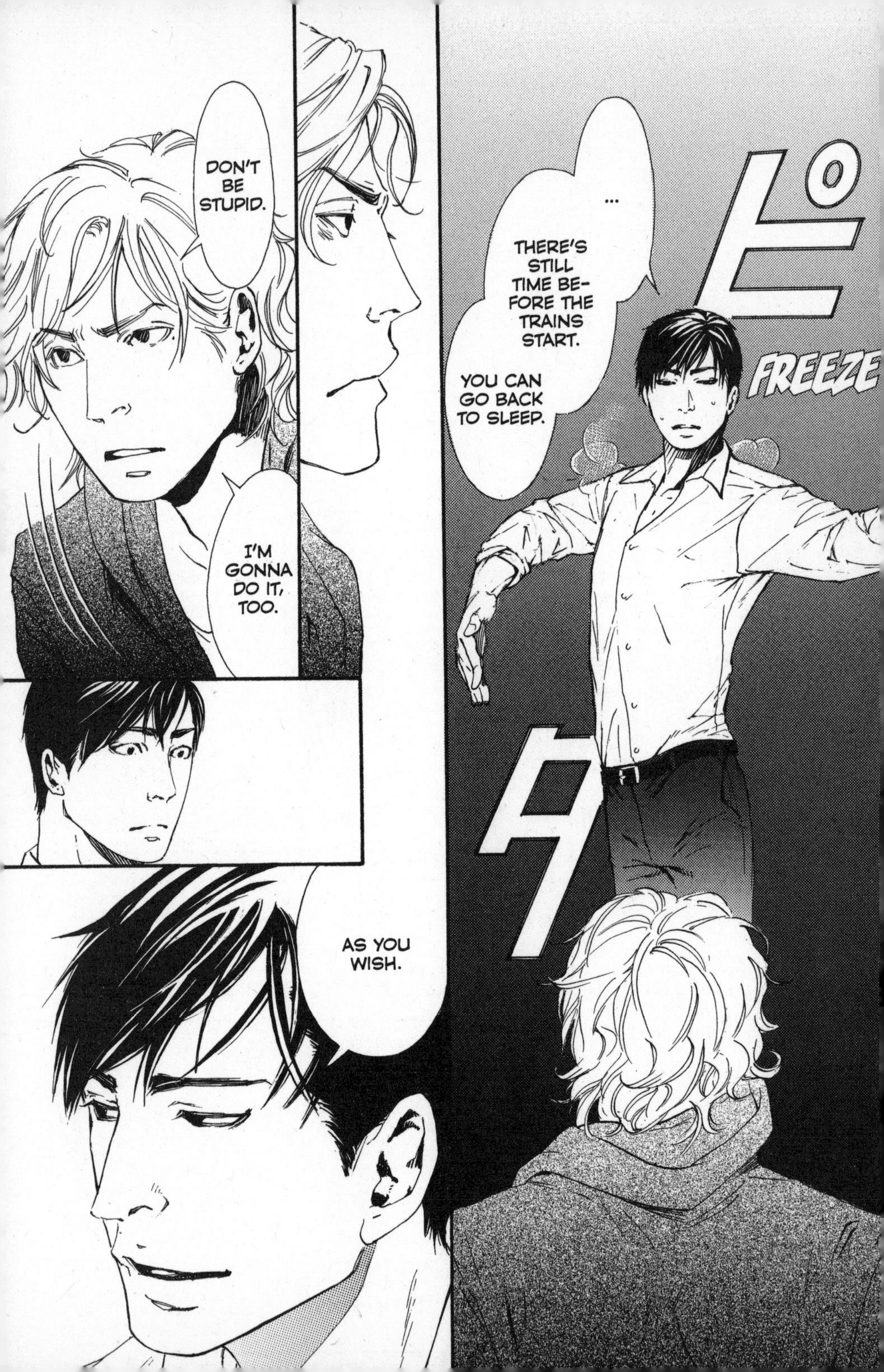
...
THERE'S STILL TIME BE-FORE THE TRAINS START.
YOU CAN GO BACK TO SLEEP.
ピ
FREEZE
タ
DON'T BE STUPID.
I'M GONNA DO IT, TOO.
AS YOU WISH.

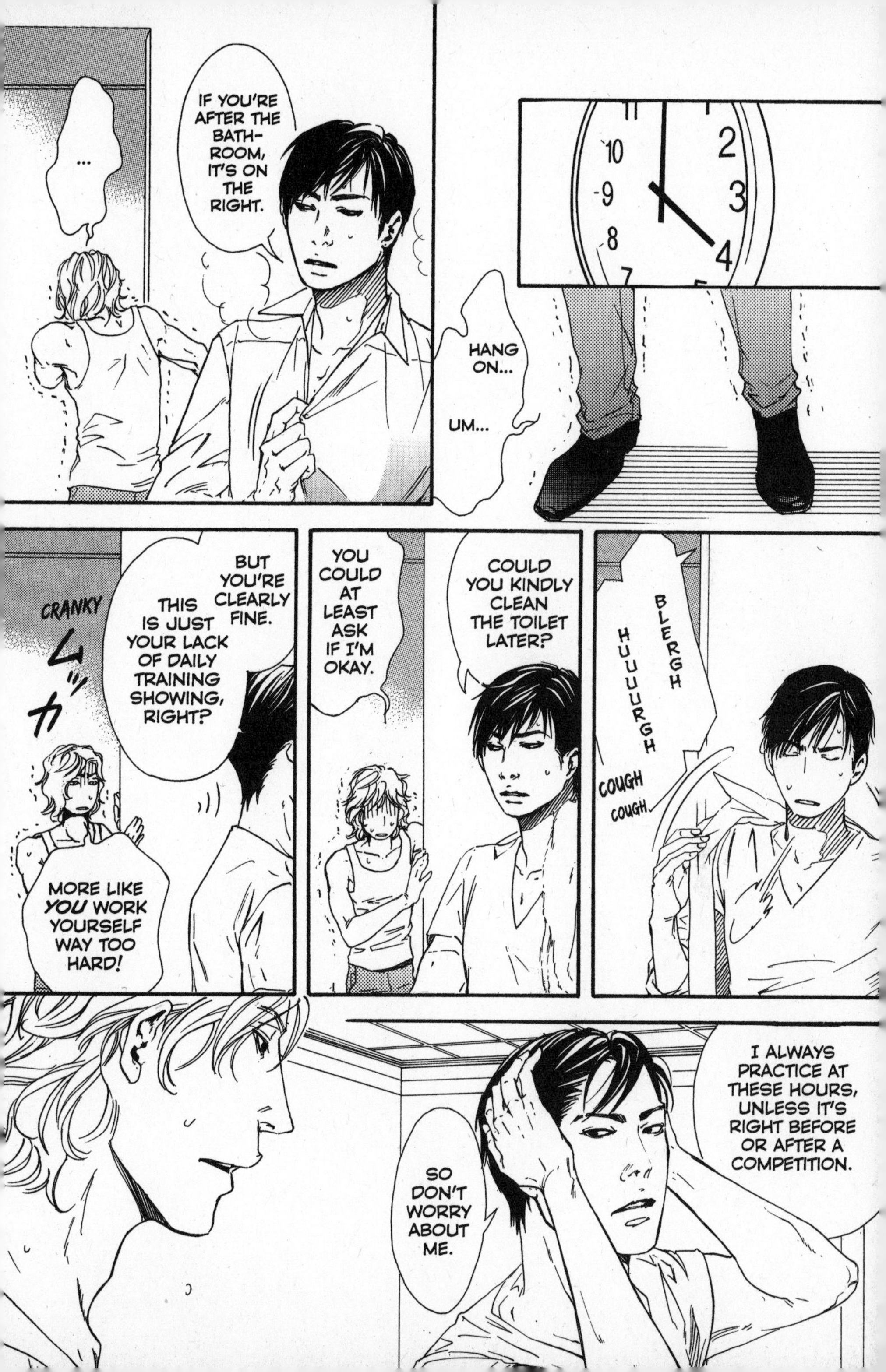
HANG ON...
UM...
IF YOU'RE AFTER THE BATH-ROOM, IT'S ON THE RIGHT.
...
BLERGH
HUUUURGH
COUGH
COUGH
COULD YOU KINDLY CLEAN THE TOILET LATER?
YOU COULD AT LEAST ASK IF I'M OKAY.
BUT YOU'RE CLEARLY FINE.
THIS IS JUST YOUR LACK OF DAILY TRAINING SHOWING, RIGHT?
CRANKY
MORE LIKE *YOU* WORK YOURSELF WAY TOO HARD!
I ALWAYS PRACTICE AT THESE HOURS, UNLESS IT'S RIGHT BEFORE OR AFTER A COMPETITION.
SO DON'T WORRY ABOUT ME.

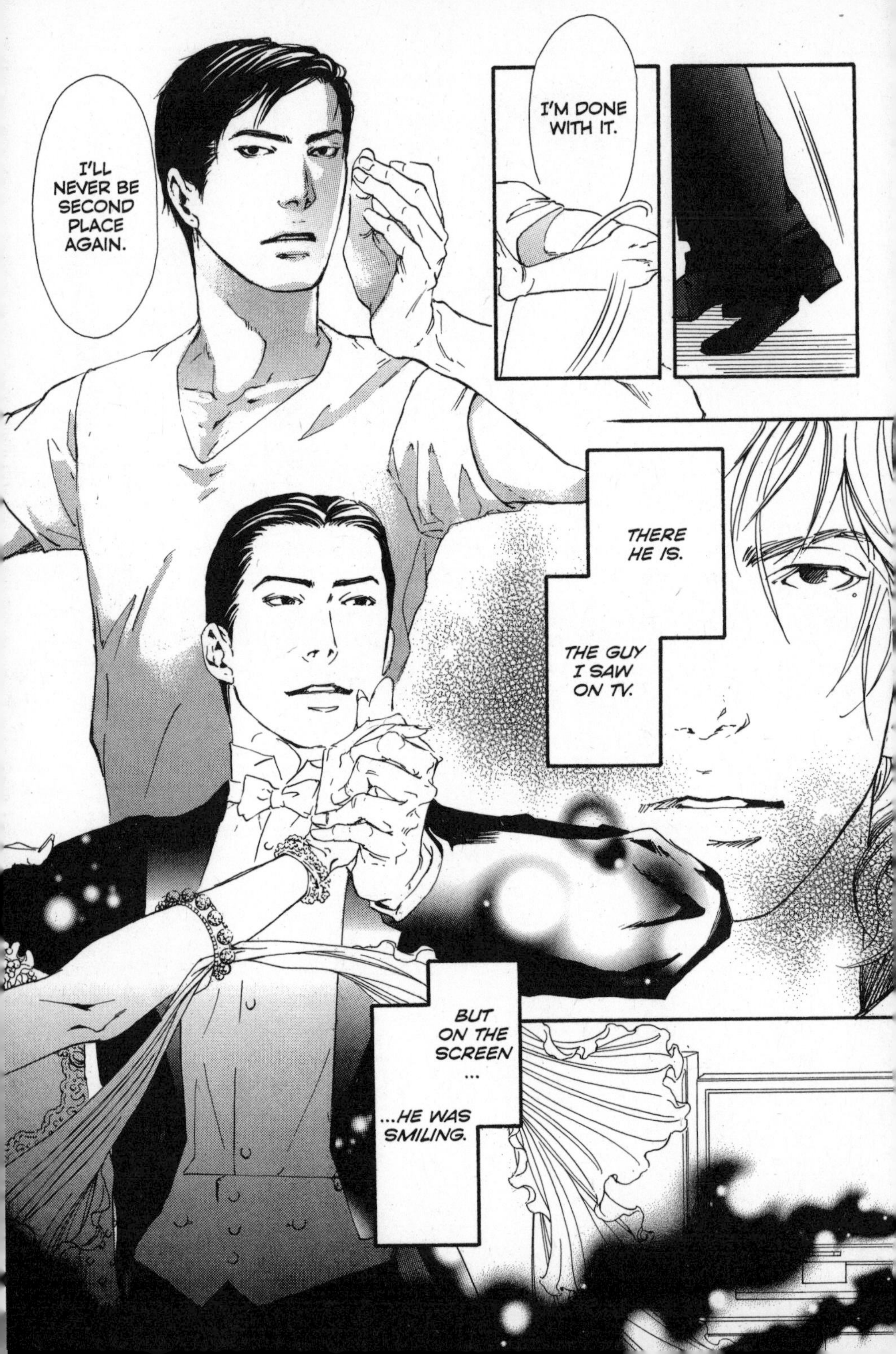
I'M DONE WITH IT.
I'LL NEVER BE SECOND PLACE AGAIN.
THERE HE IS.
THE GUY I SAW ON TV.
BUT ON THE SCREEN...
...HE WAS SMILING.

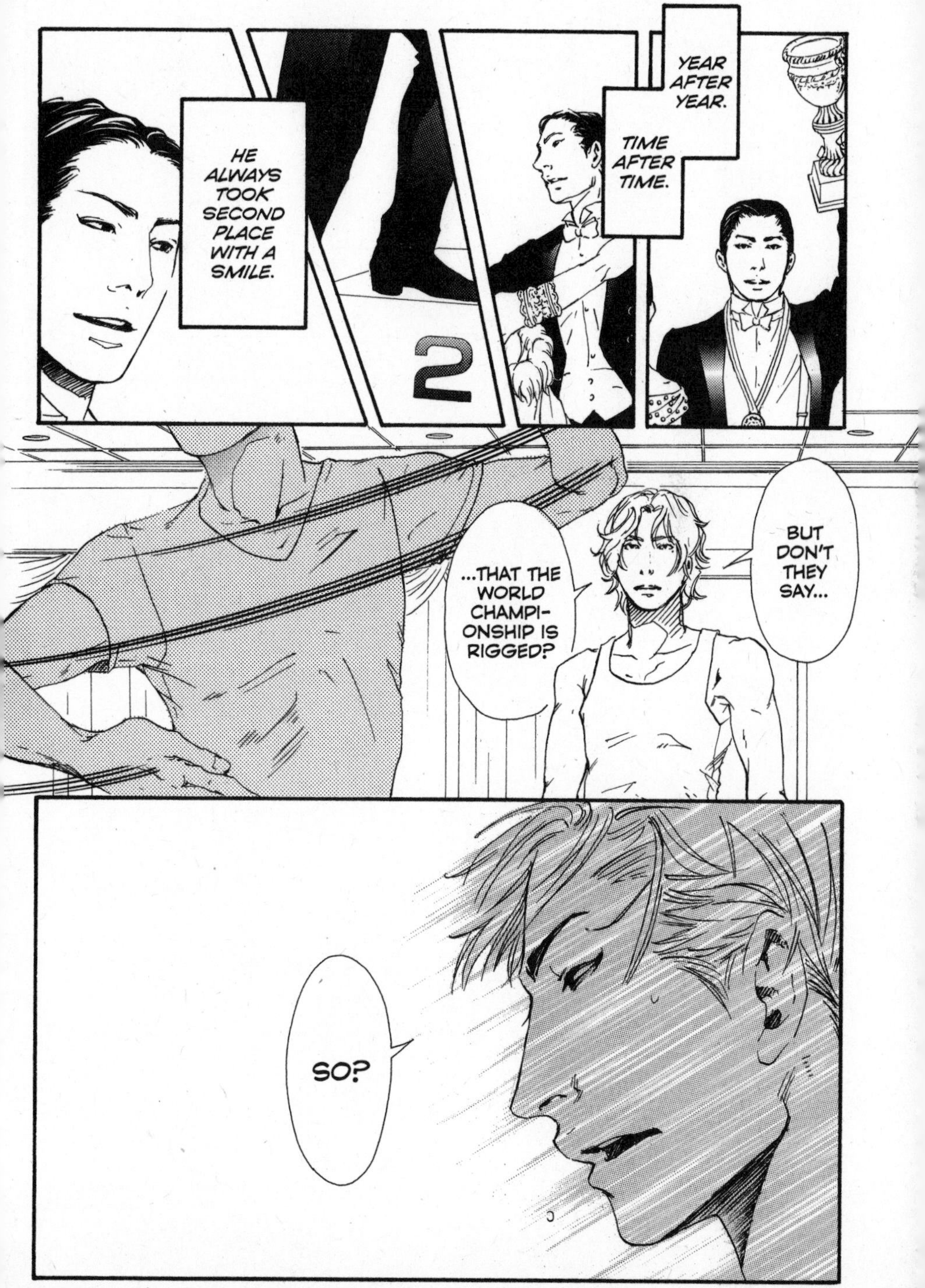
YEAR AFTER YEAR.
TIME AFTER TIME.
HE ALWAYS TOOK SECOND PLACE WITH A SMILE.
2
BUT DON'T THEY SAY...
...THAT THE WORLD CHAMPIONSHIP IS RIGGED?
SO?

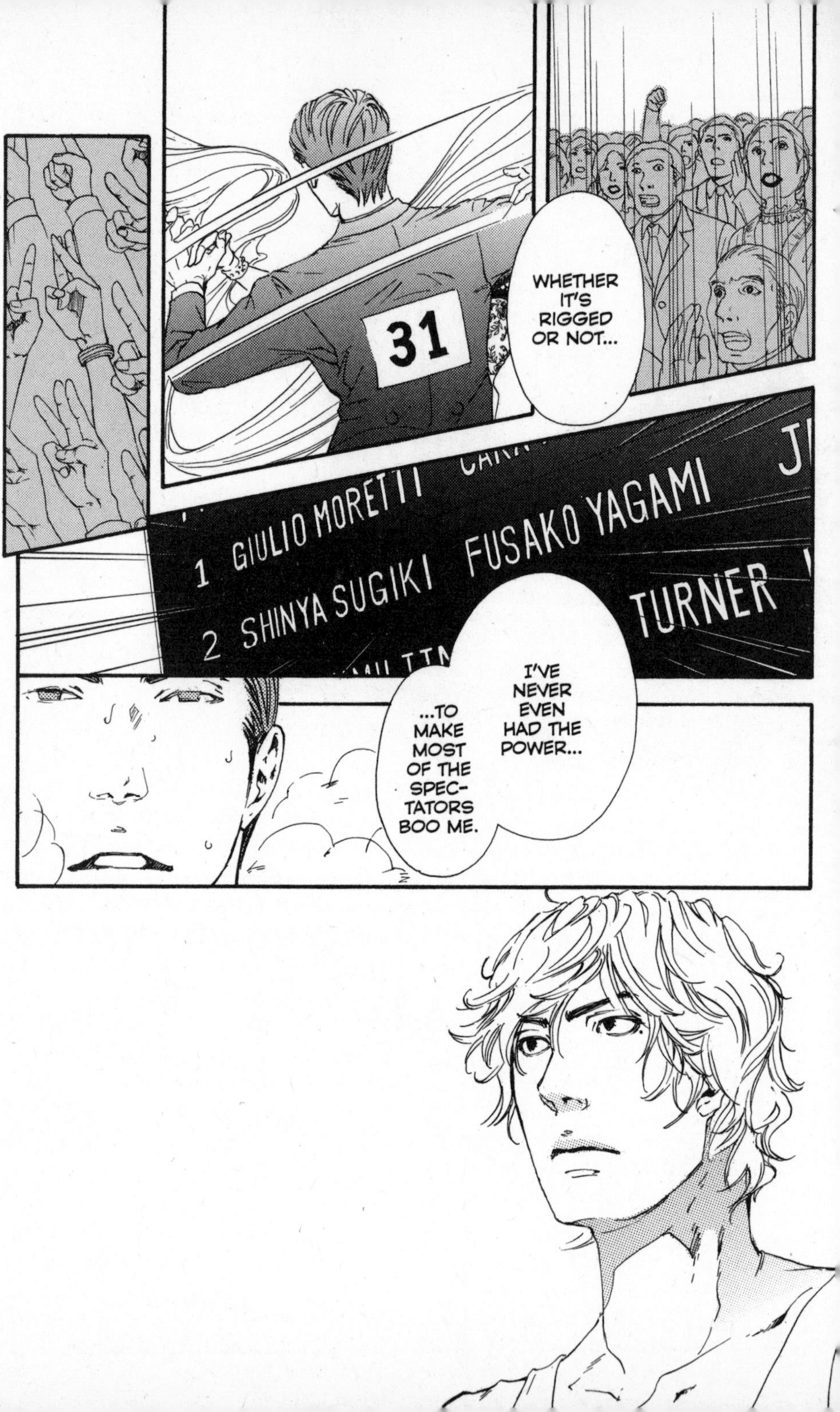
WHETHER IT'S RIGGED OR NOT...
1 GIULIO MORETTI
2 SHINYA SUGIKI
FUSAKO YAGAMI
TURNER
I'VE NEVER EVEN HAD THE POWER...
...TO MAKE MOST OF THE SPECTATORS BOO ME.

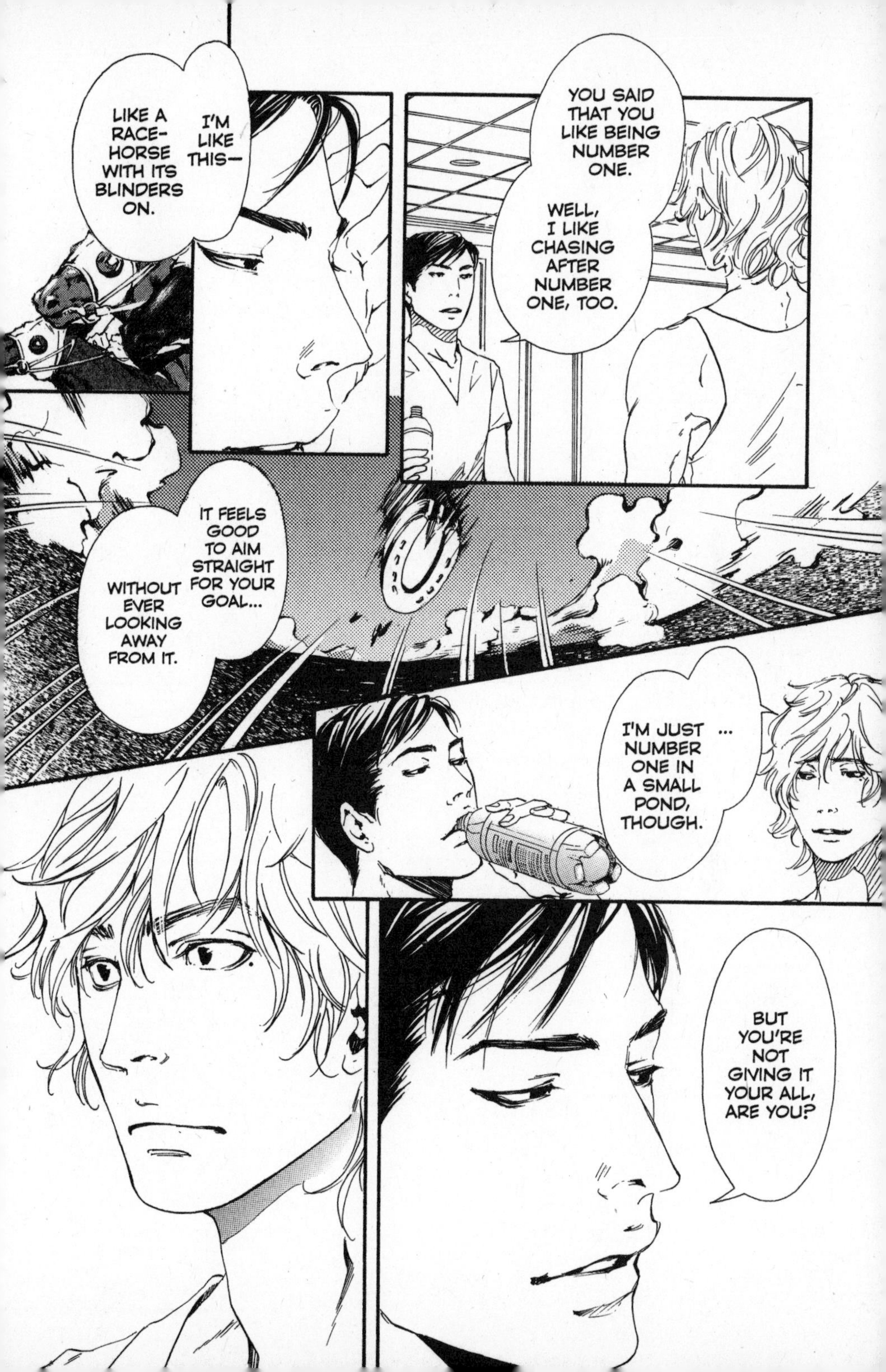
YOU SAID THAT YOU LIKE BEING NUMBER ONE.
WELL, I LIKE CHASING AFTER NUMBER ONE, TOO.
I'M LIKE THIS—
LIKE A RACE-HORSE WITH ITS BLINDERS ON.
IT FEELS GOOD TO AIM STRAIGHT FOR YOUR GOAL...
WITHOUT EVER LOOKING AWAY FROM IT.
...
I'M JUST NUMBER ONE IN A SMALL POND, THOUGH.
BUT YOU'RE NOT GIVING IT YOUR ALL, ARE YOU?

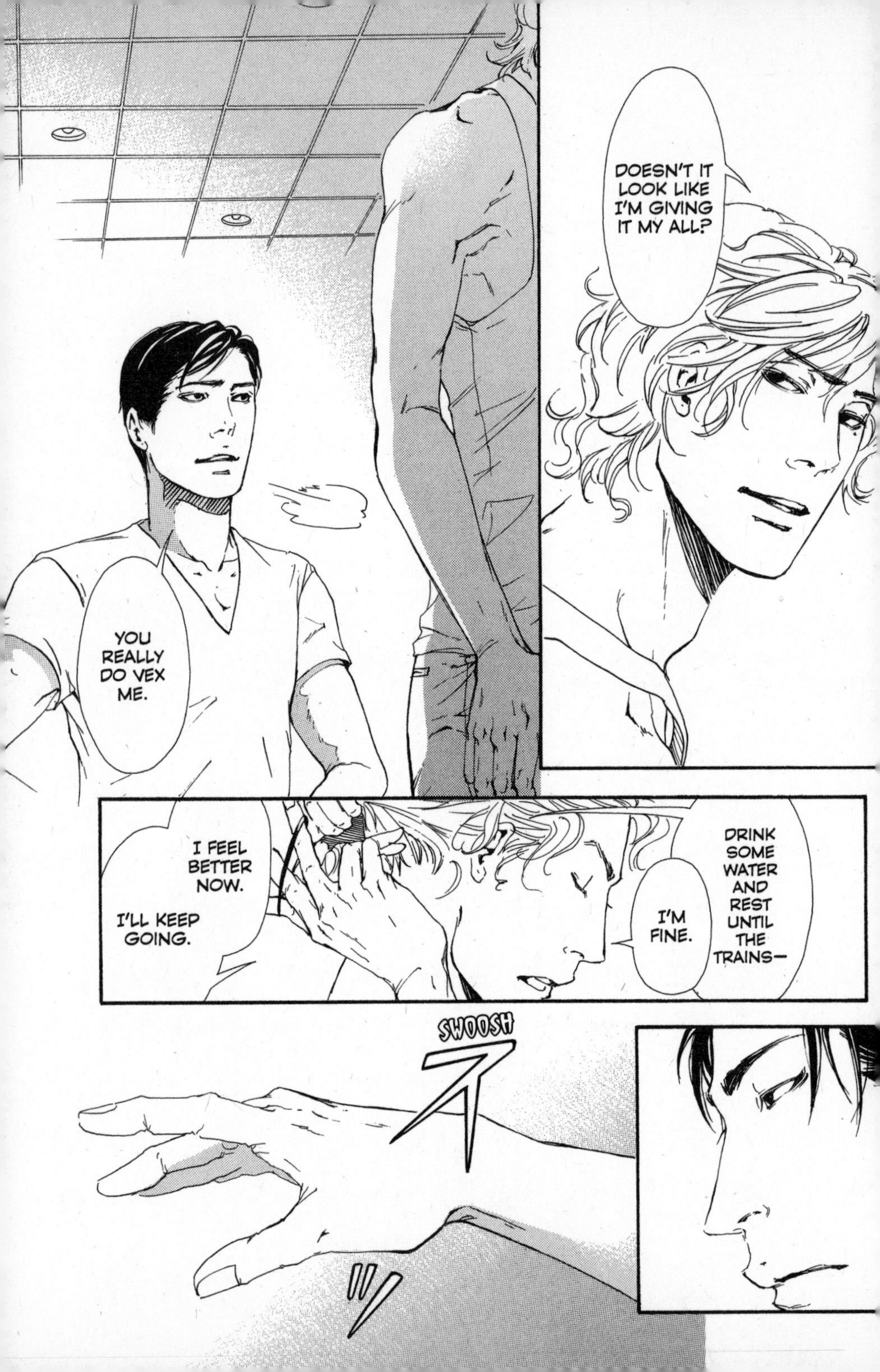
DOESN'T IT LOOK LIKE I'M GIVING IT MY ALL?
YOU REALLY DO VEX ME.
DRINK SOME WATER AND REST UNTIL THE TRAINS—
I'M FINE.
I FEEL BETTER NOW.
I'LL KEEP GOING.
SWOOSH

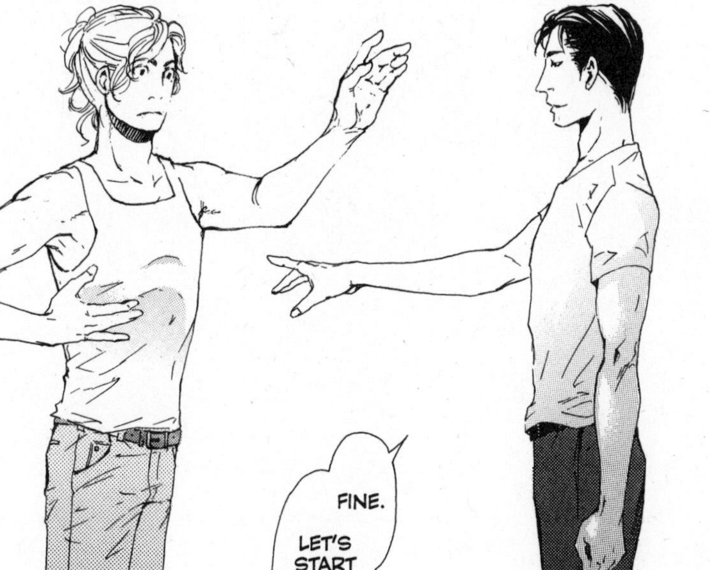
FINE.
LET'S START WITH A WALTZ.
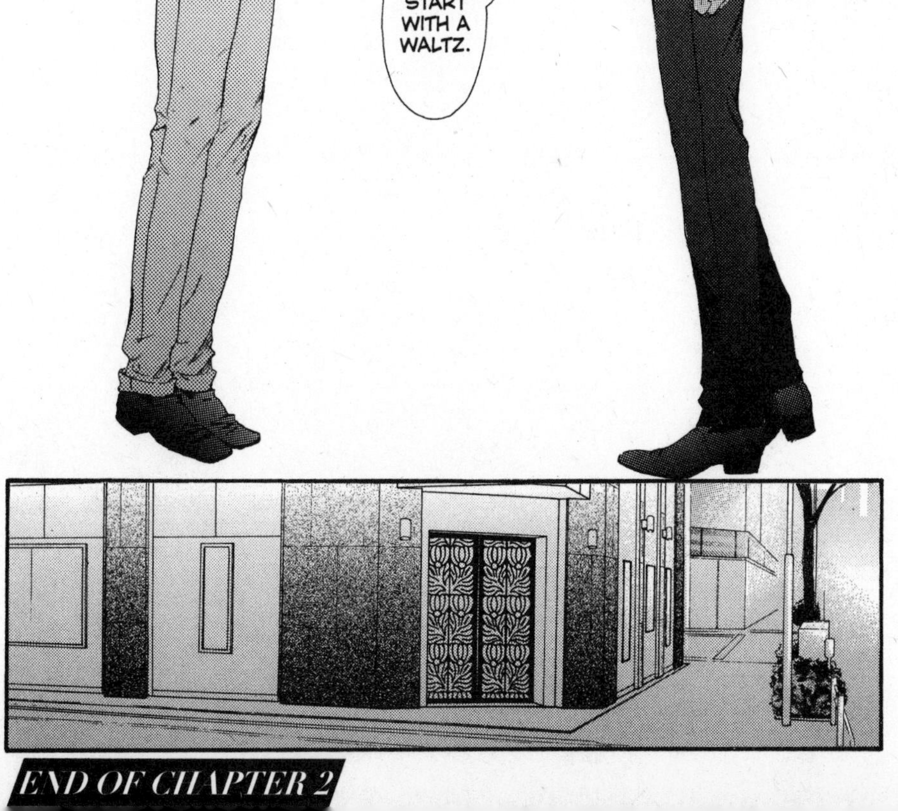

END OF CHAPTER 2

BONUS COMIC

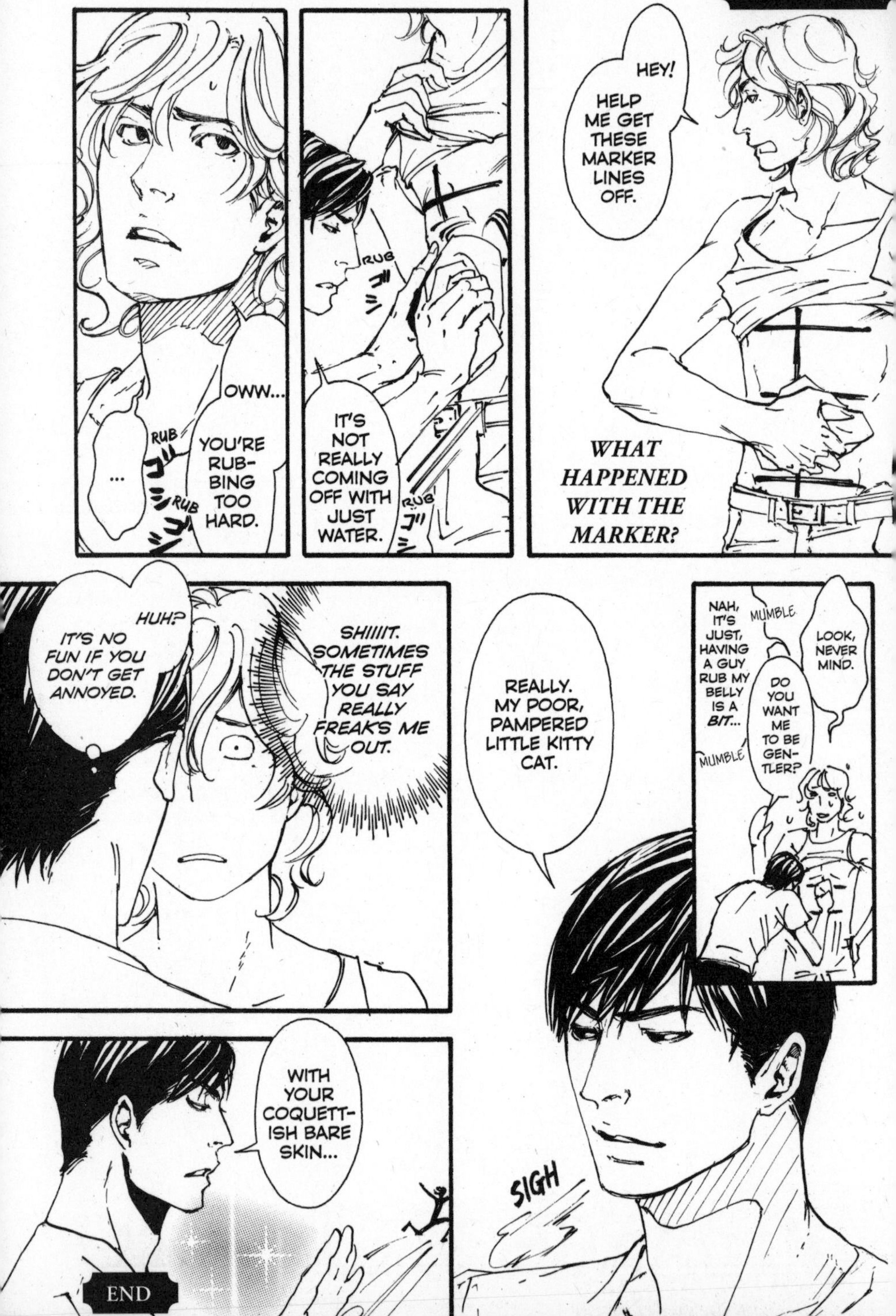
HEY!
HELP ME GET THESE MARKER LINES OFF.
WHAT HAPPENED WITH THE MARKER?
RUB
IT'S NOT REALLY COMING OFF WITH JUST WATER.
RUB
OWW...
YOU'RE RUB-BING TOO HARD.
RUB
RUB
...
LOOK, NEVER MIND.
NAH, IT'S JUST, HAVING A GUY RUB MY BELLY IS A *BIT*...
MUMBLE
MUMBLE
DO YOU WANT ME TO BE GEN-TLER?
REALLY. MY POOR, PAMPERED LITTLE KITTY CAT.
SIGH
SHIIIIT. SOMETIMES THE STUFF YOU SAY REALLY FREAKS ME OUT.
HUH?
IT'S NO FUN IF YOU DON'T GET ANNOYED.
WITH YOUR COQUETT-ISH BARE SKIN...
END

10 DANCE

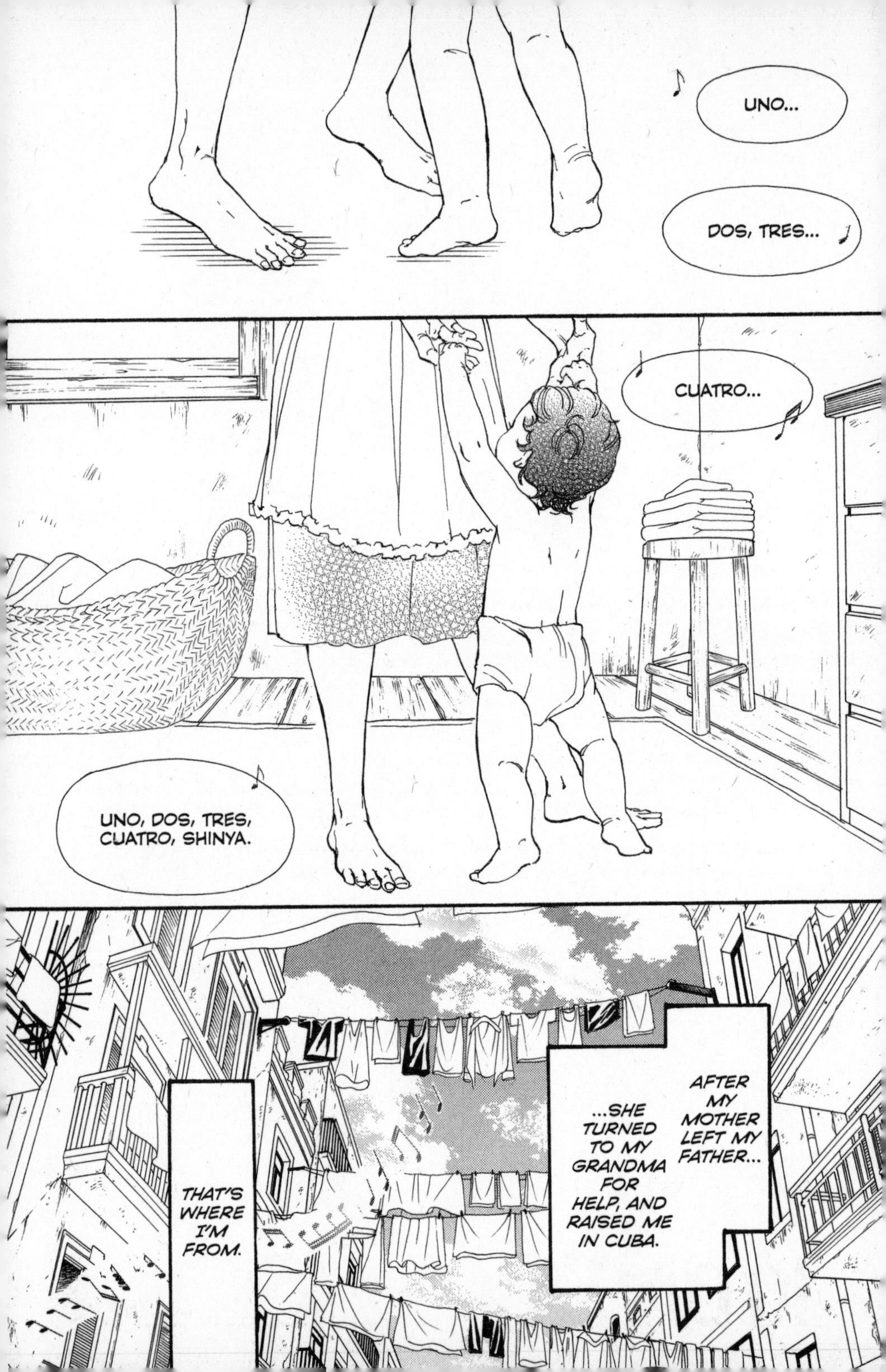
UNO...
DOS, TRES...
CUATRO...
UNO, DOS, TRES, CUATRO, SHINYA.
AFTER MY MOTHER LEFT MY FATHER...
...SHE TURNED TO MY GRANDMA FOR HELP, AND RAISED ME IN CUBA.
THAT'S WHERE I'M FROM.

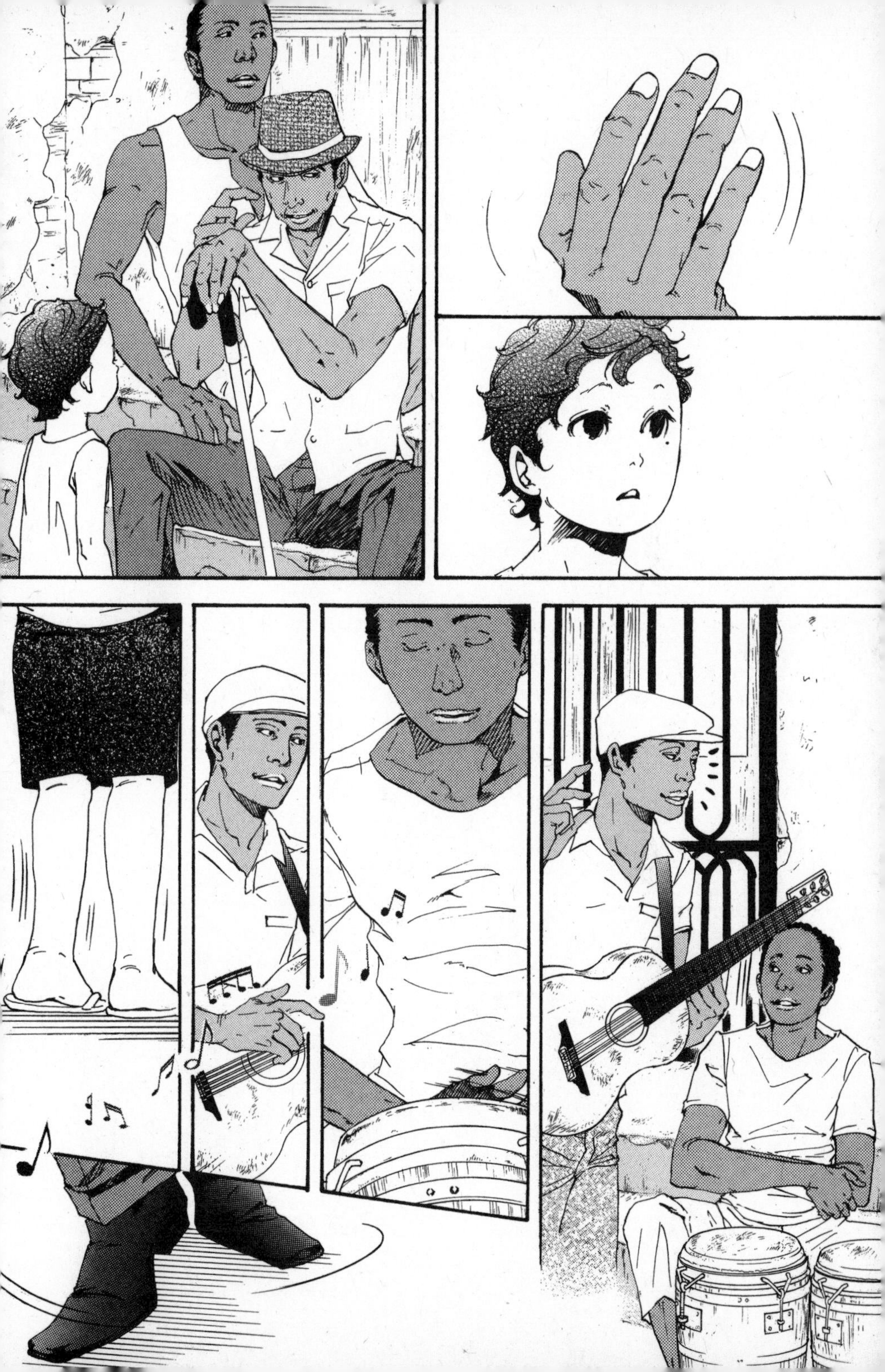

#03
A CLEAR BLUE RIVER SOMEWHERE

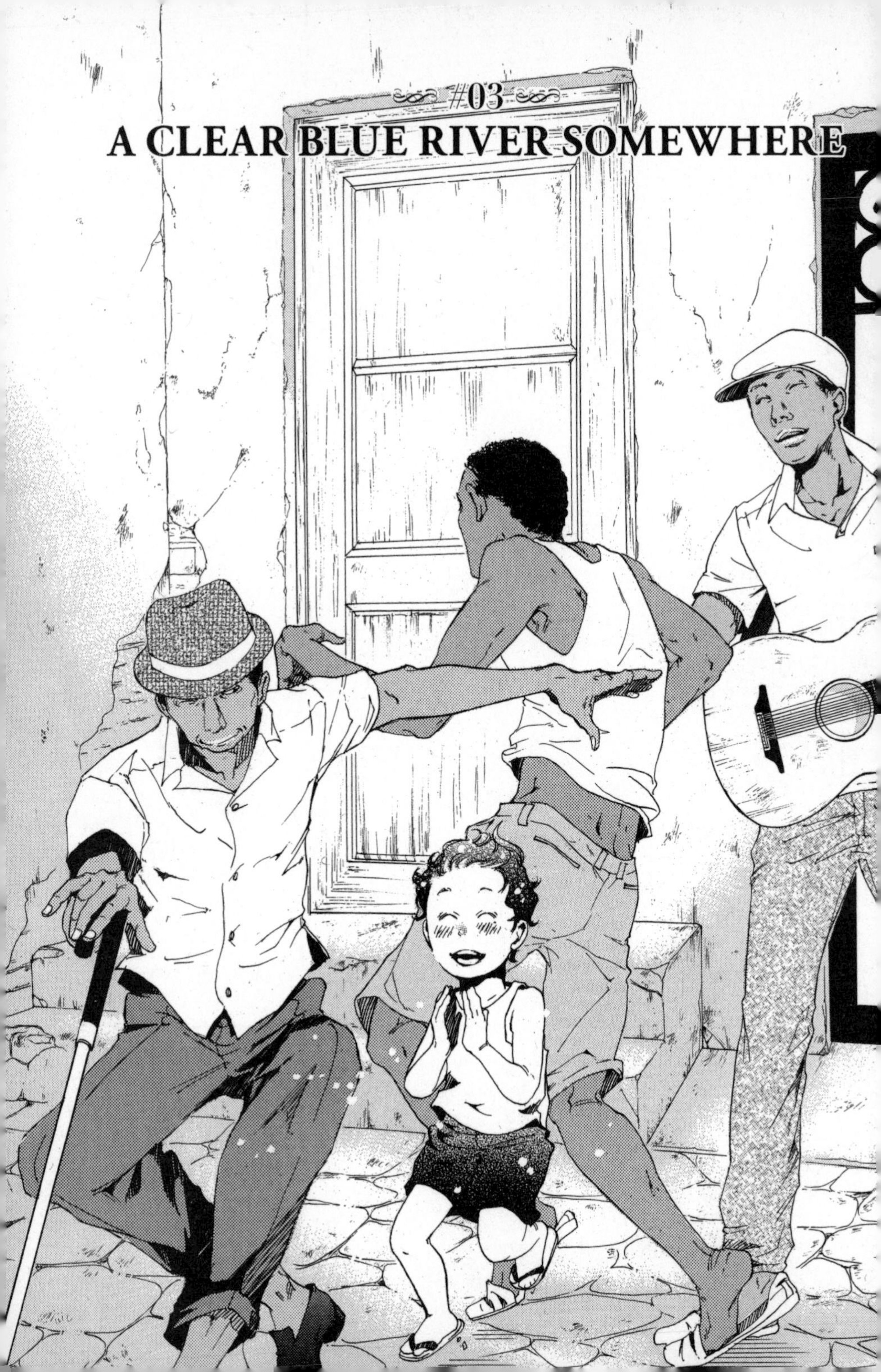

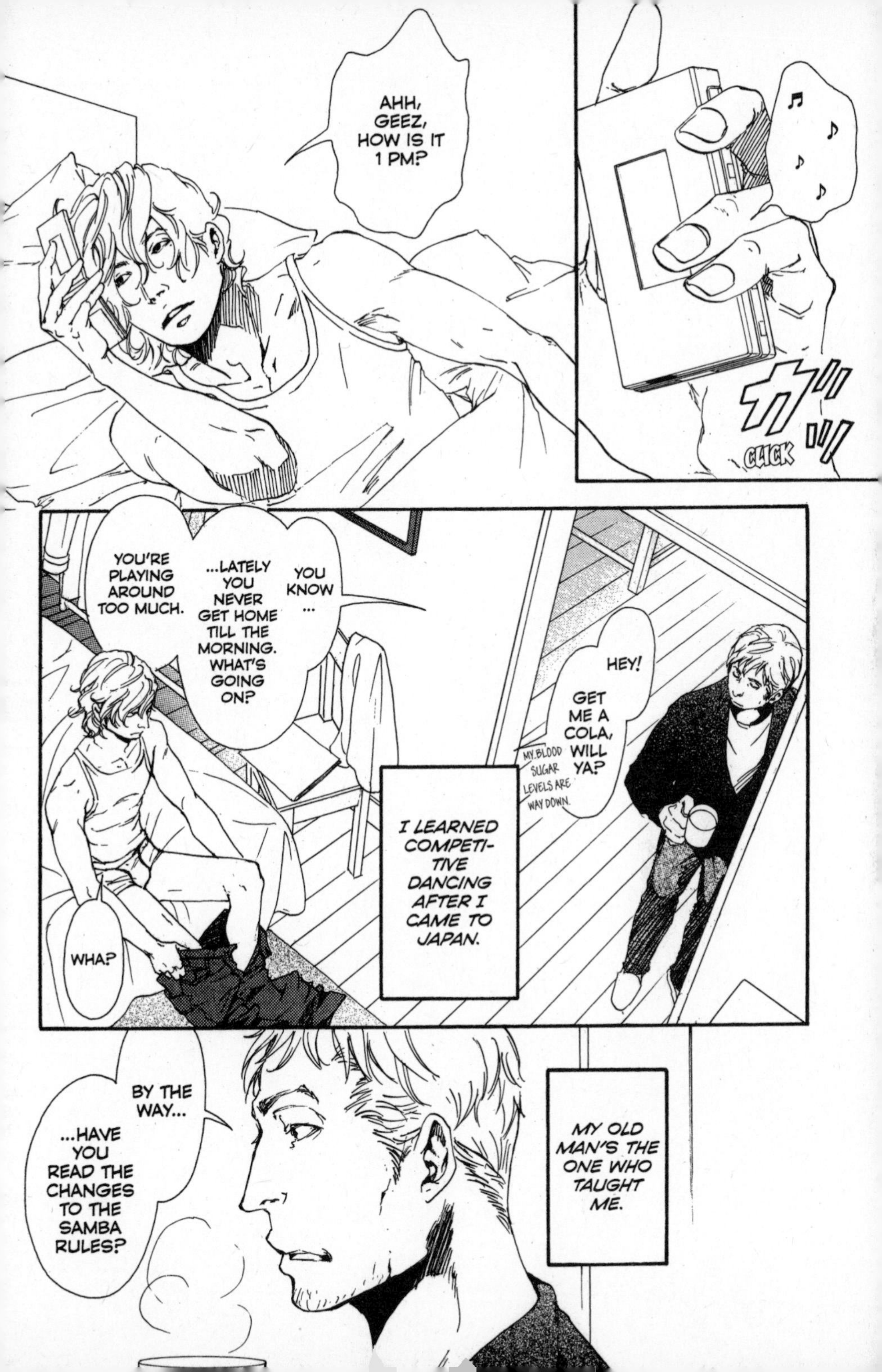
CLICK
AHH, GEEZ, HOW IS IT 1 PM?
HEY! GET ME A COLA, WILL YA?
MY BLOOD SUGAR LEVELS ARE WAY DOWN.
I LEARNED COMPETITIVE DANCING AFTER I CAME TO JAPAN.
YOU KNOW...
...LATELY YOU NEVER GET HOME TILL THE MORNING. WHAT'S GOING ON?
YOU'RE PLAYING AROUND TOO MUCH.
WHA?
MY OLD MAN'S THE ONE WHO TAUGHT ME.
BY THE WAY...
...HAVE YOU READ THE CHANGES TO THE SAMBA RULES?

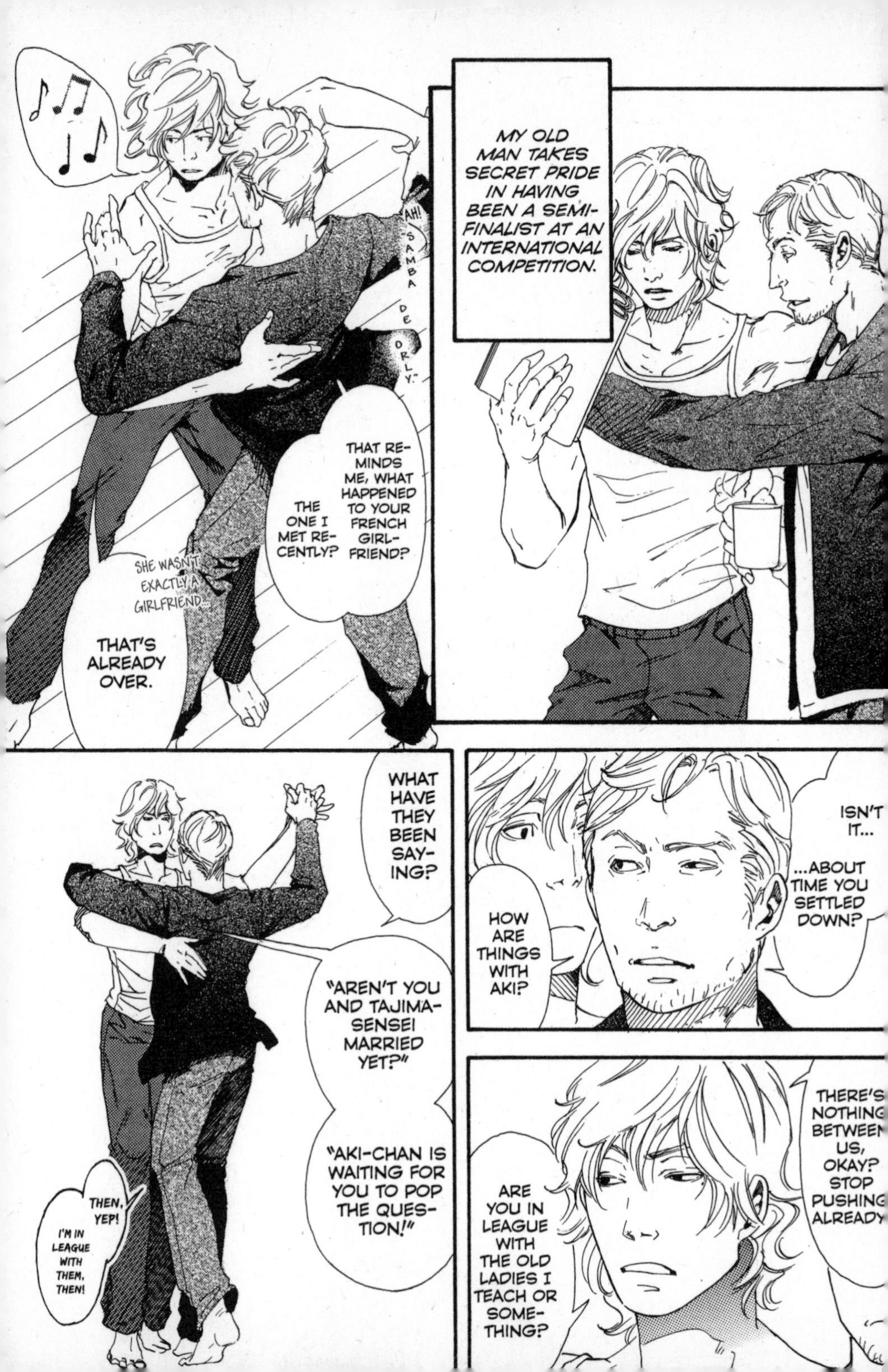
MY OLD MAN TAKES SECRET PRIDE IN HAVING BEEN A SEMI-FINALIST AT AN INTERNATIONAL COMPETITION.
AH! "SAMBA DE ORLY."
THAT RE-MINDS ME, WHAT HAPPENED TO YOUR FRENCH GIRL-FRIEND?
THE ONE I MET RE-CENTLY?
SHE WASN'T EXACTLY A GIRLFRIEND...
THAT'S ALREADY OVER.
ISN'T IT...
...ABOUT TIME YOU SETTLED DOWN?
HOW ARE THINGS WITH AKI?
THERE'S NOTHING BETWEEN US, OKAY? STOP PUSHING ALREADY
ARE YOU IN LEAGUE WITH THE OLD LADIES I TEACH OR SOME-THING?
WHAT HAVE THEY BEEN SAY-ING?
"AREN'T YOU AND TAJIMA-SENSEI MARRIED YET?"
"AKI-CHAN IS WAITING FOR YOU TO POP THE QUES-TION!"
THEN, YEP!
I'M IN LEAGUE WITH THEM, THEN!

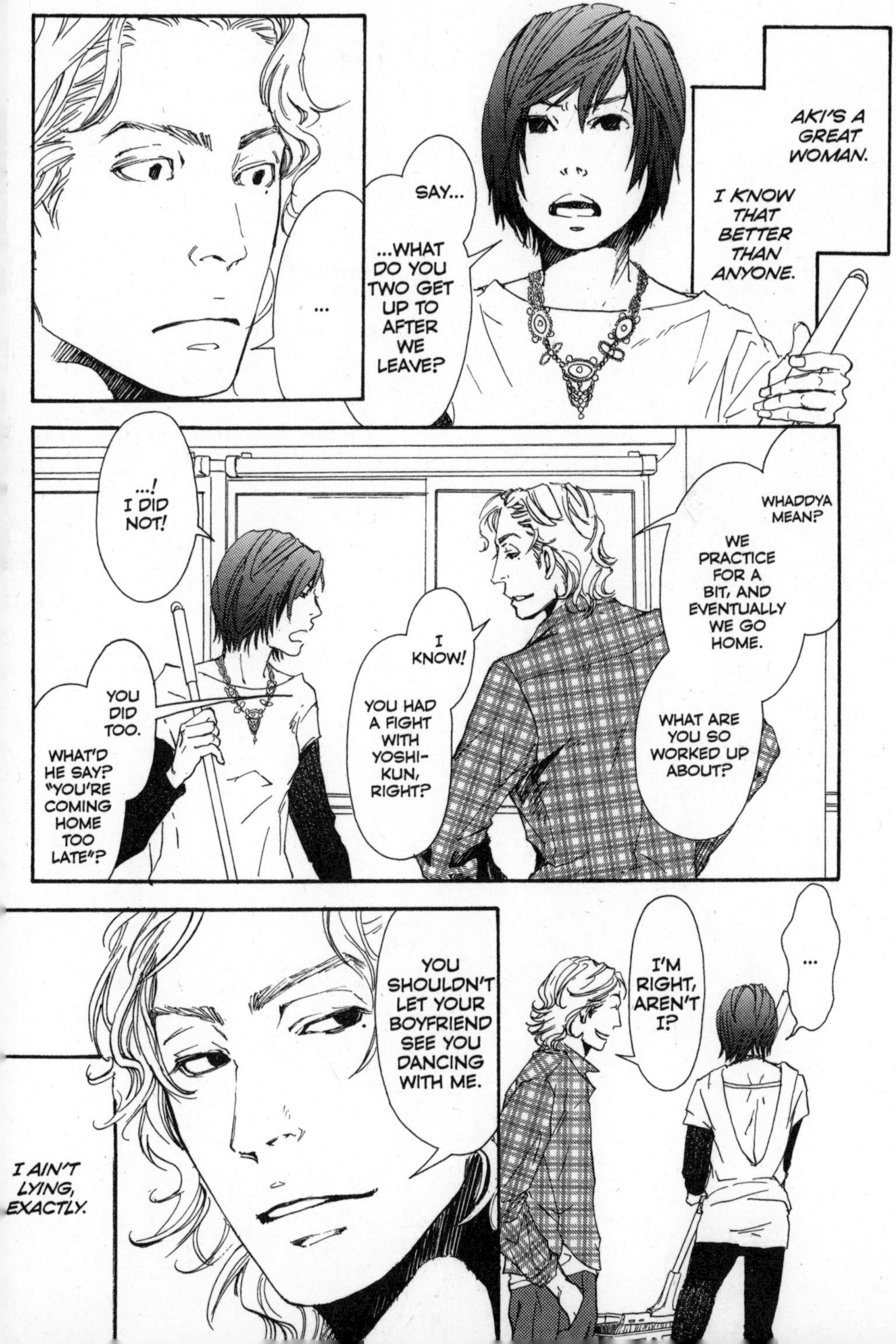
AKI'S A GREAT WOMAN.
I KNOW THAT BETTER THAN ANYONE.
SAY...
...WHAT DO YOU TWO GET UP TO AFTER WE LEAVE?
...
WHADDYA MEAN?
WE PRACTICE FOR A BIT, AND EVENTUALLY WE GO HOME.
WHAT ARE YOU SO WORKED UP ABOUT?
I KNOW!
YOU HAD A FIGHT WITH YOSHI-KUN, RIGHT?
...! I DID NOT!
YOU DID TOO.
WHAT'D HE SAY? "YOU'RE COMING HOME TOO LATE"?
...
I'M RIGHT, AREN'T I?
YOU SHOULDN'T LET YOUR BOYFRIEND SEE YOU DANCING WITH ME.
I AIN'T LYING, EXACTLY.

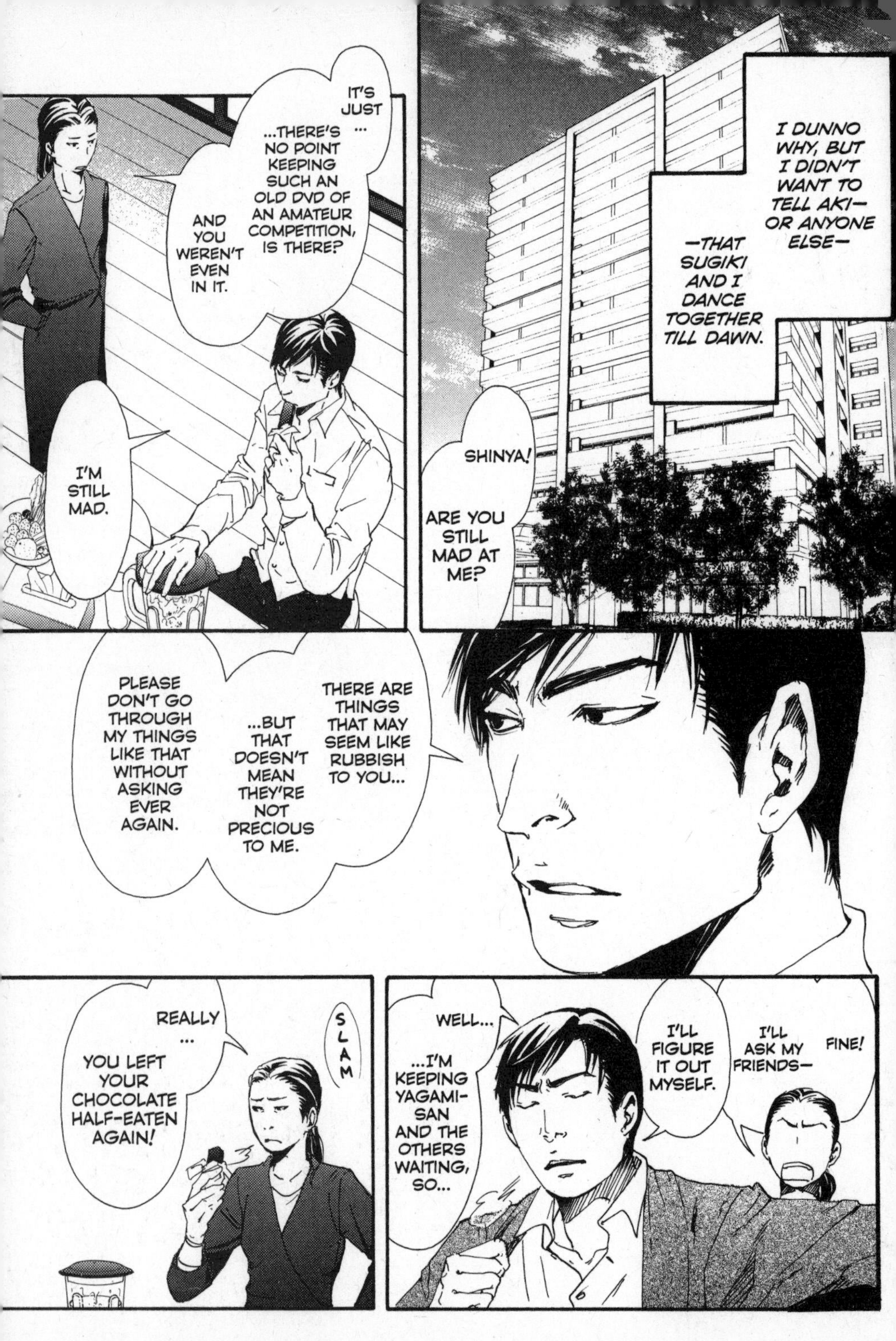
I DUNNO WHY, BUT I DIDN'T WANT TO TELL AKI— OR ANYONE ELSE—
—THAT SUGIKI AND I DANCE TOGETHER TILL DAWN.
SHINYA!
ARE YOU STILL MAD AT ME?
IT'S JUST ...
...THERE'S NO POINT KEEPING SUCH AN OLD DVD OF AN AMATEUR COMPETITION, IS THERE?
AND YOU WEREN'T EVEN IN IT.
I'M STILL MAD.
THERE ARE THINGS THAT MAY SEEM LIKE RUBBISH TO YOU...
...BUT THAT DOESN'T MEAN THEY'RE NOT PRECIOUS TO ME.
PLEASE DON'T GO THROUGH MY THINGS LIKE THAT WITHOUT ASKING EVER AGAIN.
FINE!
I'LL ASK MY FRIENDS—
I'LL FIGURE IT OUT MYSELF.
WELL...
...I'M KEEPING YAGAMI-SAN AND THE OTHERS WAITING, SO...
SLAM
REALLY ...
YOU LEFT YOUR CHOCOLATE HALF-EATEN AGAIN!

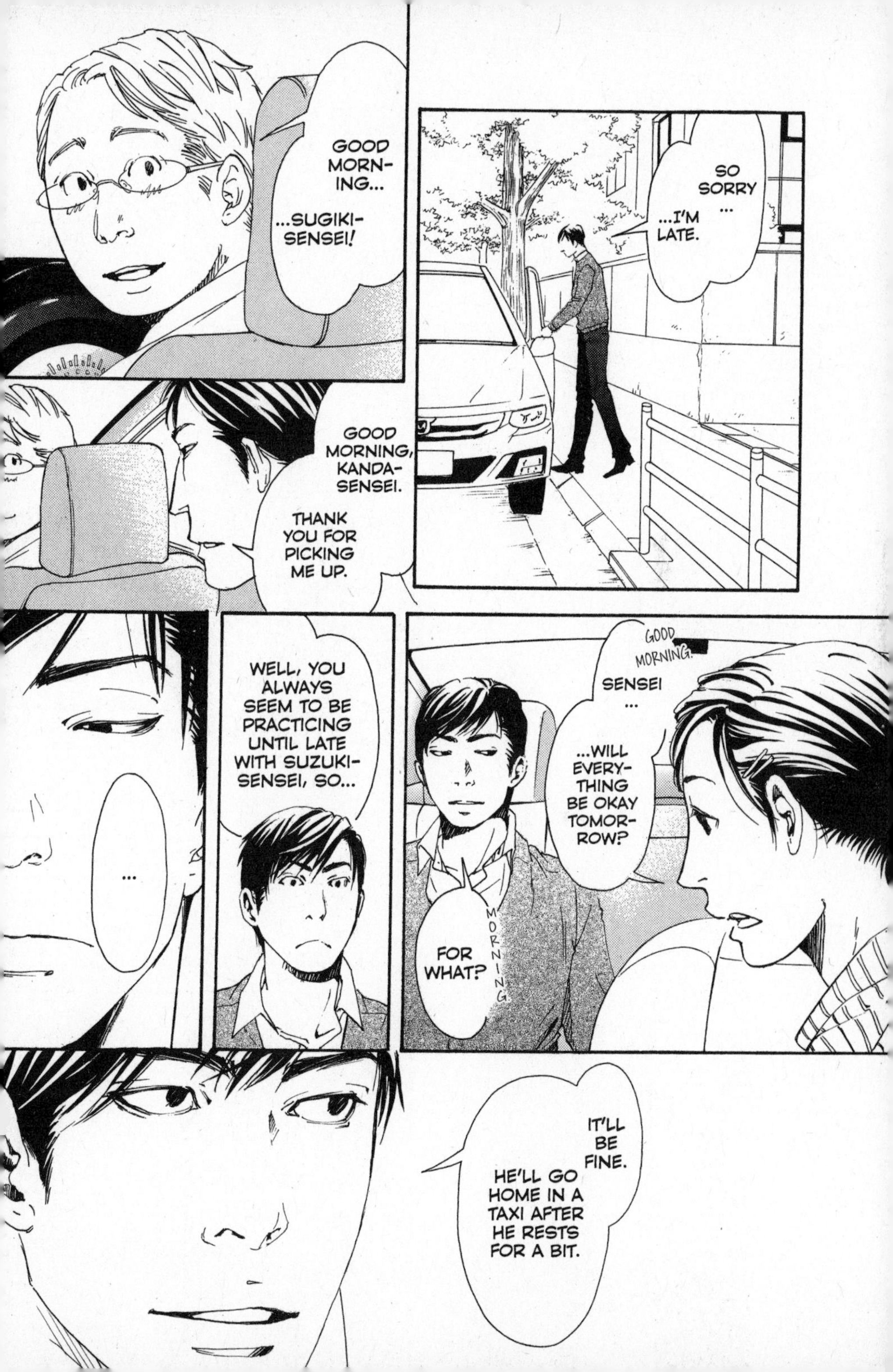
SO SORRY ... ...I'M LATE.
GOOD MORNING... ...SUGIKI-SENSEI!
GOOD MORNING, KANDA-SENSEI.
THANK YOU FOR PICKING ME UP.
GOOD MORNING.
SENSEI ...
...WILL EVERYTHING BE OKAY TOMORROW?
MORNING
FOR WHAT?
WELL, YOU ALWAYS SEEM TO BE PRACTICING UNTIL LATE WITH SUZUKI-SENSEI, SO...
...
IT'LL BE FINE.
HE'LL GO HOME IN A TAXI AFTER HE RESTS FOR A BIT.

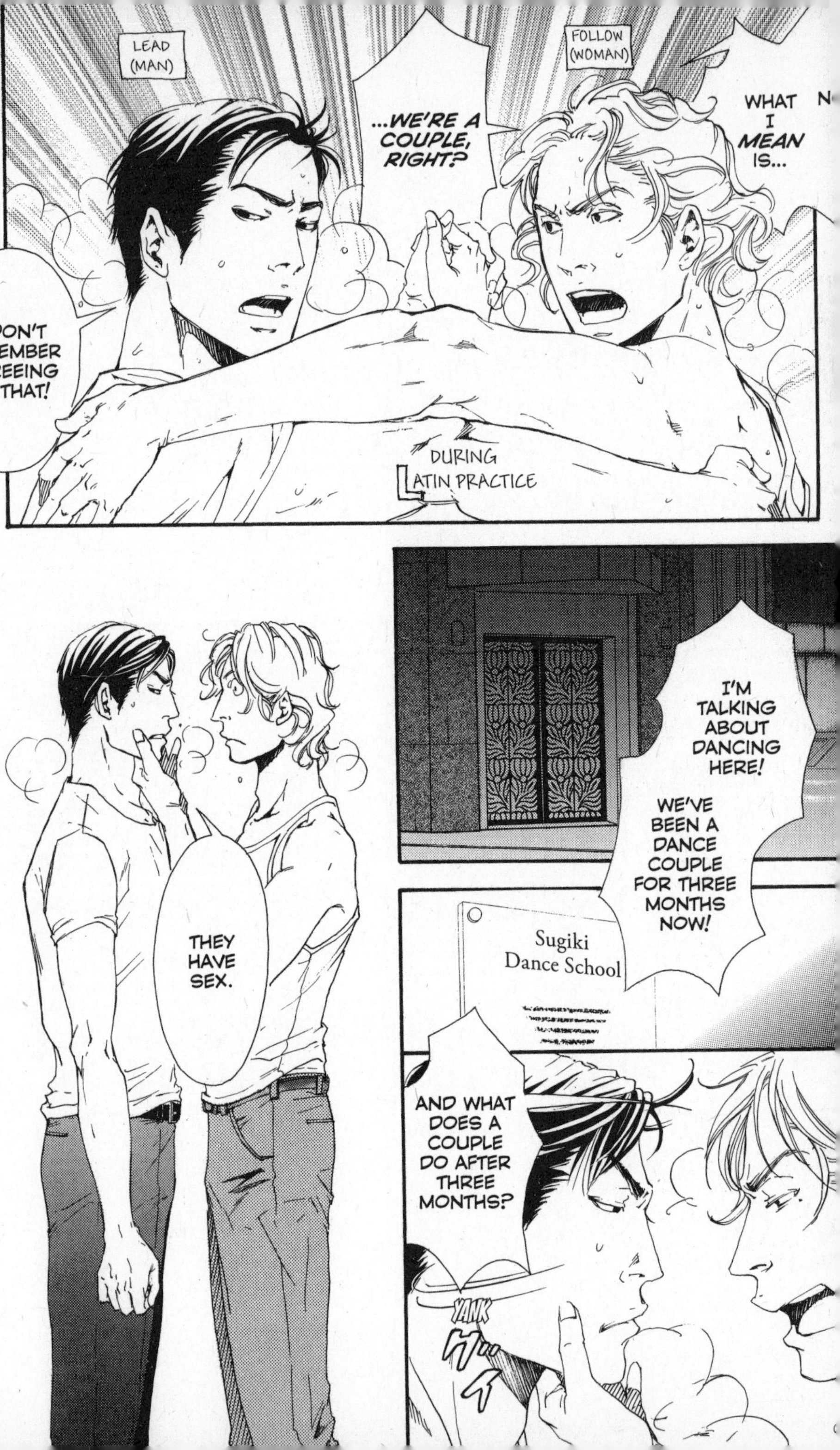
WHAT I MEAN IS...
FOLLOW (WOMAN)
...WE'RE A COUPLE, RIGHT?
LEAD (MAN)
I DON'T REMEMBER AGREEING TO THAT!
DURING LATIN PRACTICE
I'M TALKING ABOUT DANCING HERE!
WE'VE BEEN A DANCE COUPLE FOR THREE MONTHS NOW!
Sugiki Dance School
AND WHAT DOES A COUPLE DO AFTER THREE MONTHS?
YANK
THEY HAVE SEX.

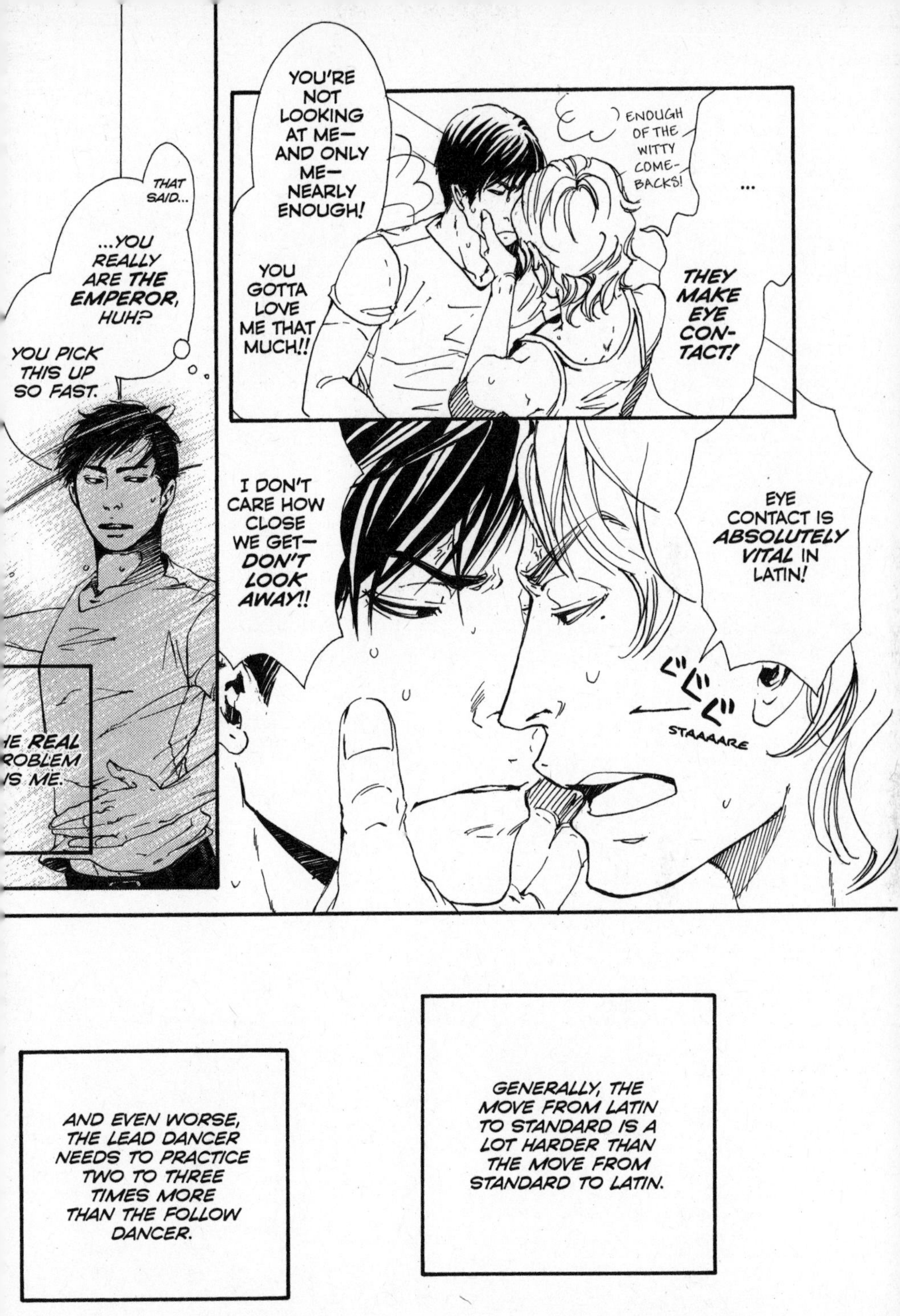
ENOUGH OF THE WITTY COMEBACKS!
...
THEY MAKE EYE CONTACT!
YOU'RE NOT LOOKING AT ME—AND ONLY ME—NEARLY ENOUGH!
YOU GOTTA LOVE ME THAT MUCH!!
EYE CONTACT IS ABSOLUTELY VITAL IN LATIN!
ぐぐぐ
STAAAARE
I DON'T CARE HOW CLOSE WE GET—DON'T LOOK AWAY!!
THAT SAID...
...YOU REALLY ARE THE EMPEROR, HUH?
YOU PICK THIS UP SO FAST.
HE REAL ROBLEM IS ME.

GENERALLY, THE MOVE FROM LATIN TO STANDARD IS A LOT HARDER THAN THE MOVE FROM STANDARD TO LATIN.

AND EVEN WORSE, THE LEAD DANCER NEEDS TO PRACTICE TWO TO THREE TIMES MORE THAN THE FOLLOW DANCER.

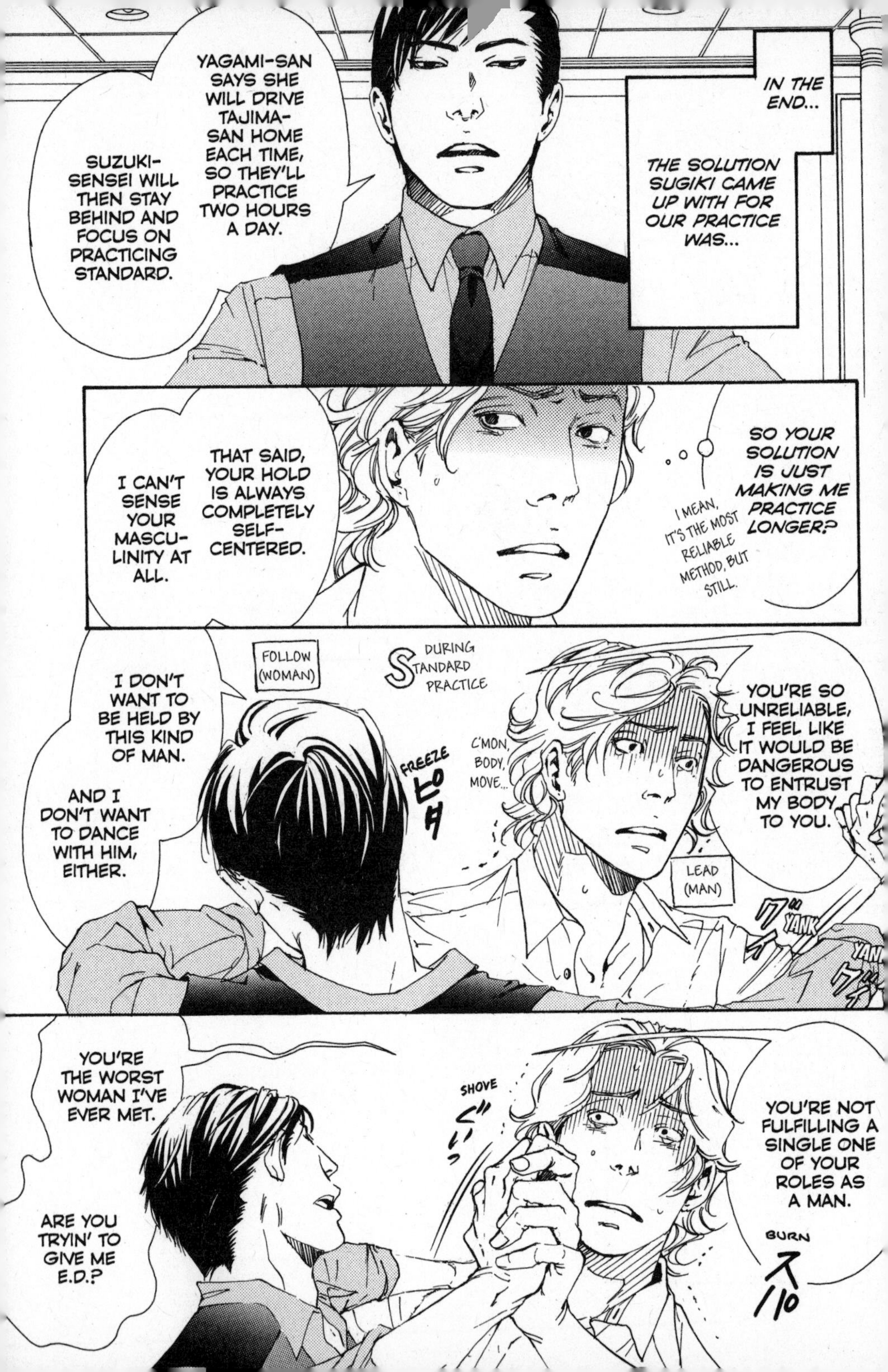
IN THE END...
THE SOLUTION SUGIKI CAME UP WITH FOR OUR PRACTICE WAS...
YAGAMI-SAN SAYS SHE WILL DRIVE TAJIMA-SAN HOME EACH TIME, SO THEY'LL PRACTICE TWO HOURS A DAY.
SUZUKI-SENSEI WILL THEN STAY BEHIND AND FOCUS ON PRACTICING STANDARD.
SO YOUR SOLUTION IS JUST MAKING ME PRACTICE LONGER?
I MEAN, IT'S THE MOST RELIABLE METHOD, BUT STILL.
THAT SAID, YOUR HOLD IS ALWAYS COMPLETELY SELF-CENTERED.
I CAN'T SENSE YOUR MASCULINITY AT ALL.
YOU'RE SO UNRELIABLE, I FEEL LIKE IT WOULD BE DANGEROUS TO ENTRUST MY BODY TO YOU.
YANK
YANK
LEAD (MAN)
C'MON, BODY, MOVE...
FREEZE
DURING STANDARD PRACTICE
FOLLOW (WOMAN)
I DON'T WANT TO BE HELD BY THIS KIND OF MAN.
AND I DON'T WANT TO DANCE WITH HIM, EITHER.
YOU'RE NOT FULFILLING A SINGLE ONE OF YOUR ROLES AS A MAN.
BURN
SHOVE
YOU'RE THE WORST WOMAN I'VE EVER MET.
ARE YOU TRYIN' TO GIVE ME E.D.?

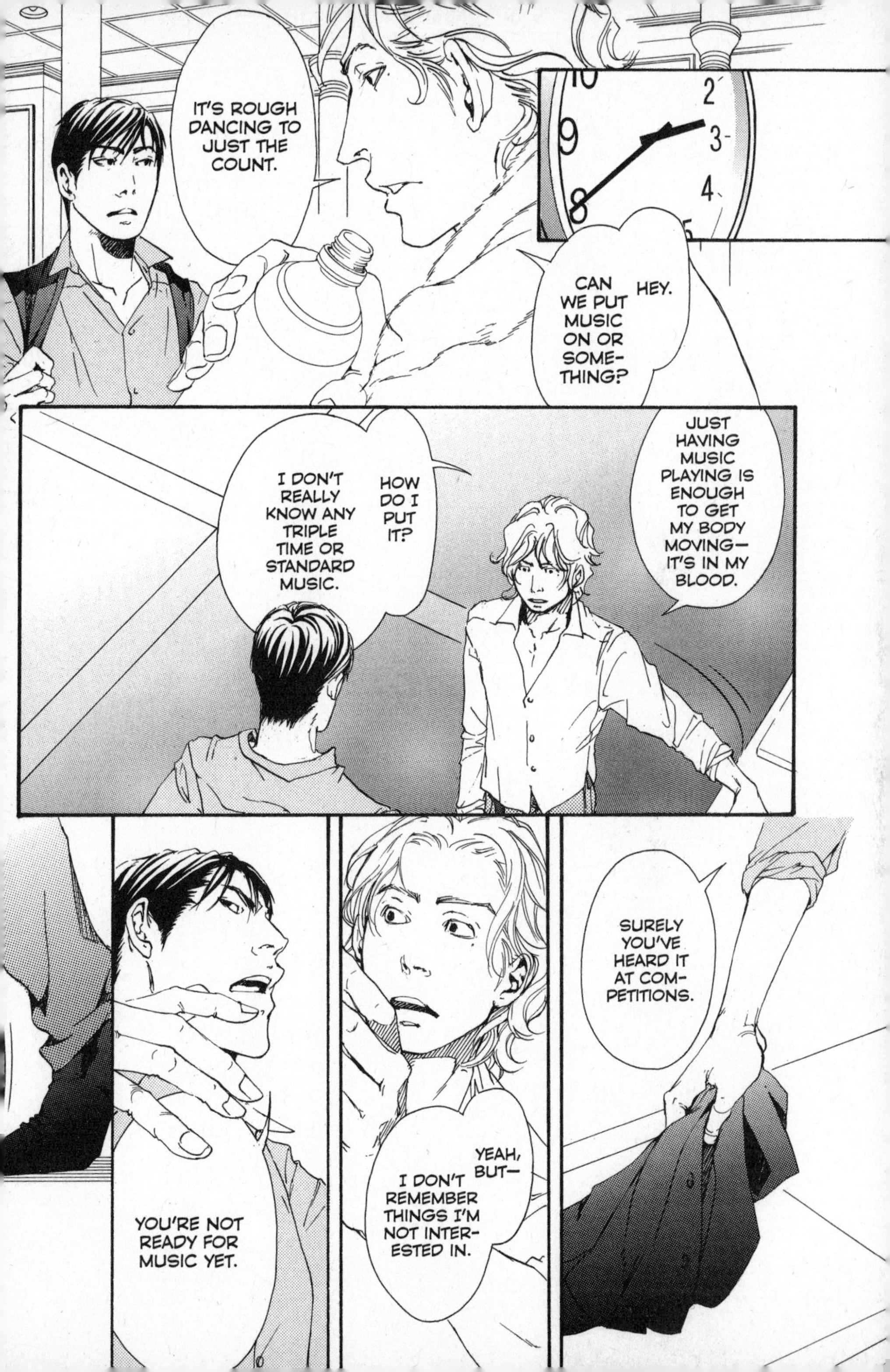
HEY.
CAN WE PUT MUSIC ON OR SOMETHING?
IT'S ROUGH DANCING TO JUST THE COUNT.
JUST HAVING MUSIC PLAYING IS ENOUGH TO GET MY BODY MOVING—IT'S IN MY BLOOD.
HOW DO I PUT IT?
I DON'T REALLY KNOW ANY TRIPLE TIME OR STANDARD MUSIC.
SURELY YOU'VE HEARD IT AT COMPETITIONS.
YEAH, BUT—
I DON'T REMEMBER THINGS I'M NOT INTERESTED IN.
YOU'RE NOT READY FOR MUSIC YET.

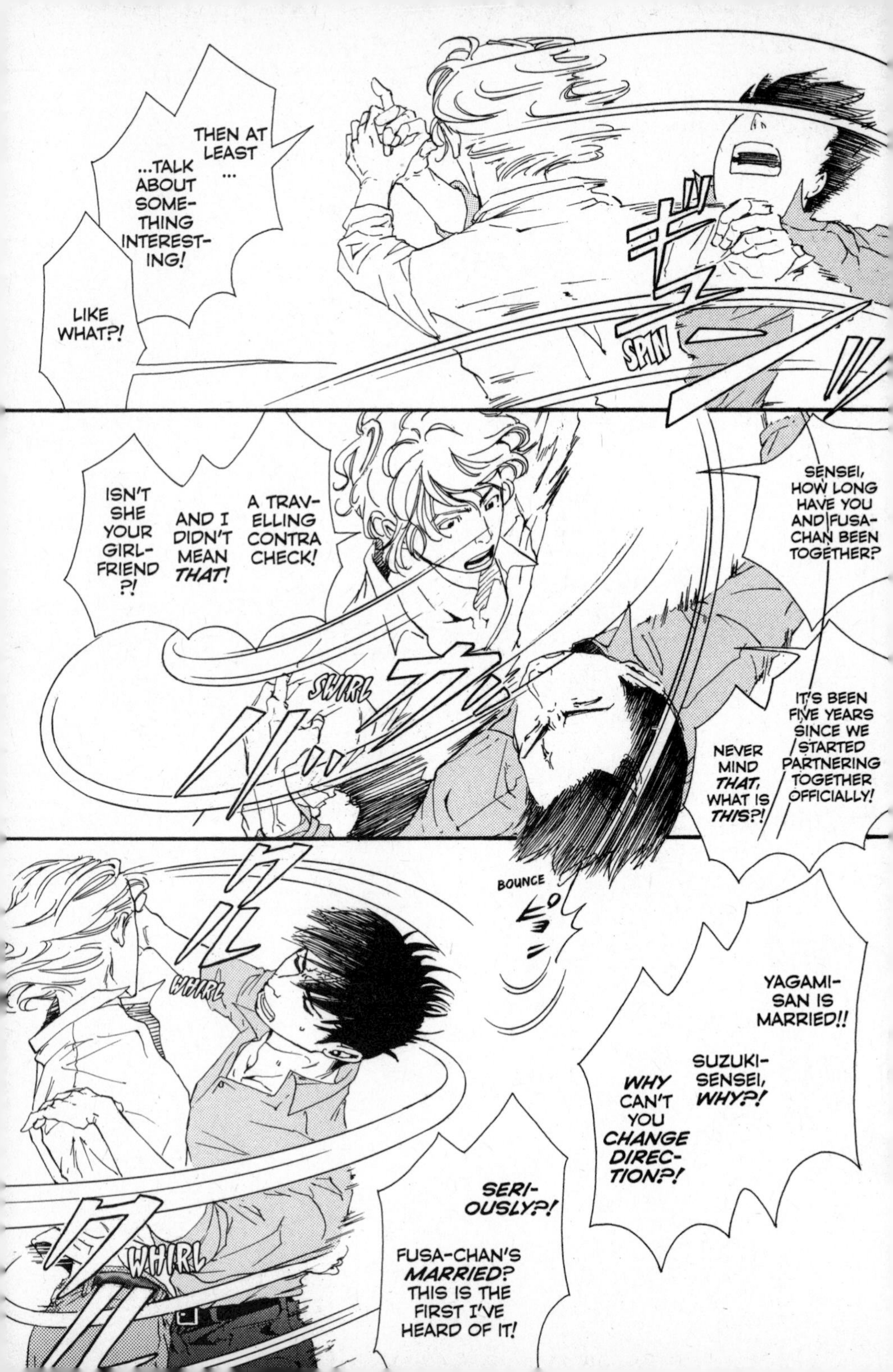
THEN AT LEAST ...
...TALK ABOUT SOMETHING INTERESTING!
LIKE WHAT?!
SPIN
SENSEI, HOW LONG HAVE YOU AND FUSA-CHAN BEEN TOGETHER?
IT'S BEEN FIVE YEARS SINCE WE STARTED PARTNERING TOGETHER OFFICIALLY!
NEVER MIND THAT, WHAT IS THIS?!
A TRAVELLING CONTRA CHECK!
AND I DIDN'T MEAN THAT!
ISN'T SHE YOUR GIRLFRIEND?!
SWIRL
BOUNCE
YAGAMI-SAN IS MARRIED!!
SUZUKI-SENSEI, WHY?!
WHY CAN'T YOU CHANGE DIRECTION?!
WHIRL
SERIOUSLY?!
FUSA-CHAN'S MARRIED? THIS IS THE FIRST I'VE HEARD OF IT!
WHIRL

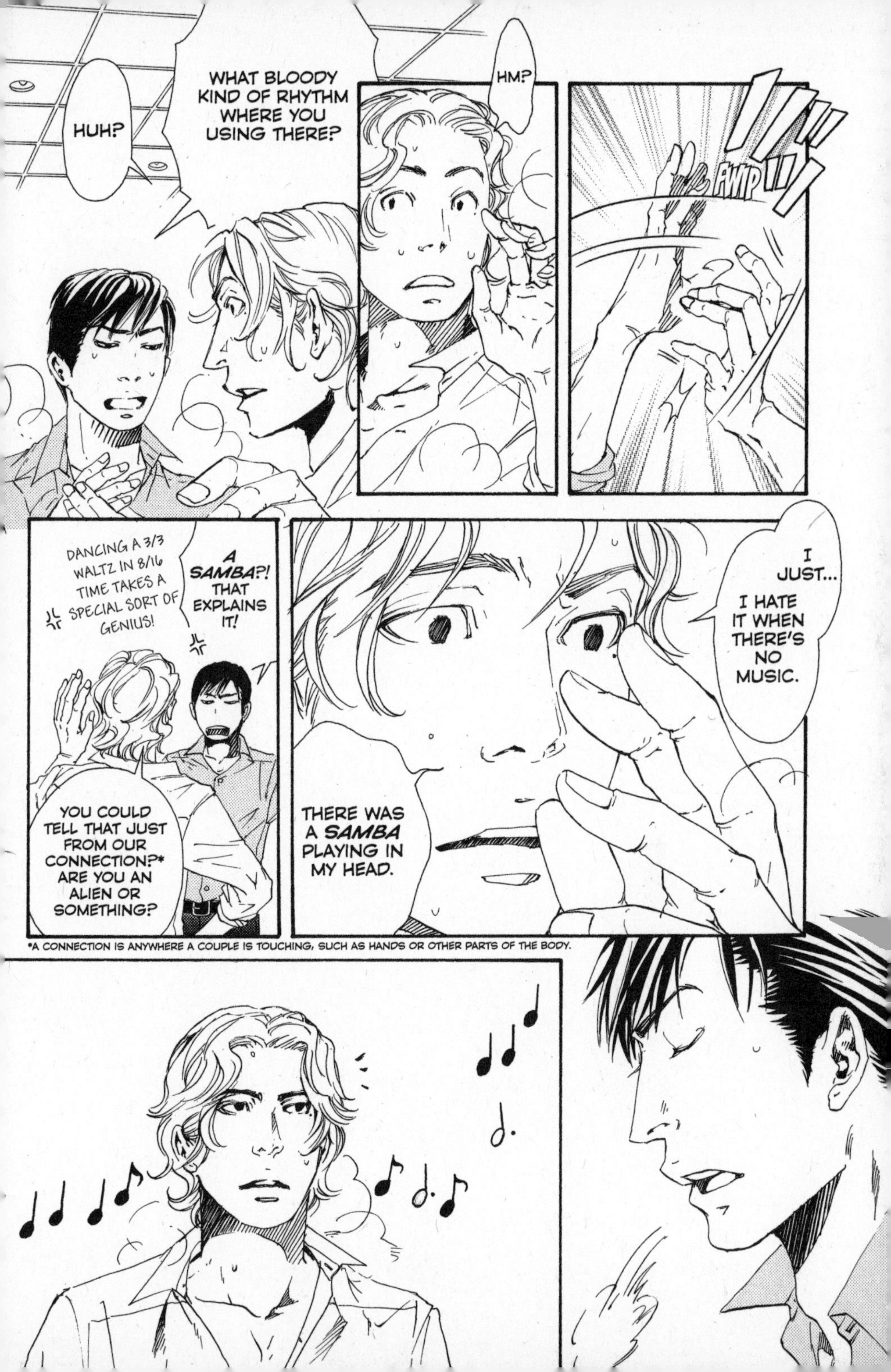
FWIP
HM?
WHAT BLOODY KIND OF RHYTHM WHERE YOU USING THERE?
HUH?
I JUST... I HATE IT WHEN THERE'S NO MUSIC.
THERE WAS A *SAMBA* PLAYING IN MY HEAD.
A *SAMBA*?! THAT EXPLAINS IT!
DANCING A 3/3 WALTZ IN 8/16 TIME TAKES A SPECIAL SORT OF GENIUS!
YOU COULD TELL THAT JUST FROM OUR CONNECTION?* ARE YOU AN ALIEN OR SOMETHING?

*A CONNECTION IS ANYWHERE A COUPLE IS TOUCHING, SUCH AS HANDS OR OTHER PARTS OF THE BODY.

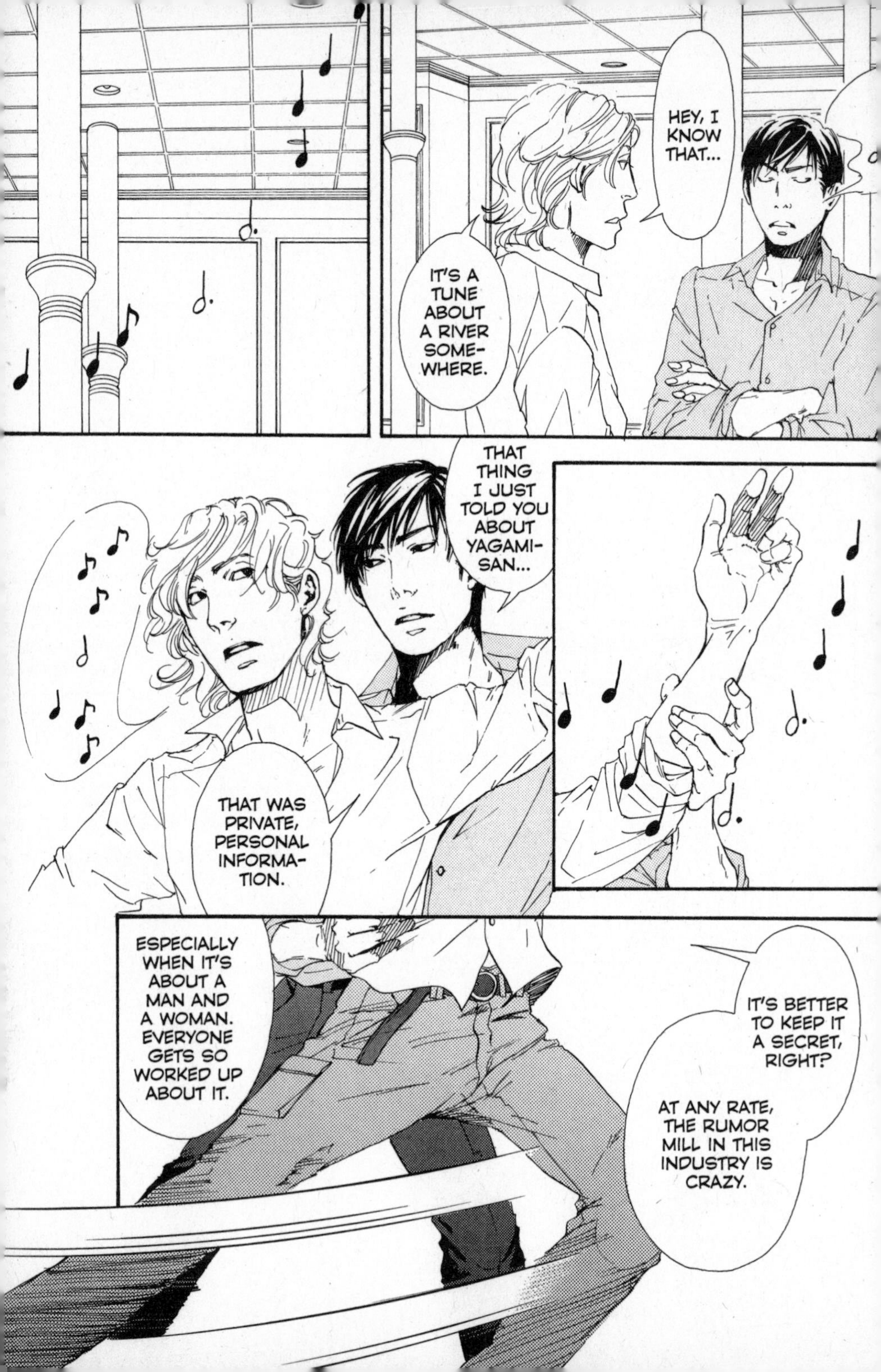
HEY, I KNOW THAT...
IT'S A TUNE ABOUT A RIVER SOME-WHERE.
THAT THING I JUST TOLD YOU ABOUT YAGAMI-SAN...
THAT WAS PRIVATE, PERSONAL INFORMA-TION.
ESPECIALLY WHEN IT'S ABOUT A MAN AND A WOMAN. EVERYONE GETS SO WORKED UP ABOUT IT.
IT'S BETTER TO KEEP IT A SECRET, RIGHT?
AT ANY RATE, THE RUMOR MILL IN THIS INDUSTRY IS CRAZY.

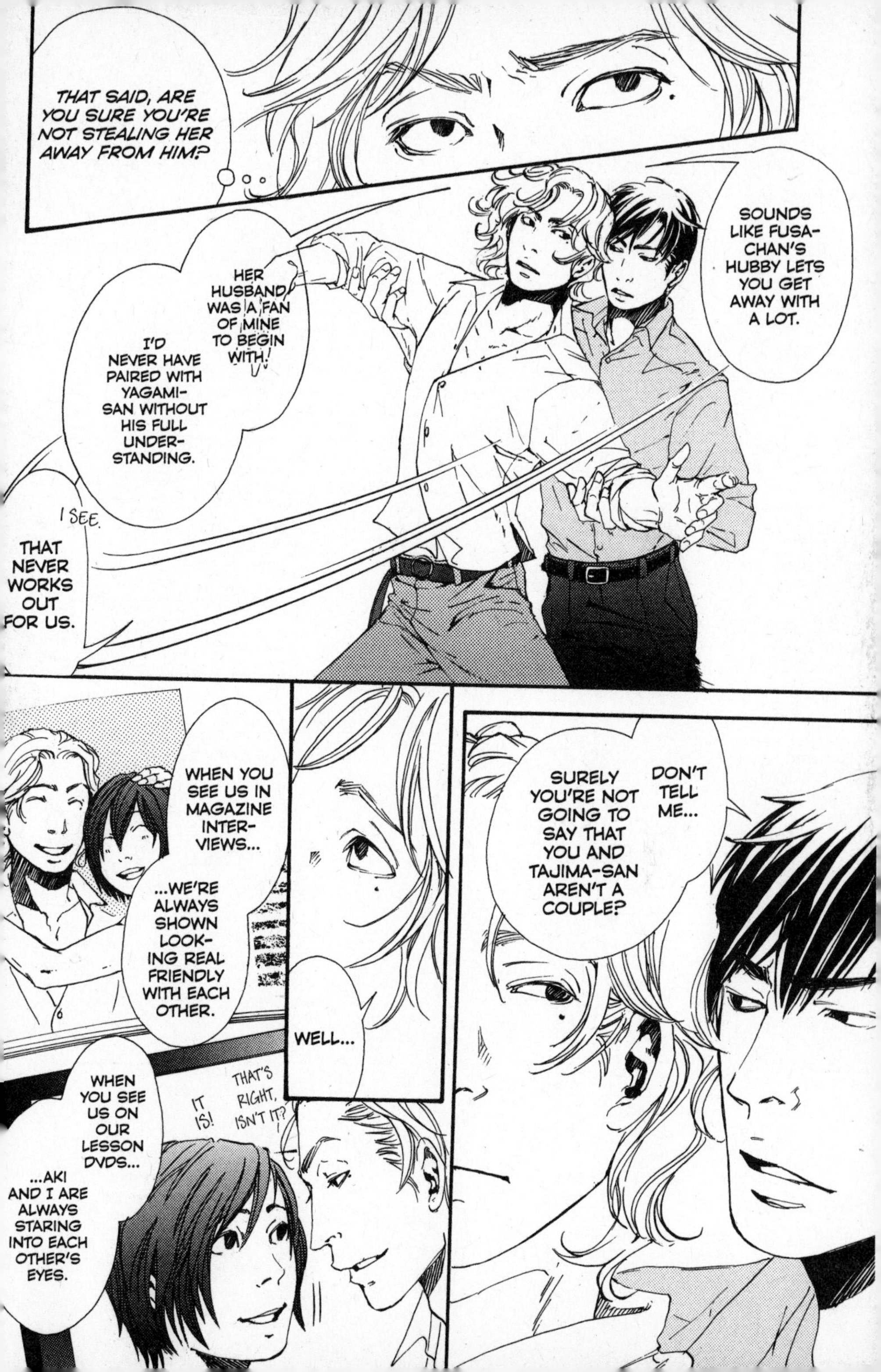
THAT SAID, ARE YOU SURE YOU'RE NOT STEALING HER AWAY FROM HIM?
SOUNDS LIKE FUSA-CHAN'S HUBBY LETS YOU GET AWAY WITH A LOT.
HER HUSBAND WAS A FAN OF MINE TO BEGIN WITH.
I'D NEVER HAVE PAIRED WITH YAGAMI-SAN WITHOUT HIS FULL UNDER-STANDING.
I SEE.
THAT NEVER WORKS OUT FOR US.
DON'T TELL ME...
SURELY YOU'RE NOT GOING TO SAY THAT YOU AND TAJIMA-SAN AREN'T A COUPLE?
WELL...
WHEN YOU SEE US IN MAGAZINE INTER-VIEWS...
...WE'RE ALWAYS SHOWN LOOK-ING REAL FRIENDLY WITH EACH OTHER.
THAT'S RIGHT, ISN'T IT?
IT IS!
WHEN YOU SEE US ON OUR LESSON DVDS...
...AKI AND I ARE ALWAYS STARING INTO EACH OTHER'S EYES.

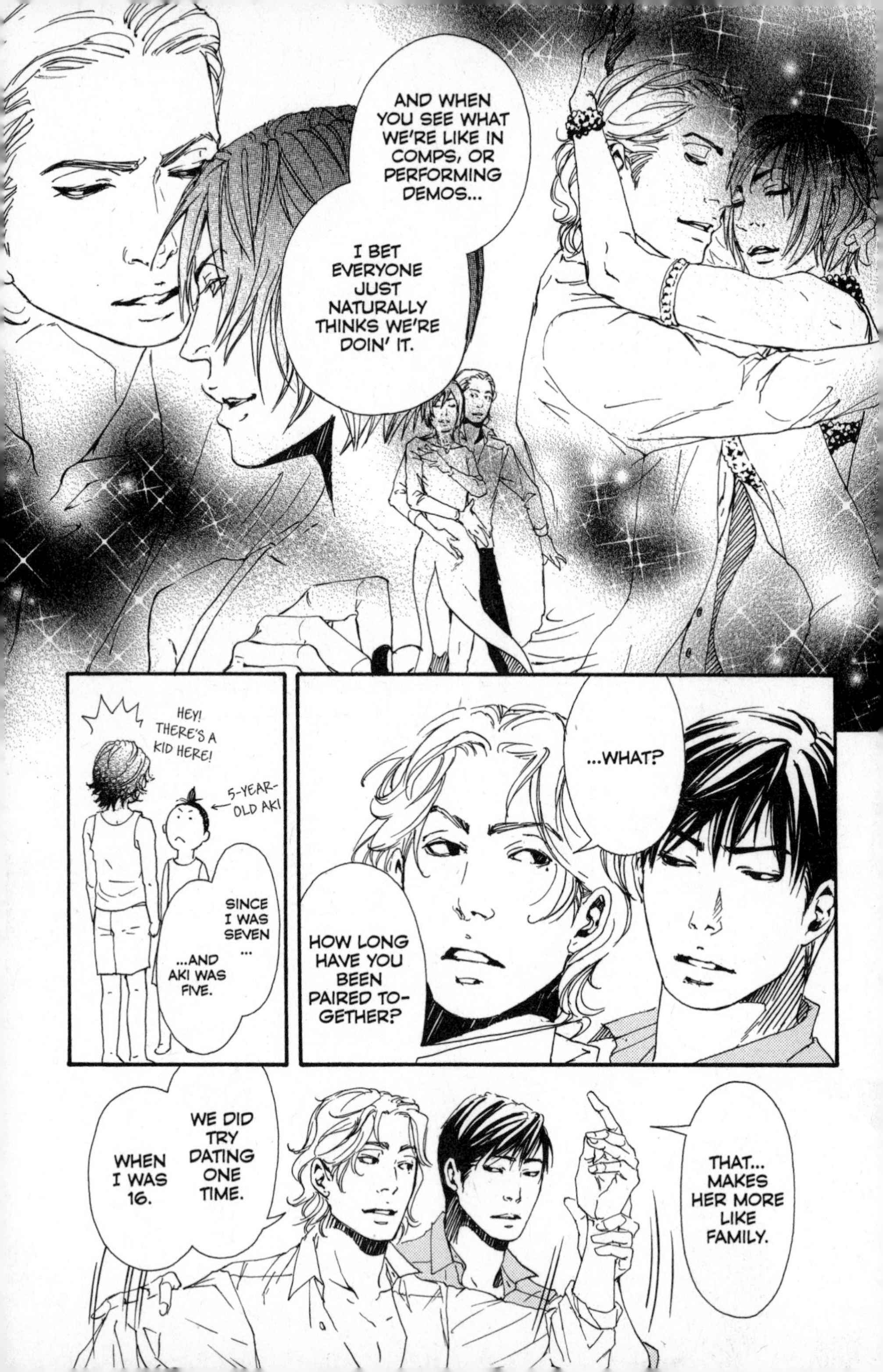
AND WHEN YOU SEE WHAT WE'RE LIKE IN COMPS, OR PERFORMING DEMOS...
I BET EVERYONE JUST NATURALLY THINKS WE'RE DOIN' IT.
...WHAT?
HOW LONG HAVE YOU BEEN PAIRED TO-GETHER?
HEY! THERE'S A KID HERE!
5-YEAR-OLD AKI
SINCE I WAS SEVEN ...
...AND AKI WAS FIVE.
THAT... MAKES HER MORE LIKE FAMILY.
WE DID TRY DATING ONE TIME.
WHEN I WAS 16.

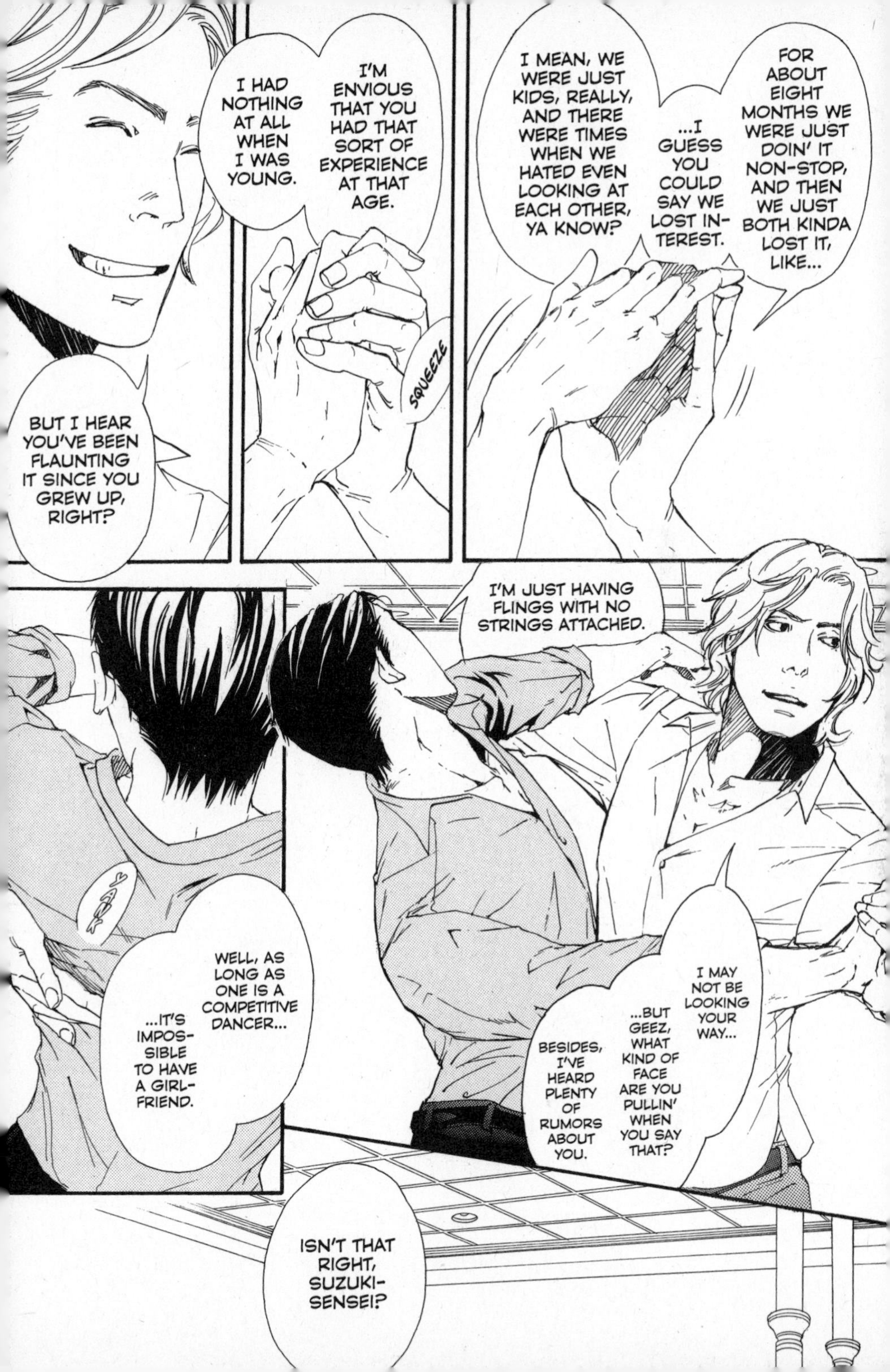
FOR ABOUT EIGHT MONTHS WE WERE JUST DOIN' IT NON-STOP, AND THEN WE JUST BOTH KINDA LOST IT, LIKE...
...I GUESS YOU COULD SAY WE LOST IN-TEREST.
I MEAN, WE WERE JUST KIDS, REALLY, AND THERE WERE TIMES WHEN WE HATED EVEN LOOKING AT EACH OTHER, YA KNOW?
I'M ENVIOUS THAT YOU HAD THAT SORT OF EXPERIENCE AT THAT AGE.
I HAD NOTHING AT ALL WHEN I WAS YOUNG.
SQUEEZE
BUT I HEAR YOU'VE BEEN FLAUNTING IT SINCE YOU GREW UP, RIGHT?
I'M JUST HAVING FLINGS WITH NO STRINGS ATTACHED.
I MAY NOT BE LOOKING YOUR WAY...
...BUT GEEZ, WHAT KIND OF FACE ARE YOU PULLIN' WHEN YOU SAY THAT?
BESIDES, I'VE HEARD PLENTY OF RUMORS ABOUT YOU.
YANK
WELL, AS LONG AS ONE IS A COMPETITIVE DANCER...
...IT'S IMPOS-SIBLE TO HAVE A GIRL-FRIEND.
ISN'T THAT RIGHT, SUZUKI-SENSEI?

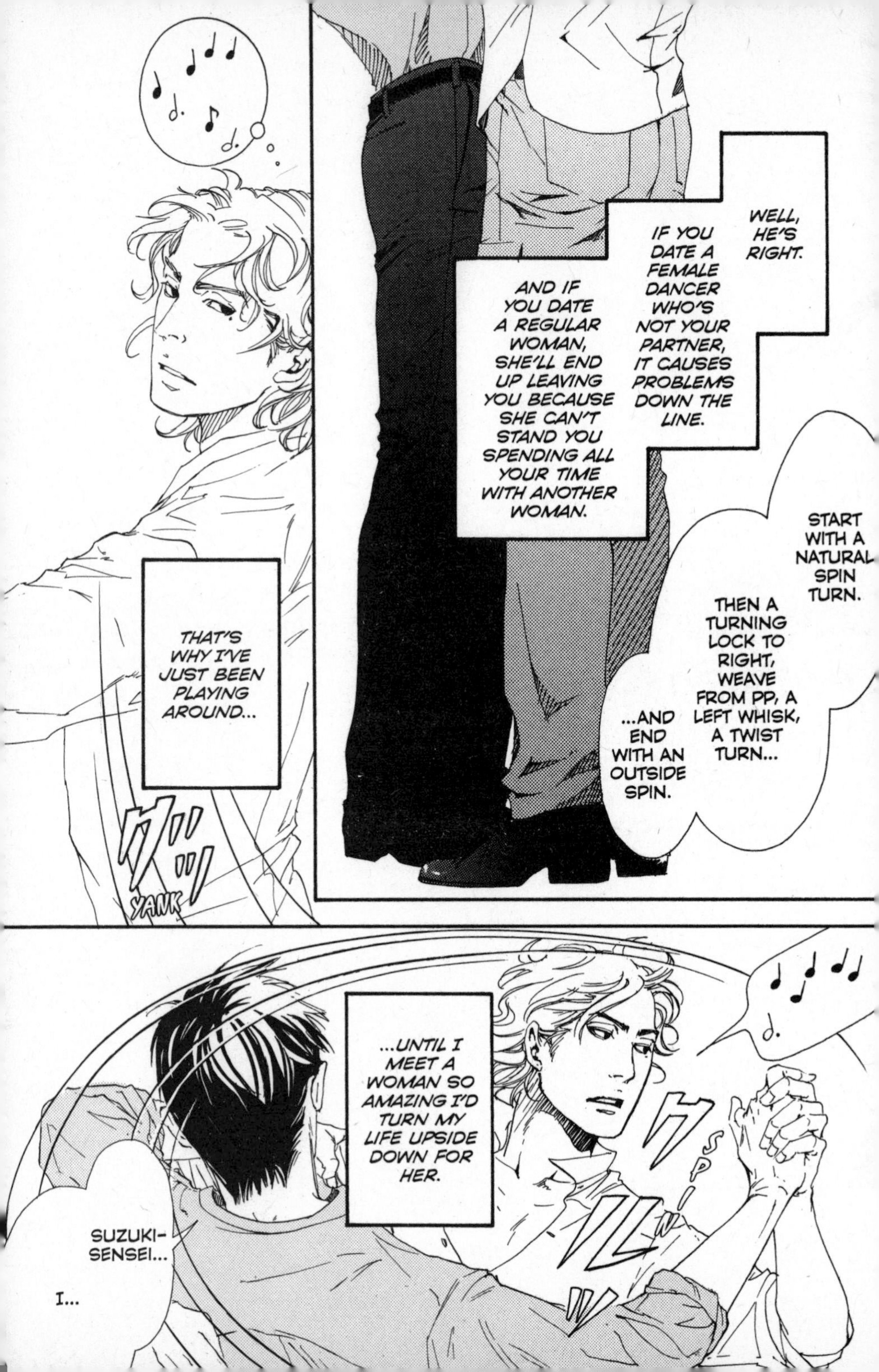
WELL, HE'S RIGHT.
IF YOU DATE A FEMALE DANCER WHO'S NOT YOUR PARTNER, IT CAUSES PROBLEMS DOWN THE LINE.
AND IF YOU DATE A REGULAR WOMAN, SHE'LL END UP LEAVING YOU BECAUSE SHE CAN'T STAND YOU SPENDING ALL YOUR TIME WITH ANOTHER WOMAN.
START WITH A NATURAL SPIN TURN.
THEN A TURNING LOCK TO RIGHT, WEAVE FROM PP, A LEFT WHISK, A TWIST TURN...
...AND END WITH AN OUTSIDE SPIN.
THAT'S WHY I'VE JUST BEEN PLAYING AROUND...
YANK
...UNTIL I MEET A WOMAN SO AMAZING I'D TURN MY LIFE UPSIDE DOWN FOR HER.
SPIN
SUZUKI-SENSEI...
I...

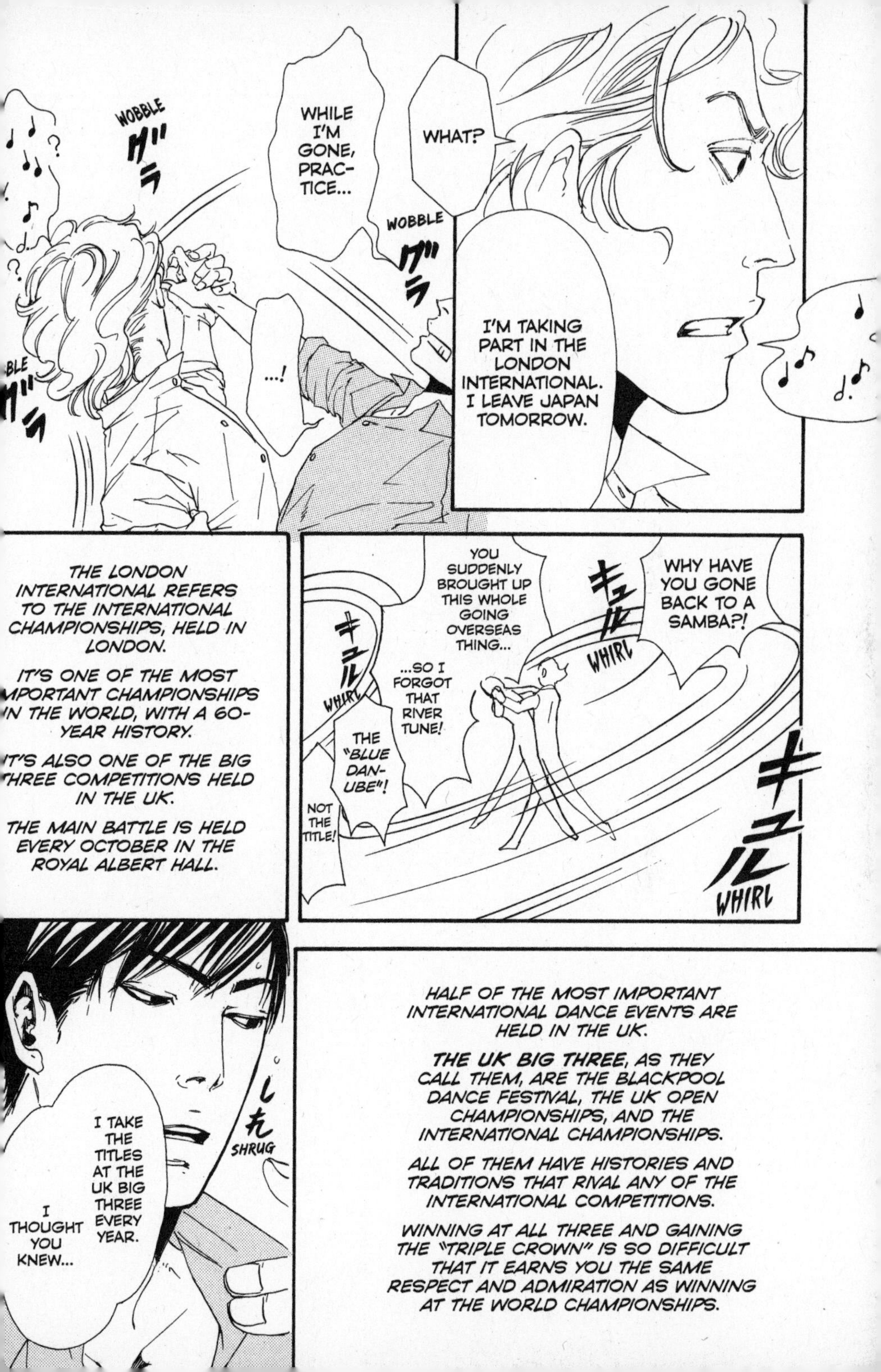
WHAT?
I'M TAKING PART IN THE LONDON INTERNATIONAL. I LEAVE JAPAN TOMORROW.
WHILE I'M GONE, PRACTICE...
WOBBLE
WOBBLE
...!
WHY HAVE YOU GONE BACK TO A SAMBA?!
WHIRL
YOU SUDDENLY BROUGHT UP THIS WHOLE GOING OVERSEAS THING...
...SO I FORGOT THAT RIVER TUNE!
WHIRL
THE "BLUE DANUBE"!
NOT THE TITLE!
WHIRL
THE LONDON INTERNATIONAL REFERS TO THE INTERNATIONAL CHAMPIONSHIPS, HELD IN LONDON.
IT'S ONE OF THE MOST IMPORTANT CHAMPIONSHIPS IN THE WORLD, WITH A 60-YEAR HISTORY.
IT'S ALSO ONE OF THE BIG THREE COMPETITIONS HELD IN THE UK.
THE MAIN BATTLE IS HELD EVERY OCTOBER IN THE ROYAL ALBERT HALL.
HALF OF THE MOST IMPORTANT INTERNATIONAL DANCE EVENTS ARE HELD IN THE UK.
THE UK BIG THREE, AS THEY CALL THEM, ARE THE BLACKPOOL DANCE FESTIVAL, THE UK OPEN CHAMPIONSHIPS, AND THE INTERNATIONAL CHAMPIONSHIPS.
ALL OF THEM HAVE HISTORIES AND TRADITIONS THAT RIVAL ANY OF THE INTERNATIONAL COMPETITIONS.
WINNING AT ALL THREE AND GAINING THE "TRIPLE CROWN" IS SO DIFFICULT THAT IT EARNS YOU THE SAME RESPECT AND ADMIRATION AS WINNING AT THE WORLD CHAMPIONSHIPS.
SHRUG
I TAKE THE TITLES AT THE UK BIG THREE EVERY YEAR.
I THOUGHT YOU KNEW...

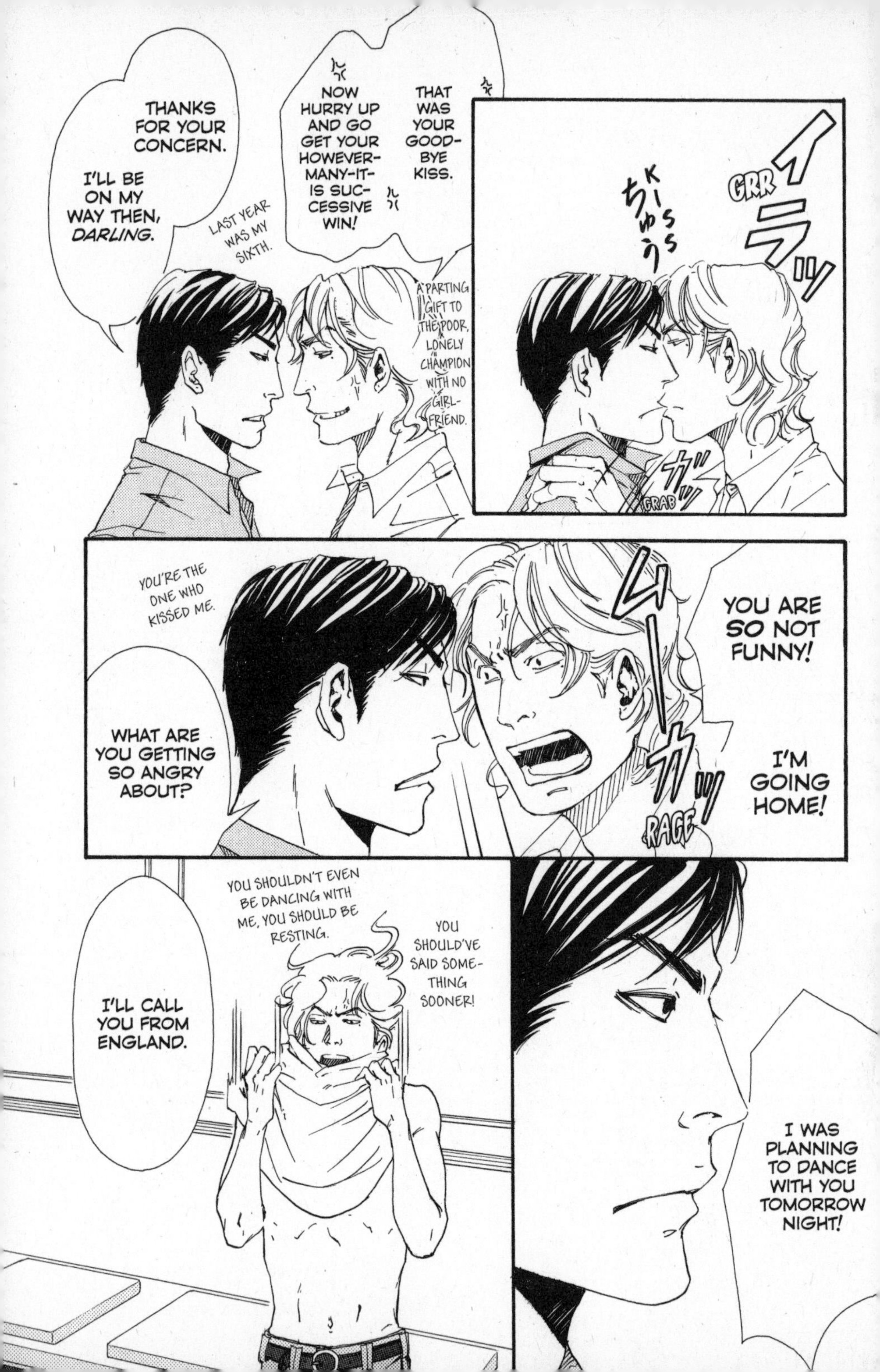
GRR
KISS
GRAB
THAT WAS YOUR GOOD-BYE KISS.
NOW HURRY UP AND GO GET YOUR HOWEVER-MANY-IT-IS SUCCESSIVE WIN!
A PARTING GIFT TO THE POOR, LONELY CHAMPION WITH NO GIRLFRIEND.
LAST YEAR WAS MY SIXTH.
THANKS FOR YOUR CONCERN.
I'LL BE ON MY WAY THEN, *DARLING*.
YOU ARE SO NOT FUNNY!
I'M GOING HOME!
RAGE
YOU'RE THE ONE WHO KISSED ME.
WHAT ARE YOU GETTING SO ANGRY ABOUT?
I WAS PLANNING TO DANCE WITH YOU TOMORROW NIGHT!
YOU SHOULD'VE SAID SOMETHING SOONER!
YOU SHOULDN'T EVEN BE DANCING WITH ME, YOU SHOULD BE RESTING.
I'LL CALL YOU FROM ENGLAND.

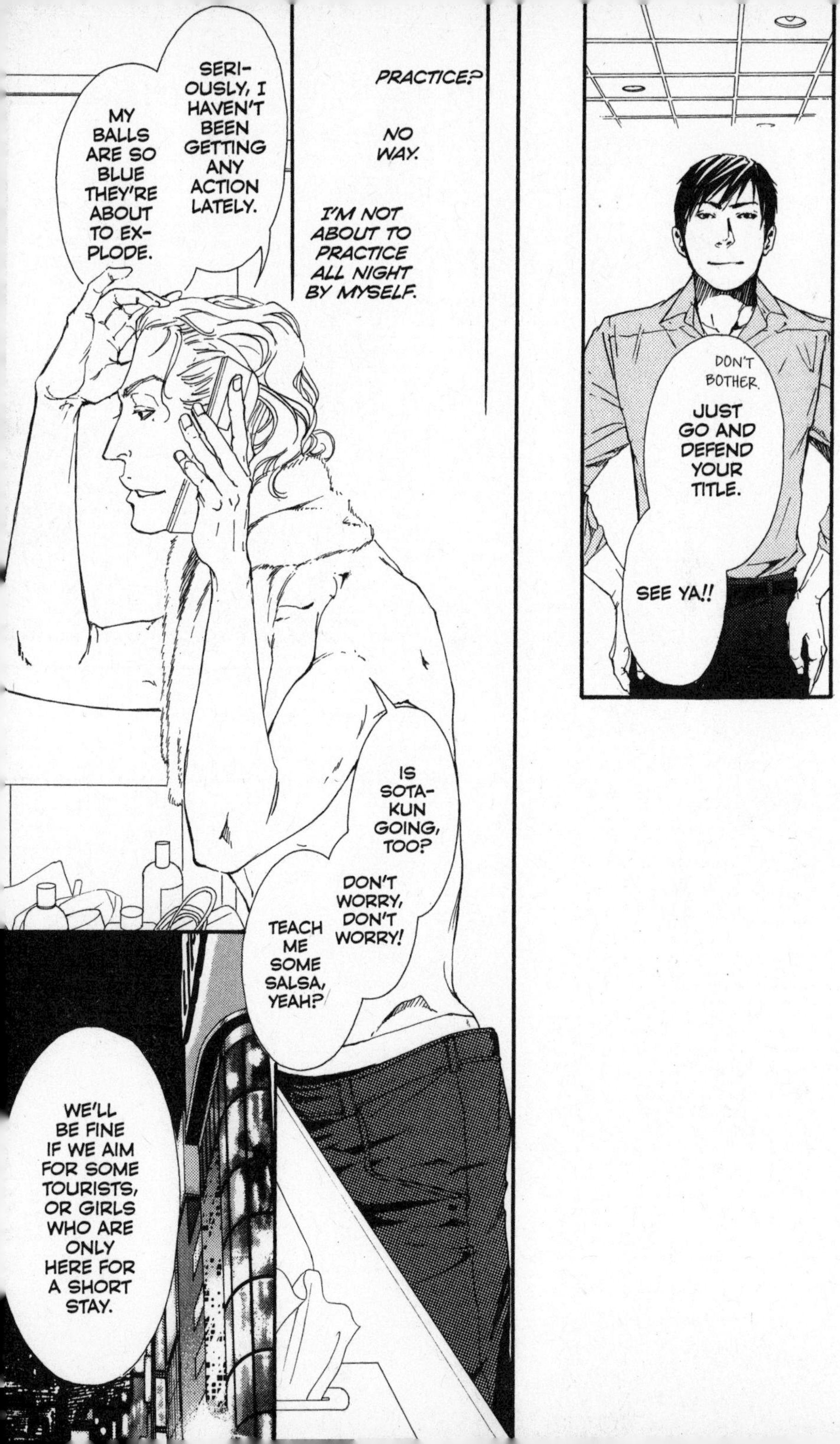
DON'T BOTHER.
JUST GO AND DEFEND YOUR TITLE.
SEE YA!!
PRACTICE?
NO WAY.
I'M NOT ABOUT TO PRACTICE ALL NIGHT BY MYSELF.
SERI-OUSLY, I HAVEN'T BEEN GETTING ANY ACTION LATELY.
MY BALLS ARE SO BLUE THEY'RE ABOUT TO EX-PLODE.
IS SOTA-KUN GOING, TOO?
DON'T WORRY, DON'T WORRY!
TEACH ME SOME SALSA, YEAH?
WE'LL BE FINE IF WE AIM FOR SOME TOURISTS, OR GIRLS WHO ARE ONLY HERE FOR A SHORT STAY.

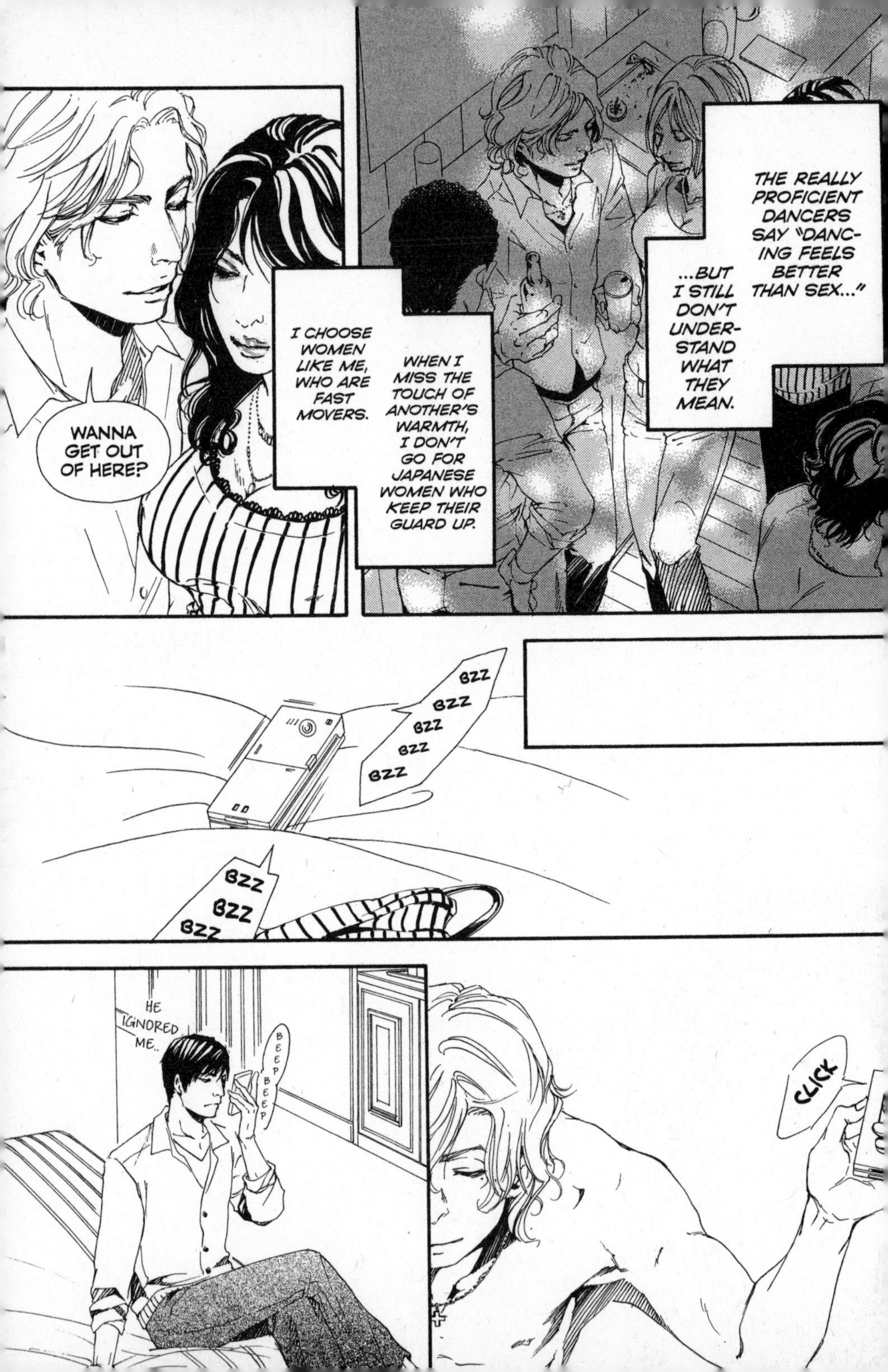
THE REALLY PROFICIENT DANCERS SAY "DANCING FEELS BETTER THAN SEX..."
...BUT I STILL DON'T UNDERSTAND WHAT THEY MEAN.
WHEN I MISS THE TOUCH OF ANOTHER'S WARMTH, I DON'T GO FOR JAPANESE WOMEN WHO KEEP THEIR GUARD UP.
I CHOOSE WOMEN LIKE ME, WHO ARE FAST MOVERS.
WANNA GET OUT OF HERE?
BZZ BZZ BZZ BZZ BZZ
BZZ BZZ BZZ
CLICK
HE IGNORED ME..
BEEP BEEP

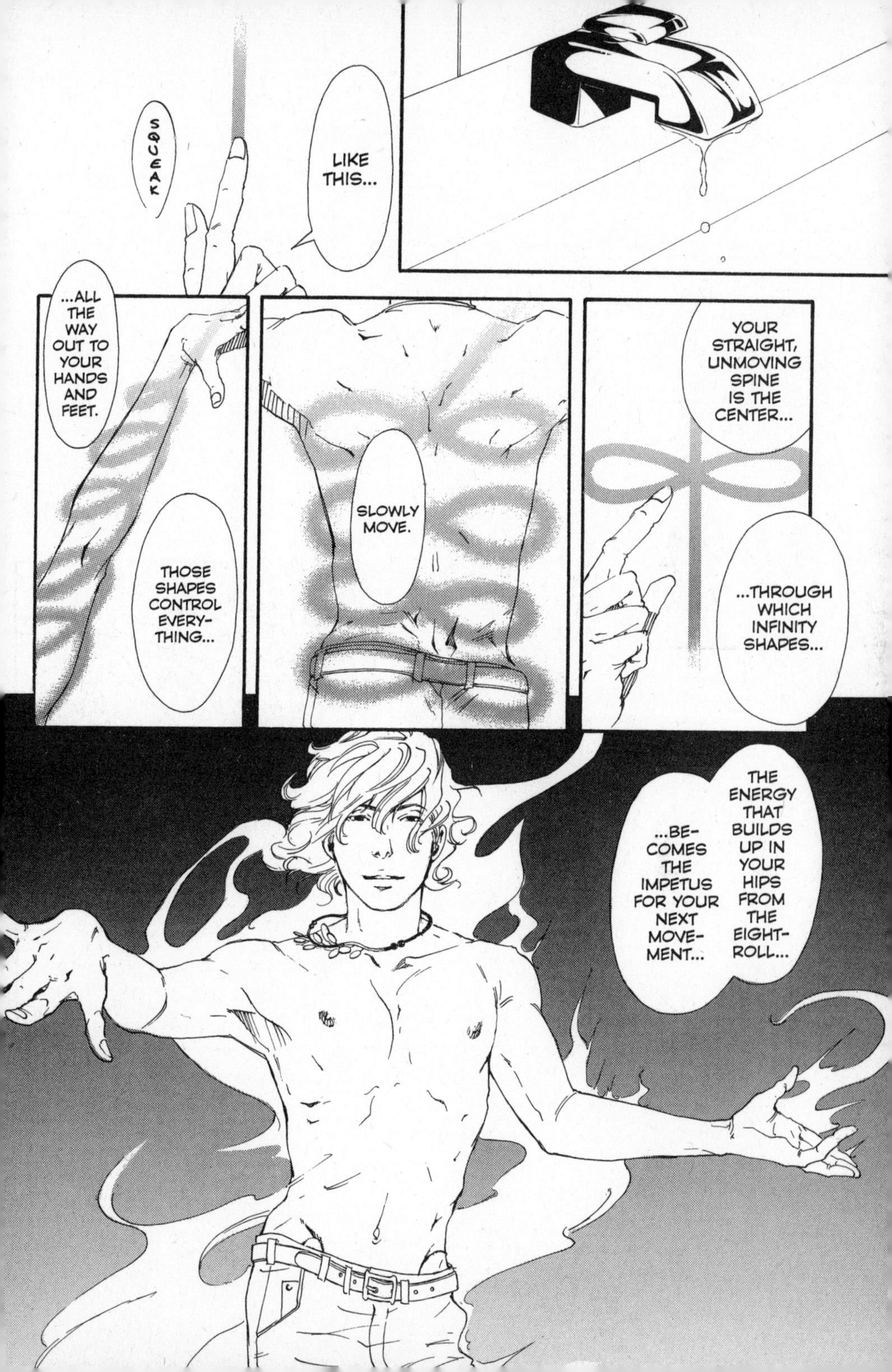
LIKE THIS...
SQUEAK
YOUR STRAIGHT, UNMOVING SPINE IS THE CENTER...
...THROUGH WHICH INFINITY SHAPES...
SLOWLY MOVE.
...ALL THE WAY OUT TO YOUR HANDS AND FEET.
THOSE SHAPES CONTROL EVERY-THING...
THE ENERGY THAT BUILDS UP IN YOUR HIPS FROM THE EIGHT-ROLL...
...BE-COMES THE IMPETUS FOR YOUR NEXT MOVE-MENT...

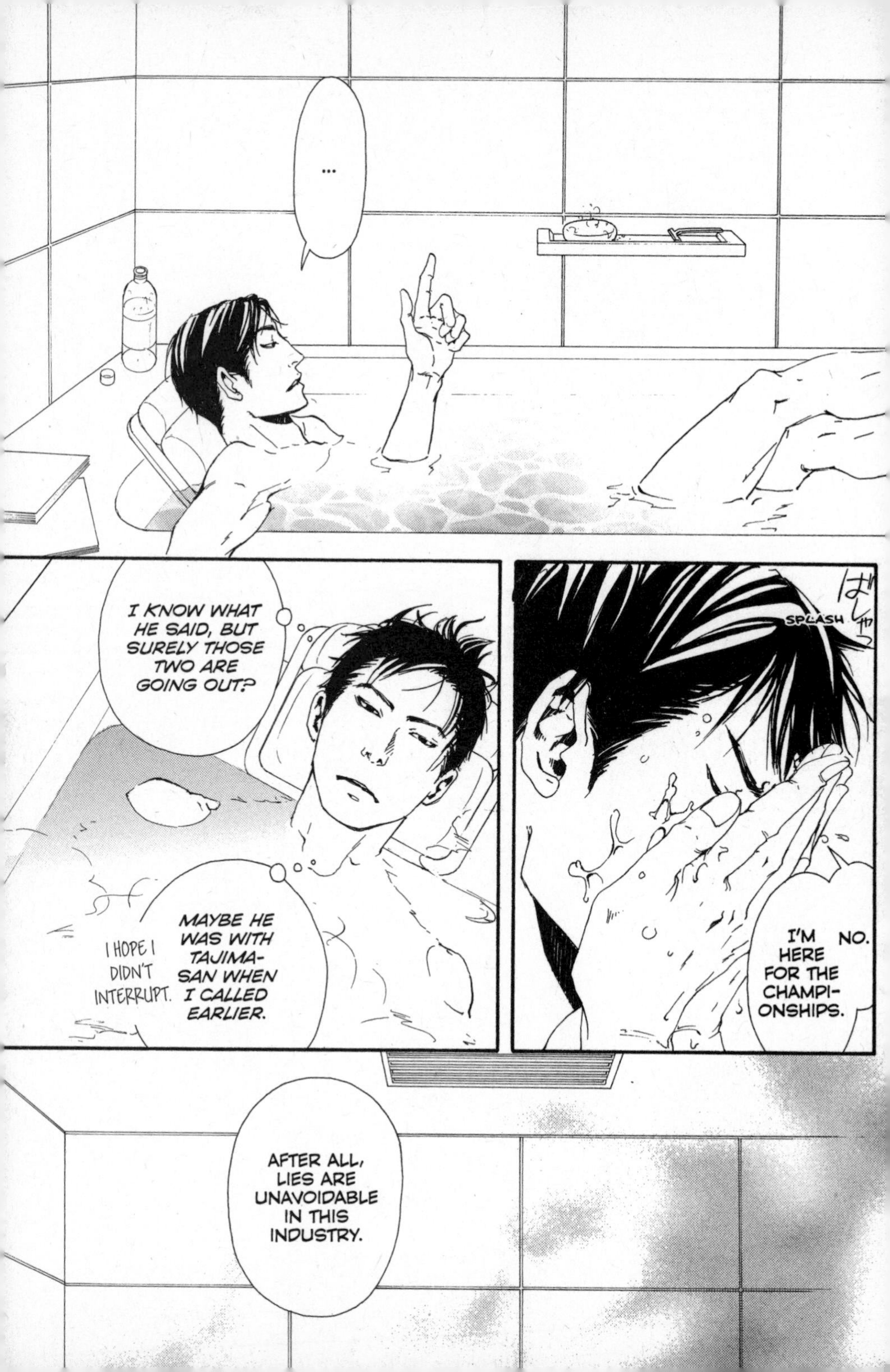
...
ばしゃっ
SPLASH
NO.
I'M HERE FOR THE CHAMPIONSHIPS.
I KNOW WHAT HE SAID, BUT SURELY THOSE TWO ARE GOING OUT?
MAYBE HE WAS WITH TAJIMA-SAN WHEN I CALLED EARLIER.
I HOPE I DIDN'T INTERRUPT.
AFTER ALL, LIES ARE UNAVOIDABLE IN THIS INDUSTRY.

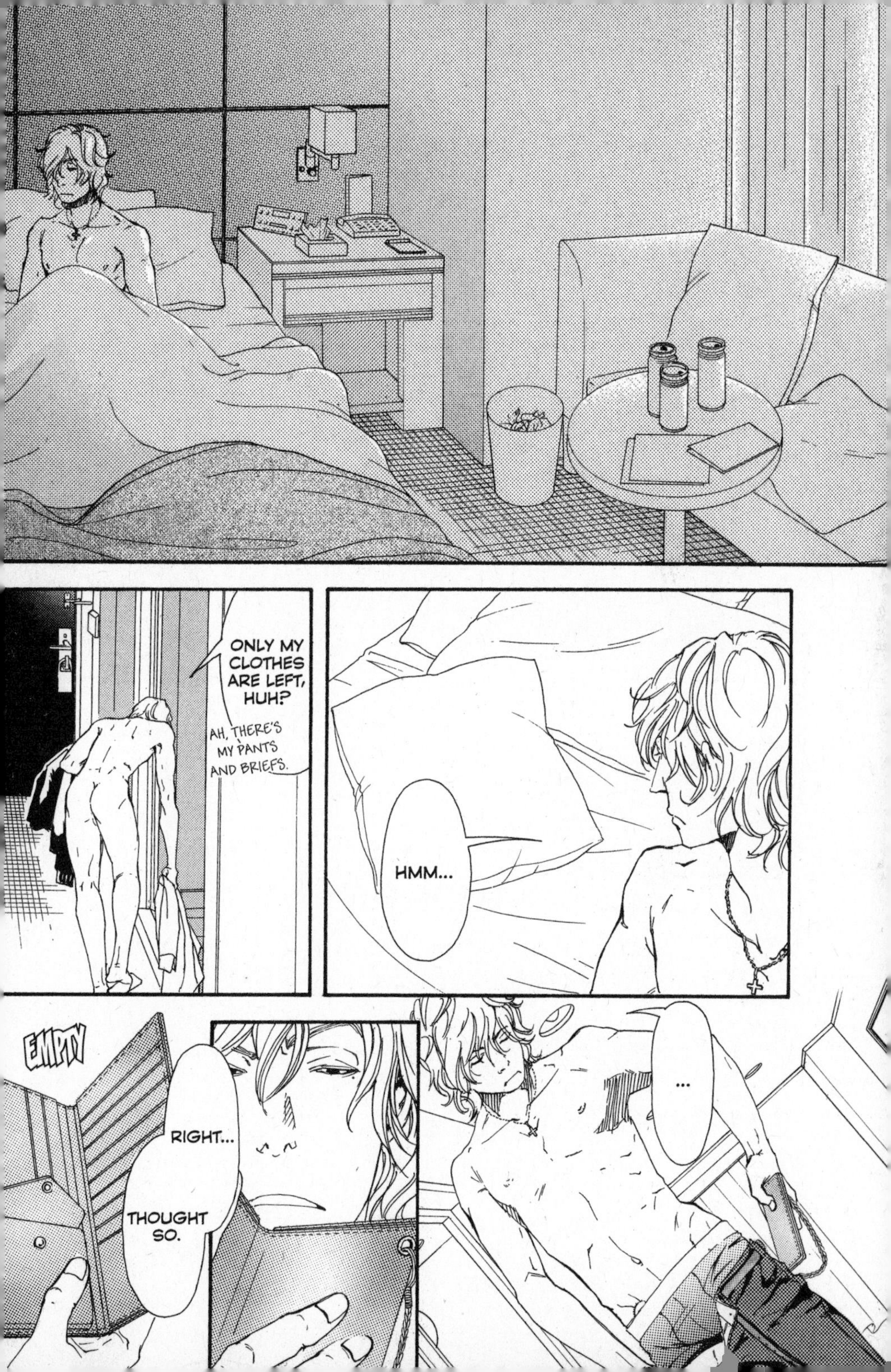
HMM...
ONLY MY CLOTHES ARE LEFT, HUH?
AH, THERE'S MY PANTS AND BRIEFS.
...
RIGHT...
THOUGHT SO.
EMPTY

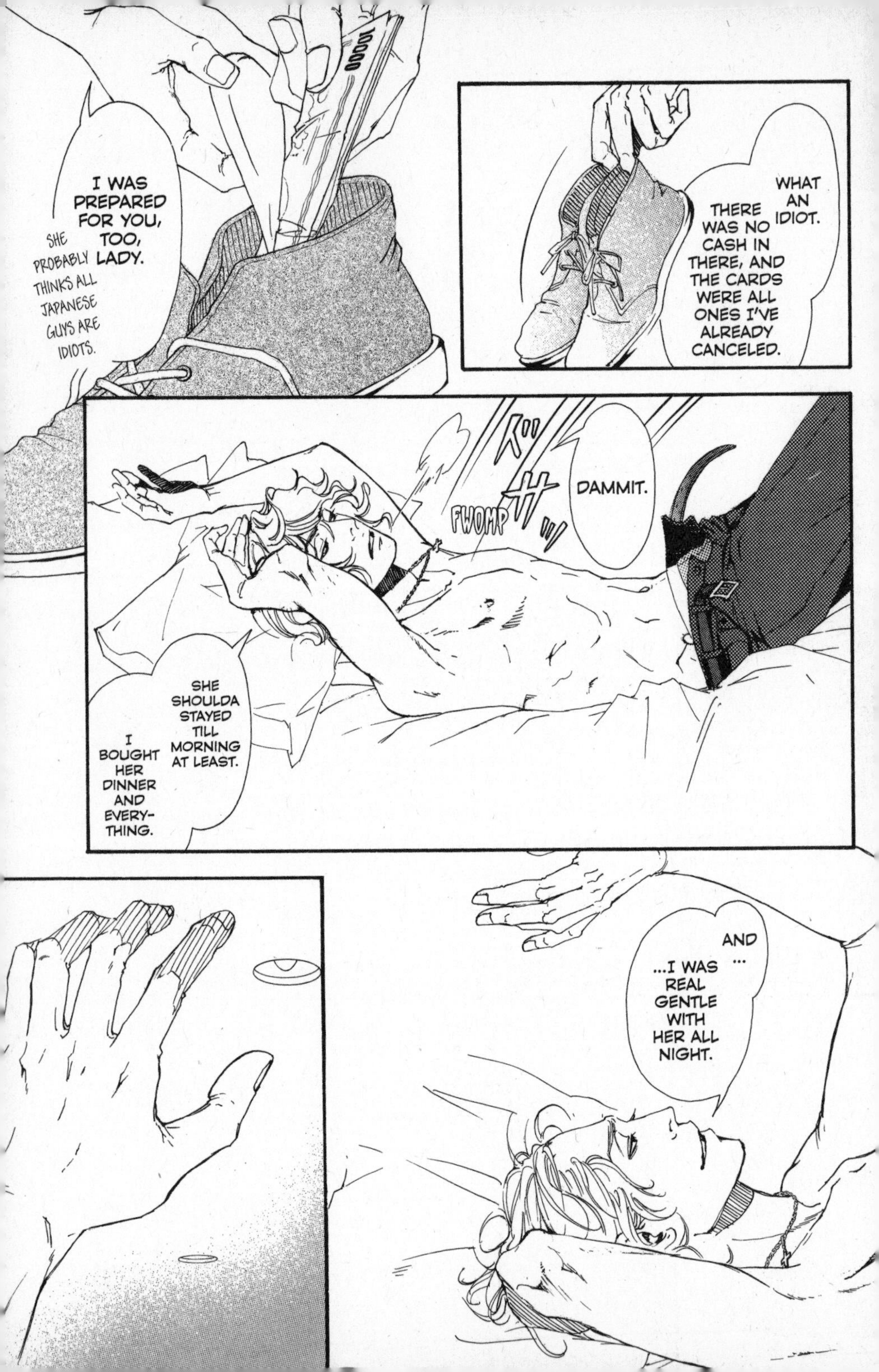
WHAT AN IDIOT.
THERE WAS NO CASH IN THERE, AND THE CARDS WERE ALL ONES I'VE ALREADY CANCELED.
I WAS PREPARED FOR YOU, TOO, LADY.
SHE PROBABLY THINKS ALL JAPANESE GUYS ARE IDIOTS.
DAMMIT.
FWOMP
SHE SHOULDA STAYED TILL MORNING AT LEAST.
I BOUGHT HER DINNER AND EVERY-THING.
AND ...
...I WAS REAL GENTLE WITH HER ALL NIGHT.

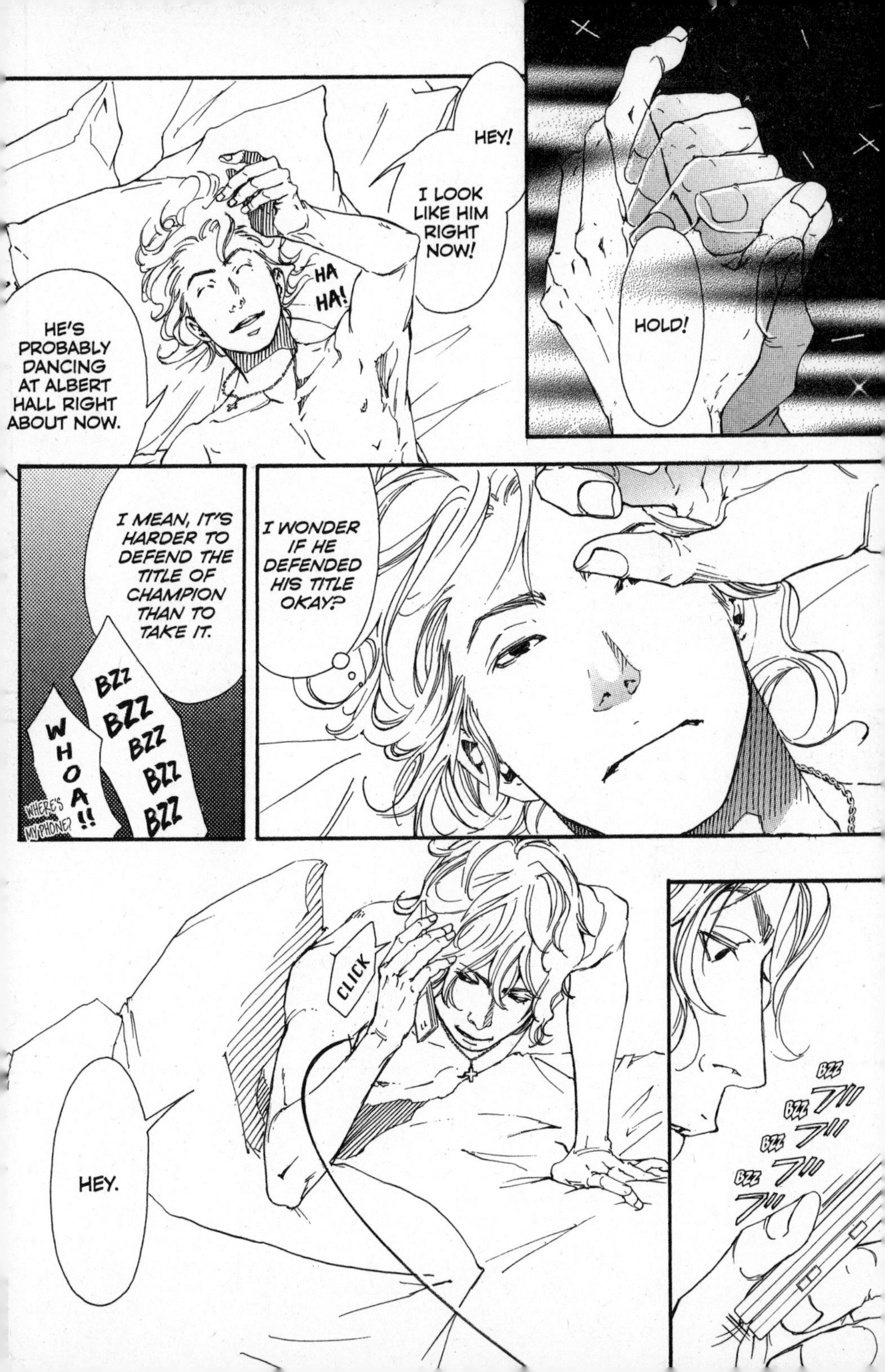
HOLD!
HEY!
I LOOK LIKE HIM RIGHT NOW!
HA HA!
HE'S PROBABLY DANCING AT ALBERT HALL RIGHT ABOUT NOW.
I WONDER IF HE DEFENDED HIS TITLE OKAY?
I MEAN, IT'S HARDER TO DEFEND THE TITLE OF CHAMPION THAN TO TAKE IT.
BZZ BZZ BZZ BZZ BZZ
WHOA!!
WHERE'S MY PHONE?
BZZ BZZ BZZ BZZ
CLICK
HEY.

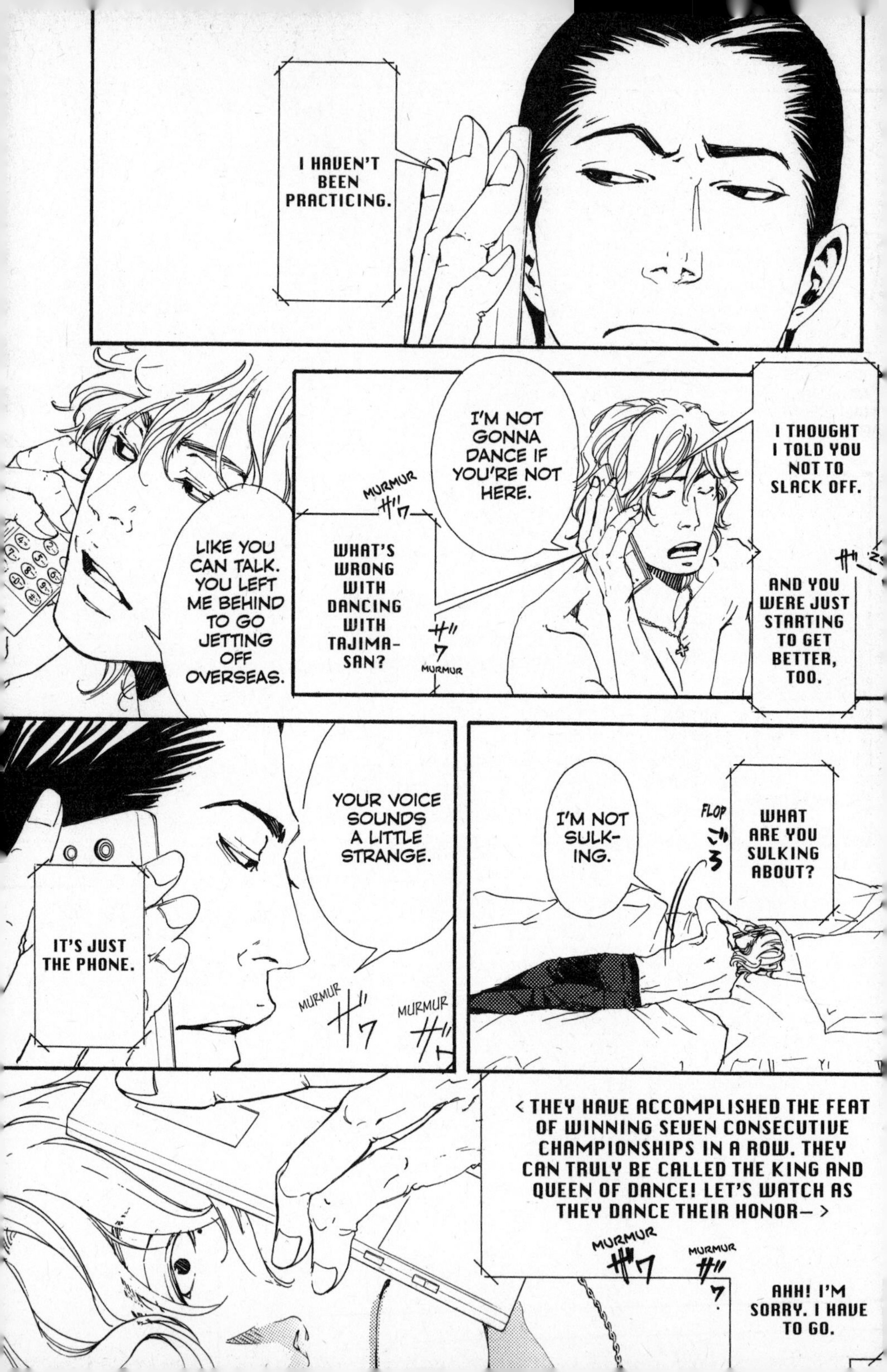
I HAVEN'T BEEN PRACTICING.
I THOUGHT I TOLD YOU NOT TO SLACK OFF.
AND YOU WERE JUST STARTING TO GET BETTER, TOO.
I'M NOT GONNA DANCE IF YOU'RE NOT HERE.
MURMUR
WHAT'S WRONG WITH DANCING WITH TAJIMA-SAN?
MURMUR
LIKE YOU CAN TALK. YOU LEFT ME BEHIND TO GO JETTING OFF OVERSEAS.
WHAT ARE YOU SULKING ABOUT?
FLOP
I'M NOT SULKING.
YOUR VOICE SOUNDS A LITTLE STRANGE.
IT'S JUST THE PHONE.
MURMUR
MURMUR
< THEY HAVE ACCOMPLISHED THE FEAT OF WINNING SEVEN CONSECUTIVE CHAMPIONSHIPS IN A ROW. THEY CAN TRULY BE CALLED THE KING AND QUEEN OF DANCE! LET'S WATCH AS THEY DANCE THEIR HONOR— >
MURMUR
MURMUR
AHH! I'M SORRY. I HAVE TO GO.

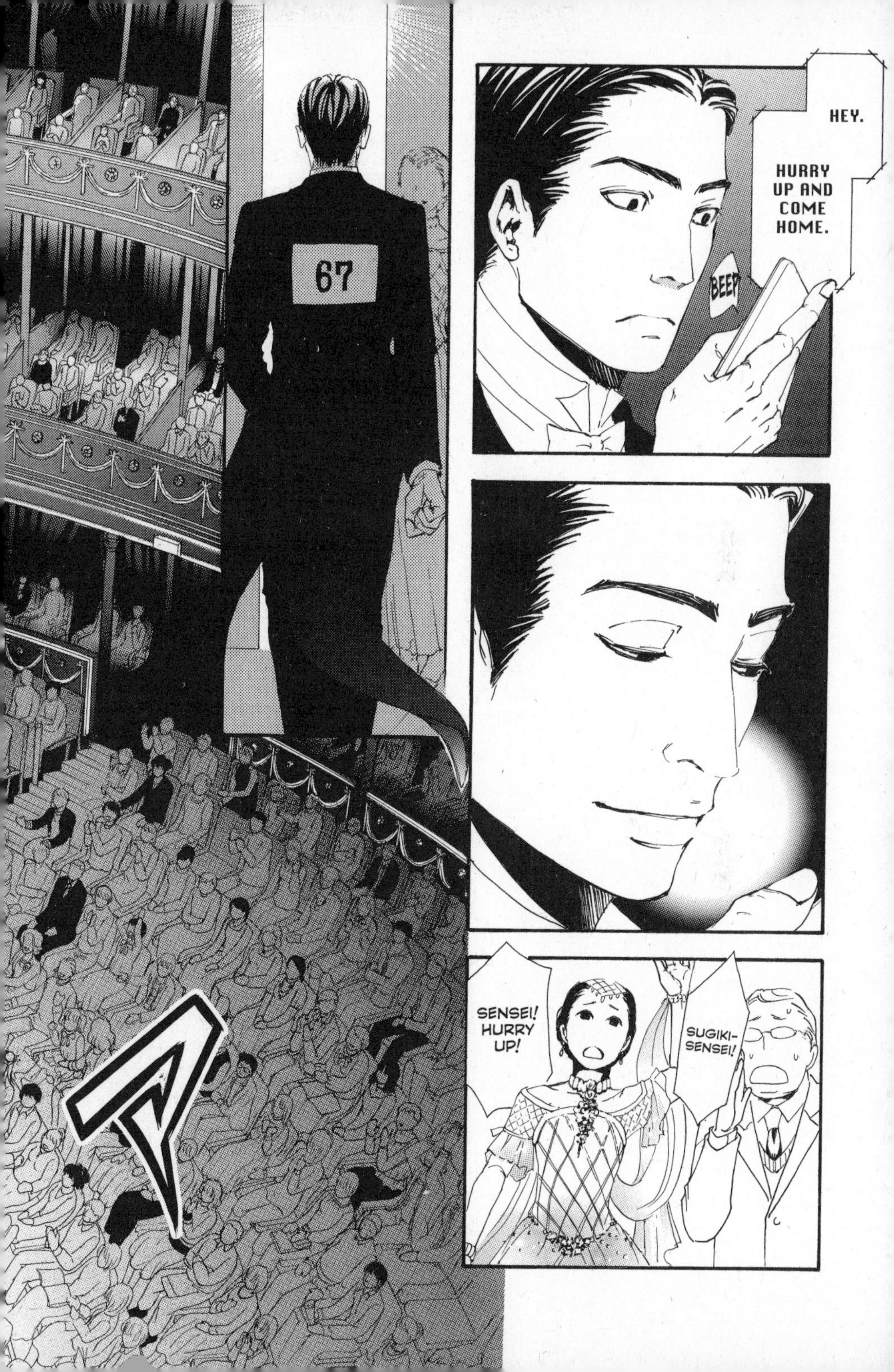
HEY.
HURRY UP AND COME HOME.
BEEP
SUGIKI-SENSEI!
SENSEI! HURRY UP!
67

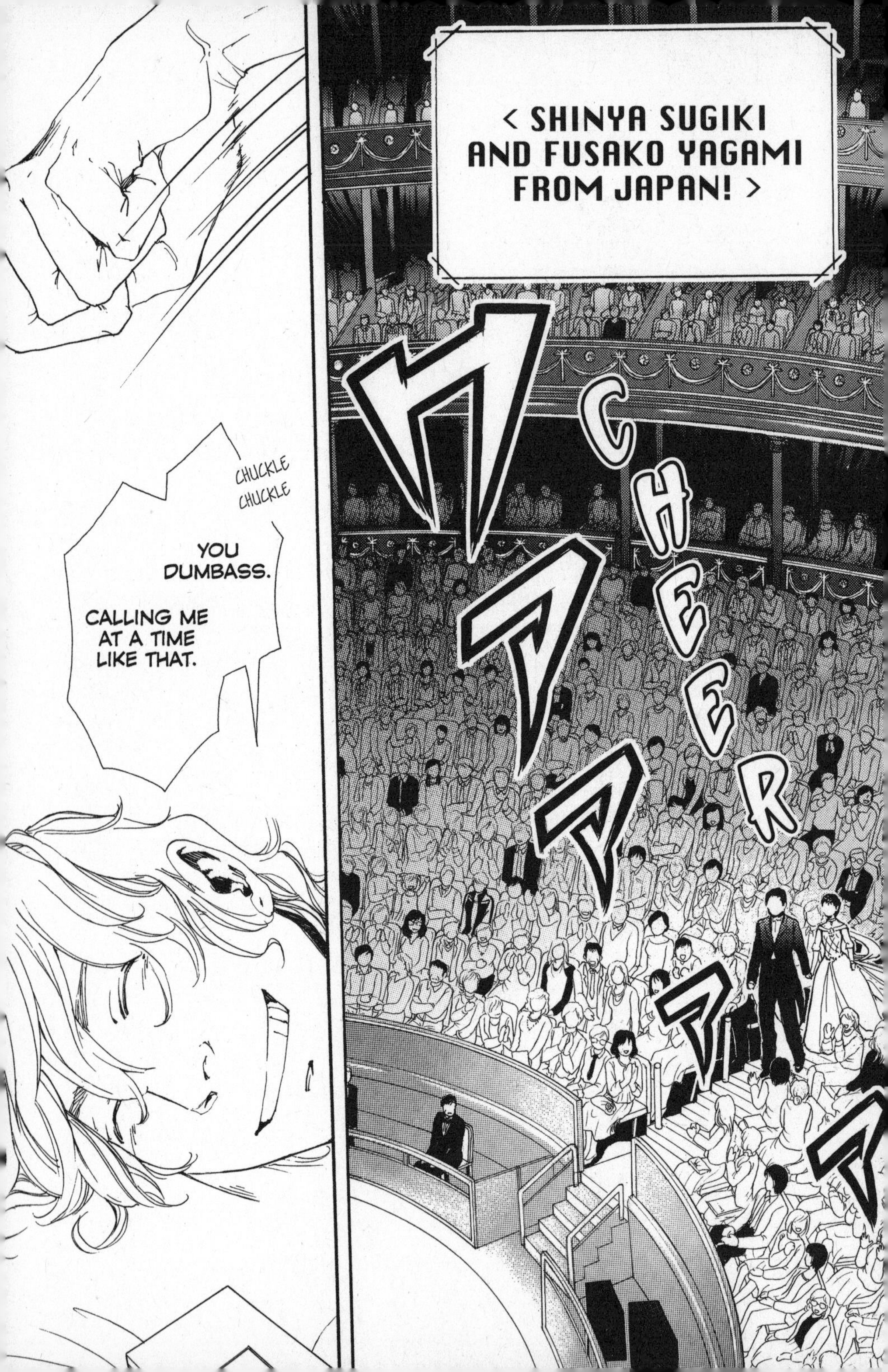
< SHINYA SUGIKI AND FUSAKO YAGAMI FROM JAPAN! >
CHEER
CHUCKLE CHUCKLE
YOU DUMBASS.
CALLING ME AT A TIME LIKE THAT.

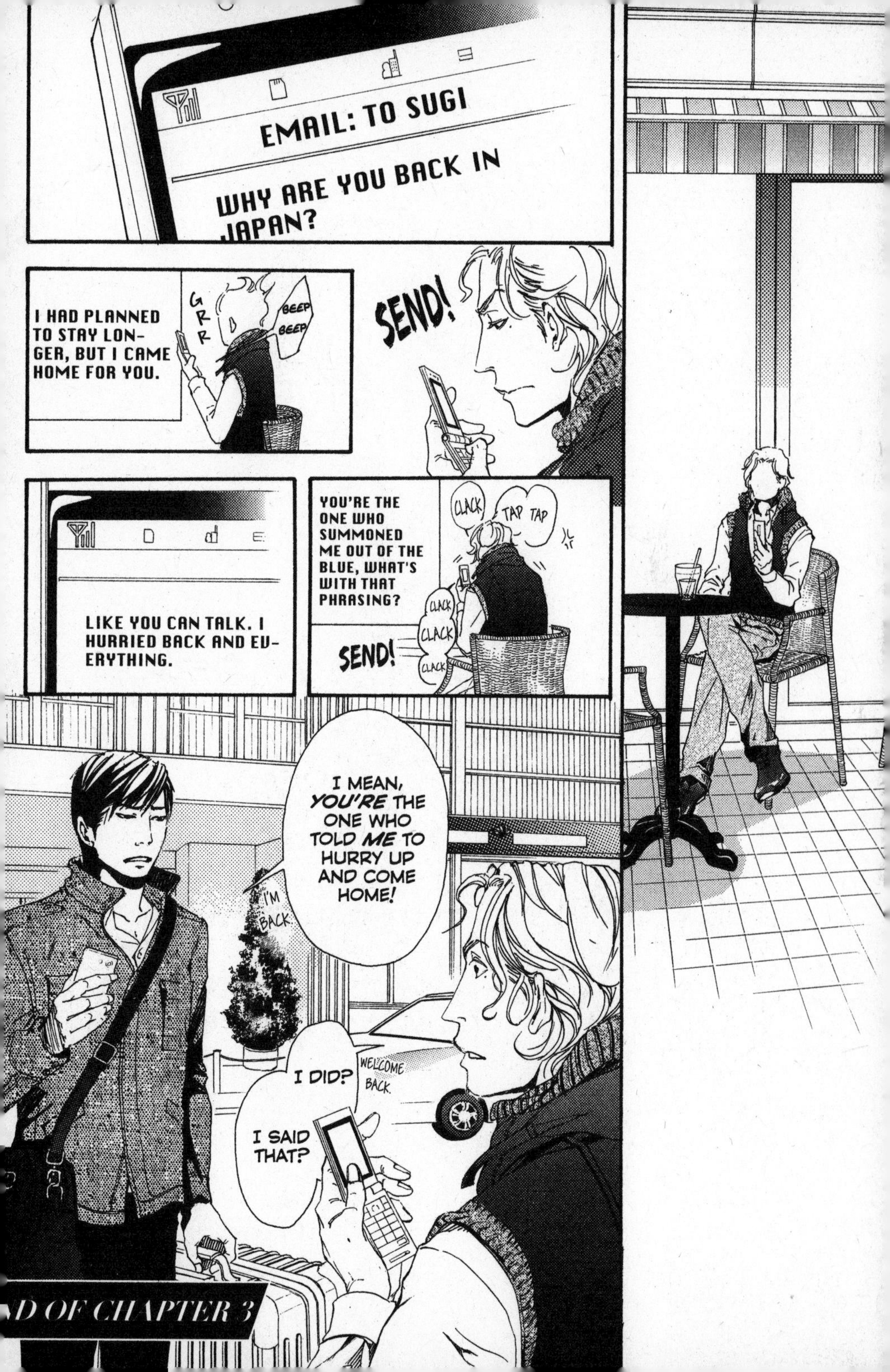
EMAIL: TO SUGI
WHY ARE YOU BACK IN JAPAN?
SEND!
GRR
BEEP BEEP
I HAD PLANNED TO STAY LONGER, BUT I CAME HOME FOR YOU.
CLACK
TAP TAP
YOU'RE THE ONE WHO SUMMONED ME OUT OF THE BLUE, WHAT'S WITH THAT PHRASING?
CLACK
CLACK
CLACK
SEND!
LIKE YOU CAN TALK. I HURRIED BACK AND EVERYTHING.
I MEAN, *YOU'RE* THE ONE WHO TOLD *ME* TO HURRY UP AND COME HOME!
I'M BACK.
WELCOME BACK.
I DID?
I SAID THAT?
ND OF CHAPTER 3

#04
SOMEDAY MY KING WILL COME

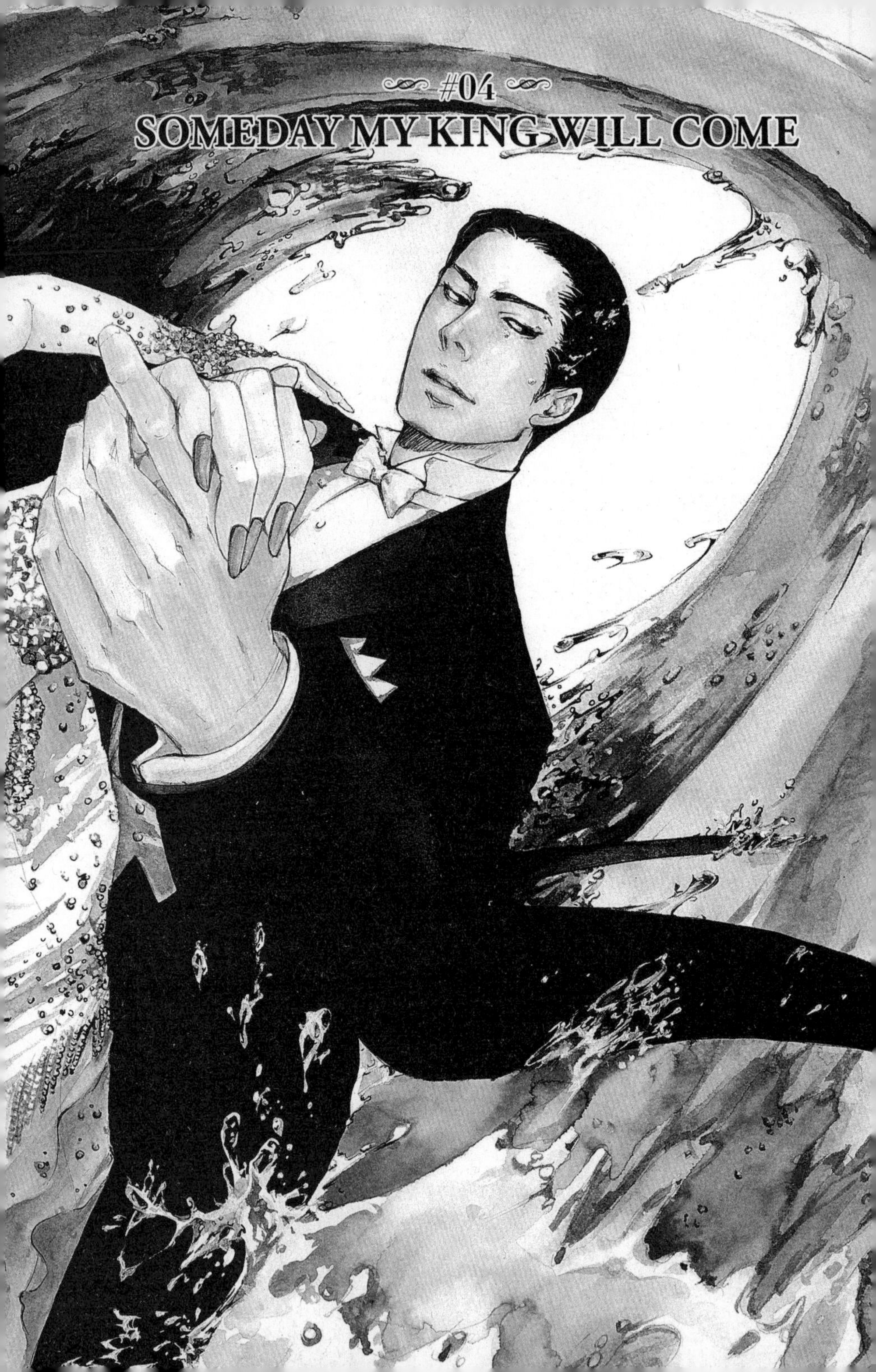

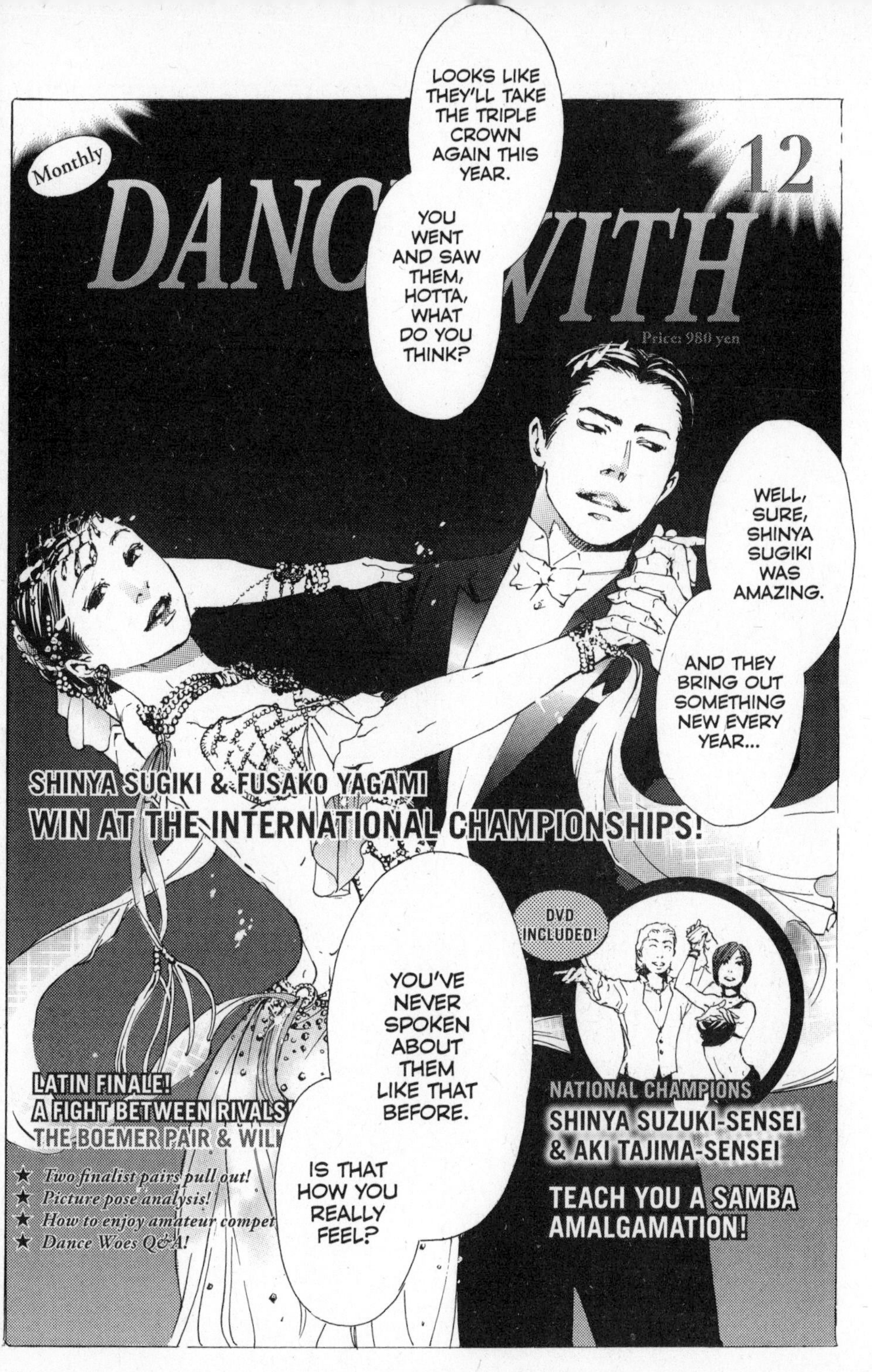
Monthly
DANC
WITH
12
Price: 980 yen
LOOKS LIKE THEY'LL TAKE THE TRIPLE CROWN AGAIN THIS YEAR.
YOU WENT AND SAW THEM, HOTTA, WHAT DO YOU THINK?
WELL, SURE, SHINYA SUGIKI WAS AMAZING.
AND THEY BRING OUT SOMETHING NEW EVERY YEAR...
SHINYA SUGIKI & FUSAKO YAGAMI
WIN AT THE INTERNATIONAL CHAMPIONSHIPS!
DVD INCLUDED!
YOU'VE NEVER SPOKEN ABOUT THEM LIKE THAT BEFORE.
IS THAT HOW YOU REALLY FEEL?
LATIN FINALE!
A FIGHT BETWEEN RIVALS
THE BOEMER PAIR & WIL
★ Two finalist pairs pull out!
★ Picture pose analysis!
★ How to enjoy amateur compet
★ Dance Woes Q&A!
NATIONAL CHAMPIONS
SHINYA SUZUKI-SENSEI & AKI TAJIMA-SENSEI
TEACH YOU A SAMBA AMALGAMATION!

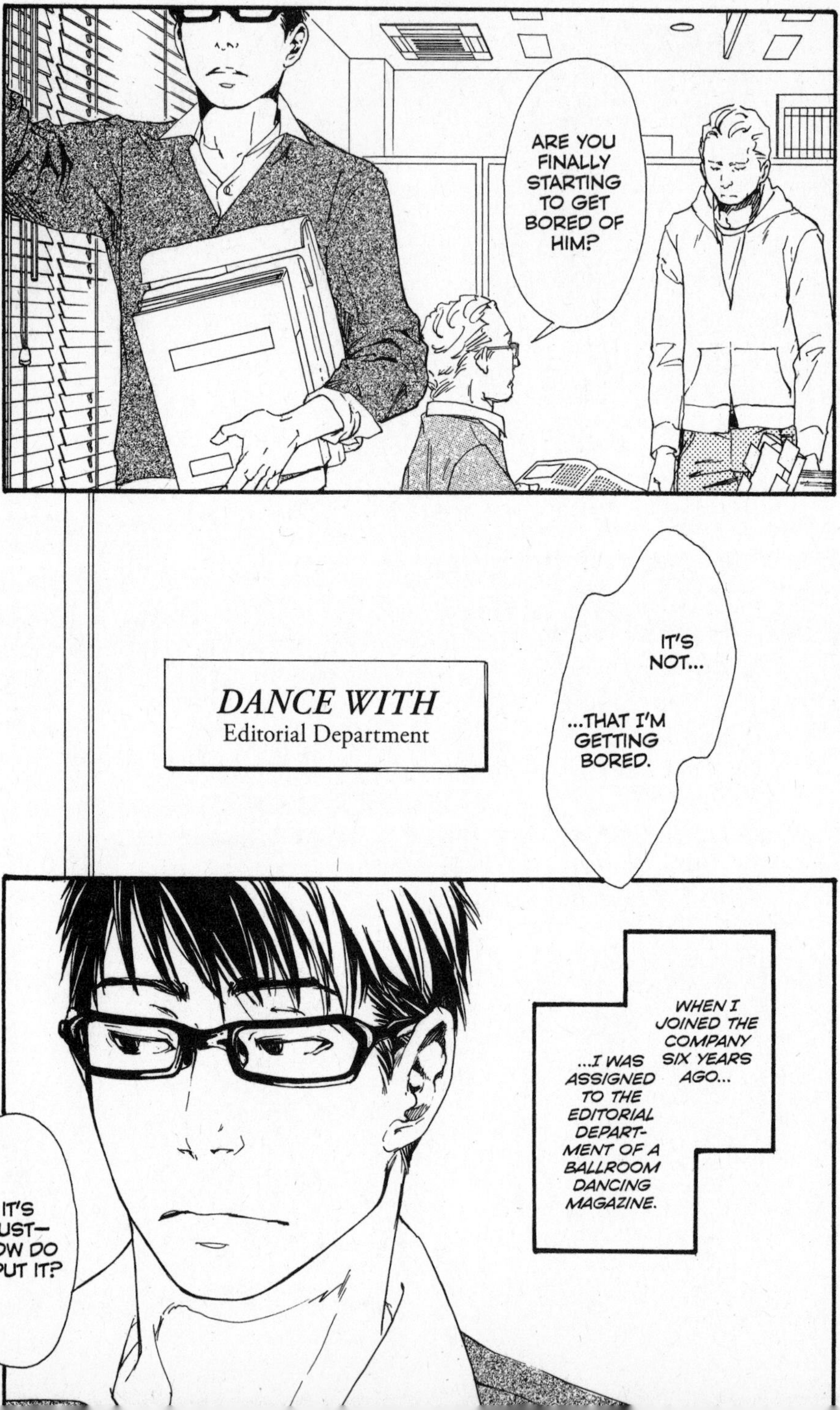
ARE YOU FINALLY STARTING TO GET BORED OF HIM?
IT'S NOT...
...THAT I'M GETTING BORED.
DANCE WITH
Editorial Department
WHEN I JOINED THE COMPANY SIX YEARS AGO...
...I WAS ASSIGNED TO THE EDITORIAL DEPART-MENT OF A BALLROOM DANCING MAGAZINE.
IT'S JUST—HOW DO I PUT IT?

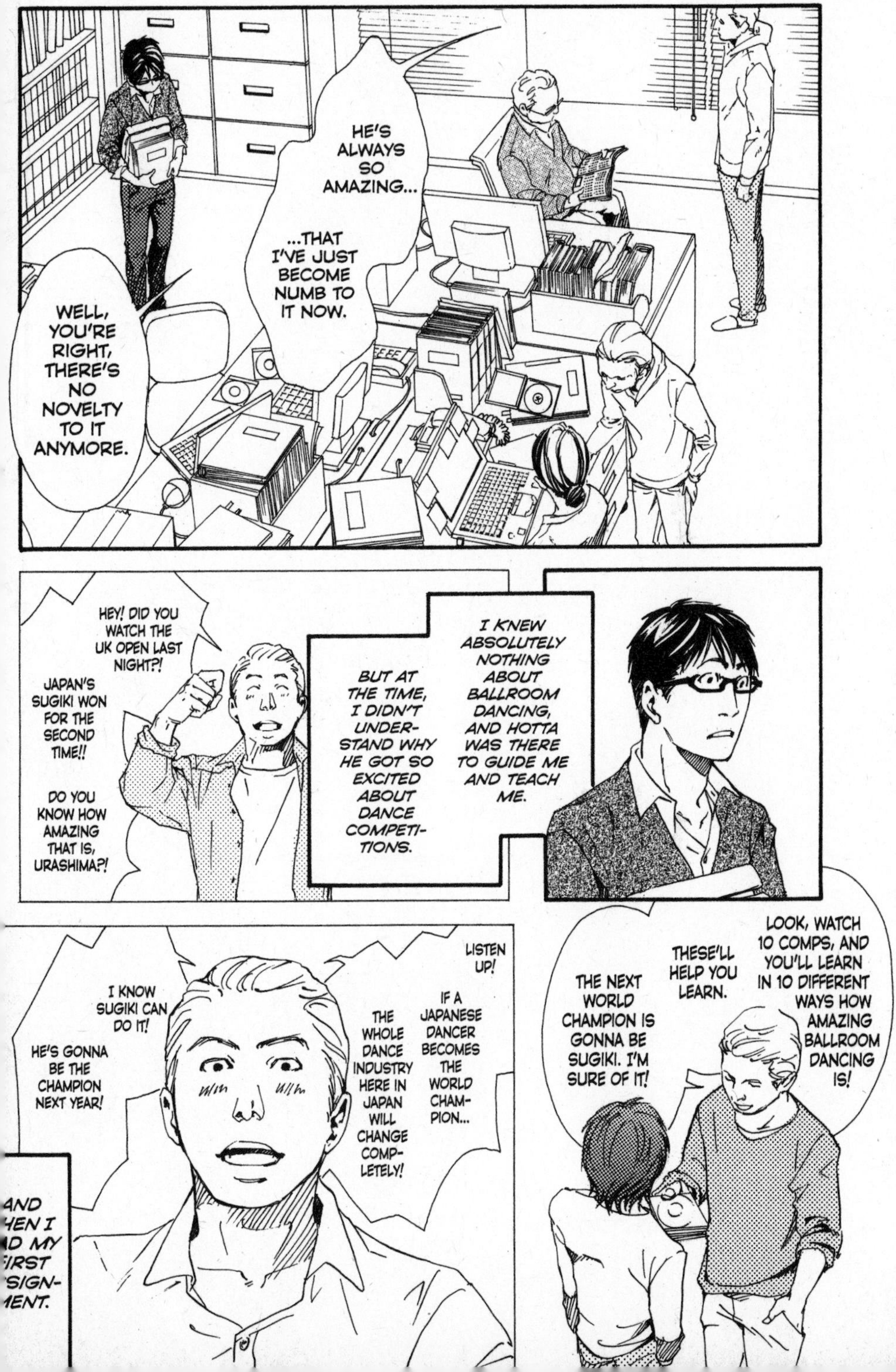
HE'S ALWAYS SO AMAZING...
...THAT I'VE JUST BECOME NUMB TO IT NOW.
WELL, YOU'RE RIGHT, THERE'S NO NOVELTY TO IT ANYMORE.
I KNEW ABSOLUTELY NOTHING ABOUT BALLROOM DANCING, AND HOTTA WAS THERE TO GUIDE ME AND TEACH ME.
BUT AT THE TIME, I DIDN'T UNDER-STAND WHY HE GOT SO EXCITED ABOUT DANCE COMPETI-TIONS.
HEY! DID YOU WATCH THE UK OPEN LAST NIGHT?!
JAPAN'S SUGIKI WON FOR THE SECOND TIME!!
DO YOU KNOW HOW AMAZING THAT IS, URASHIMA?!
LOOK, WATCH 10 COMPS, AND YOU'LL LEARN IN 10 DIFFERENT WAYS HOW AMAZING BALLROOM DANCING IS!
THESE'LL HELP YOU LEARN.
THE NEXT WORLD CHAMPION IS GONNA BE SUGIKI. I'M SURE OF IT!
LISTEN UP!
IF A JAPANESE DANCER BECOMES THE WORLD CHAM-PION...
THE WHOLE DANCE INDUSTRY HERE IN JAPAN WILL CHANGE COMP-LETELY!
I KNOW SUGIKI CAN DO IT!
HE'S GONNA BE THE CHAMPION NEXT YEAR!

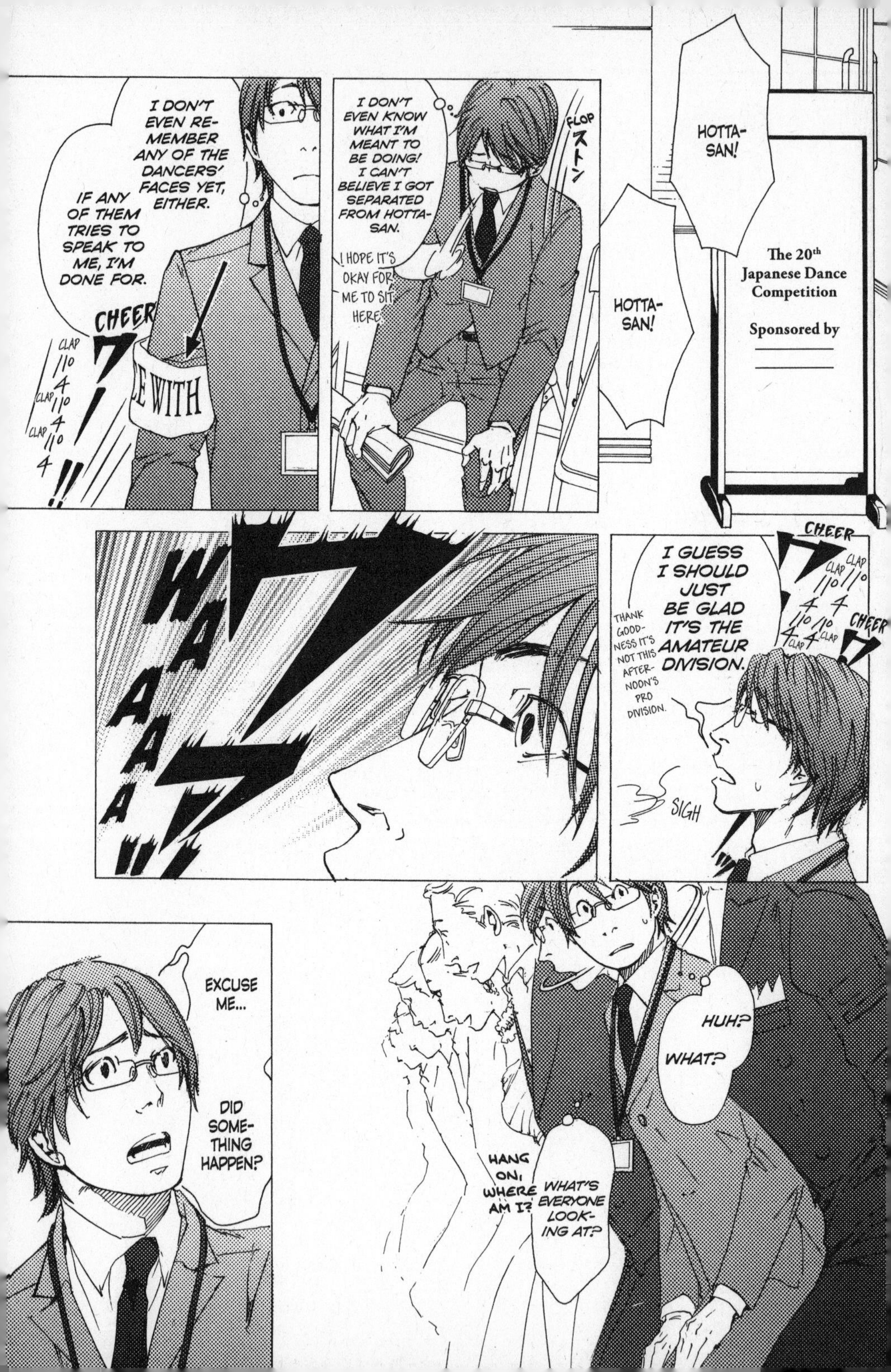
HOTTA-SAN!
HOTTA-SAN!
The 20th Japanese Dance Competition
Sponsored by
I DON'T EVEN KNOW WHAT I'M MEANT TO BE DOING! I CAN'T BELIEVE I GOT SEPARATED FROM HOTTA-SAN.
FLOP
ストン
I HOPE IT'S OKAY FOR ME TO SIT HERE.
I DON'T EVEN REMEMBER ANY OF THE DANCERS' FACES YET, EITHER.
IF ANY OF THEM TRIES TO SPEAK TO ME, I'M DONE FOR.
CHEER
CLAP CLAP CLAP
CHEER
CLAP CLAP CLAP CLAP
CHEER
I GUESS I SHOULD JUST BE GLAD IT'S THE AMATEUR DIVISION.
THANK GOODNESS IT'S NOT THIS AFTERNOON'S PRO DIVISION.
SIGH
WAAAA!!
HUH?
WHAT?
WHAT'S EVERYONE LOOKING AT?
HANG ON, WHERE AM I?
EXCUSE ME...
DID SOMETHING HAPPEN?

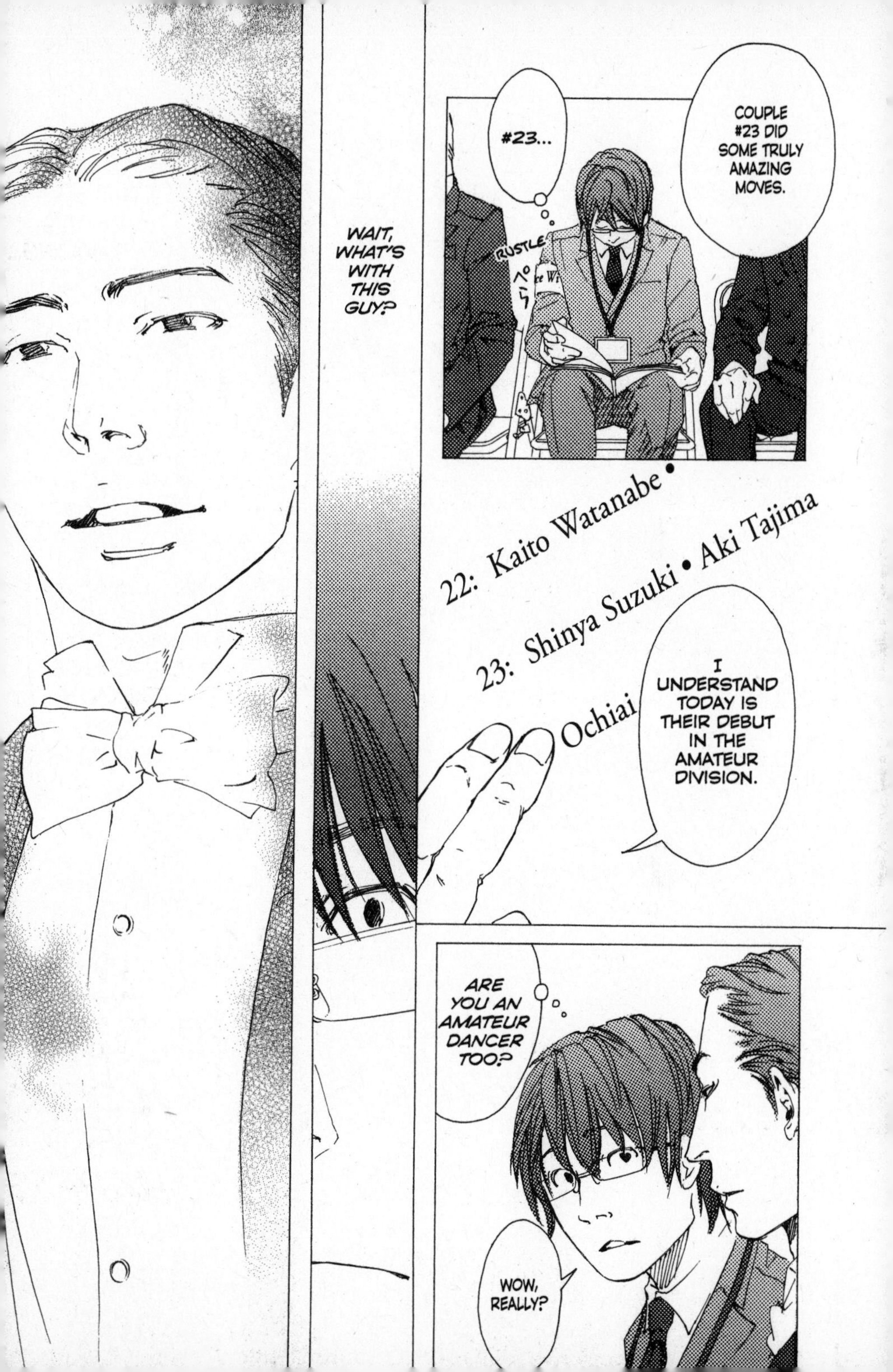
COUPLE #23 DID SOME TRULY AMAZING MOVES.
#23...
RUSTLE
ぺら
22: Kaito Watanabe •
23: Shinya Suzuki • Aki Tajima
Ochiai
I UNDERSTAND TODAY IS THEIR DEBUT IN THE AMATEUR DIVISION.
ARE YOU AN AMATEUR DANCER TOO?
WOW, REALLY?
WAIT, WHAT'S WITH THIS GUY?

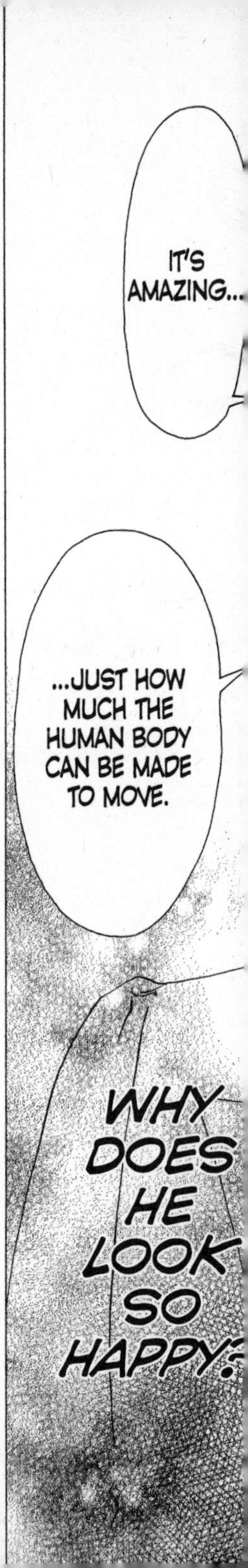
IT'S AMAZING...
...JUST HOW MUCH THE HUMAN BODY CAN BE MADE TO MOVE.
WHY DOES HE LOOK SO HAPPY?

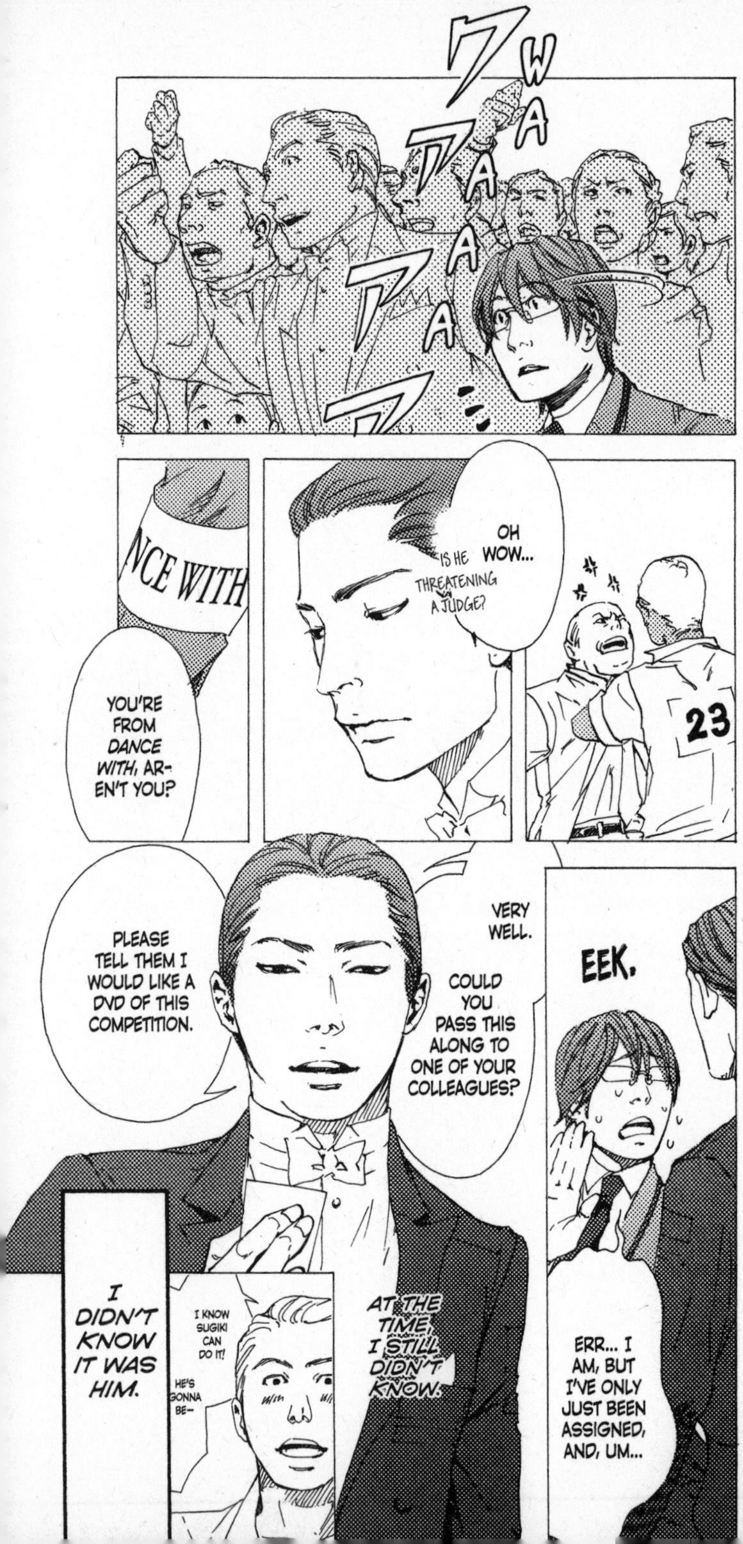
WAAAA
OH WOW...
IS HE THREATENING A JUDGE?
NCE WITH
YOU'RE FROM *DANCE WITH*, AREN'T YOU?
EEK.
ERR... I AM, BUT I'VE ONLY JUST BEEN ASSIGNED, AND, UM...
VERY WELL.
COULD YOU PASS THIS ALONG TO ONE OF YOUR COLLEAGUES?
PLEASE TELL THEM I WOULD LIKE A DVD OF THIS COMPETITION.
AT THE TIME, I STILL DIDN'T KNOW.
I KNOW SUGIKI CAN DO IT!
HE'S GONNA BE–
I DIDN'T KNOW IT WAS HIM.

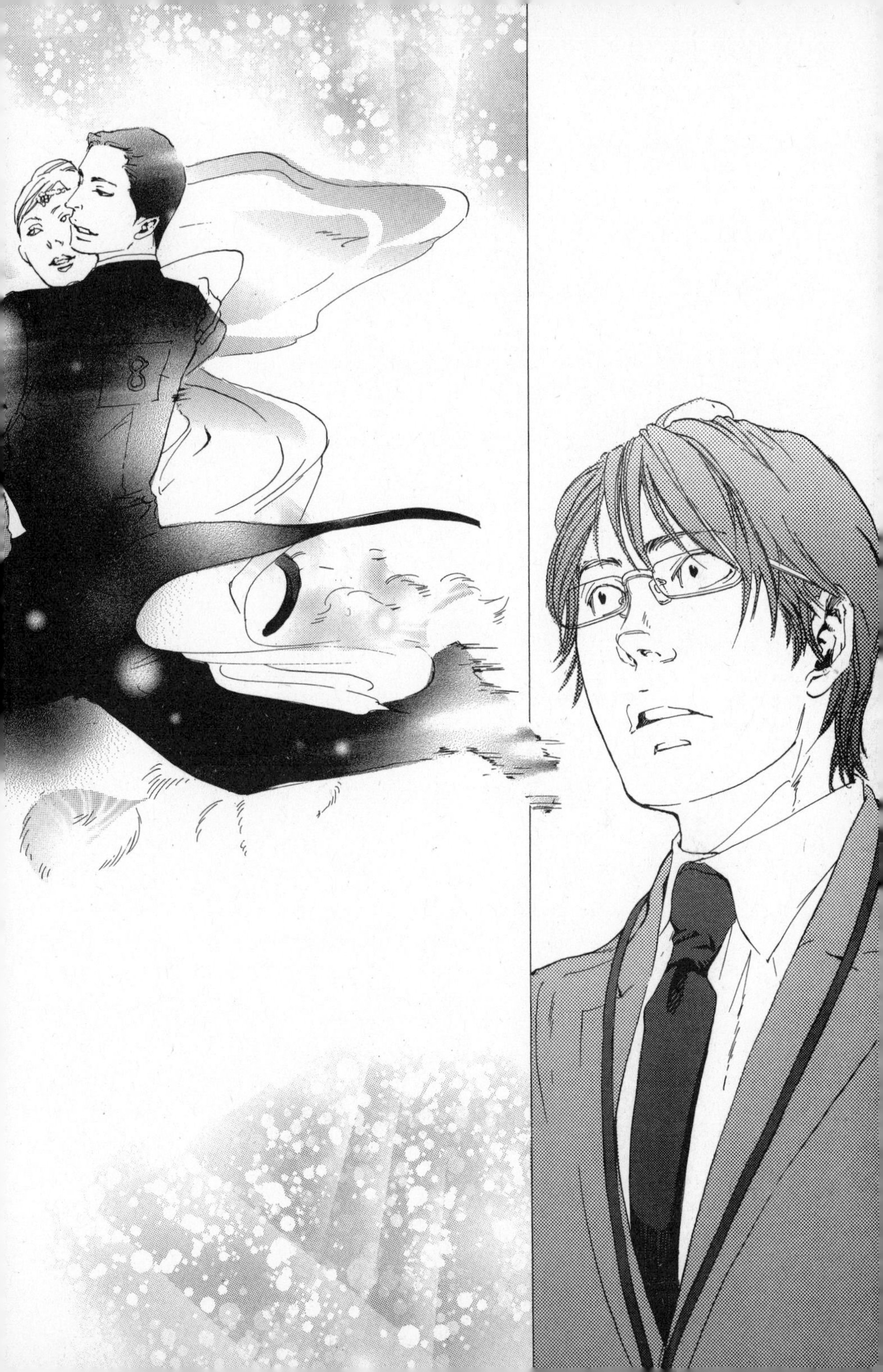

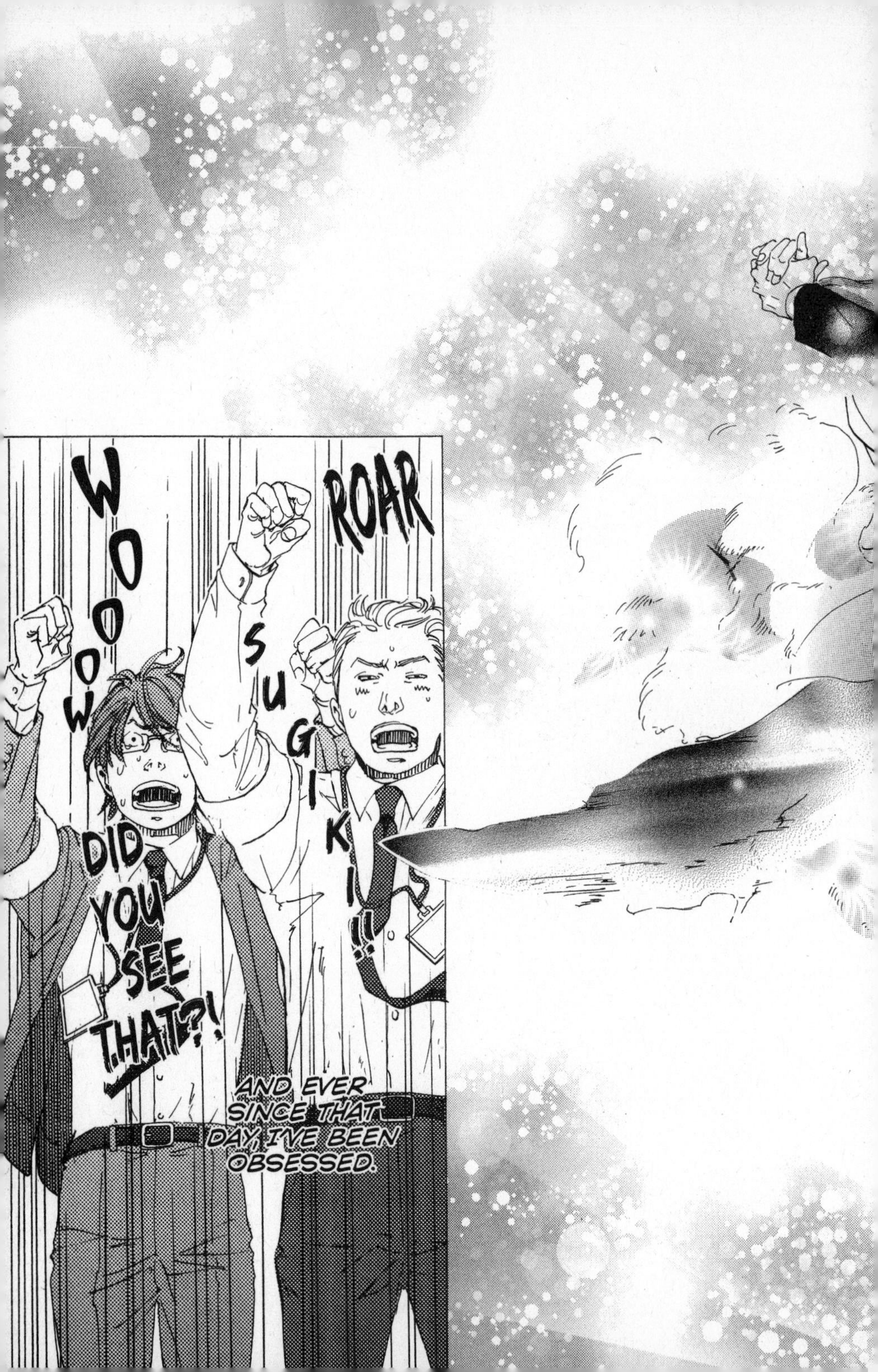
ROAR
SUGIKI!!
WOOOOW
DID YOU SEE THAT?!
AND EVER SINCE THAT DAY, I'VE BEEN OBSESSED.

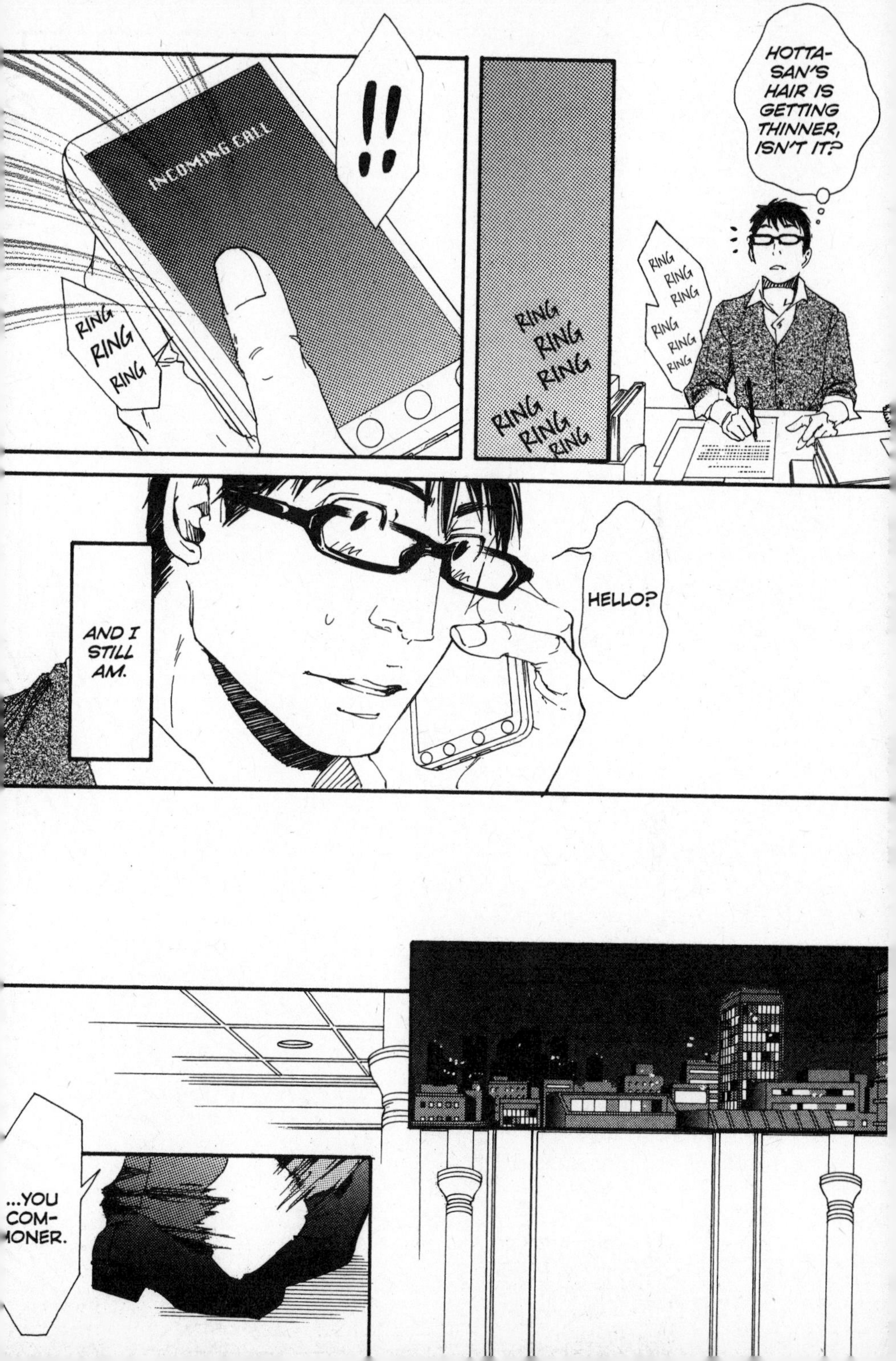
HOTTA-SAN'S HAIR IS GETTING THINNER, ISN'T IT?
RING RING RING RING RING RING
RING RING RING RING RING RING
!!
INCOMING CALL
RING RING RING
HELLO?
AND I STILL AM.
...YOU COM-MONER.

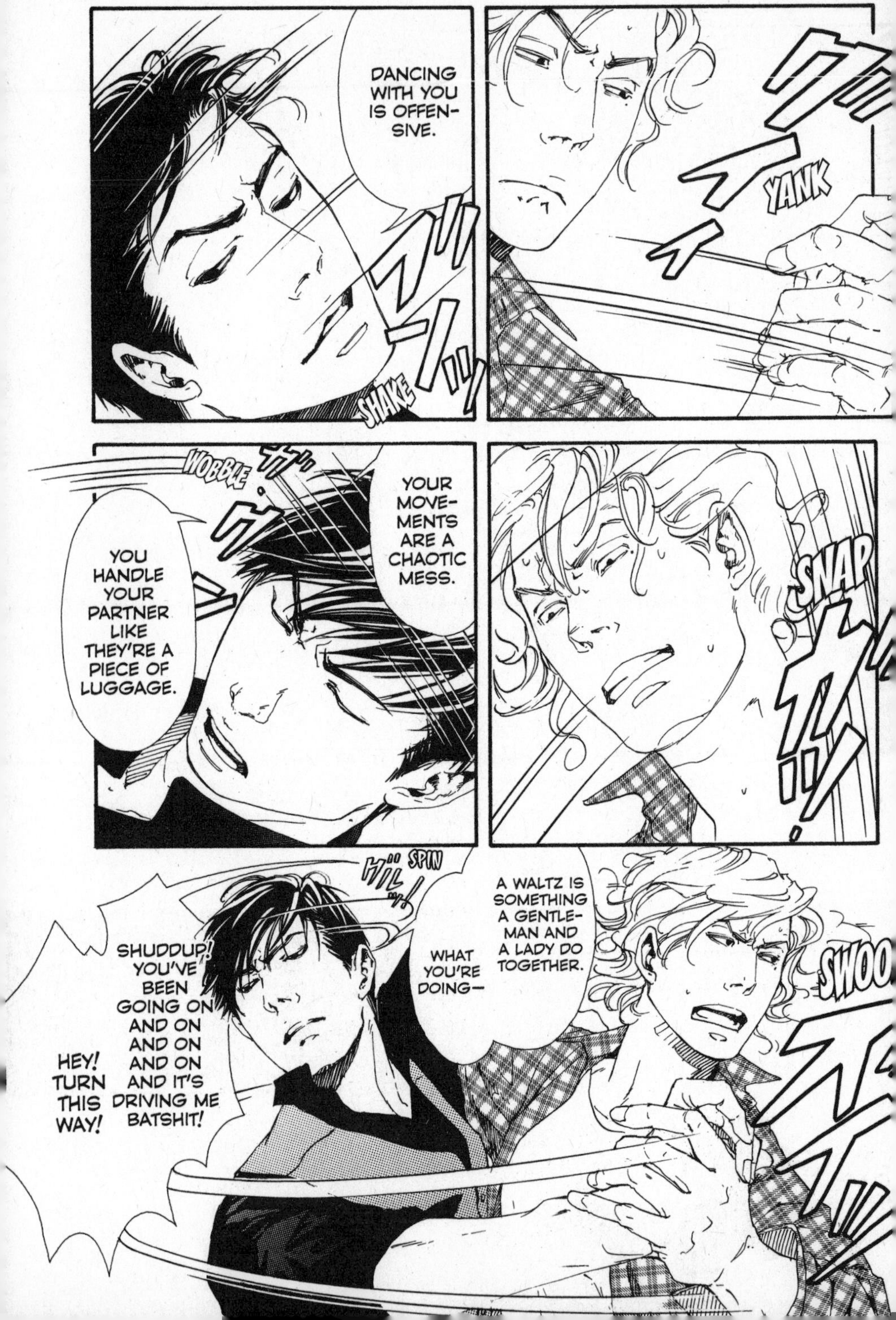
YANK
DANCING WITH YOU IS OFFENSIVE.
SHAKE
SNAP
YOUR MOVEMENTS ARE A CHAOTIC MESS.
WOBBLE
YOU HANDLE YOUR PARTNER LIKE THEY'RE A PIECE OF LUGGAGE.
A WALTZ IS SOMETHING A GENTLEMAN AND A LADY DO TOGETHER.
WHAT YOU'RE DOING—
SPIN
SHUDDUP! YOU'VE BEEN GOING ON AND ON AND ON AND ON AND IT'S DRIVING ME BATSHIT!
HEY! TURN THIS WAY!

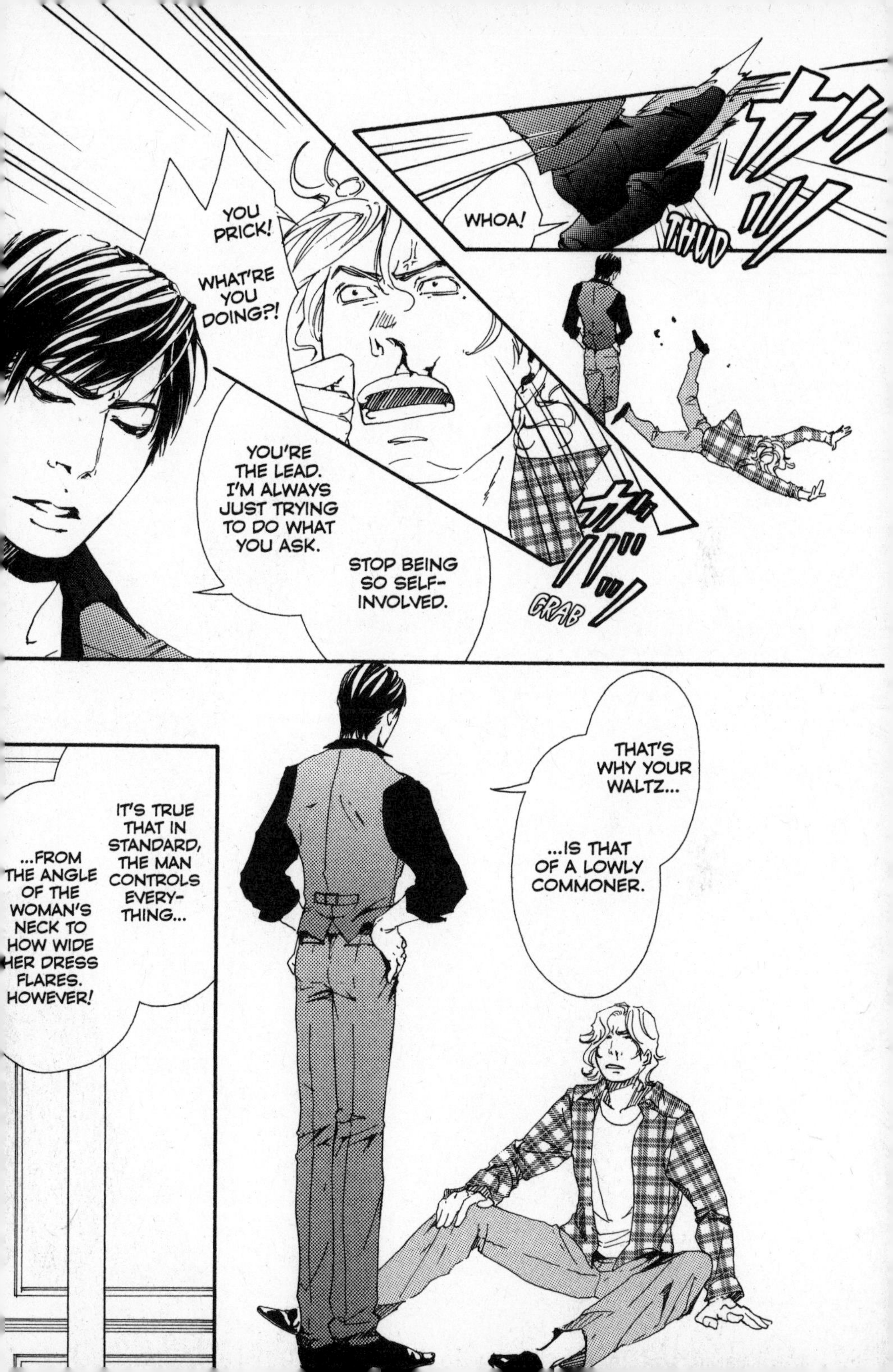
WHOA!
THUD
GRAB
YOU PRICK!
WHAT'RE YOU DOING?!
YOU'RE THE LEAD. I'M ALWAYS JUST TRYING TO DO WHAT YOU ASK.
STOP BEING SO SELF-INVOLVED.
THAT'S WHY YOUR WALTZ...
...IS THAT OF A LOWLY COMMONER.
IT'S TRUE THAT IN STANDARD, THE MAN CONTROLS EVERY-THING...
...FROM THE ANGLE OF THE WOMAN'S NECK TO HOW WIDE HER DRESS FLARES. HOWEVER!

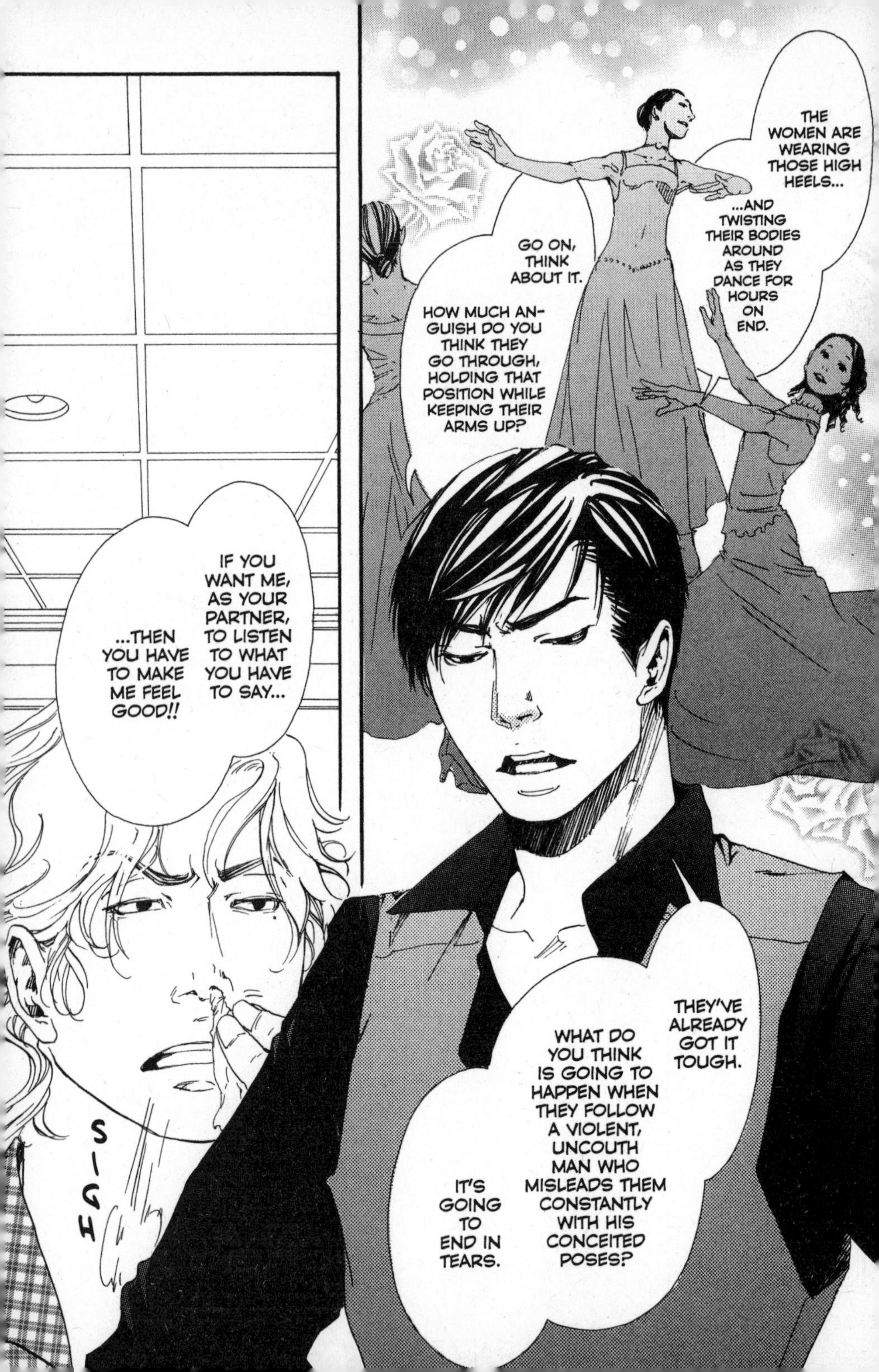
THE WOMEN ARE WEARING THOSE HIGH HEELS...
...AND TWISTING THEIR BODIES AROUND AS THEY DANCE FOR HOURS ON END.
GO ON, THINK ABOUT IT.
HOW MUCH AN-GUISH DO YOU THINK THEY GO THROUGH, HOLDING THAT POSITION WHILE KEEPING THEIR ARMS UP?
THEY'VE ALREADY GOT IT TOUGH.
WHAT DO YOU THINK IS GOING TO HAPPEN WHEN THEY FOLLOW A VIOLENT, UNCOUTH MAN WHO MISLEADS THEM CONSTANTLY WITH HIS CONCEITED POSES?
IT'S GOING TO END IN TEARS.
IF YOU WANT ME, AS YOUR PARTNER, TO LISTEN TO WHAT YOU HAVE TO SAY...
...THEN YOU HAVE TO MAKE ME FEEL GOOD!!
SIGH

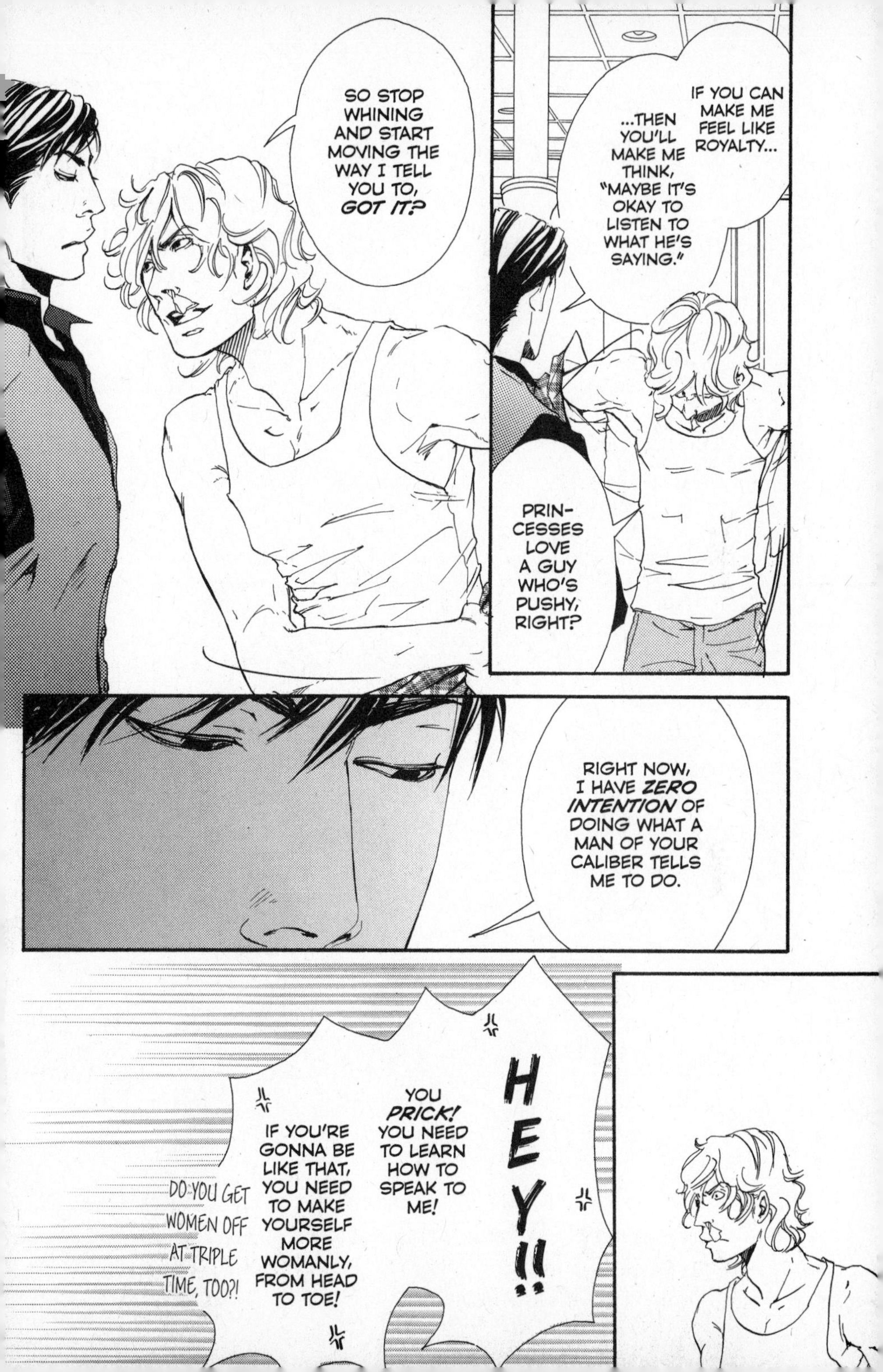
IF YOU CAN MAKE ME FEEL LIKE ROYALTY...
...THEN YOU'LL MAKE ME THINK, "MAYBE IT'S OKAY TO LISTEN TO WHAT HE'S SAYING."
PRIN-CESSES LOVE A GUY WHO'S PUSHY, RIGHT?
SO STOP WHINING AND START MOVING THE WAY I TELL YOU TO, *GOT IT?*
RIGHT NOW, I HAVE *ZERO INTENTION* OF DOING WHAT A MAN OF YOUR CALIBER TELLS ME TO DO.
HEY!!
YOU *PRICK!* YOU NEED TO LEARN HOW TO SPEAK TO ME!
IF YOU'RE GONNA BE LIKE THAT, YOU NEED TO MAKE YOURSELF MORE WOMANLY, FROM HEAD TO TOE!
DO YOU GET WOMEN OFF AT TRIPLE TIME, TOO?!

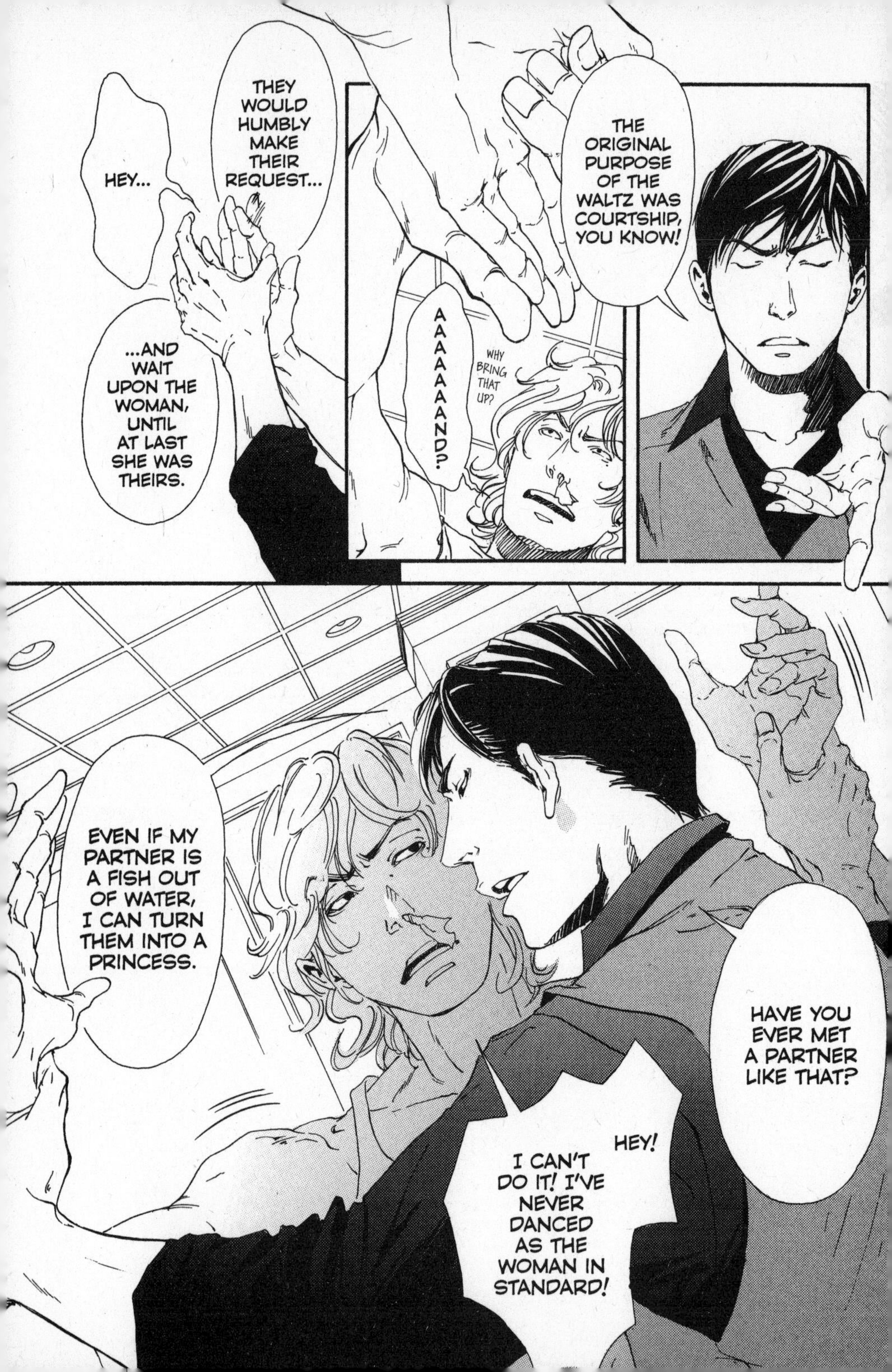
THE ORIGINAL PURPOSE OF THE WALTZ WAS COURTSHIP, YOU KNOW!
AAAAAAAND?
WHY BRING THAT UP?
THEY WOULD HUMBLY MAKE THEIR REQUEST...
HEY...
...AND WAIT UPON THE WOMAN, UNTIL AT LAST SHE WAS THEIRS.
EVEN IF MY PARTNER IS A FISH OUT OF WATER, I CAN TURN THEM INTO A PRINCESS.
HAVE YOU EVER MET A PARTNER LIKE THAT?
HEY!
I CAN'T DO IT! I'VE NEVER DANCED AS THE WOMAN IN STANDARD!

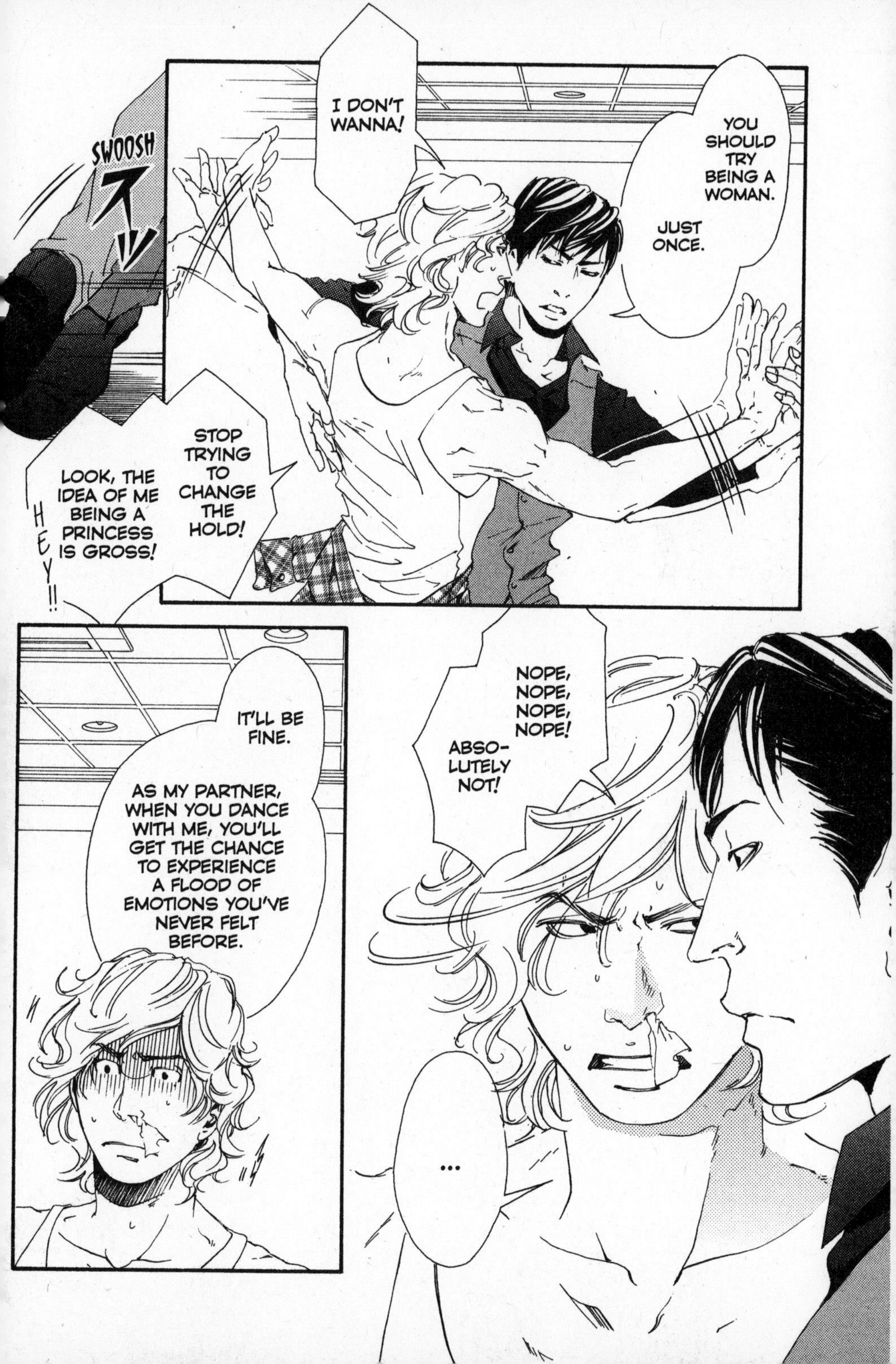
YOU SHOULD TRY BEING A WOMAN.
JUST ONCE.
I DON'T WANNA!
SWOOSH
STOP TRYING TO CHANGE THE HOLD!
LOOK, THE IDEA OF ME BEING A PRINCESS IS GROSS!
HEY!!
NOPE, NOPE, NOPE, NOPE!
ABSOLUTELY NOT!
...
IT'LL BE FINE.
AS MY PARTNER, WHEN YOU DANCE WITH ME, YOU'LL GET THE CHANCE TO EXPERIENCE A FLOOD OF EMOTIONS YOU'VE NEVER FELT BEFORE.

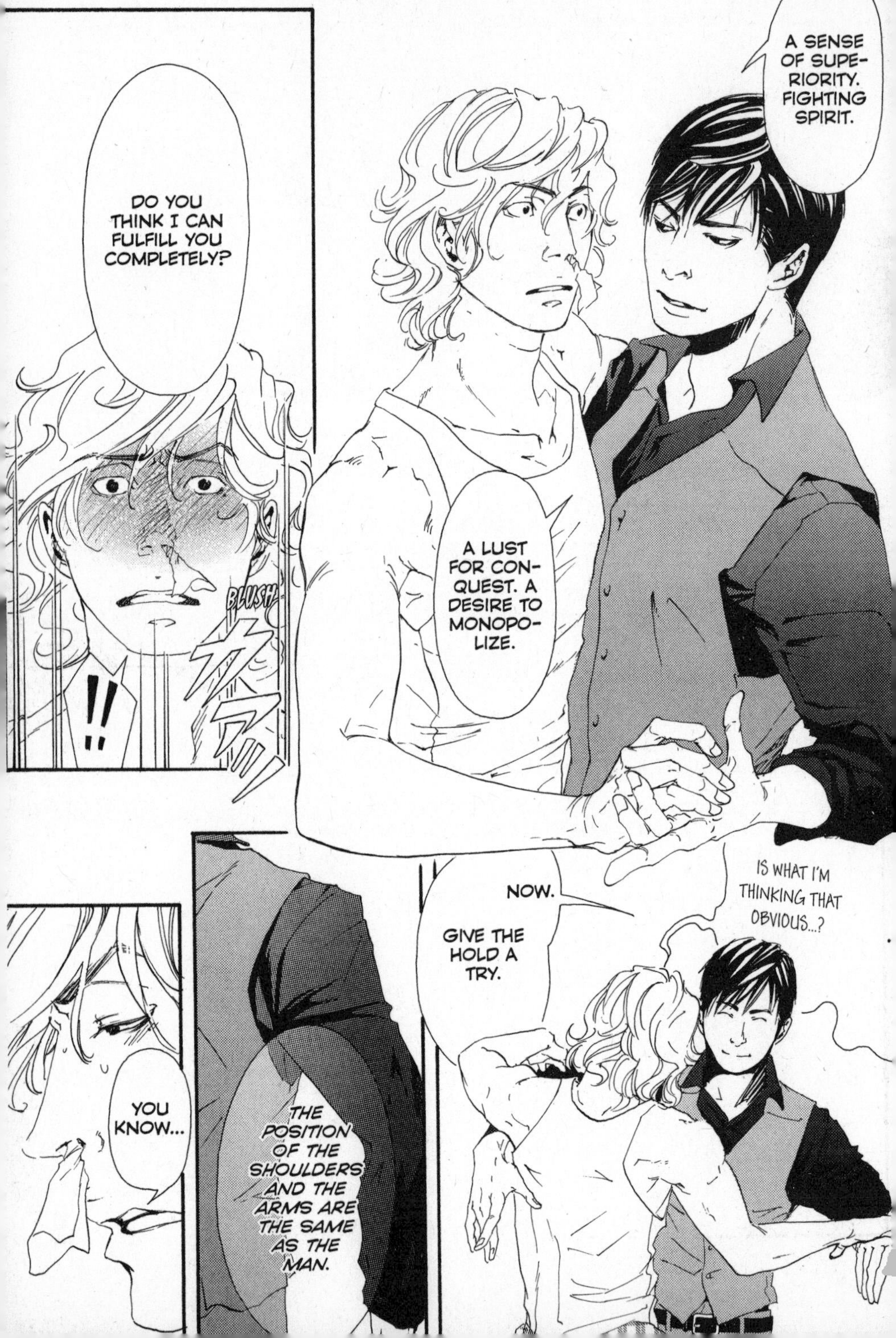
A SENSE OF SUPERIORITY. FIGHTING SPIRIT.
A LUST FOR CONQUEST. A DESIRE TO MONOPOLIZE.
DO YOU THINK I CAN FULFILL YOU COMPLETELY?
BLUSH
!!
IS WHAT I'M THINKING THAT OBVIOUS...?
NOW.
GIVE THE HOLD A TRY.
THE POSITION OF THE SHOULDERS AND THE ARMS ARE THE SAME AS THE MAN.
YOU KNOW...

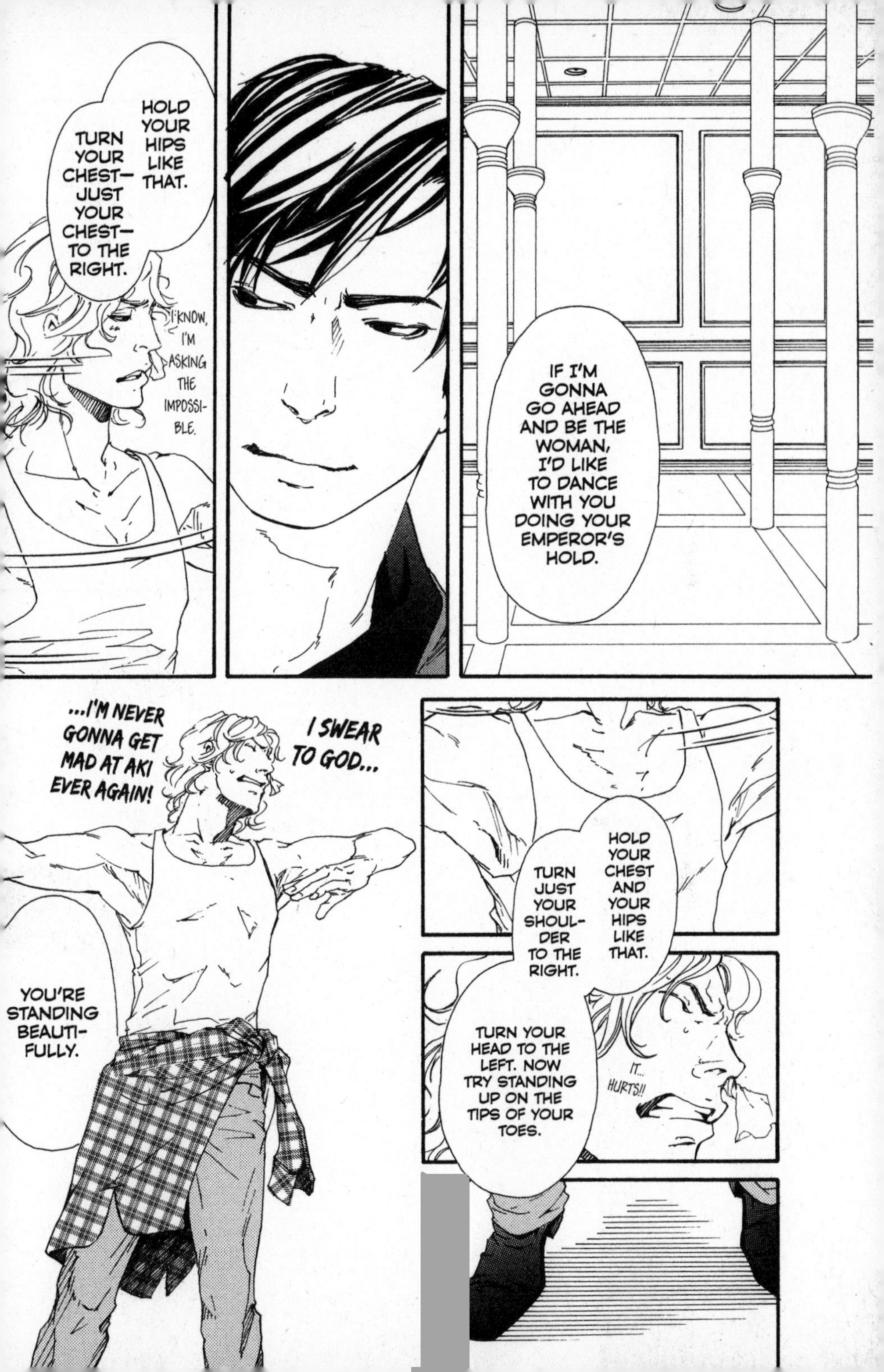
IF I'M GONNA GO AHEAD AND BE THE WOMAN, I'D LIKE TO DANCE WITH YOU DOING YOUR EMPEROR'S HOLD.
TURN YOUR CHEST— JUST YOUR CHEST— TO THE RIGHT. HOLD YOUR HIPS LIKE THAT.
I KNOW, I'M ASKING THE IMPOSSI- BLE.
TURN JUST YOUR SHOUL- DER TO THE RIGHT. HOLD YOUR CHEST AND YOUR HIPS LIKE THAT.
TURN YOUR HEAD TO THE LEFT. NOW TRY STANDING UP ON THE TIPS OF YOUR TOES.
IT... HURTS!!
I SWEAR TO GOD...
...I'M NEVER GONNA GET MAD AT AKI EVER AGAIN!
YOU'RE STANDING BEAUTI- FULLY.

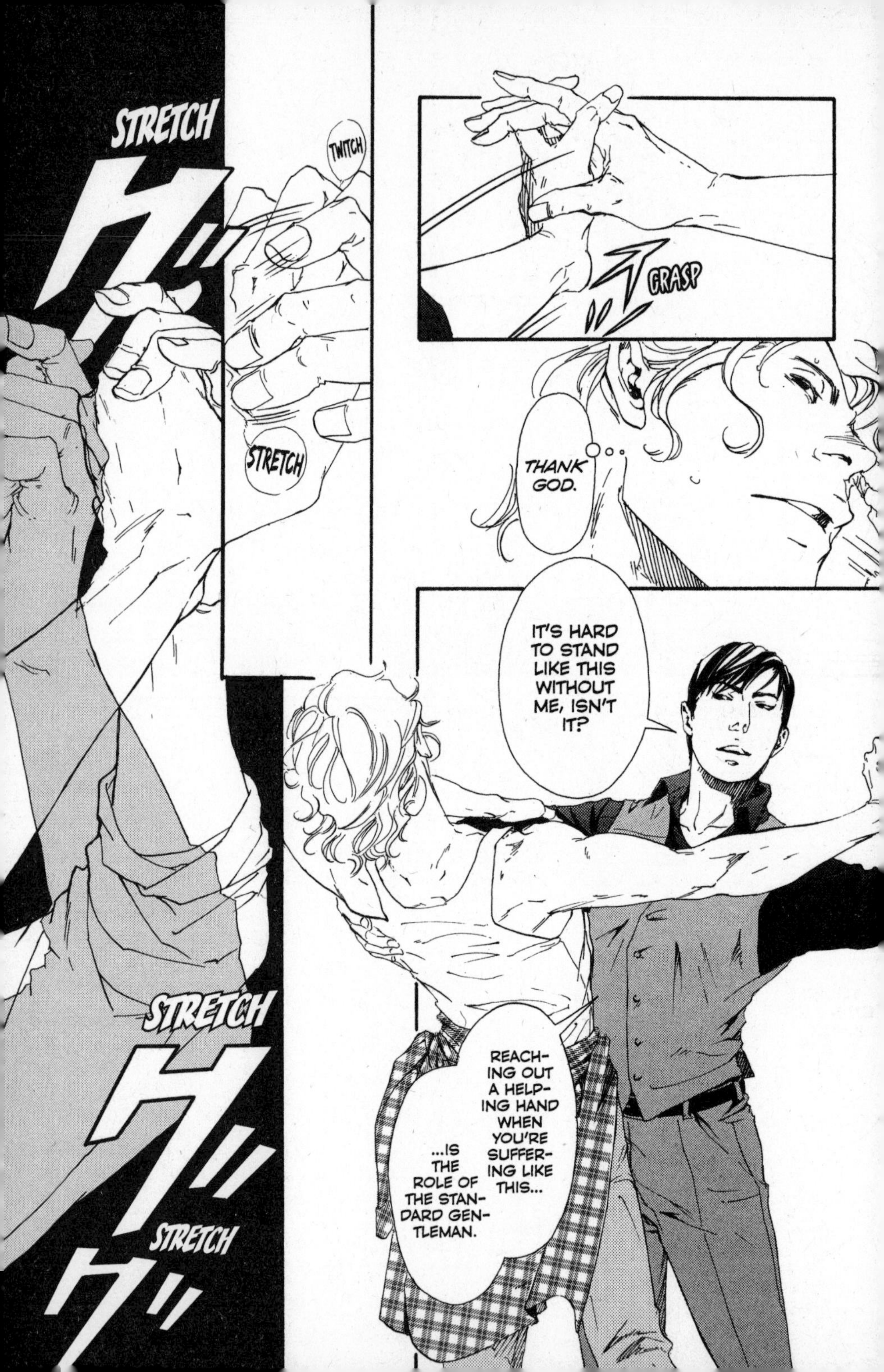
GRASP
THANK GOD.
TWITCH
STRETCH
STRETCH
IT'S HARD TO STAND LIKE THIS WITHOUT ME, ISN'T IT?
REACHING OUT A HELPING HAND WHEN YOU'RE SUFFERING LIKE THIS...
...IS THE ROLE OF THE STANDARD GENTLEMAN.
STRETCH
STRETCH

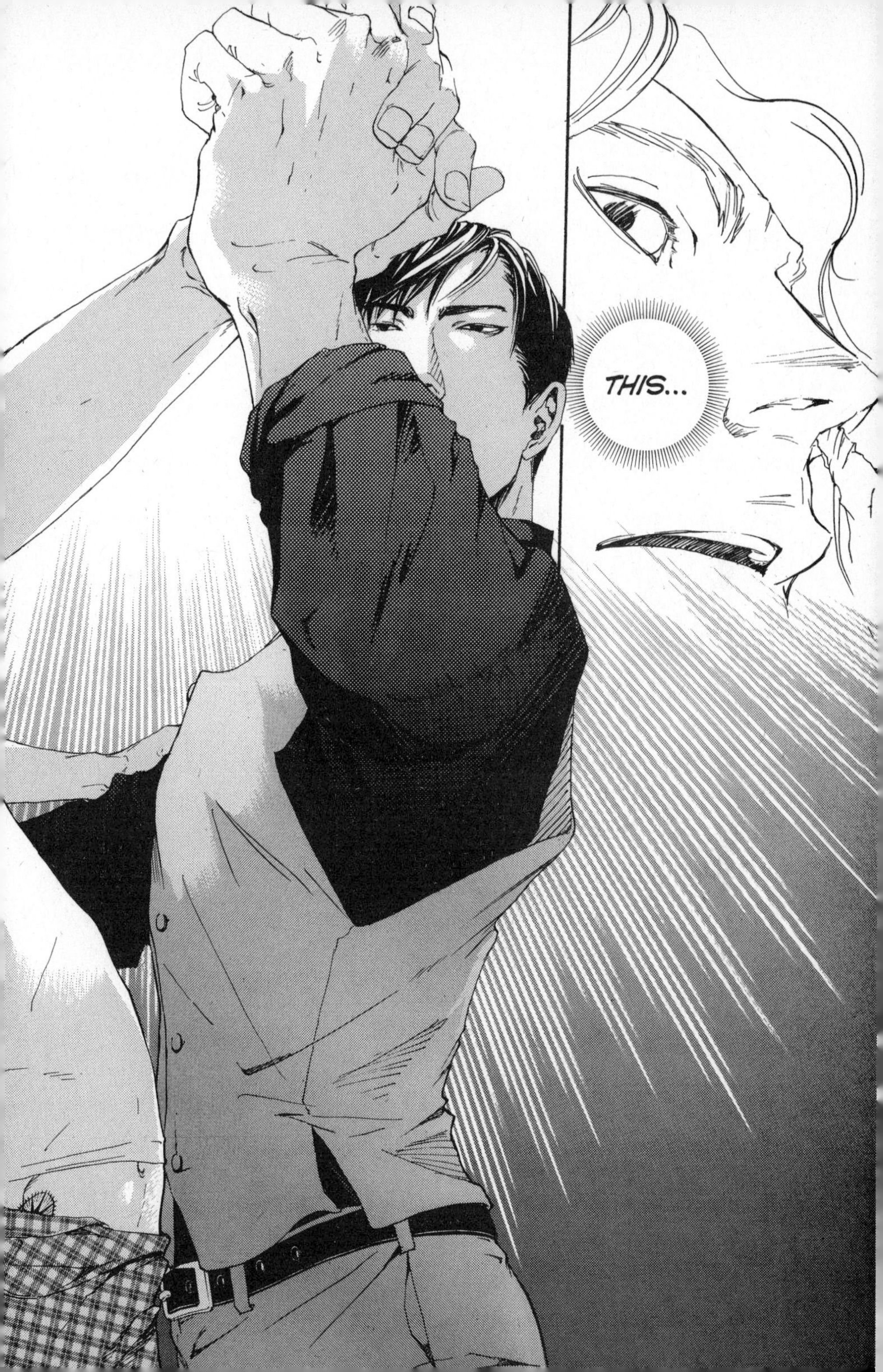
THIS...

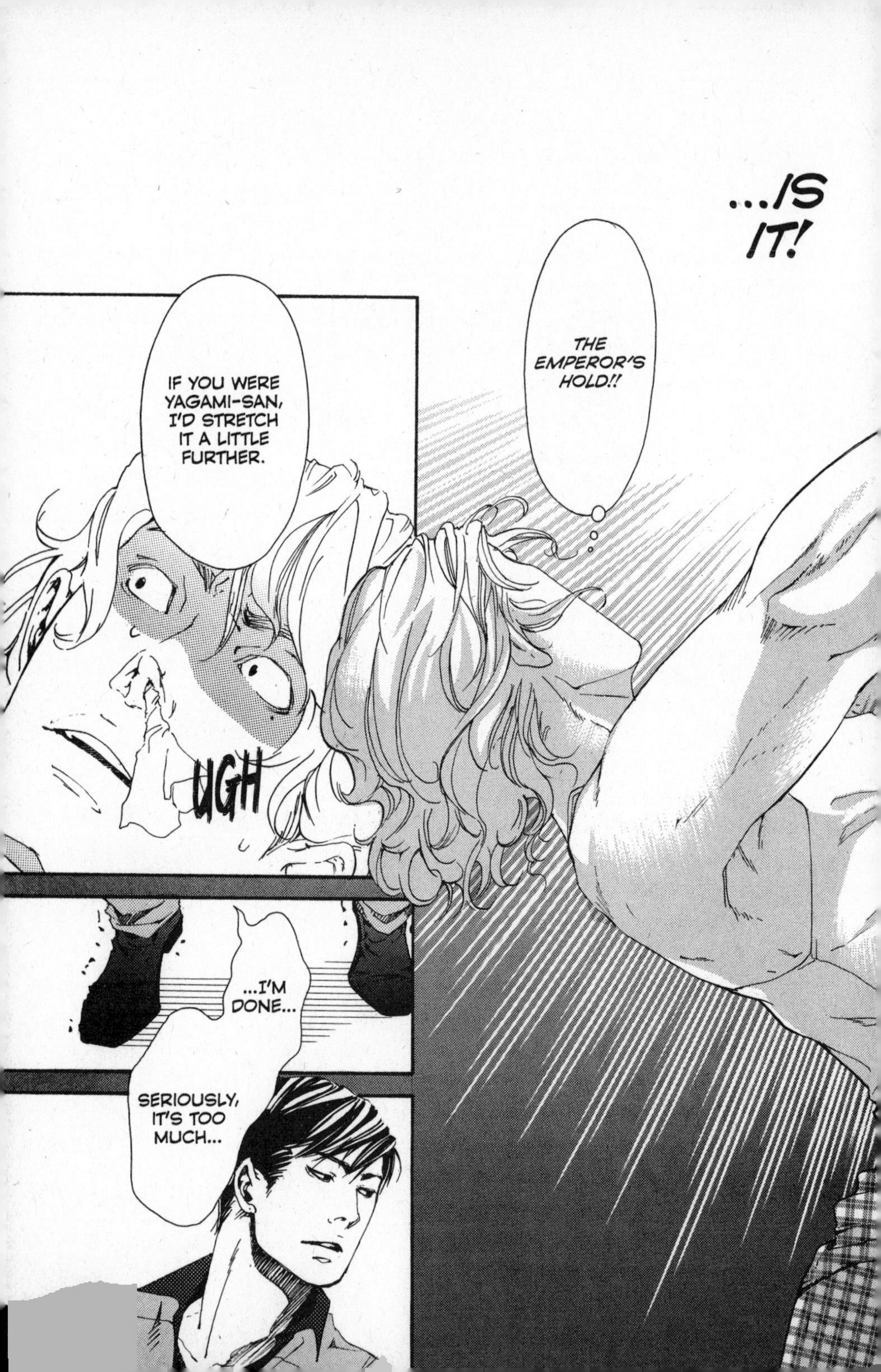
...IS IT!
THE EMPEROR'S HOLD!!
IF YOU WERE YAGAMI-SAN, I'D STRETCH IT A LITTLE FURTHER.
UGH
...I'M DONE...
SERIOUSLY, IT'S TOO MUCH...

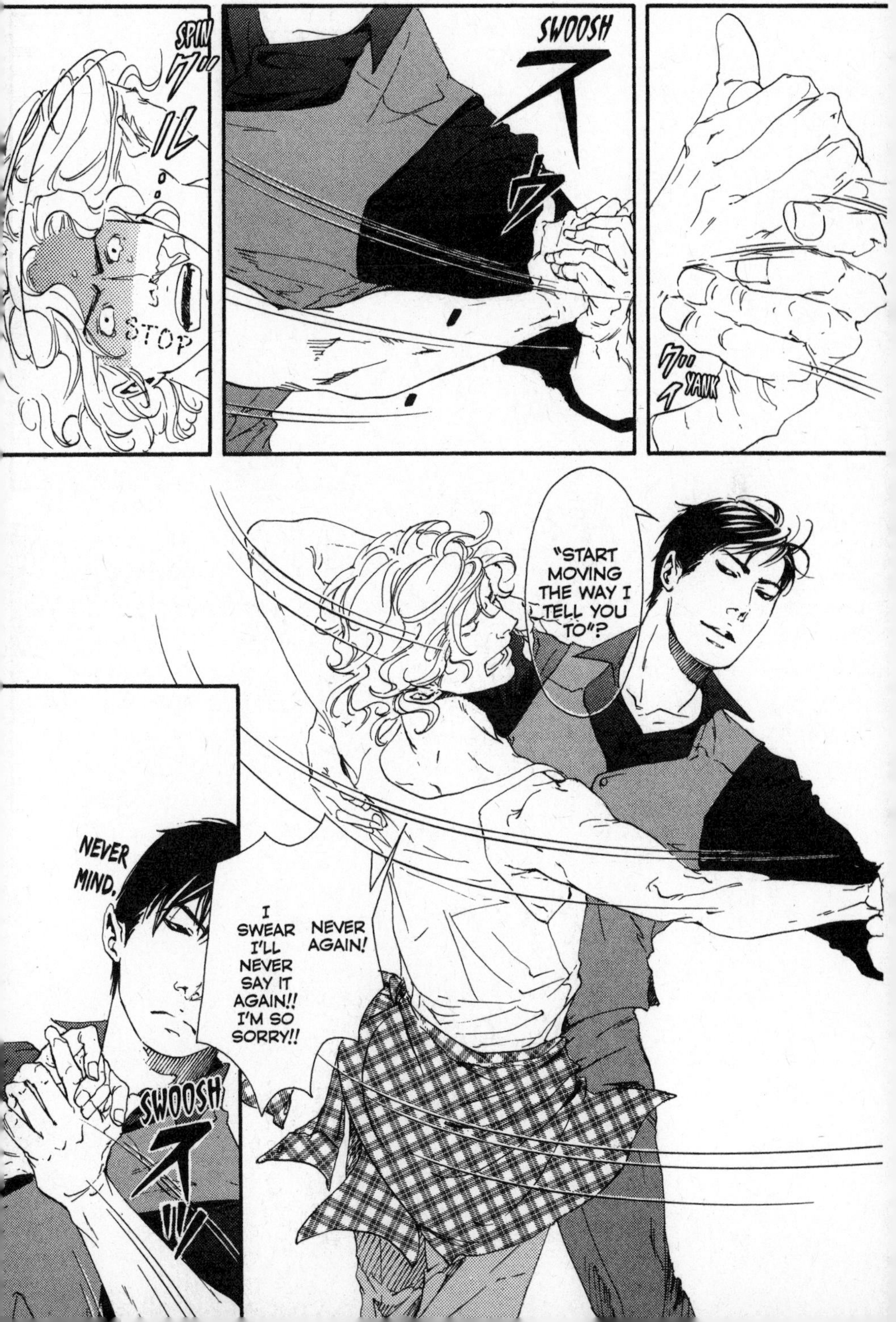
YANK
SWOOSH
SPIN
STOP
"START MOVING THE WAY I TELL YOU TO"?
NEVER AGAIN!
I SWEAR I'LL NEVER SAY IT AGAIN!! I'M SO SORRY!!
NEVER MIND.
SWOOSH

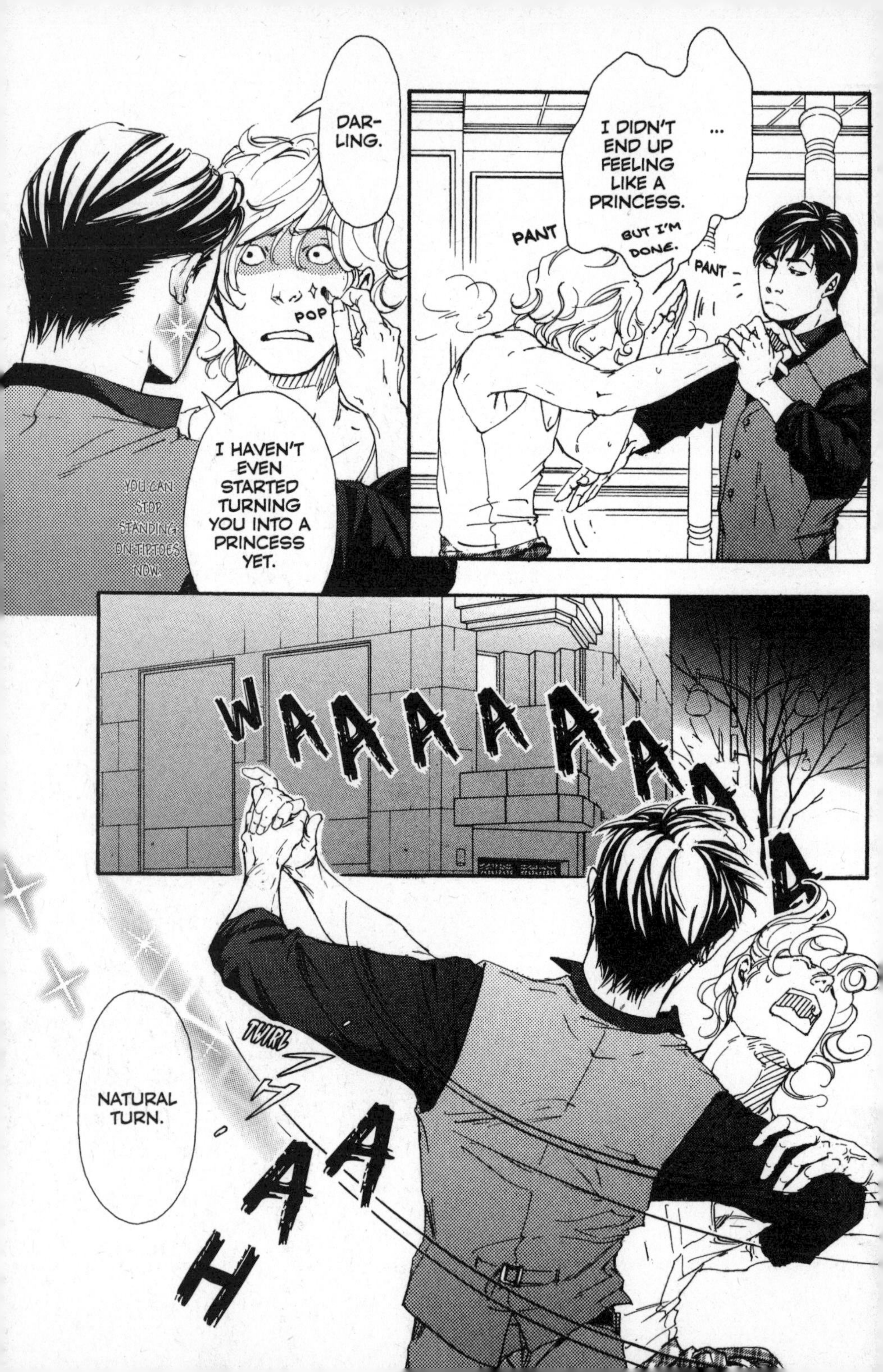
I DIDN'T END UP FEELING LIKE A PRINCESS.
...
PANT
BUT I'M DONE.
PANT
DAR-LING.
POP
I HAVEN'T EVEN STARTED TURNING YOU INTO A PRINCESS YET.
YOU CAN STOP STANDING ON TIPTOES NOW.
WAAAAAAAAAA
TWIRL
NATURAL TURN.
AAH

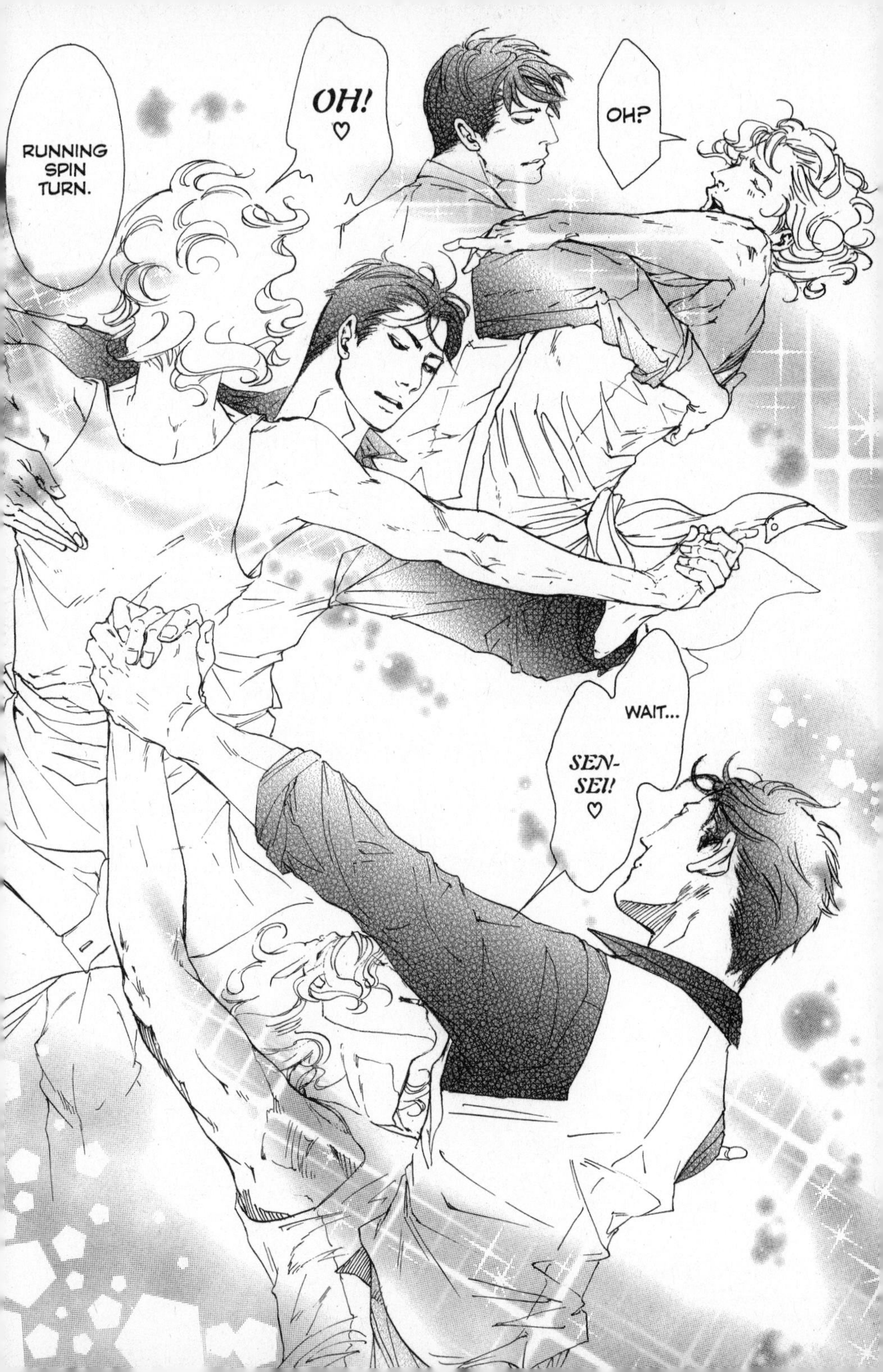
OH?
OH! ♡
RUNNING SPIN TURN.
WAIT... SEN-SEI! ♡

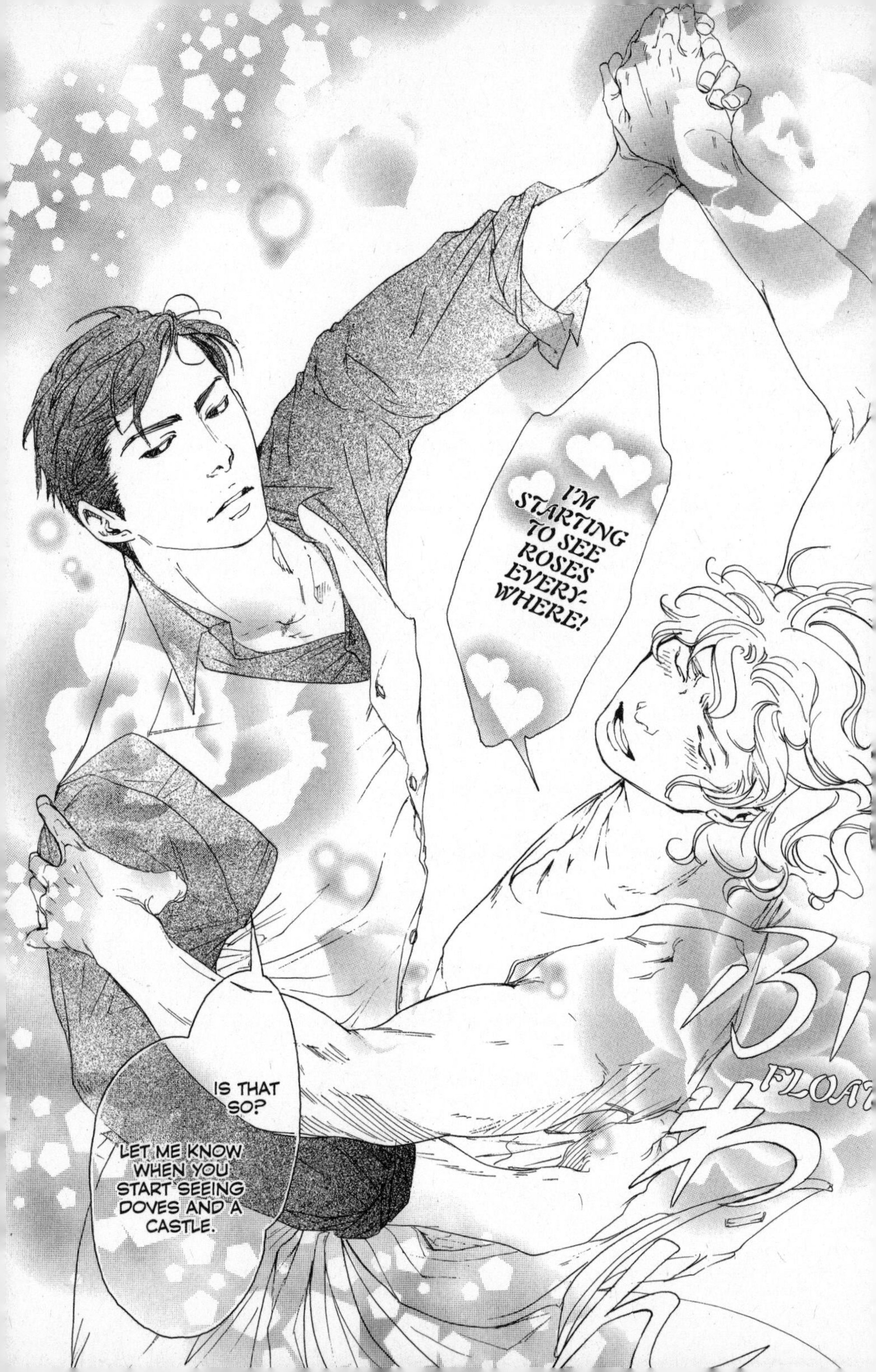
I'M STARTING TO SEE ROSES EVERY-WHERE!
FLOAT
IS THAT SO?
LET ME KNOW WHEN YOU START SEEING DOVES AND A CASTLE.

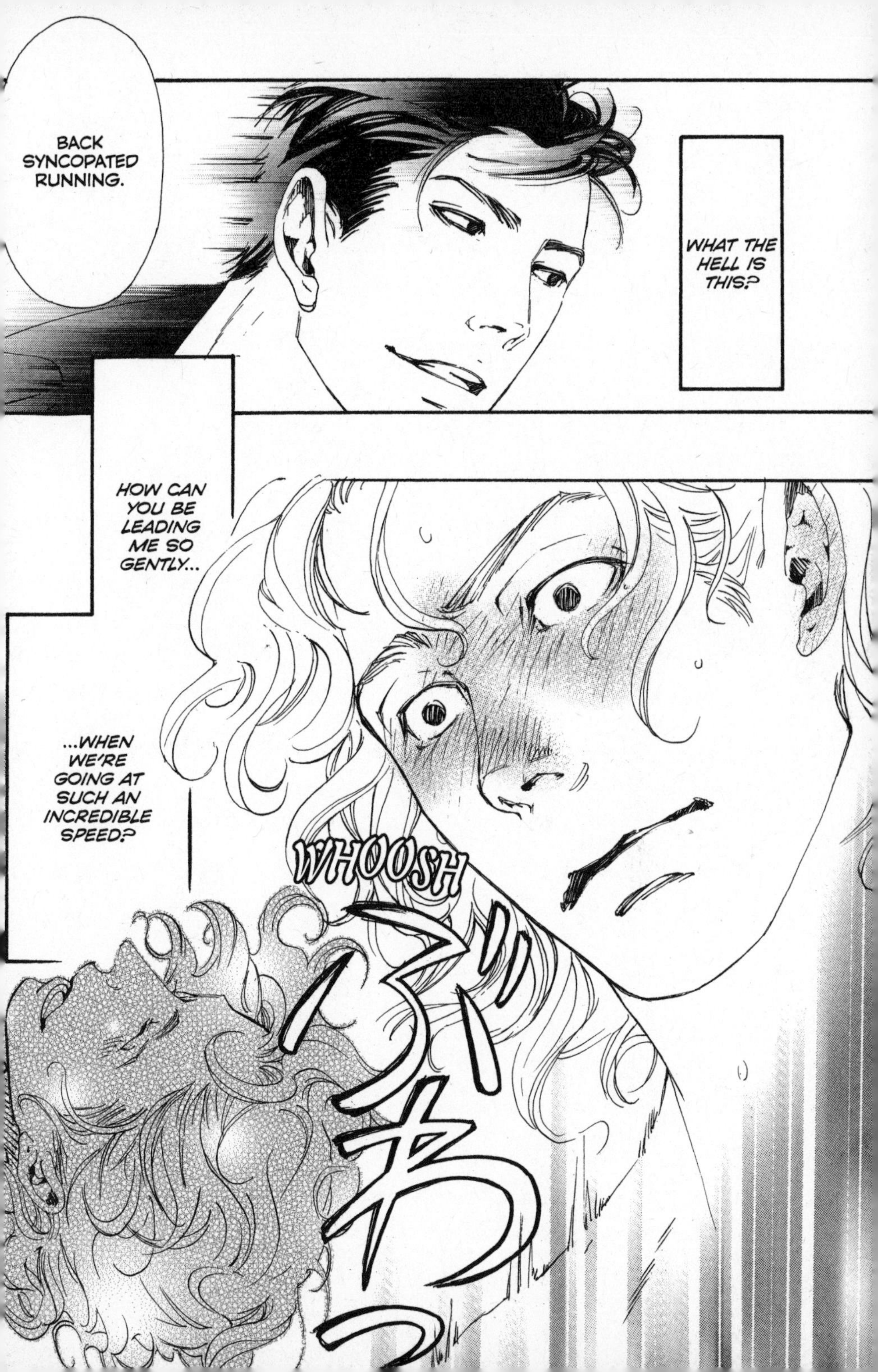
BACK SYNCOPATED RUNNING.
WHAT THE HELL IS THIS?
HOW CAN YOU BE LEADING ME SO GENTLY...
...WHEN WE'RE GOING AT SUCH AN INCREDIBLE SPEED?
WHOOSH

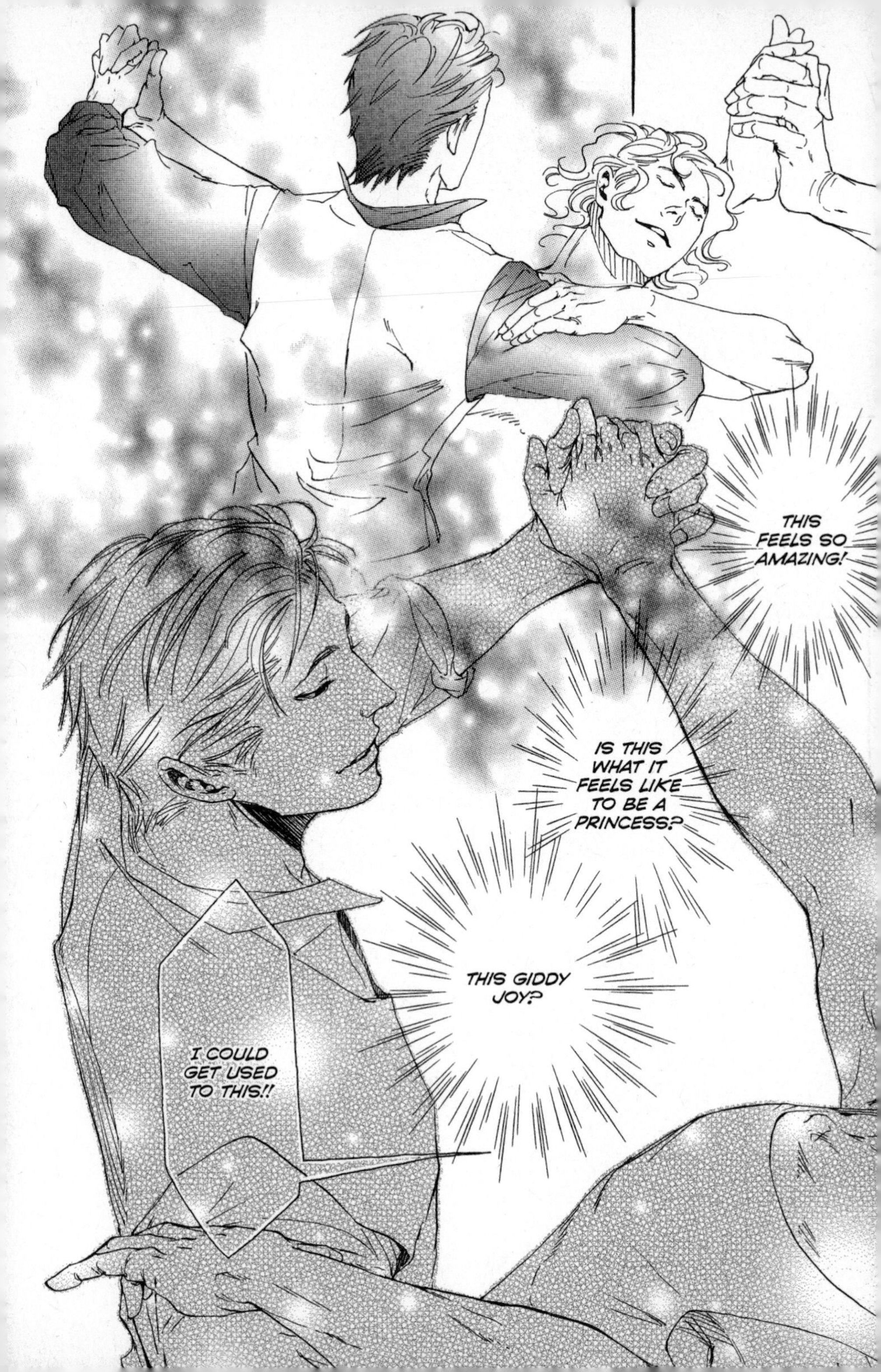
THIS FEELS SO AMAZING!
IS THIS WHAT IT FEELS LIKE TO BE A PRINCESS?
THIS GIDDY JOY?
I COULD GET USED TO THIS!!

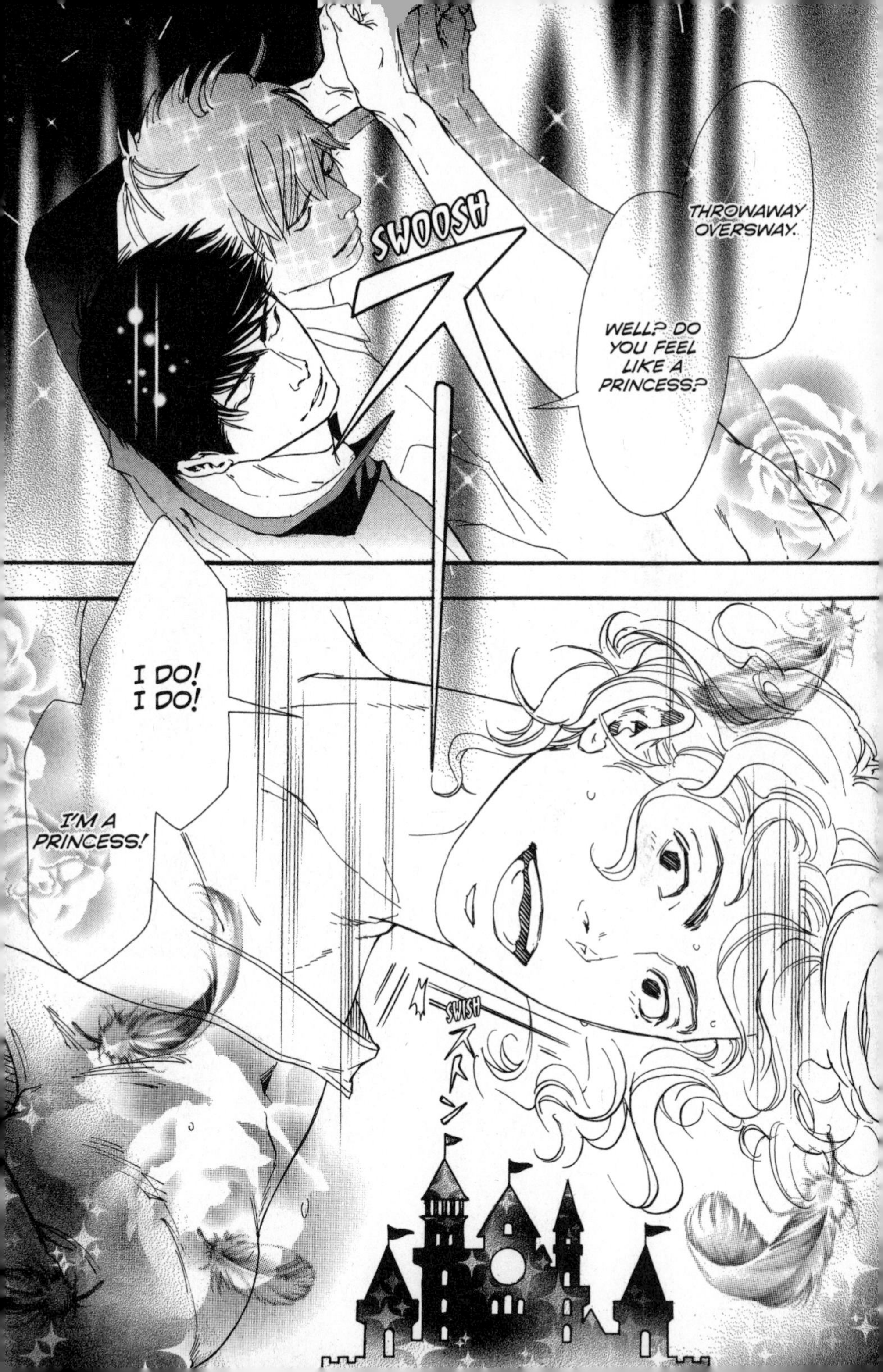
THROWAWAY OVERSWAY.
SWOOSH
WELL? DO YOU FEEL LIKE A PRINCESS?
I DO! I DO!
I'M A PRINCESS!
SWISH

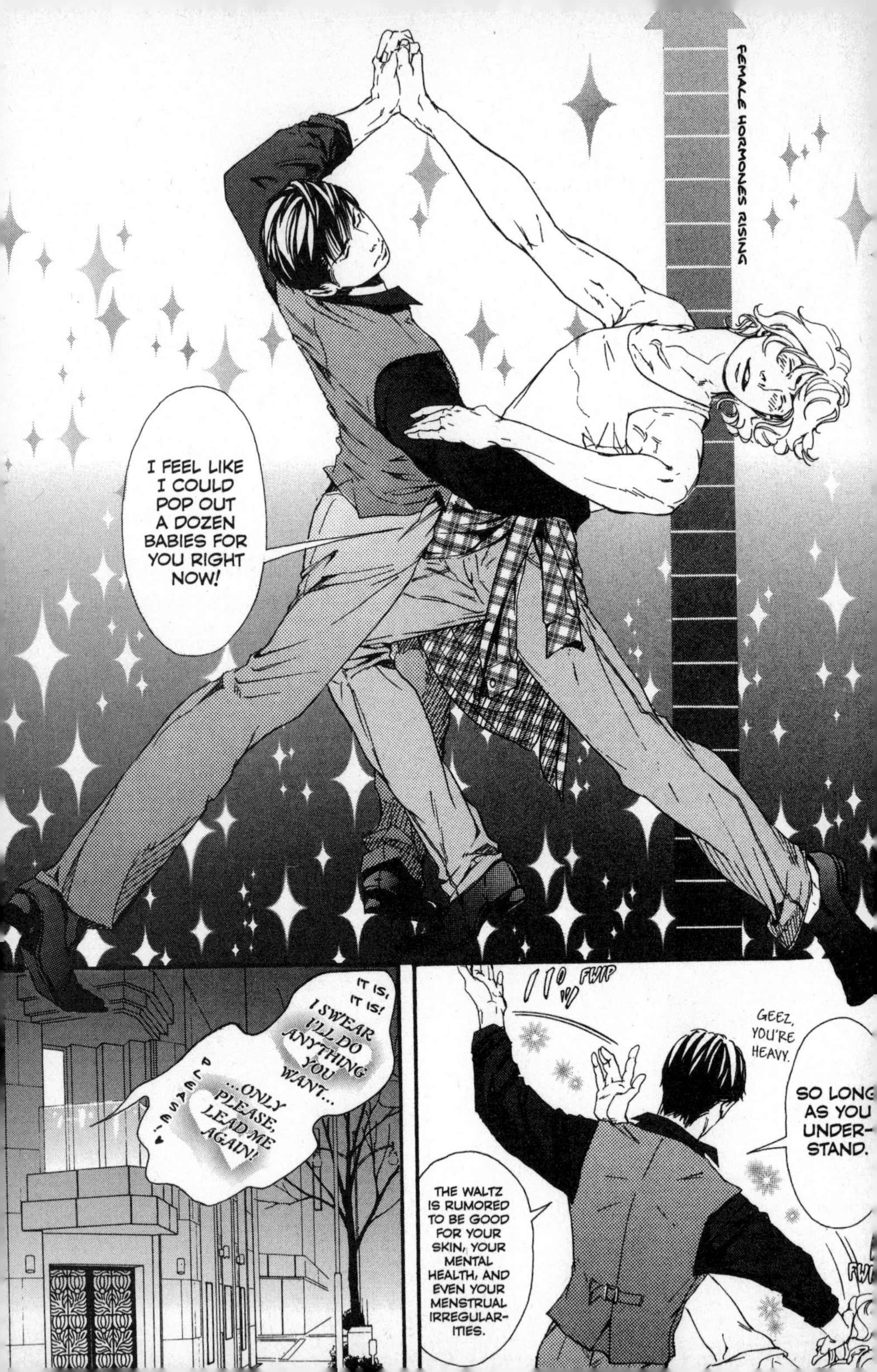
FEMALE HORMONES RISING
I FEEL LIKE I COULD POP OUT A DOZEN BABIES FOR YOU RIGHT NOW!
FWIP
GEEZ, YOU'RE HEAVY.
SO LONG AS YOU UNDER-STAND.
THE WALTZ IS RUMORED TO BE GOOD FOR YOUR SKIN, YOUR MENTAL HEALTH, AND EVEN YOUR MENSTRUAL IRREGULAR-ITIES.
IT IS, IT IS! I SWEAR I'LL DO ANYTHING YOU WANT...
...ONLY PLEASE, LEAD ME AGAIN!
PLEASE!

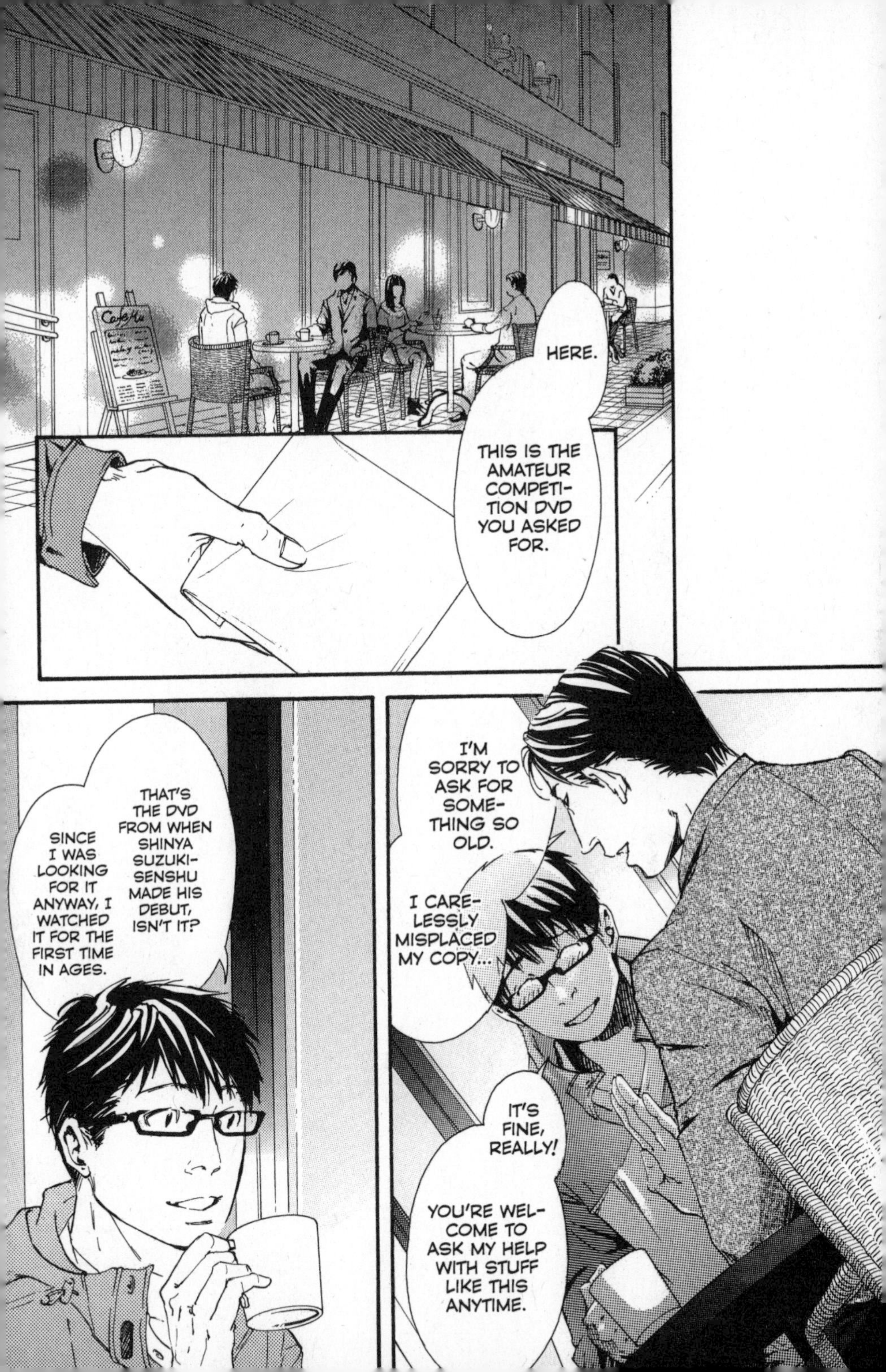
HERE.
THIS IS THE AMATEUR COMPETI-TION DVD YOU ASKED FOR.
I'M SORRY TO ASK FOR SOME-THING SO OLD.
I CARE-LESSLY MISPLACED MY COPY...
IT'S FINE, REALLY!
YOU'RE WEL-COME TO ASK MY HELP WITH STUFF LIKE THIS ANYTIME.
THAT'S THE DVD FROM WHEN SHINYA SUZUKI-SENSHU MADE HIS DEBUT, ISN'T IT?
SINCE I WAS LOOKING FOR IT ANYWAY, I WATCHED IT FOR THE FIRST TIME IN AGES.

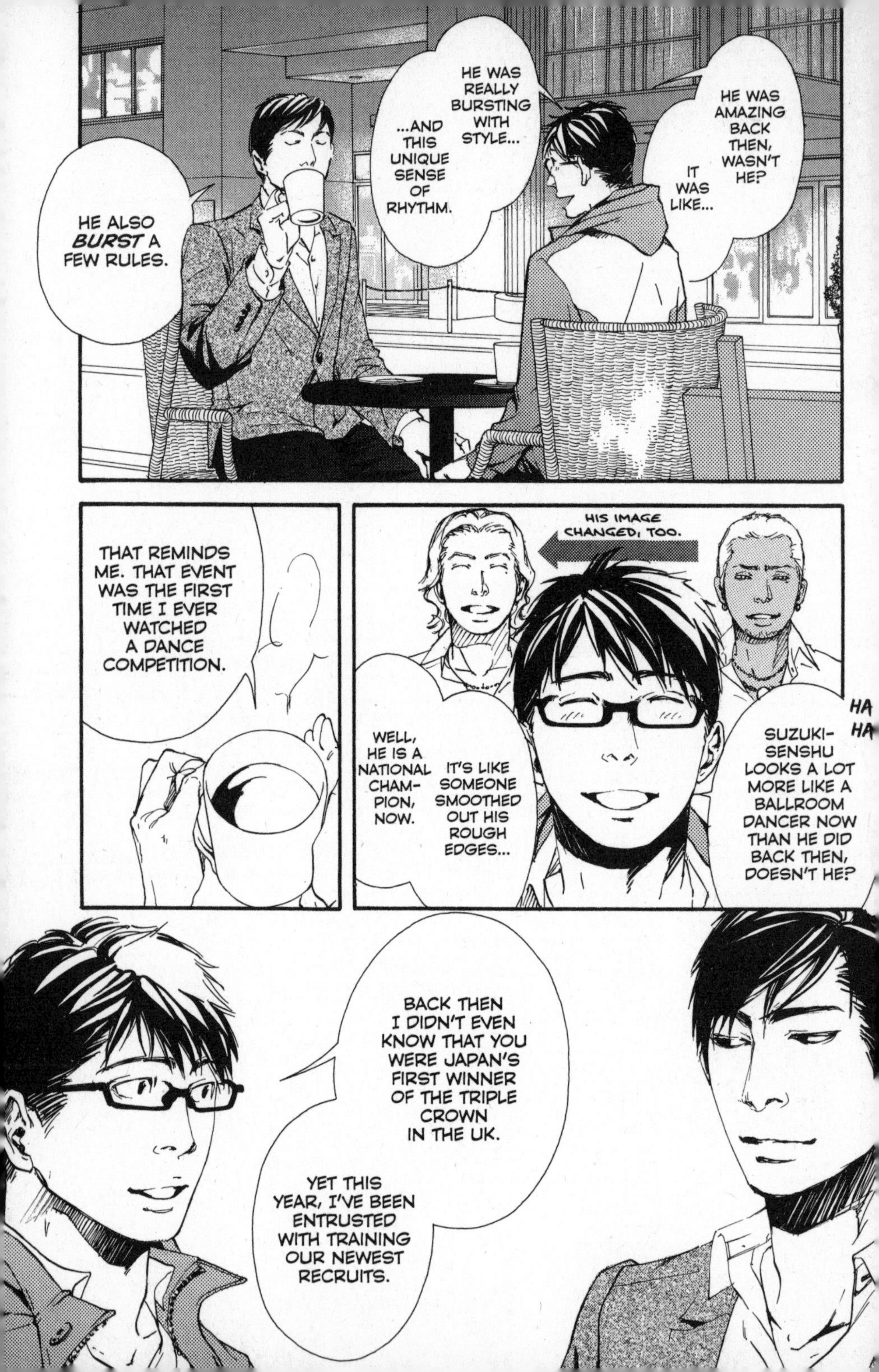
HE WAS AMAZING BACK THEN, WASN'T HE?
IT WAS LIKE...
HE WAS REALLY BURSTING WITH STYLE...
...AND THIS UNIQUE SENSE OF RHYTHM.
HE ALSO *BURST* A FEW RULES.
HIS IMAGE CHANGED, TOO.
HA HA
SUZUKI-SENSHU LOOKS A LOT MORE LIKE A BALLROOM DANCER NOW THAN HE DID BACK THEN, DOESN'T HE?
IT'S LIKE SOMEONE SMOOTHED OUT HIS ROUGH EDGES...
WELL, HE IS A NATIONAL CHAMPION, NOW.
THAT REMINDS ME. THAT EVENT WAS THE FIRST TIME I EVER WATCHED A DANCE COMPETITION.
BACK THEN I DIDN'T EVEN KNOW THAT YOU WERE JAPAN'S FIRST WINNER OF THE TRIPLE CROWN IN THE UK.
YET THIS YEAR, I'VE BEEN ENTRUSTED WITH TRAINING OUR NEWEST RECRUITS.

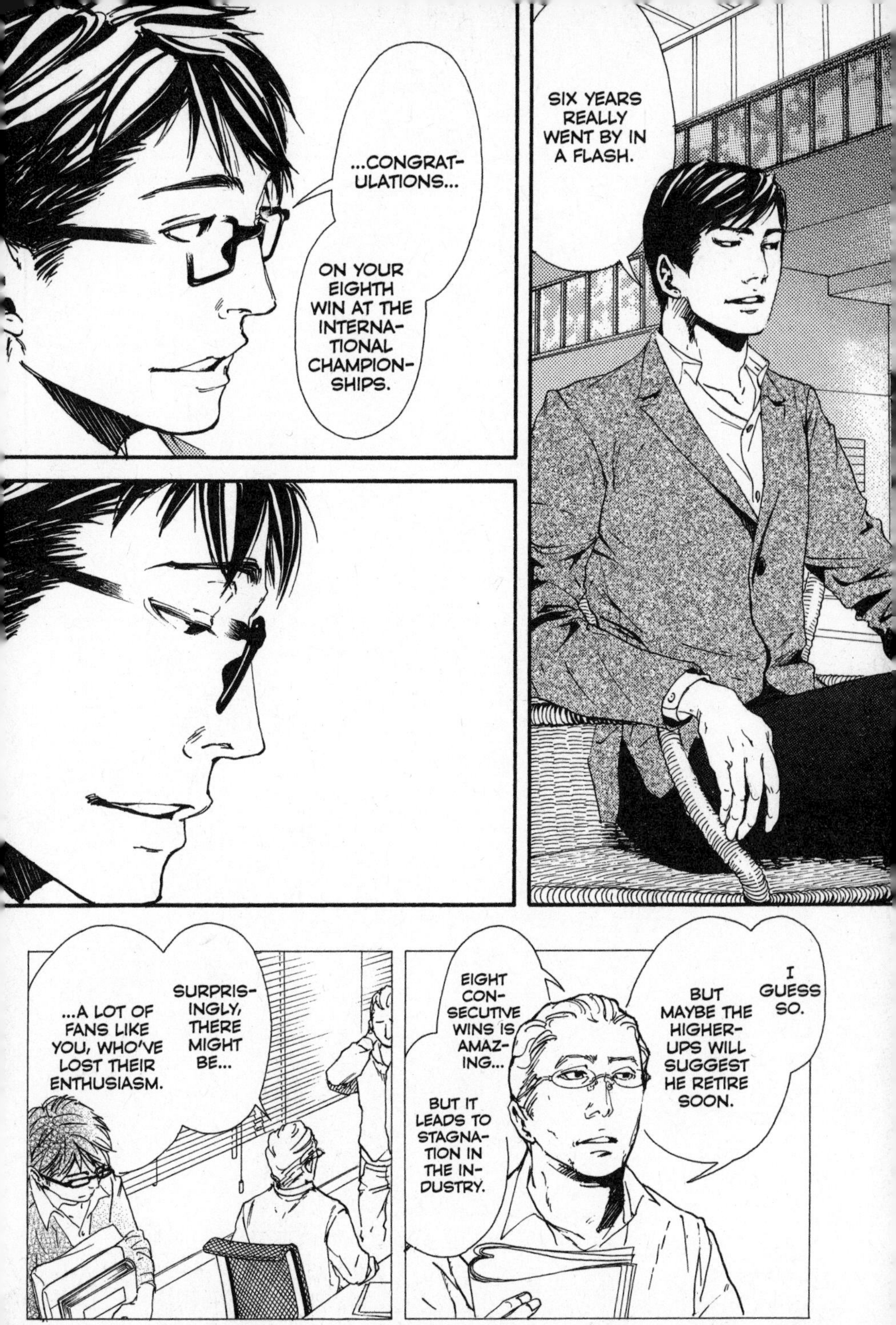
SIX YEARS REALLY WENT BY IN A FLASH.
...CONGRATULATIONS...
ON YOUR EIGHTH WIN AT THE INTERNATIONAL CHAMPIONSHIPS.
I GUESS SO.
BUT MAYBE THE HIGHER-UPS WILL SUGGEST HE RETIRE SOON.
EIGHT CONSECUTIVE WINS IS AMAZING...
BUT IT LEADS TO STAGNATION IN THE INDUSTRY.
SURPRISINGLY, THERE MIGHT BE...
...A LOT OF FANS LIKE YOU, WHO'VE LOST THEIR ENTHUSIASM.

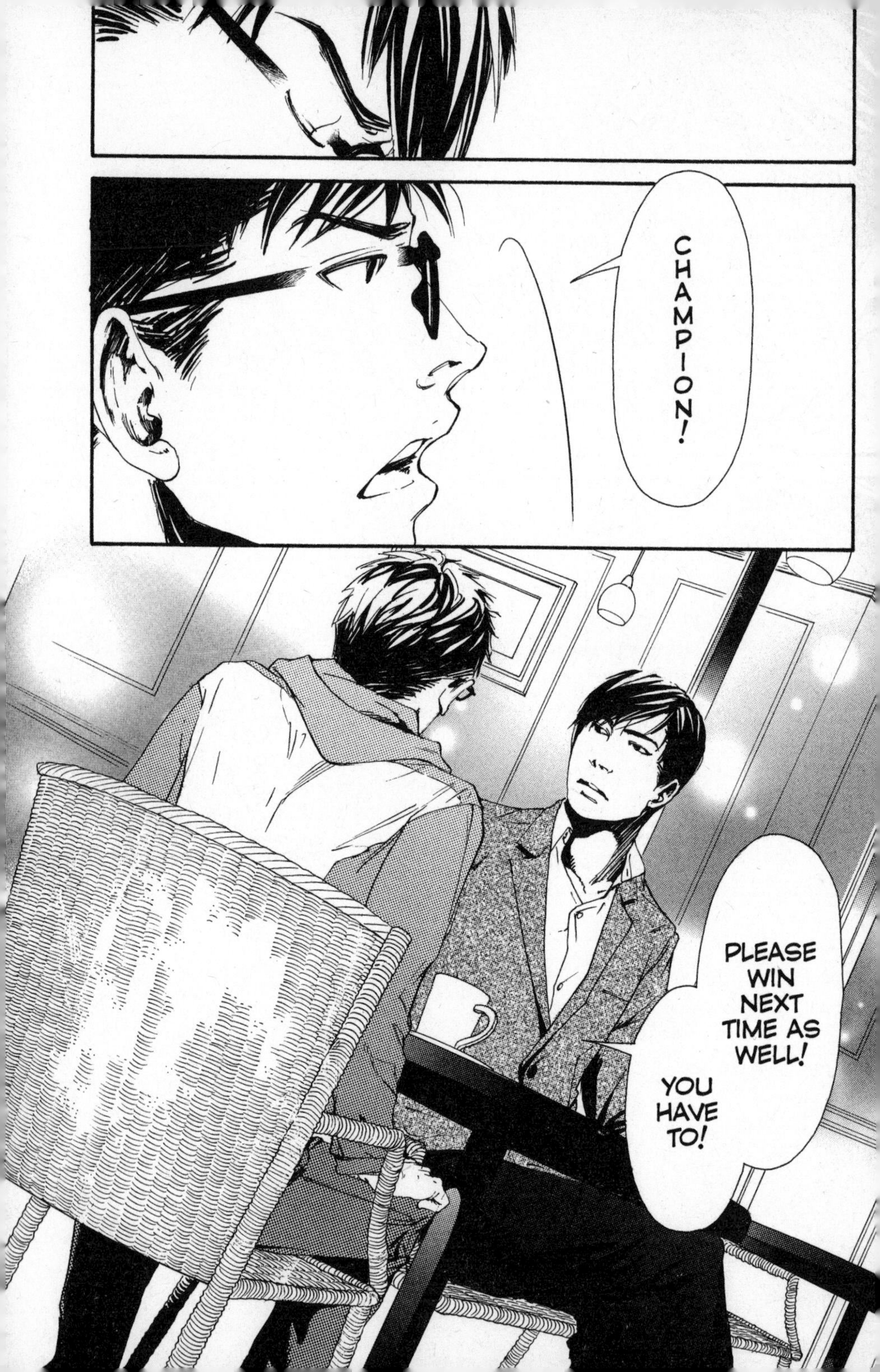
CHAMPION!
PLEASE WIN NEXT TIME AS WELL!
YOU HAVE TO!

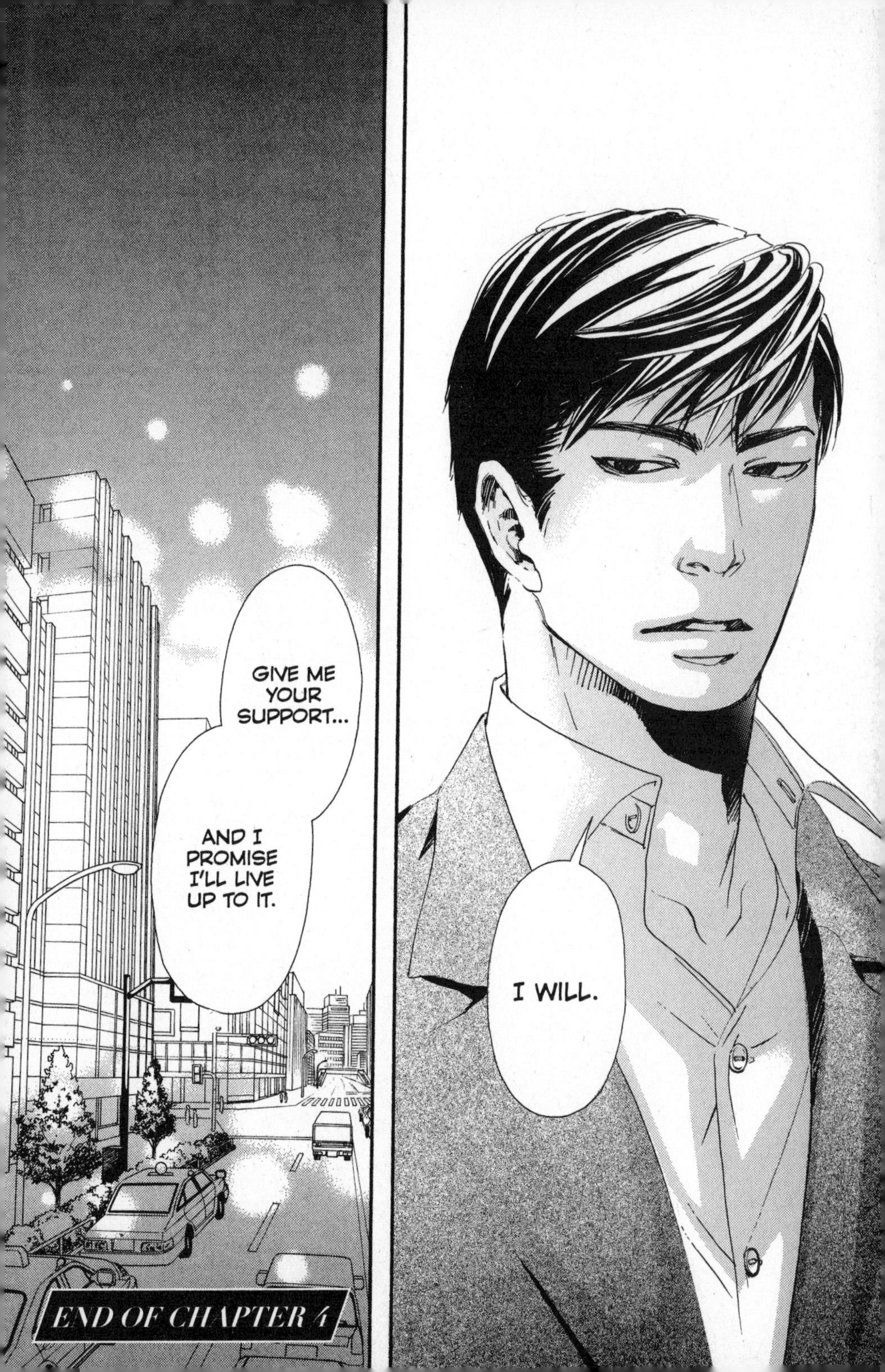
I WILL.
GIVE ME YOUR SUPPORT...
AND I PROMISE I'LL LIVE UP TO IT.
END OF CHAPTER 4

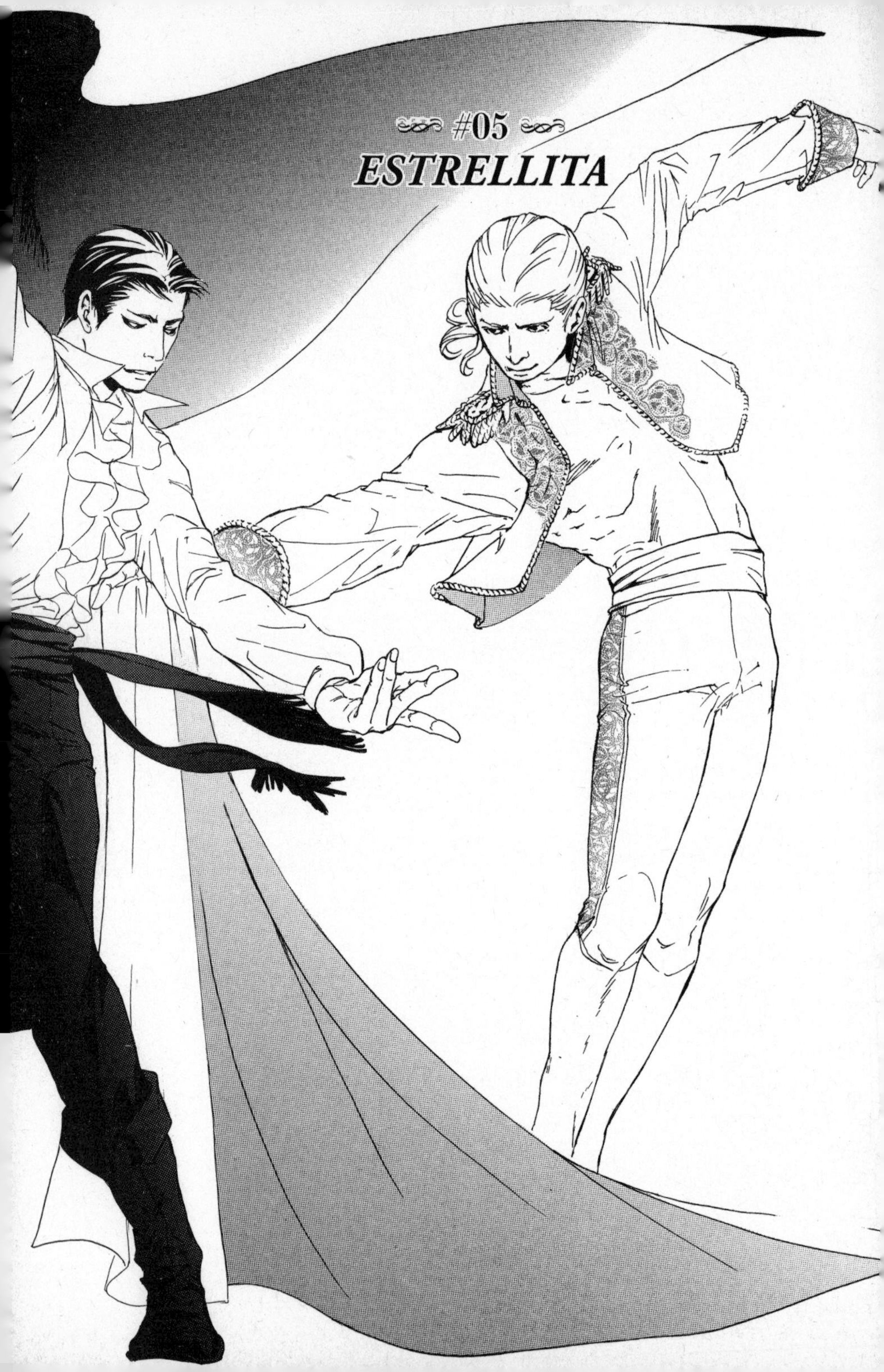
#05
ESTRELLITA

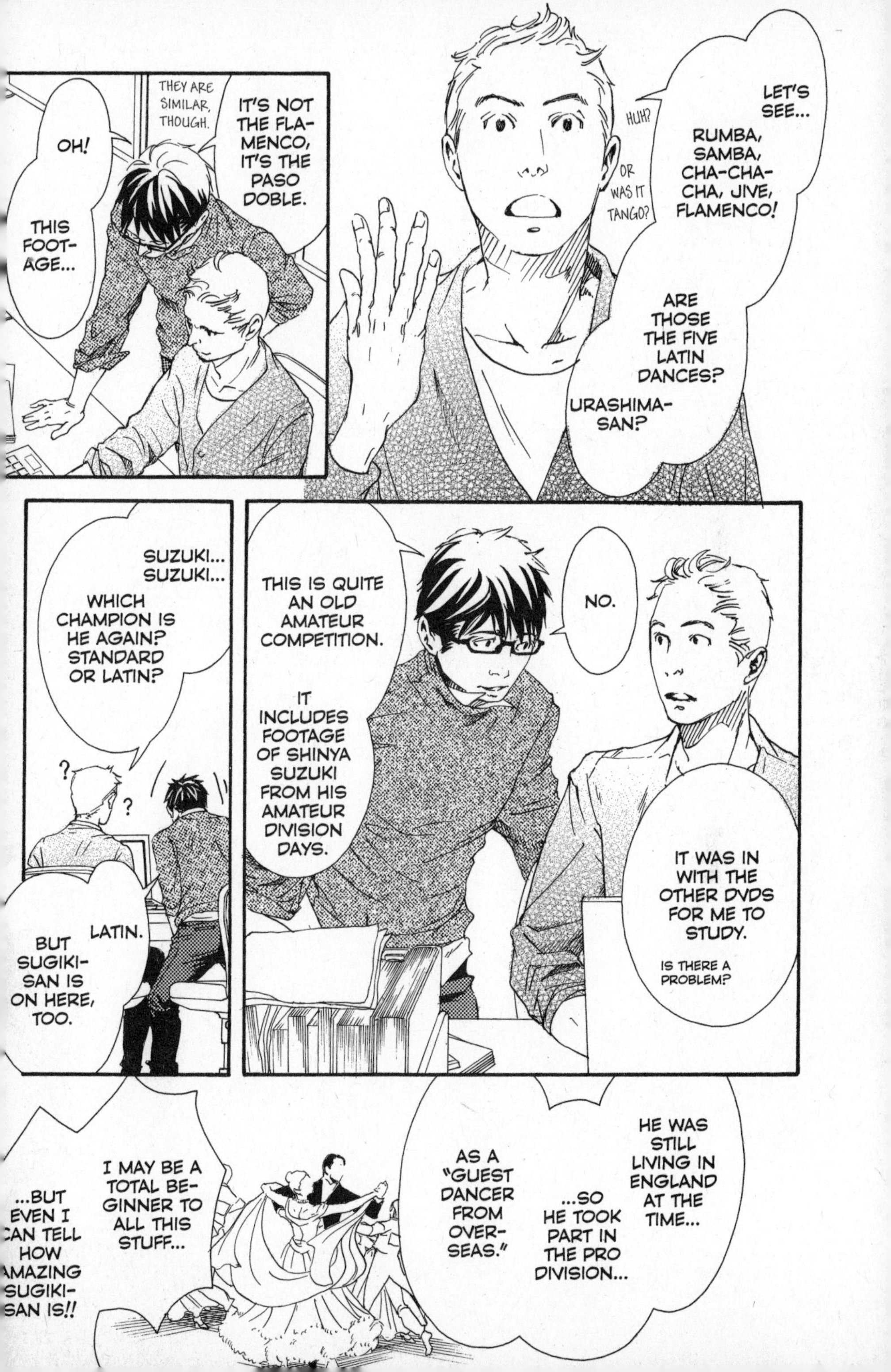
LET'S SEE... RUMBA, SAMBA, CHA-CHA-CHA, JIVE, FLAMENCO!
HUH?
OR WAS IT TANGO?
ARE THOSE THE FIVE LATIN DANCES?
URASHIMA-SAN?
IT'S NOT THE FLAMENCO, IT'S THE PASO DOBLE.
THEY ARE SIMILAR, THOUGH.
OH!
THIS FOOTAGE...
NO.
THIS IS QUITE AN OLD AMATEUR COMPETITION.
IT INCLUDES FOOTAGE OF SHINYA SUZUKI FROM HIS AMATEUR DIVISION DAYS.
IT WAS IN WITH THE OTHER DVDS FOR ME TO STUDY.
IS THERE A PROBLEM?
SUZUKI... SUZUKI...
WHICH CHAMPION IS HE AGAIN? STANDARD OR LATIN?
LATIN.
BUT SUGIKI-SAN IS ON HERE, TOO.
HE WAS STILL LIVING IN ENGLAND AT THE TIME...
...SO HE TOOK PART IN THE PRO DIVISION...
AS A "GUEST DANCER FROM OVERSEAS."
I MAY BE A TOTAL BEGINNER TO ALL THIS STUFF...
...BUT EVEN I CAN TELL HOW AMAZING SUGIKI-SAN IS!!

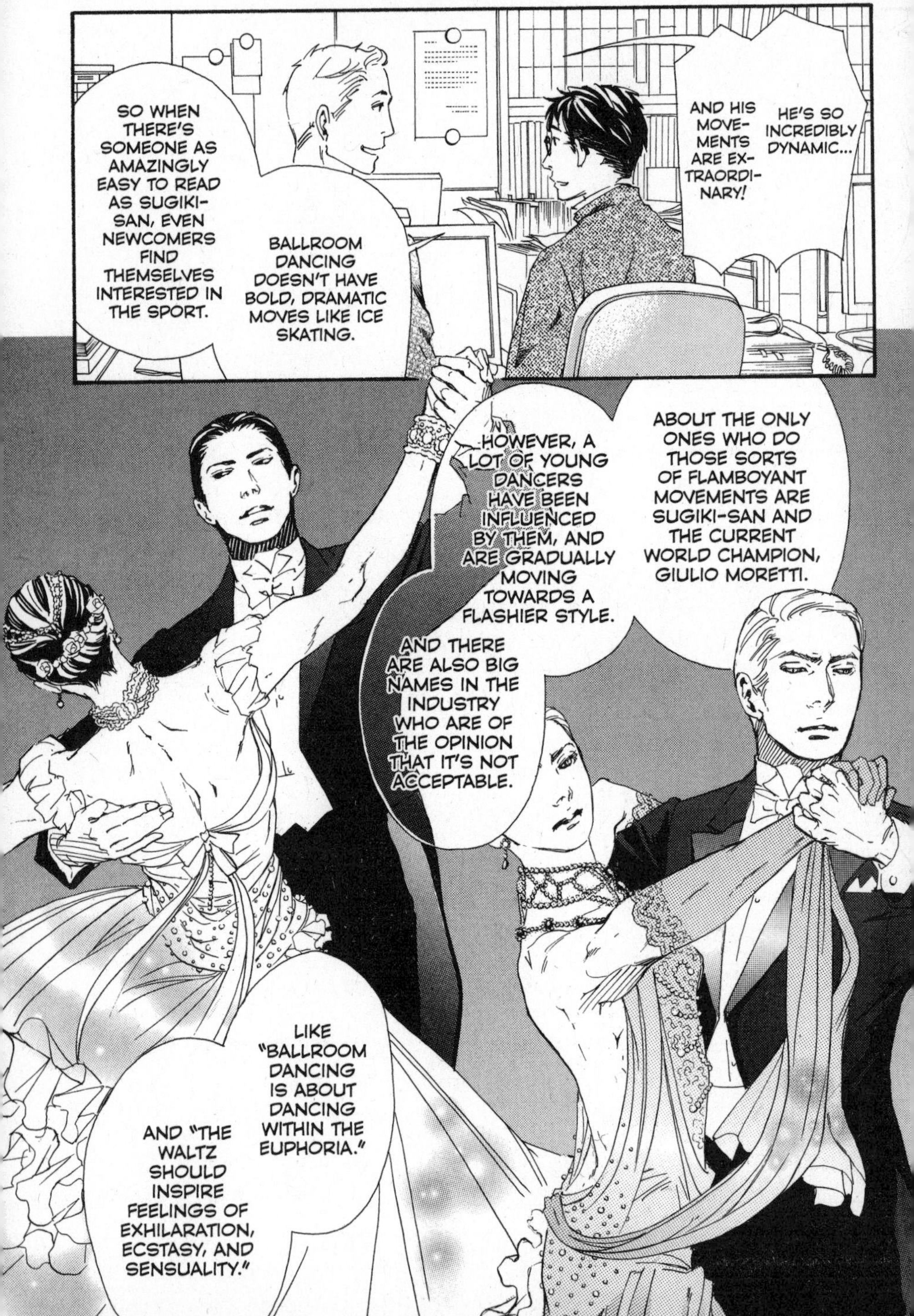
HE'S SO INCREDIBLY DYNAMIC...
AND HIS MOVEMENTS ARE EXTRAORDINARY!
SO WHEN THERE'S SOMEONE AS AMAZINGLY EASY TO READ AS SUGIKI-SAN, EVEN NEWCOMERS FIND THEMSELVES INTERESTED IN THE SPORT.
BALLROOM DANCING DOESN'T HAVE BOLD, DRAMATIC MOVES LIKE ICE SKATING.
ABOUT THE ONLY ONES WHO DO THOSE SORTS OF FLAMBOYANT MOVEMENTS ARE SUGIKI-SAN AND THE CURRENT WORLD CHAMPION, GIULIO MORETTI.
HOWEVER, A LOT OF YOUNG DANCERS HAVE BEEN INFLUENCED BY THEM, AND ARE GRADUALLY MOVING TOWARDS A FLASHIER STYLE.
AND THERE ARE ALSO BIG NAMES IN THE INDUSTRY WHO ARE OF THE OPINION THAT IT'S NOT ACCEPTABLE.
LIKE "BALLROOM DANCING IS ABOUT DANCING WITHIN THE EUPHORIA."
AND "THE WALTZ SHOULD INSPIRE FEELINGS OF EXHILARATION, ECSTASY, AND SENSUALITY."

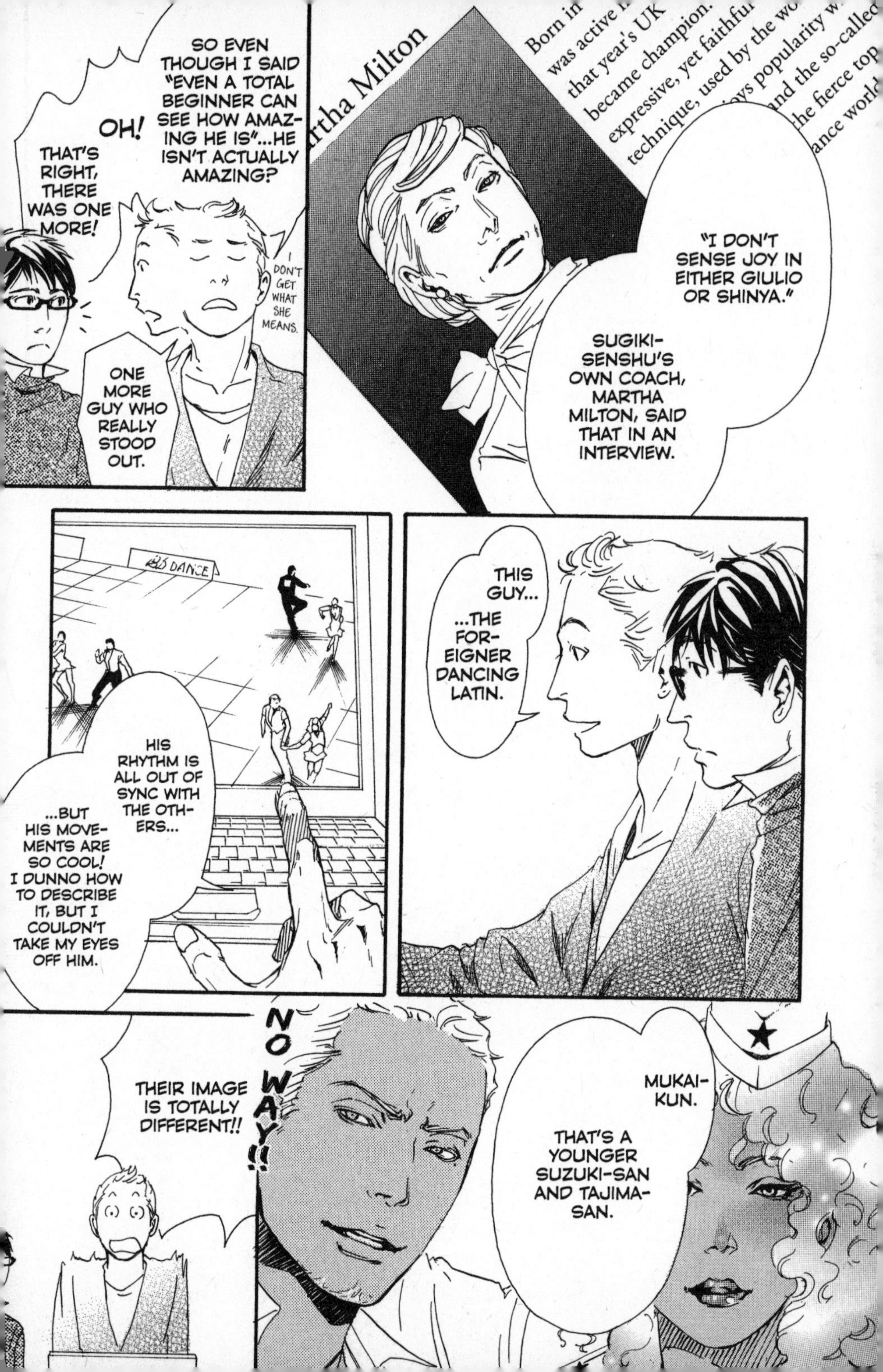
rtha Milton
Born in
was active i
that year's UK
became champion.
expressive, yet faithfu
technique, used by the wo
joys popularity w
nd the so-called
he fierce top
ance world
"I DON'T SENSE JOY IN EITHER GIULIO OR SHINYA."
SUGIKI-SENSHU'S OWN COACH, MARTHA MILTON, SAID THAT IN AN INTERVIEW.
SO EVEN THOUGH I SAID "EVEN A TOTAL BEGINNER CAN SEE HOW AMAZING HE IS"...HE ISN'T ACTUALLY AMAZING?
I DON'T GET WHAT SHE MEANS.
OH!
THAT'S RIGHT, THERE WAS ONE MORE!
ONE MORE GUY WHO REALLY STOOD OUT.
THIS GUY...
...THE FOREIGNER DANCING LATIN.
DANCE
HIS RHYTHM IS ALL OUT OF SYNC WITH THE OTHERS...
...BUT HIS MOVEMENTS ARE SO COOL! I DUNNO HOW TO DESCRIBE IT, BUT I COULDN'T TAKE MY EYES OFF HIM.
MUKAI-KUN.
THAT'S A YOUNGER SUZUKI-SAN AND TAJIMA-SAN.
NO WAY!!
THEIR IMAGE IS TOTALLY DIFFERENT!!

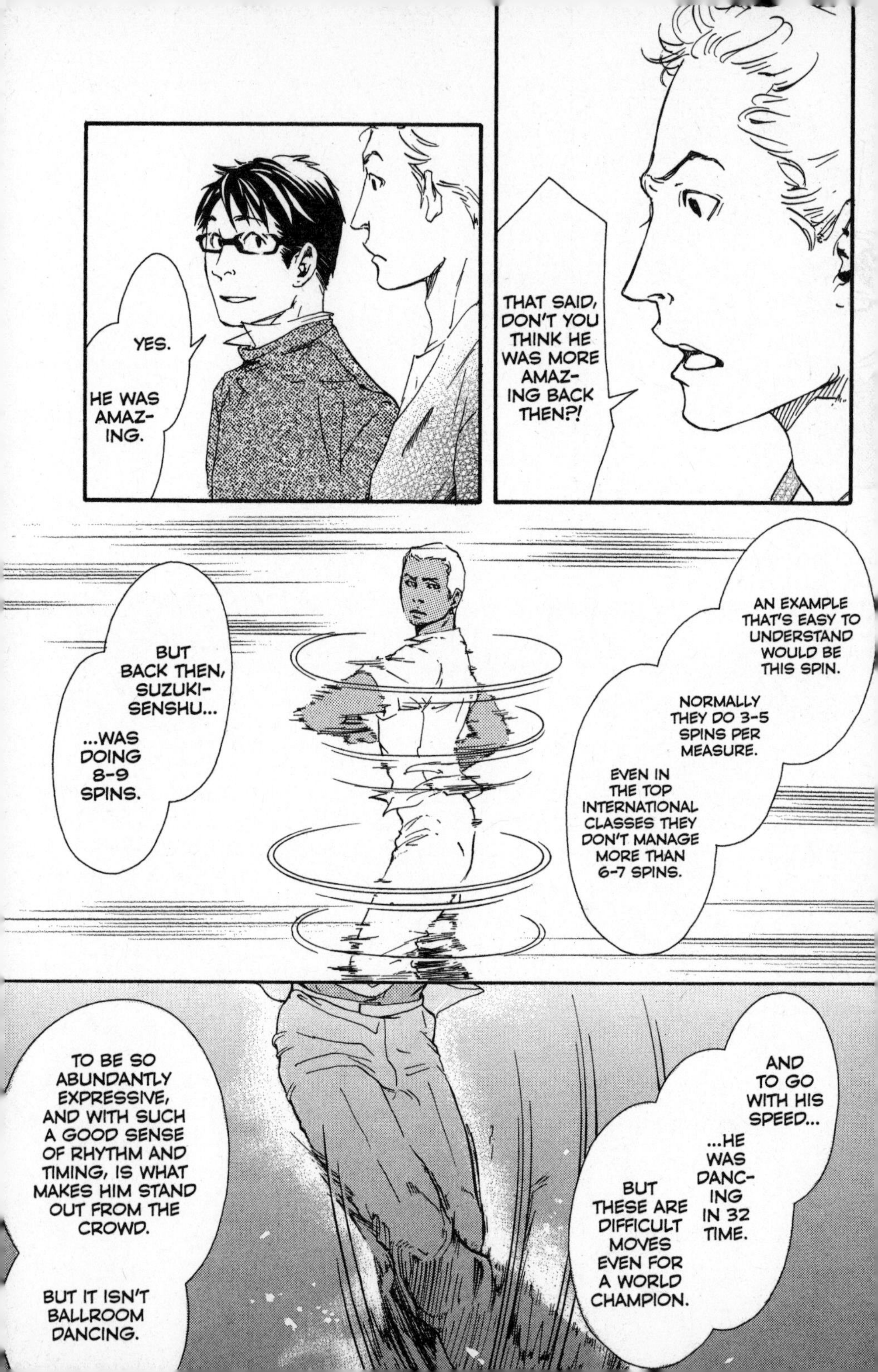
THAT SAID, DON'T YOU THINK HE WAS MORE AMAZ-ING BACK THEN?!
YES.
HE WAS AMAZ-ING.
AN EXAMPLE THAT'S EASY TO UNDERSTAND WOULD BE THIS SPIN.
NORMALLY THEY DO 3-5 SPINS PER MEASURE.
EVEN IN THE TOP INTERNATIONAL CLASSES THEY DON'T MANAGE MORE THAN 6-7 SPINS.
BUT BACK THEN, SUZUKI-SENSHU...
...WAS DOING 8-9 SPINS.
AND TO GO WITH HIS SPEED...
...HE WAS DANC-ING IN 32 TIME.
BUT THESE ARE DIFFICULT MOVES EVEN FOR A WORLD CHAMPION.
TO BE SO ABUNDANTLY EXPRESSIVE, AND WITH SUCH A GOOD SENSE OF RHYTHM AND TIMING, IS WHAT MAKES HIM STAND OUT FROM THE CROWD.
BUT IT ISN'T BALLROOM DANCING.

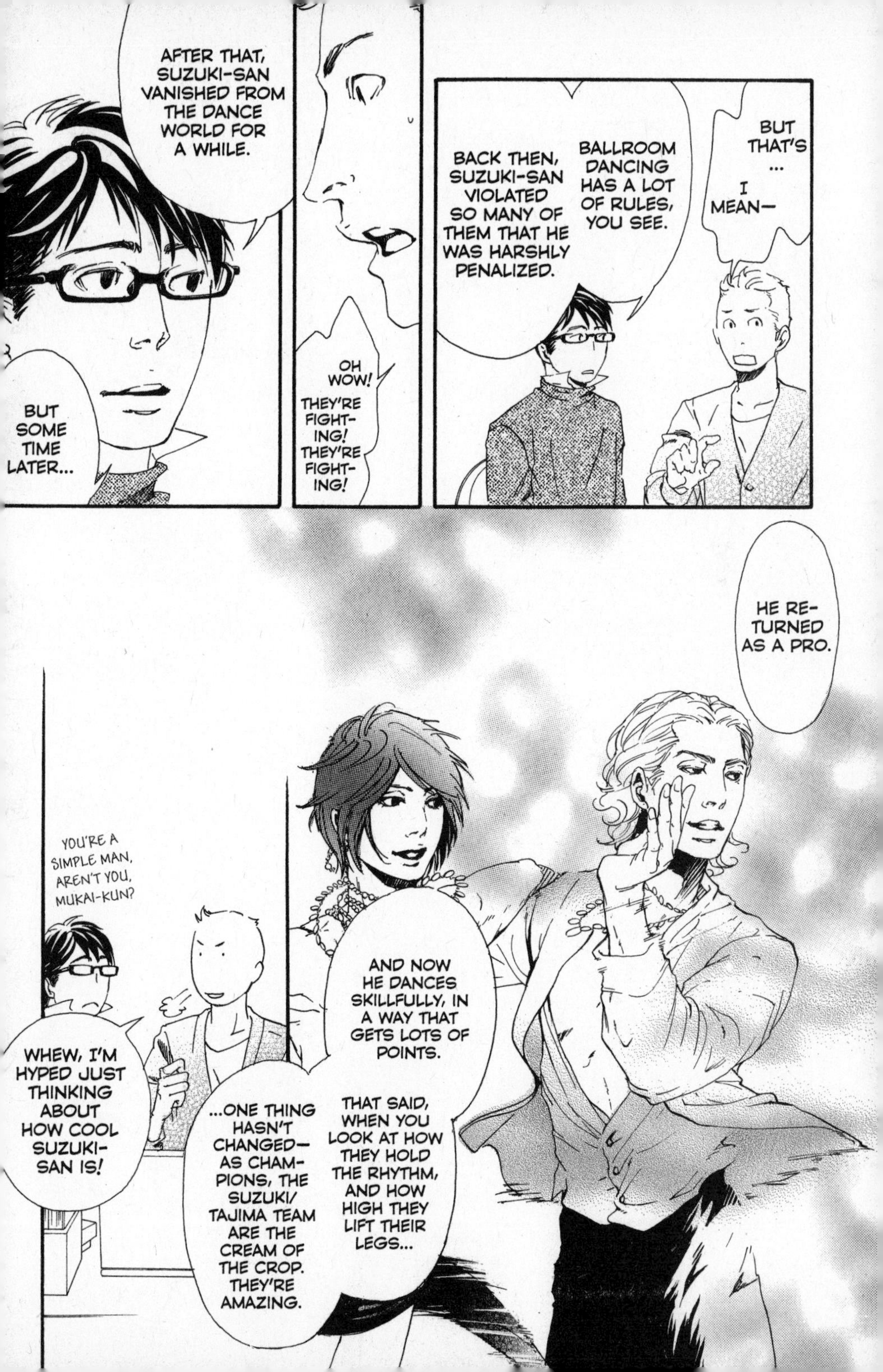
BUT THAT'S ... I MEAN—
BALLROOM DANCING HAS A LOT OF RULES, YOU SEE.
BACK THEN, SUZUKI-SAN VIOLATED SO MANY OF THEM THAT HE WAS HARSHLY PENALIZED.
OH WOW! THEY'RE FIGHT-ING! THEY'RE FIGHT-ING!
AFTER THAT, SUZUKI-SAN VANISHED FROM THE DANCE WORLD FOR A WHILE.
BUT SOME TIME LATER...
HE RE-TURNED AS A PRO.
AND NOW HE DANCES SKILLFULLY, IN A WAY THAT GETS LOTS OF POINTS.
THAT SAID, WHEN YOU LOOK AT HOW THEY HOLD THE RHYTHM, AND HOW HIGH THEY LIFT THEIR LEGS...
...ONE THING HASN'T CHANGED—AS CHAM-PIONS, THE SUZUKI/TAJIMA TEAM ARE THE CREAM OF THE CROP. THEY'RE AMAZING.
WHEW, I'M HYPED JUST THINKING ABOUT HOW COOL SUZUKI-SAN IS!
YOU'RE A SIMPLE MAN, AREN'T YOU, MUKAI-KUN?

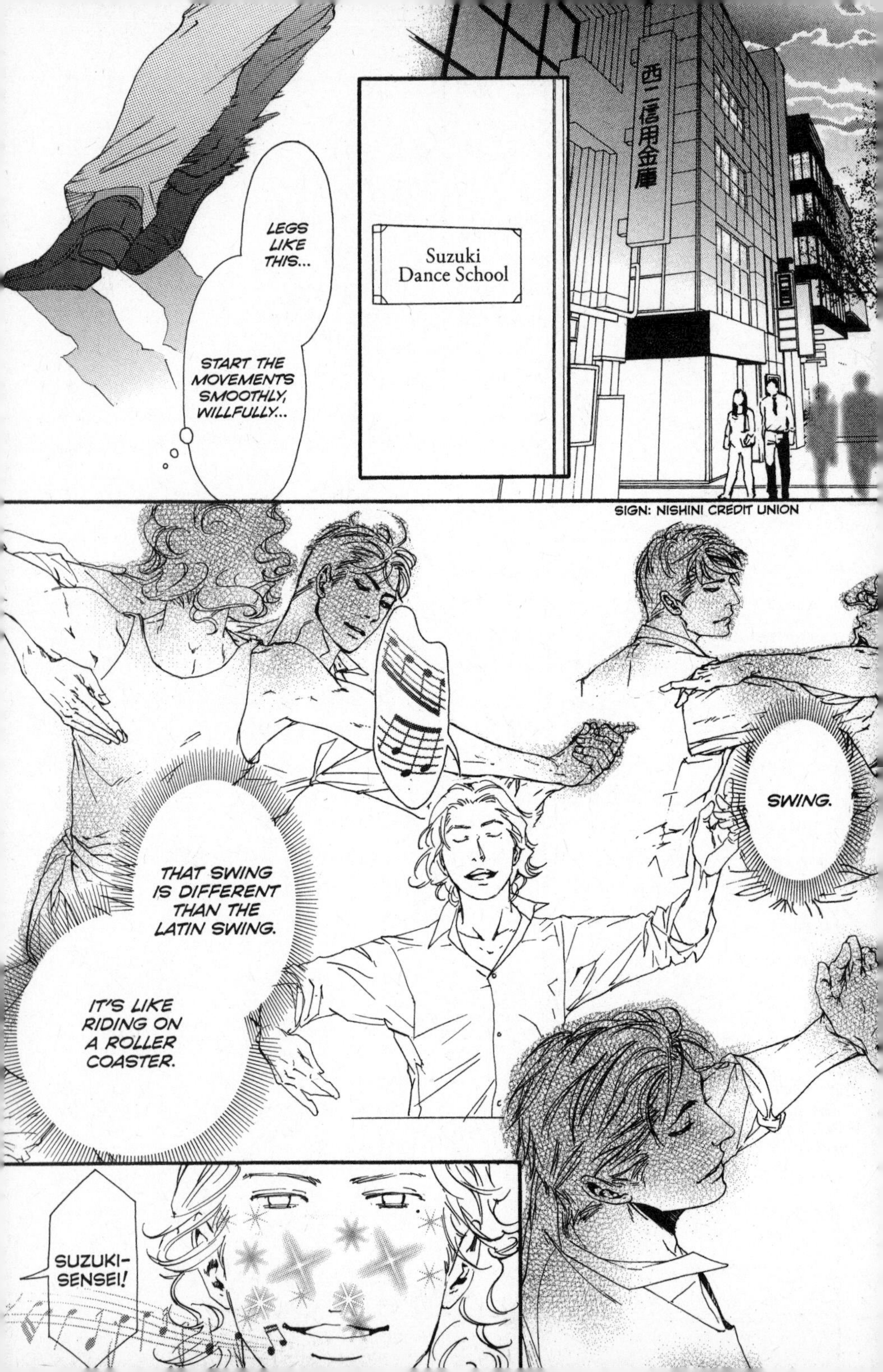
Suzuki Dance School
西二信用金庫
SIGN: NISHINI CREDIT UNION
LEGS LIKE THIS...
START THE MOVEMENTS SMOOTHLY, WILLFULLY...
SWING.
THAT SWING IS DIFFERENT THAN THE LATIN SWING.
IT'S LIKE RIDING ON A ROLLER COASTER.
SUZUKI-SENSEI!

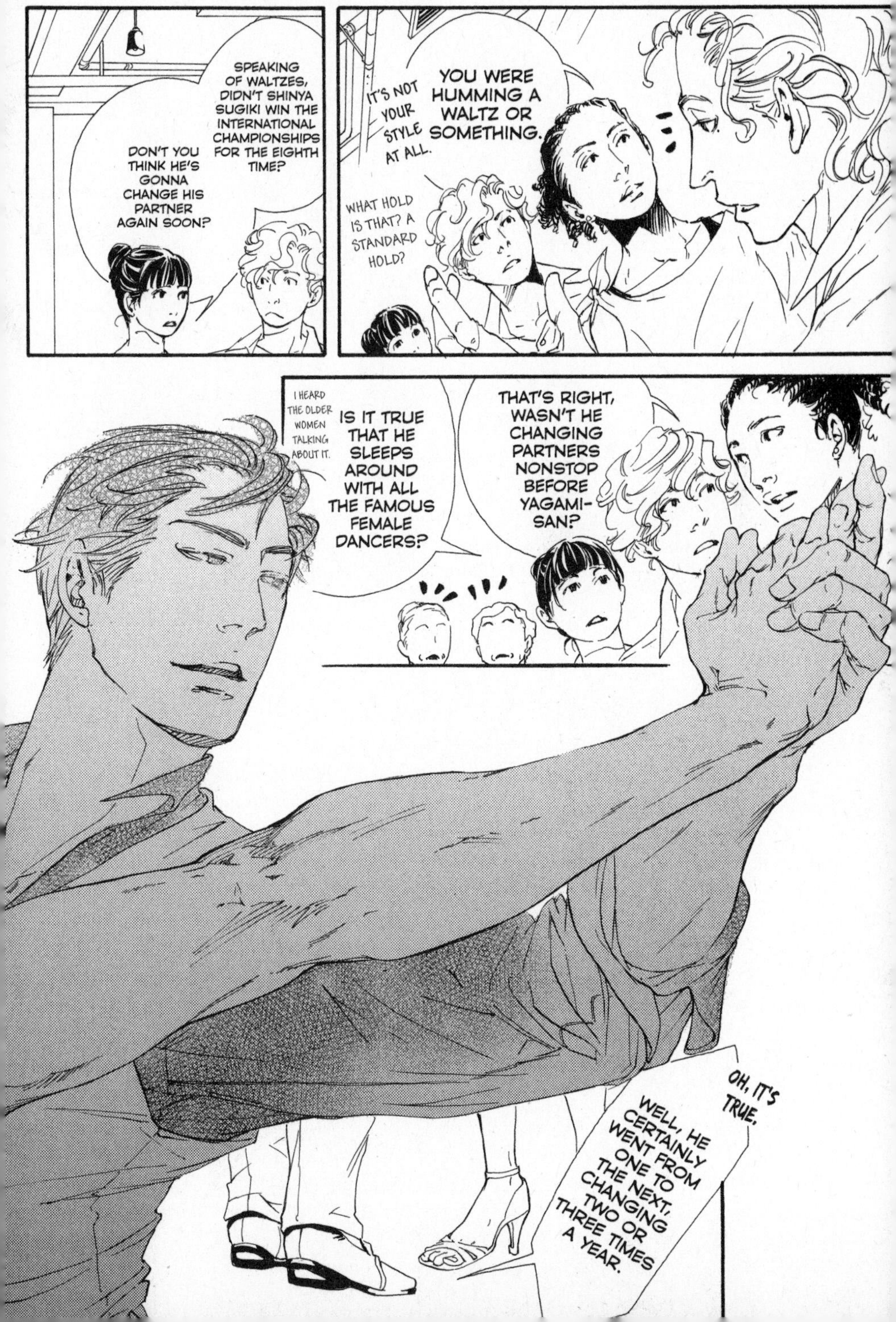
YOU WERE HUMMING A WALTZ OR SOMETHING.
IT'S NOT YOUR STYLE AT ALL.
WHAT HOLD IS THAT? A STANDARD HOLD?
SPEAKING OF WALTZES, DIDN'T SHINYA SUGIKI WIN THE INTERNATIONAL CHAMPIONSHIPS FOR THE EIGHTH TIME?
DON'T YOU THINK HE'S GONNA CHANGE HIS PARTNER AGAIN SOON?
THAT'S RIGHT, WASN'T HE CHANGING PARTNERS NONSTOP BEFORE YAGAMI-SAN?
IS IT TRUE THAT HE SLEEPS AROUND WITH ALL THE FAMOUS FEMALE DANCERS?
I HEARD THE OLDER WOMEN TALKING ABOUT IT.
OH, IT'S TRUE.
WELL, HE CERTAINLY WENT FROM ONE TO THE NEXT, CHANGING TWO OR THREE TIMES A YEAR.

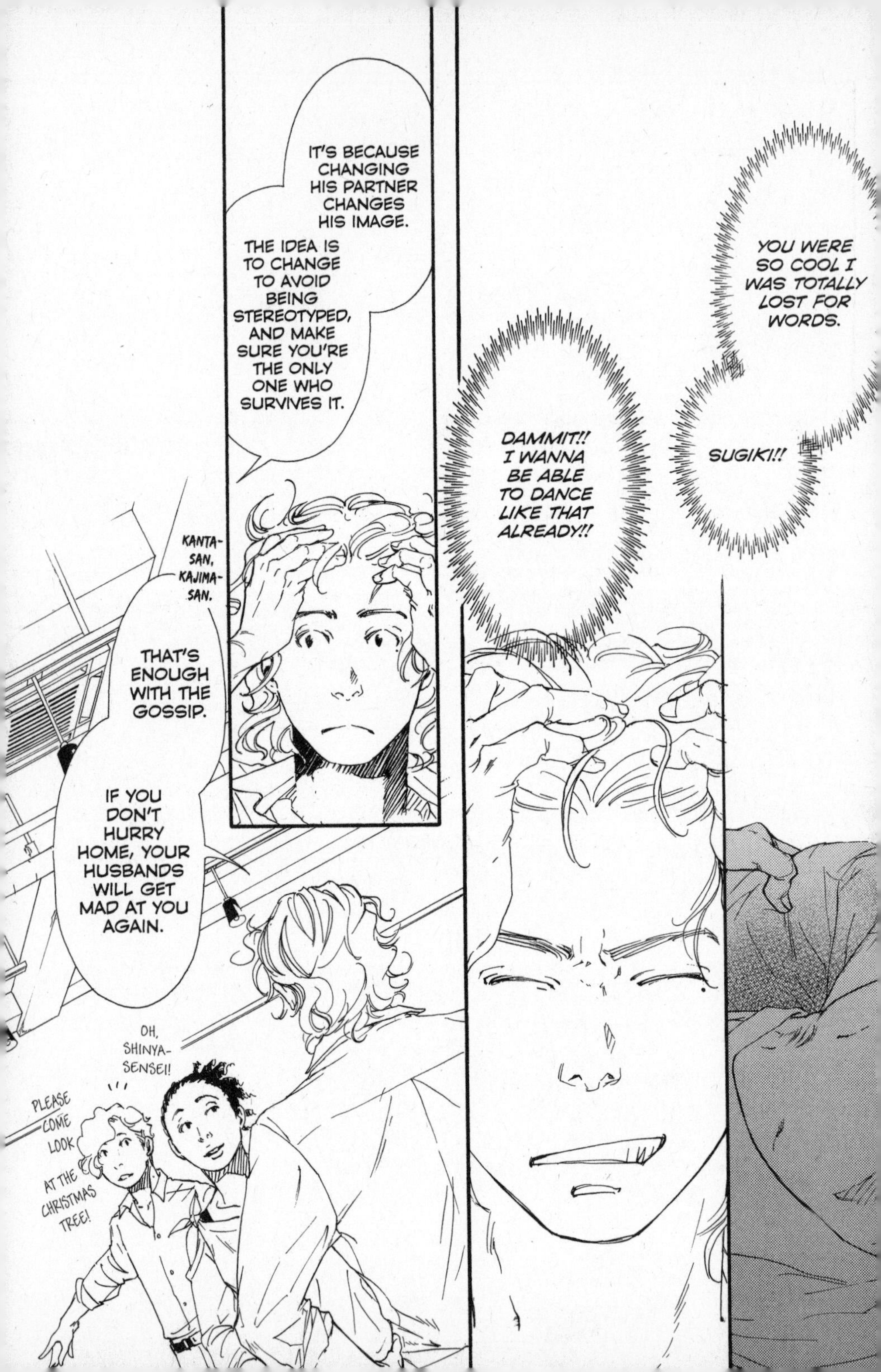
YOU WERE SO COOL I WAS TOTALLY LOST FOR WORDS.
SUGIKI!!
DAMMIT!! I WANNA BE ABLE TO DANCE LIKE THAT ALREADY!!
IT'S BECAUSE CHANGING HIS PARTNER CHANGES HIS IMAGE.
THE IDEA IS TO CHANGE TO AVOID BEING STEREOTYPED, AND MAKE SURE YOU'RE THE ONLY ONE WHO SURVIVES IT.
KANTA-SAN, KAJIMA-SAN.
THAT'S ENOUGH WITH THE GOSSIP.
IF YOU DON'T HURRY HOME, YOUR HUSBANDS WILL GET MAD AT YOU AGAIN.
OH, SHINYA-SENSEI!
PLEASE COME LOOK AT THE CHRISTMAS TREE!

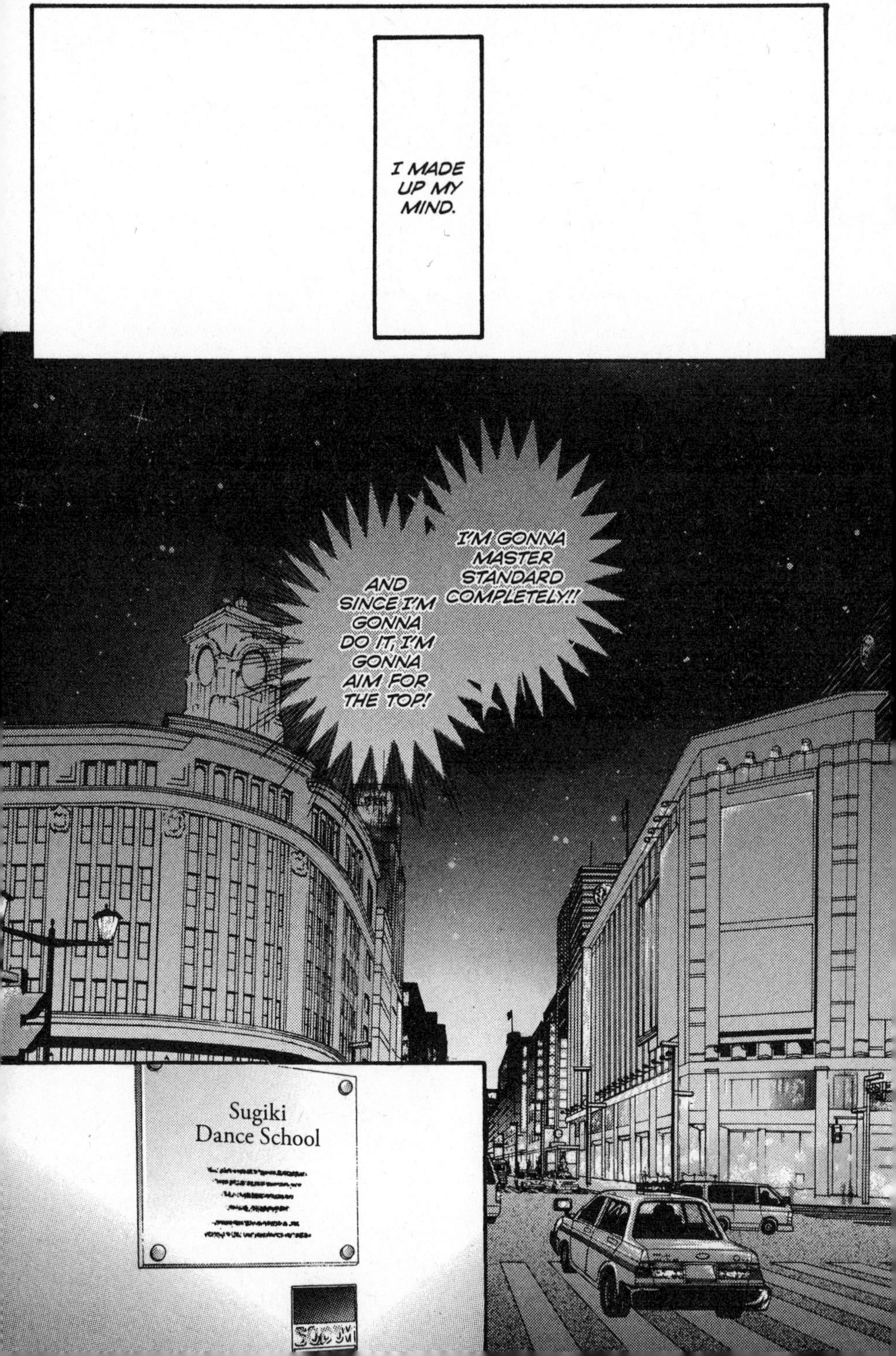
I MADE UP MY MIND.
I'M GONNA MASTER STANDARD COMPLETELY!!
AND SINCE I'M GONNA DO IT, I'M GONNA AIM FOR THE TOP!
Sugiki Dance School

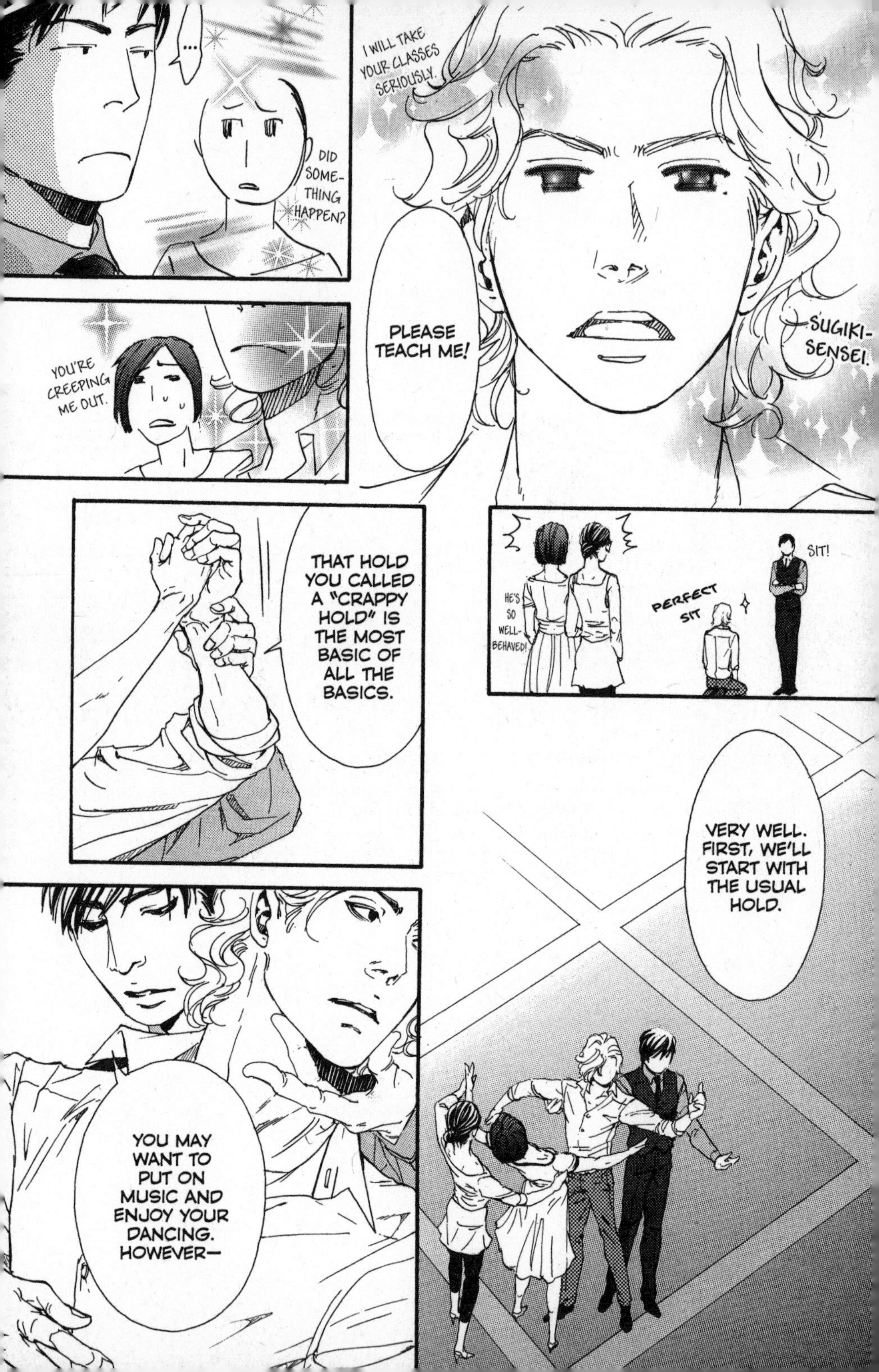
I WILL TAKE YOUR CLASSES SERIOUSLY.
SUGIKI-SENSEI.
PLEASE TEACH ME!
...
DID SOMETHING HAPPEN?
YOU'RE CREEPING ME OUT.
SIT!
PERFECT SIT
HE'S SO WELL-BEHAVED!
VERY WELL. FIRST, WE'LL START WITH THE USUAL HOLD.
THAT HOLD YOU CALLED A "CRAPPY HOLD" IS THE MOST BASIC OF ALL THE BASICS.
YOU MAY WANT TO PUT ON MUSIC AND ENJOY YOUR DANCING. HOWEVER—

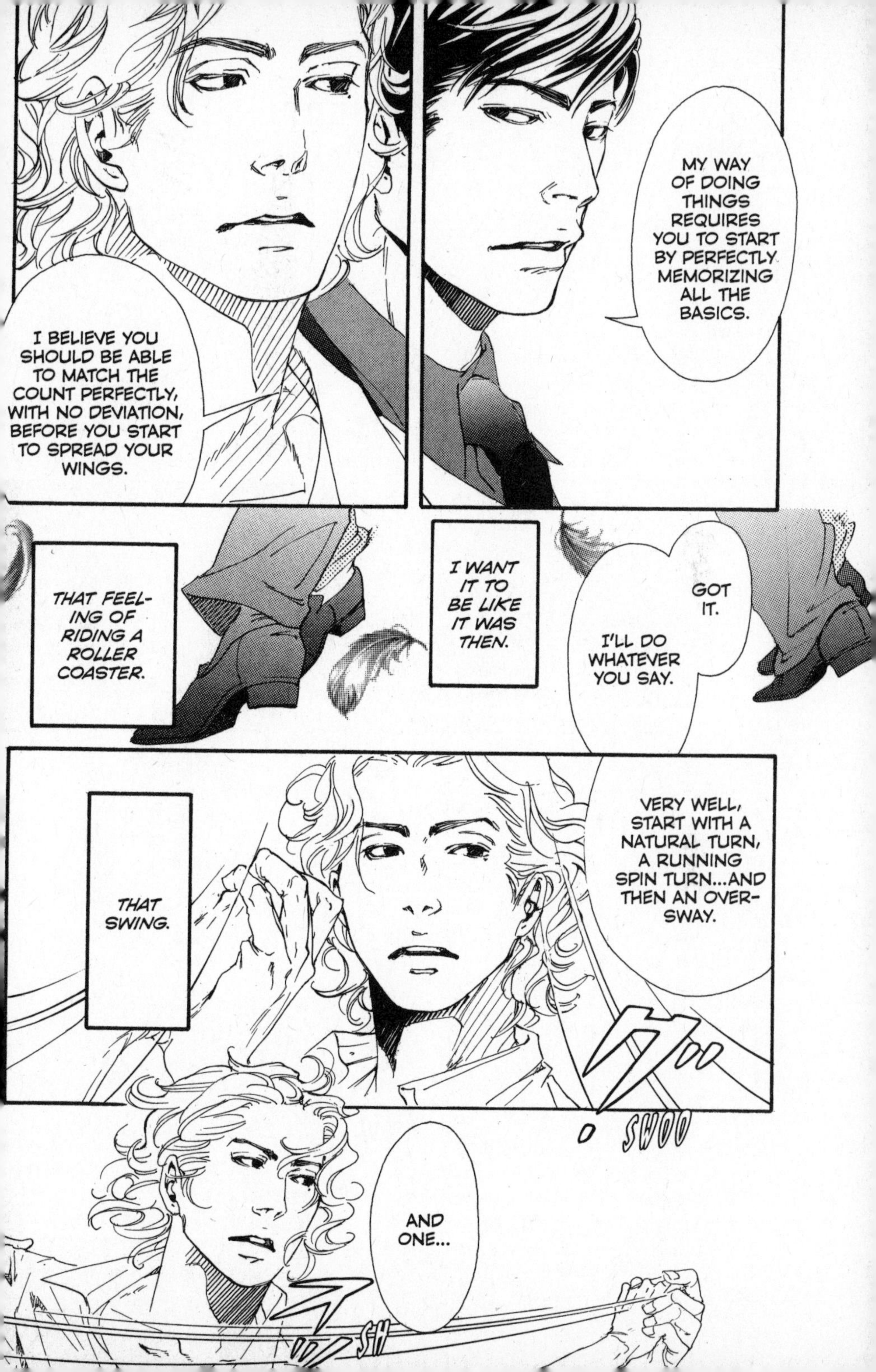
MY WAY OF DOING THINGS REQUIRES YOU TO START BY PERFECTLY MEMORIZING ALL THE BASICS.
I BELIEVE YOU SHOULD BE ABLE TO MATCH THE COUNT PERFECTLY, WITH NO DEVIATION, BEFORE YOU START TO SPREAD YOUR WINGS.
GOT IT.
I'LL DO WHATEVER YOU SAY.
I WANT IT TO BE LIKE IT WAS THEN.
THAT FEEL- ING OF RIDING A ROLLER COASTER.
VERY WELL, START WITH A NATURAL TURN, A RUNNING SPIN TURN...AND THEN AN OVER- SWAY.
THAT SWING.
SWOO
AND ONE...
SH

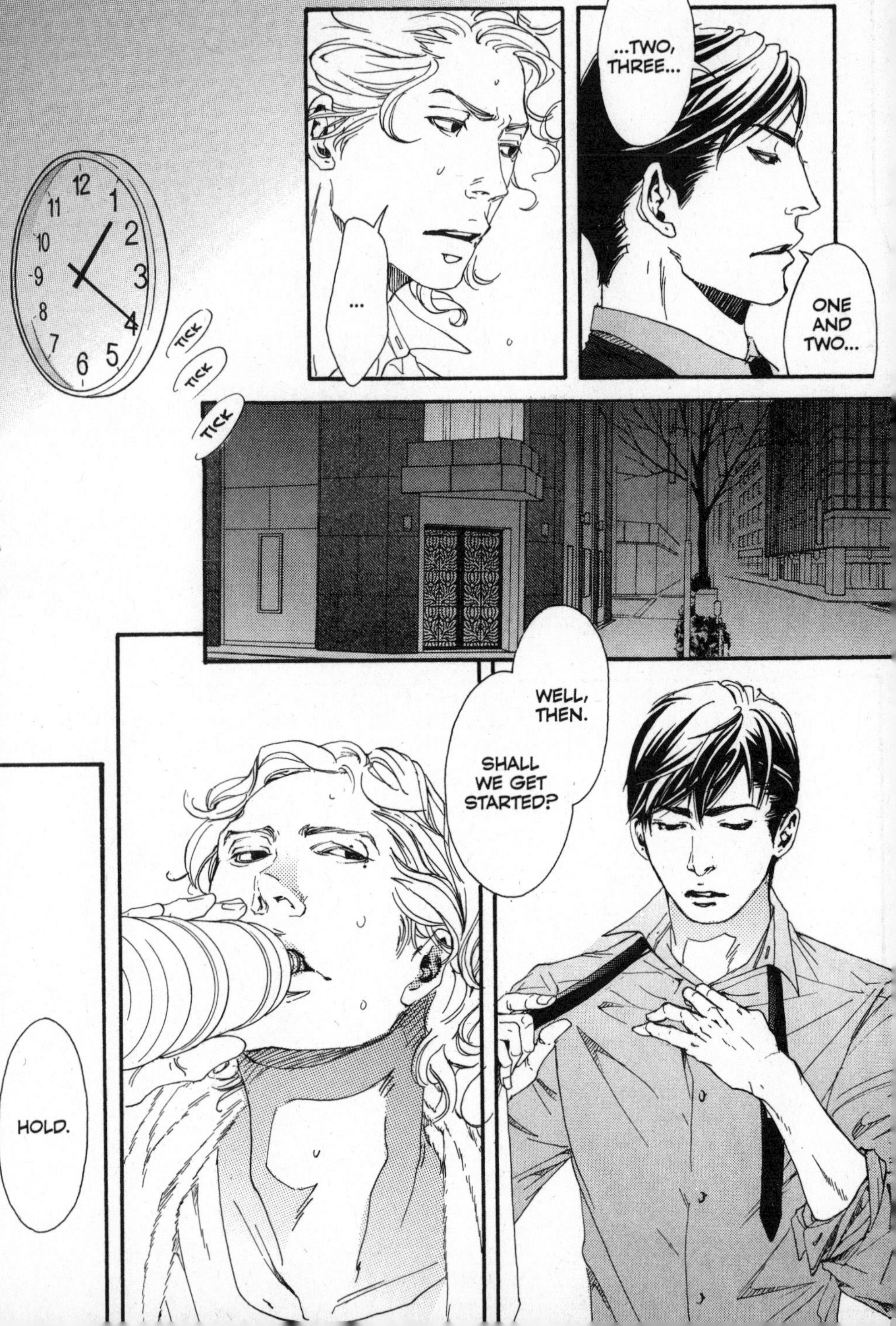
ONE AND TWO...
...TWO, THREE...
...
TICK
TICK
TICK
WELL, THEN.
SHALL WE GET STARTED?
HOLD.

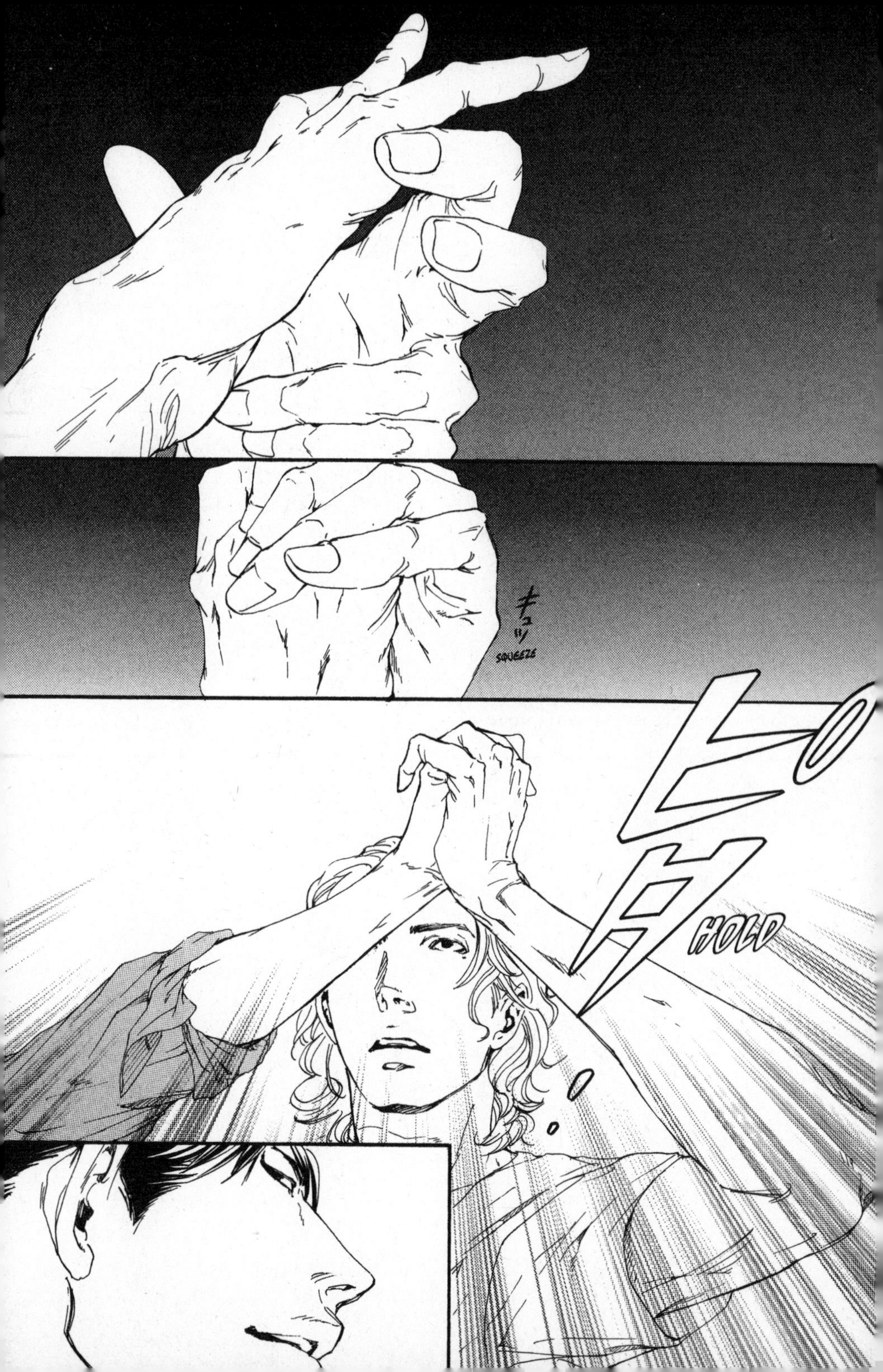
ギュッ
SQUEEZE
ピタ
HOLD

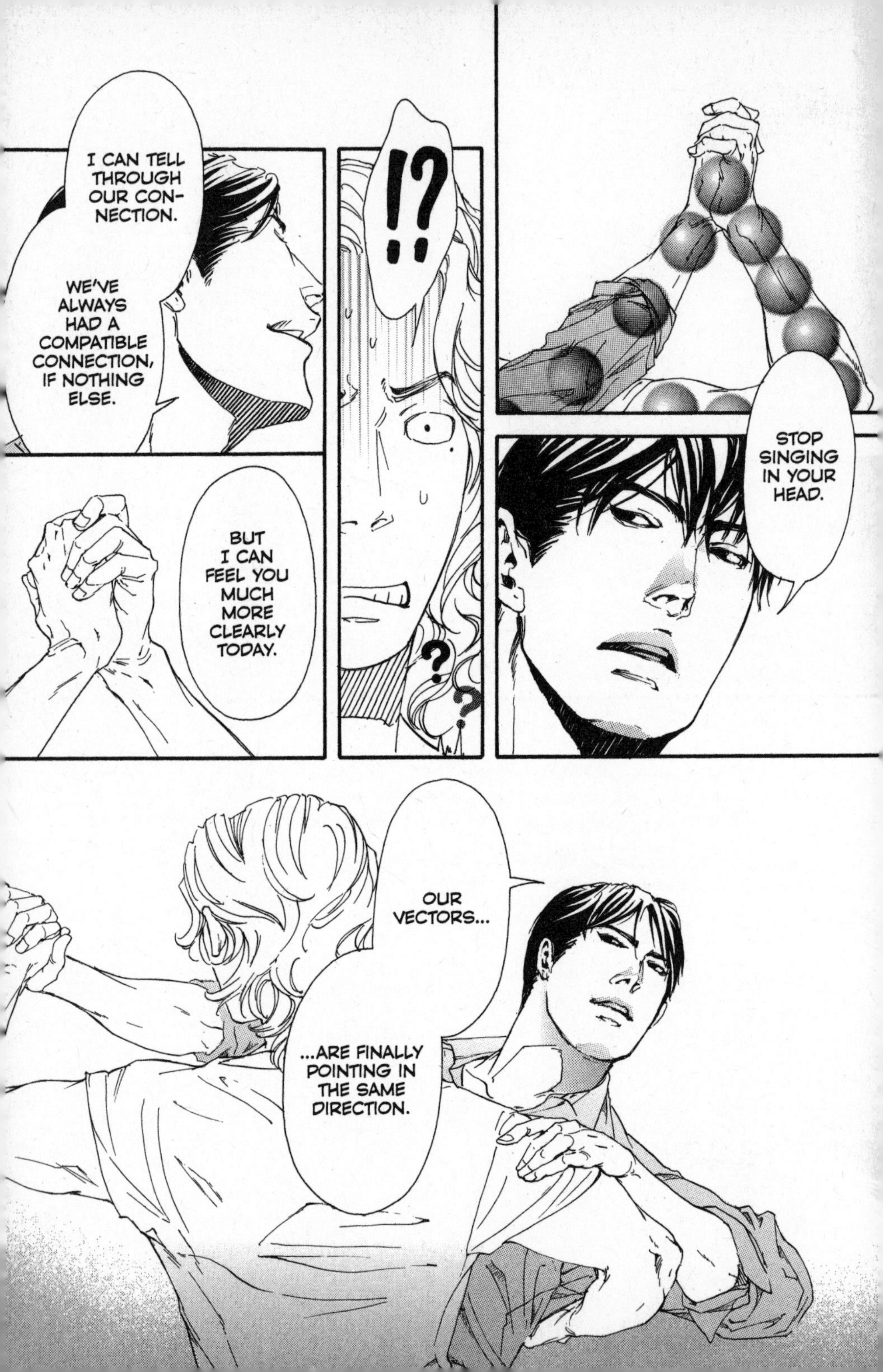
STOP SINGING IN YOUR HEAD.
!?
??
I CAN TELL THROUGH OUR CON- NECTION.
WE'VE ALWAYS HAD A COMPATIBLE CONNECTION, IF NOTHING ELSE.
BUT I CAN FEEL YOU MUCH MORE CLEARLY TODAY.
OUR VECTORS...
...ARE FINALLY POINTING IN THE SAME DIRECTION.

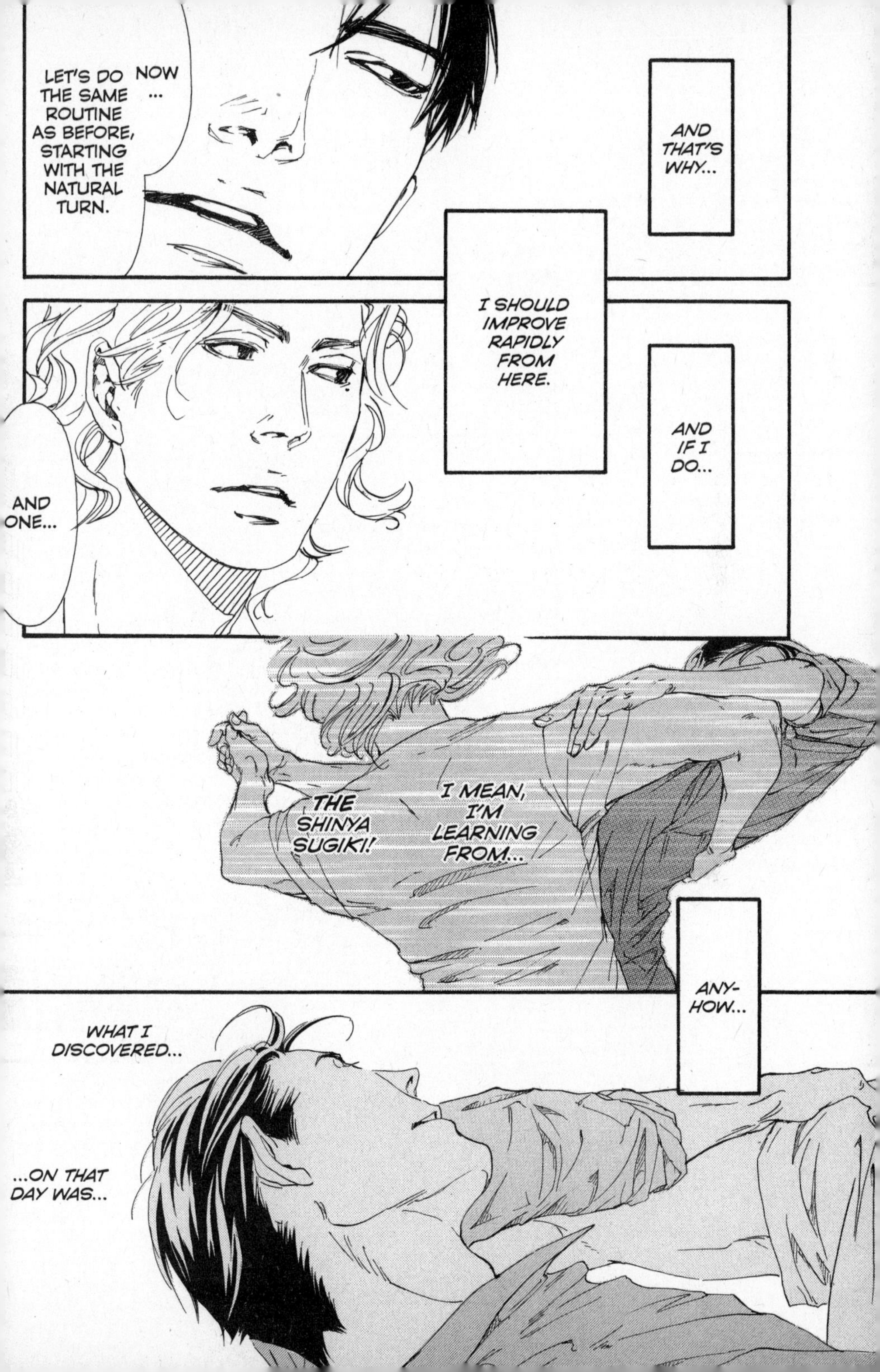
AND THAT'S WHY...
NOW ... LET'S DO THE SAME ROUTINE AS BEFORE, STARTING WITH THE NATURAL TURN.
I SHOULD IMPROVE RAPIDLY FROM HERE.
AND IF I DO...
AND ONE...
I MEAN, I'M LEARNING FROM...
THE SHINYA SUGIKI!
ANY-HOW...
WHAT I DISCOVERED...
...ON THAT DAY WAS...

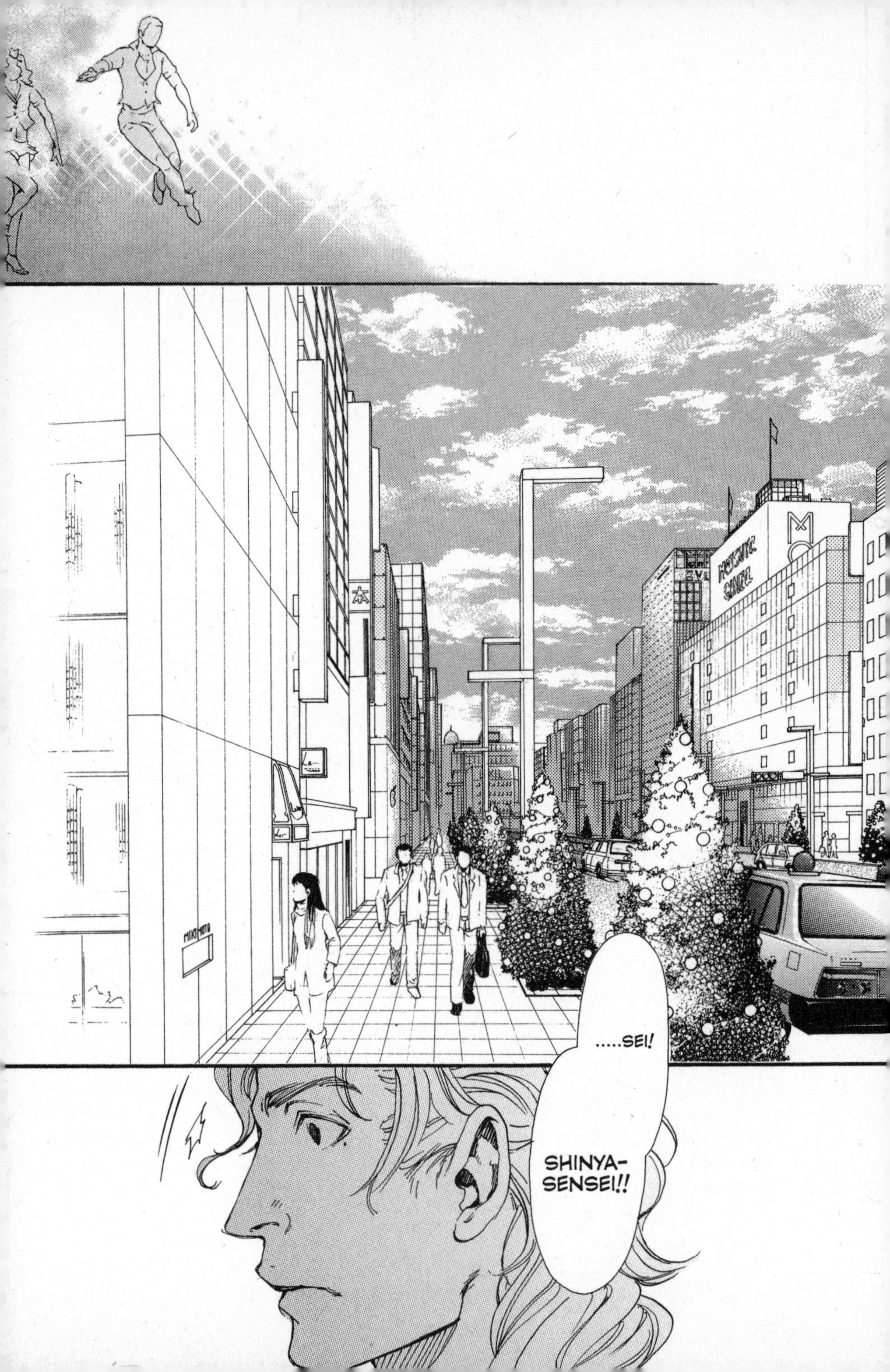
.....SEI!
SHINYA-SENSEI!!

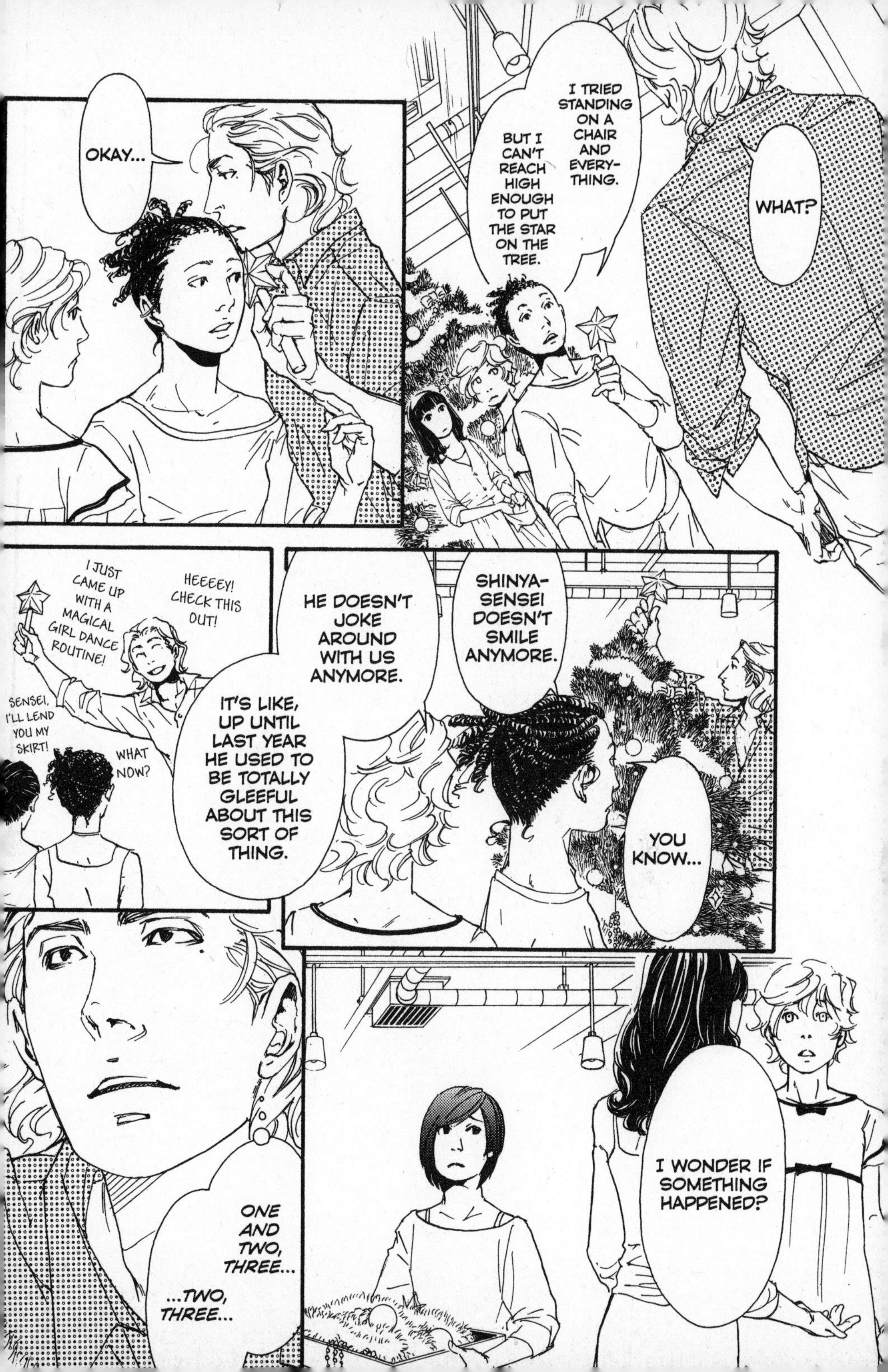
WHAT?
I TRIED STANDING ON A CHAIR AND EVERYTHING.
BUT I CAN'T REACH HIGH ENOUGH TO PUT THE STAR ON THE TREE.
OKAY...
YOU KNOW...
SHINYA-SENSEI DOESN'T SMILE ANYMORE.
HE DOESN'T JOKE AROUND WITH US ANYMORE.
IT'S LIKE, UP UNTIL LAST YEAR HE USED TO BE TOTALLY GLEEFUL ABOUT THIS SORT OF THING.
HEEEEY! CHECK THIS OUT!
I JUST CAME UP WITH A MAGICAL GIRL DANCE ROUTINE!
SENSEI, I'LL LEND YOU MY SKIRT!
WHAT NOW?
I WONDER IF SOMETHING HAPPENED?
ONE AND TWO, THREE...
...TWO, THREE...

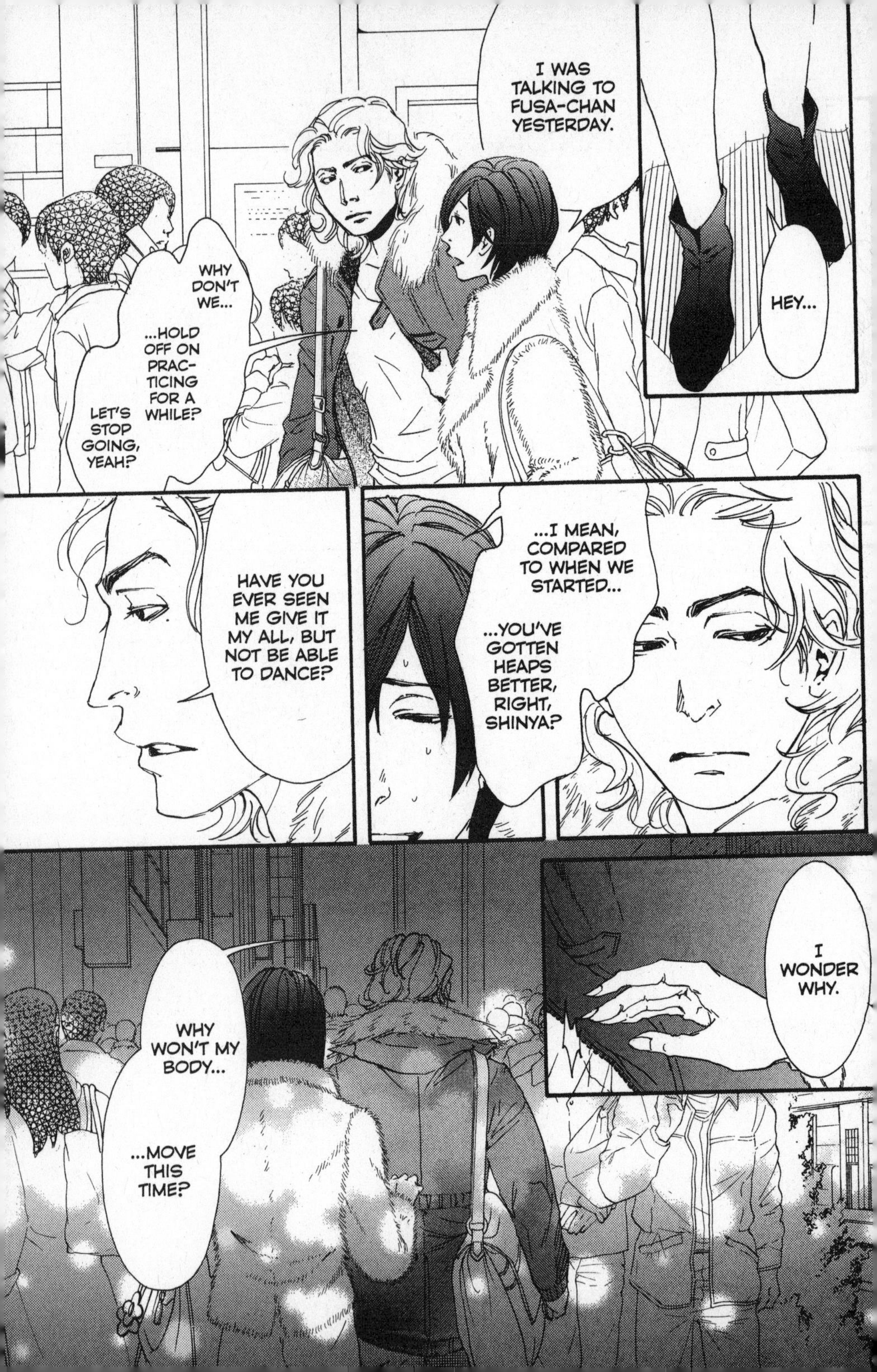
HEY...
I WAS TALKING TO FUSA-CHAN YESTERDAY.
WHY DON'T WE...
...HOLD OFF ON PRAC-TICING FOR A WHILE?
LET'S STOP GOING, YEAH?
...I MEAN, COMPARED TO WHEN WE STARTED...
...YOU'VE GOTTEN HEAPS BETTER, RIGHT, SHINYA?
HAVE YOU EVER SEEN ME GIVE IT MY ALL, BUT NOT BE ABLE TO DANCE?
I WONDER WHY.
WHY WON'T MY BODY...
...MOVE THIS TIME?

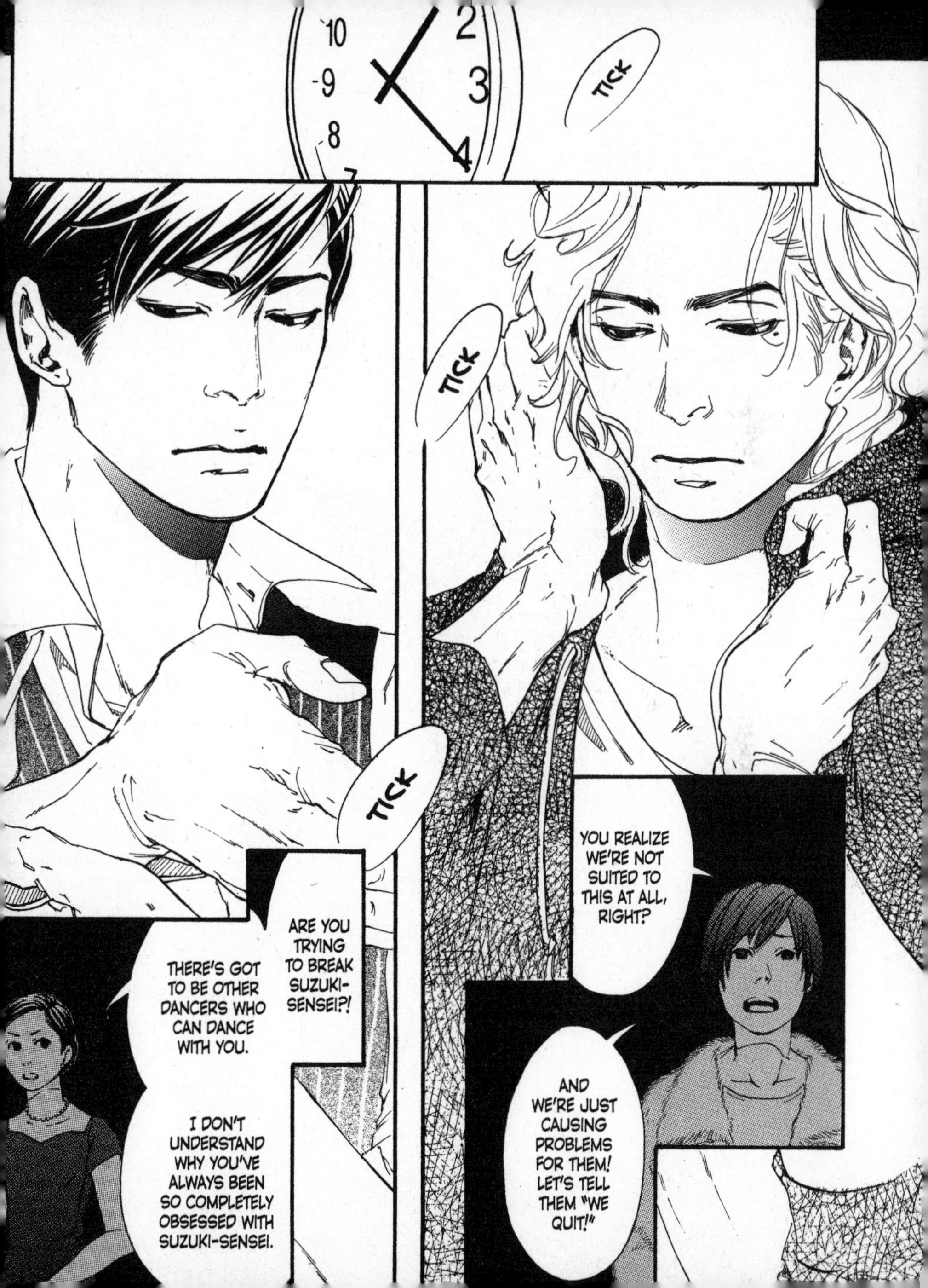
TICK
TICK
TICK
YOU REALIZE WE'RE NOT SUITED TO THIS AT ALL, RIGHT?
AND WE'RE JUST CAUSING PROBLEMS FOR THEM! LET'S TELL THEM "WE QUIT!"
ARE YOU TRYING TO BREAK SUZUKI-SENSEI?!
THERE'S GOT TO BE OTHER DANCERS WHO CAN DANCE WITH YOU.
I DON'T UNDERSTAND WHY YOU'VE ALWAYS BEEN SO COMPLETELY OBSESSED WITH SUZUKI-SENSEI.

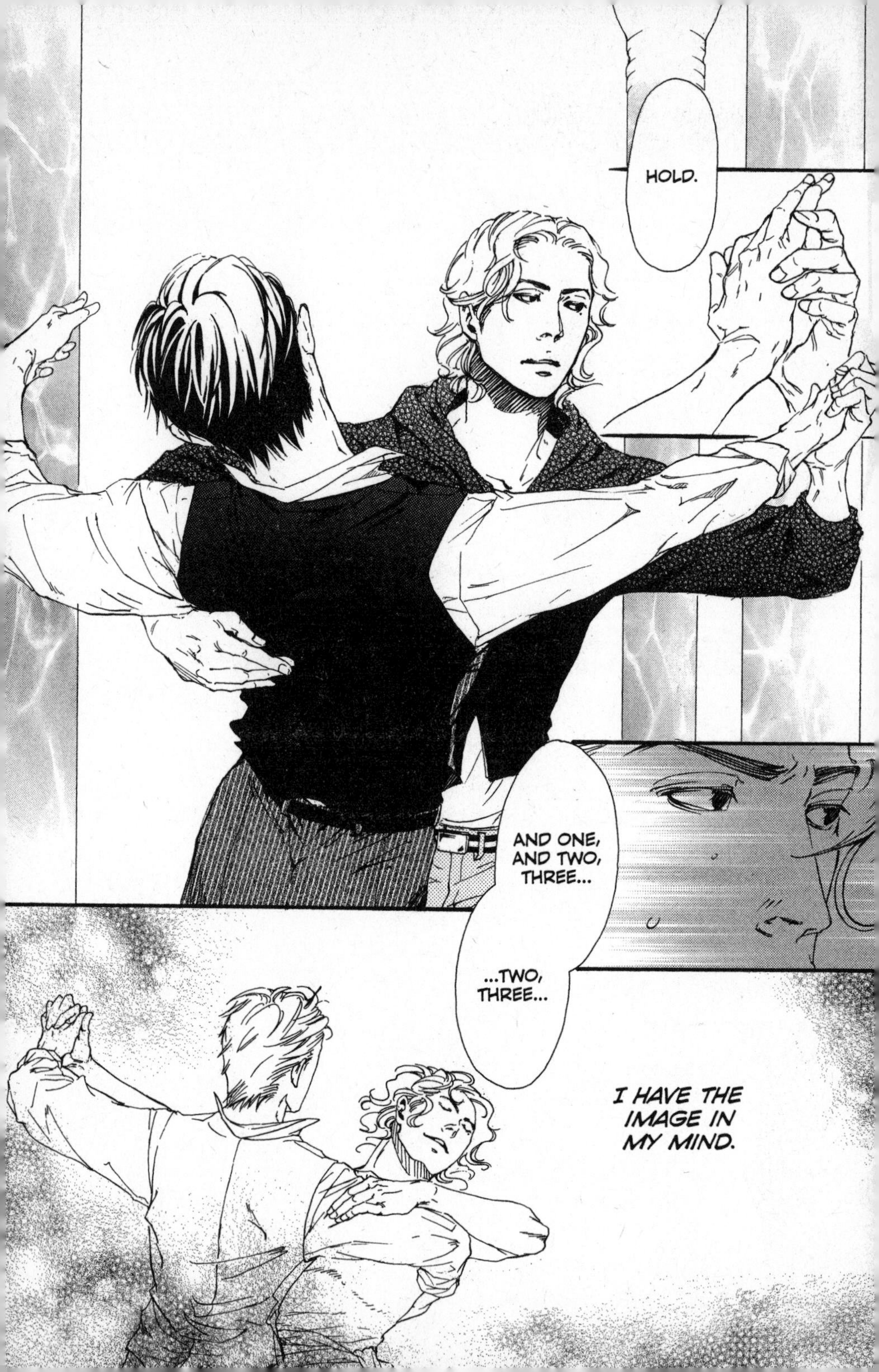
HOLD.
AND ONE, AND TWO, THREE...
...TWO, THREE...
I HAVE THE IMAGE IN MY MIND.

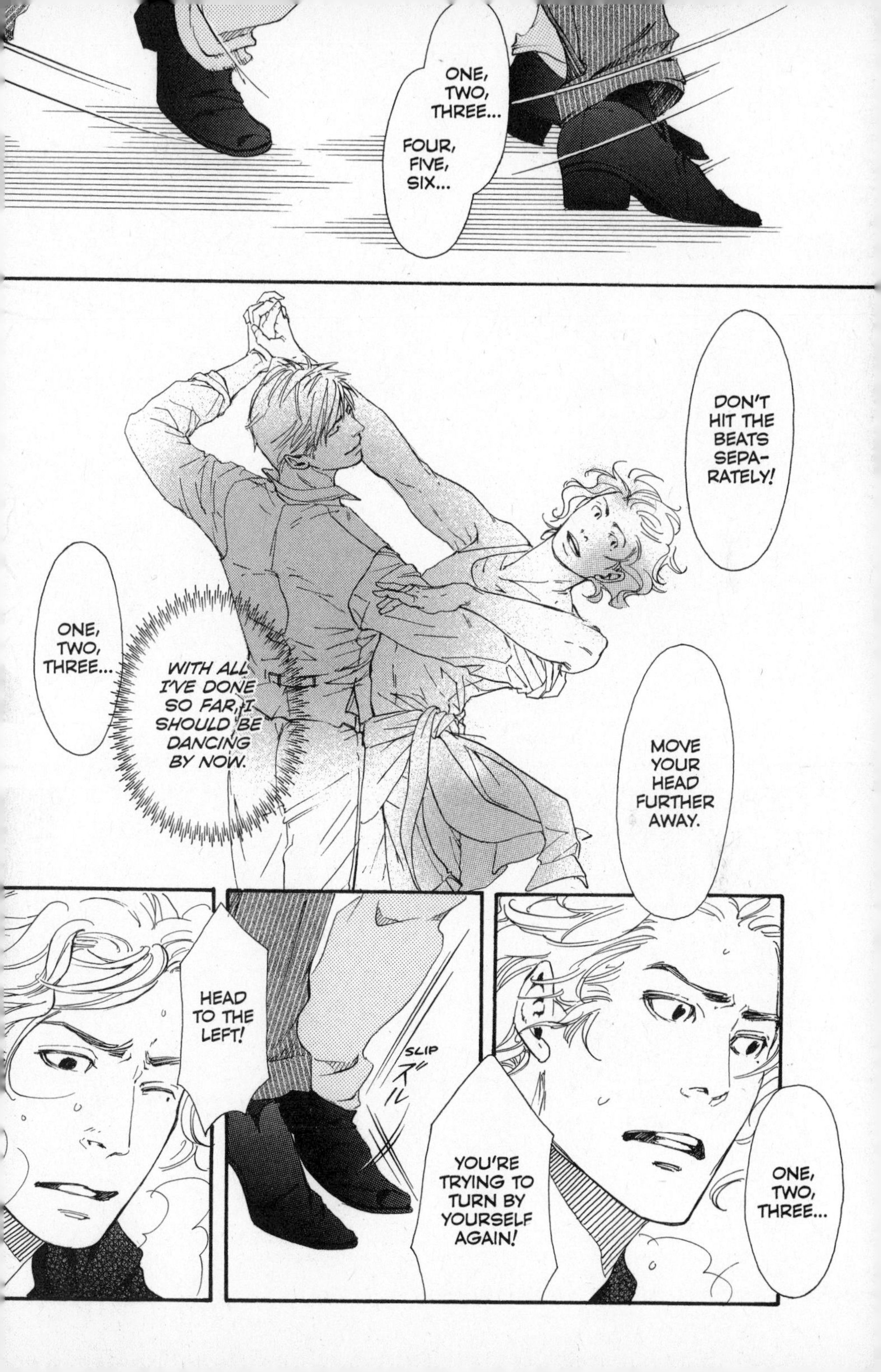
ONE, TWO, THREE... FOUR, FIVE, SIX...
DON'T HIT THE BEATS SEPA-RATELY!
MOVE YOUR HEAD FURTHER AWAY.
ONE, TWO, THREE...
WITH ALL I'VE DONE SO FAR, I SHOULD BE DANCING BY NOW.
ONE, TWO, THREE...
YOU'RE TRYING TO TURN BY YOURSELF AGAIN!
SLIP
HEAD TO THE LEFT!

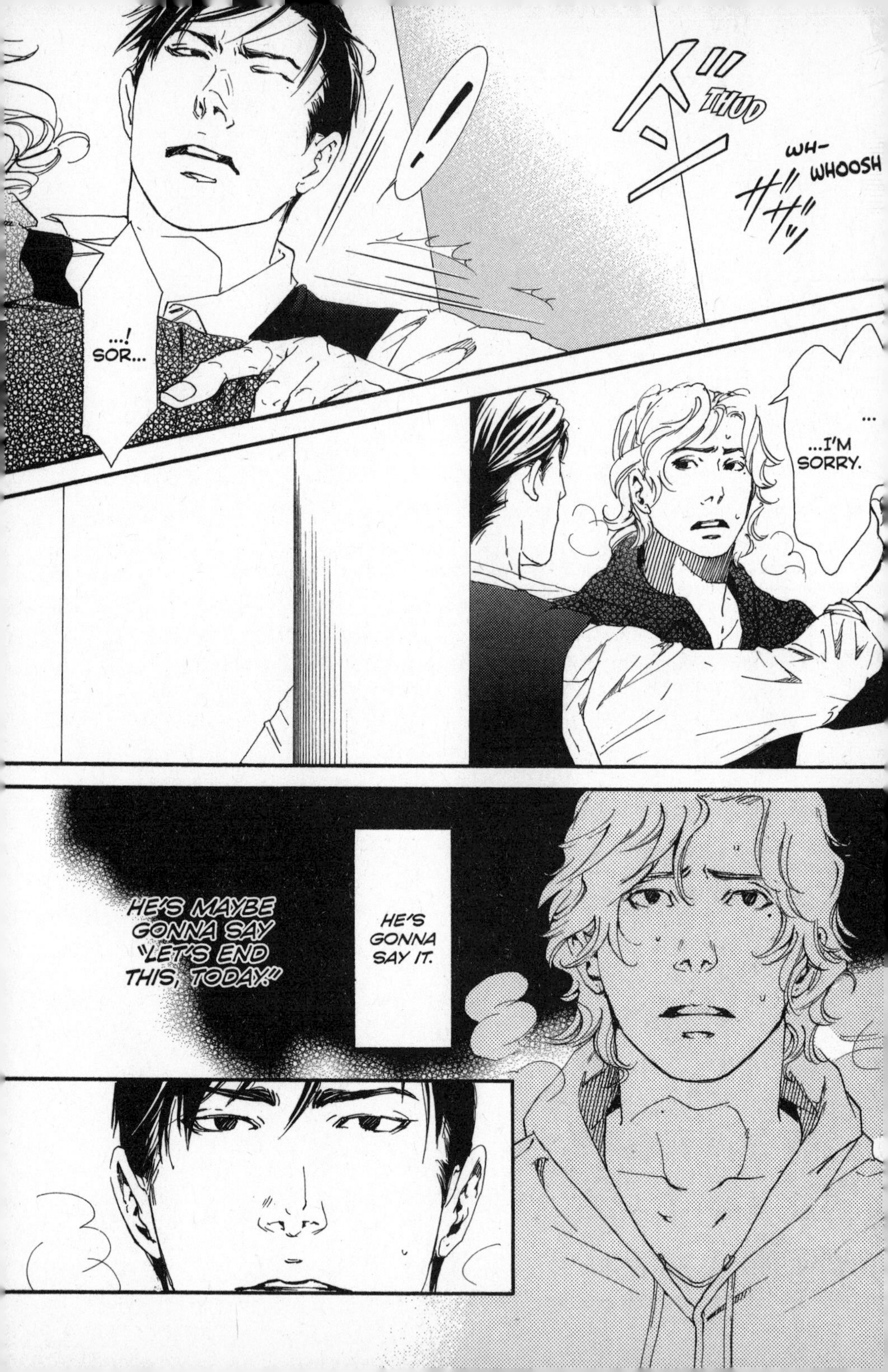
THUD
WH- WHOOSH
!
...! SOR...
...
...I'M SORRY.
HE'S GONNA SAY IT.
HE'S MAYBE GONNA SAY "LET'S END THIS, TODAY."

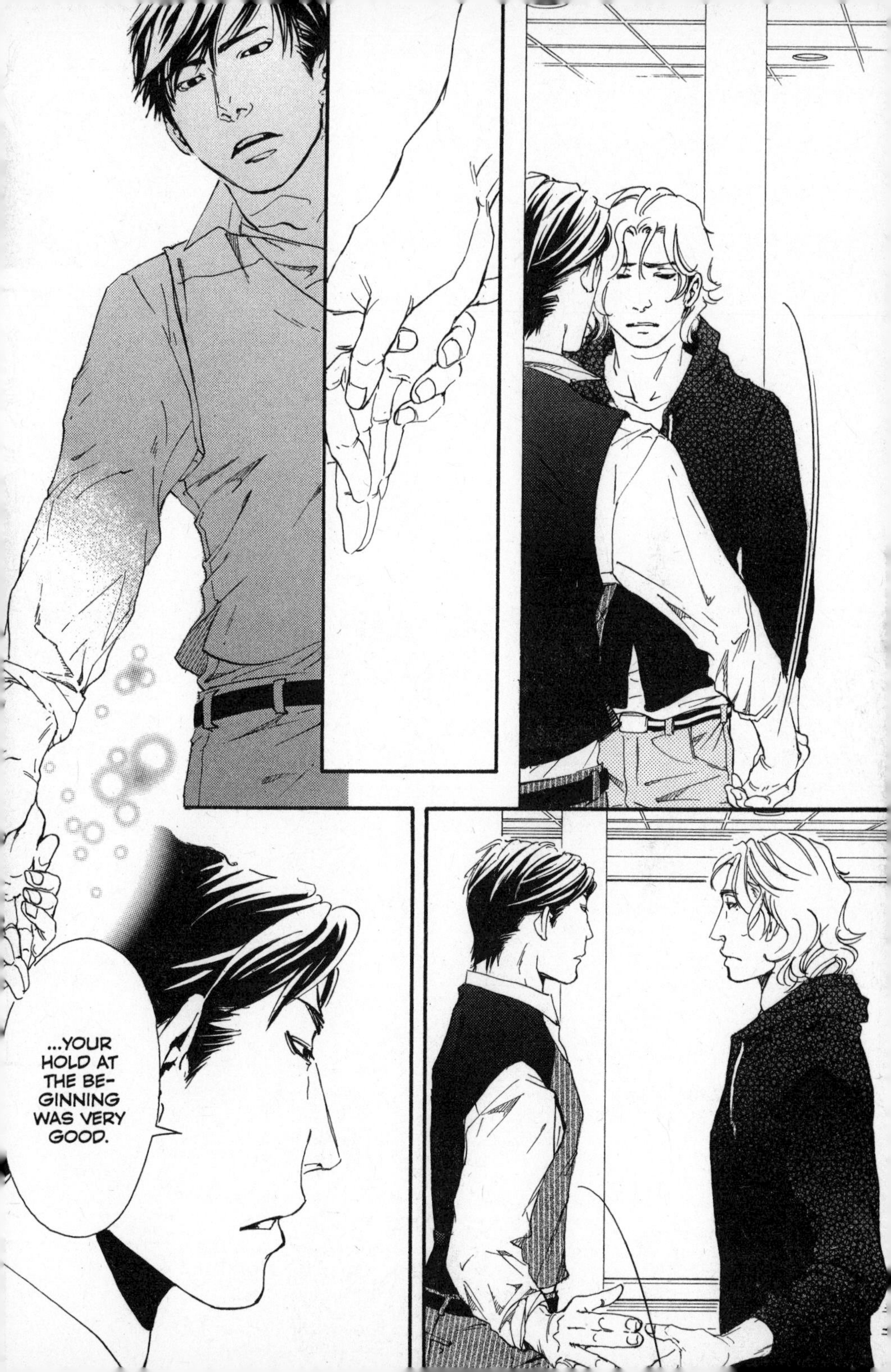
...YOUR HOLD AT THE BE- GINNING WAS VERY GOOD.

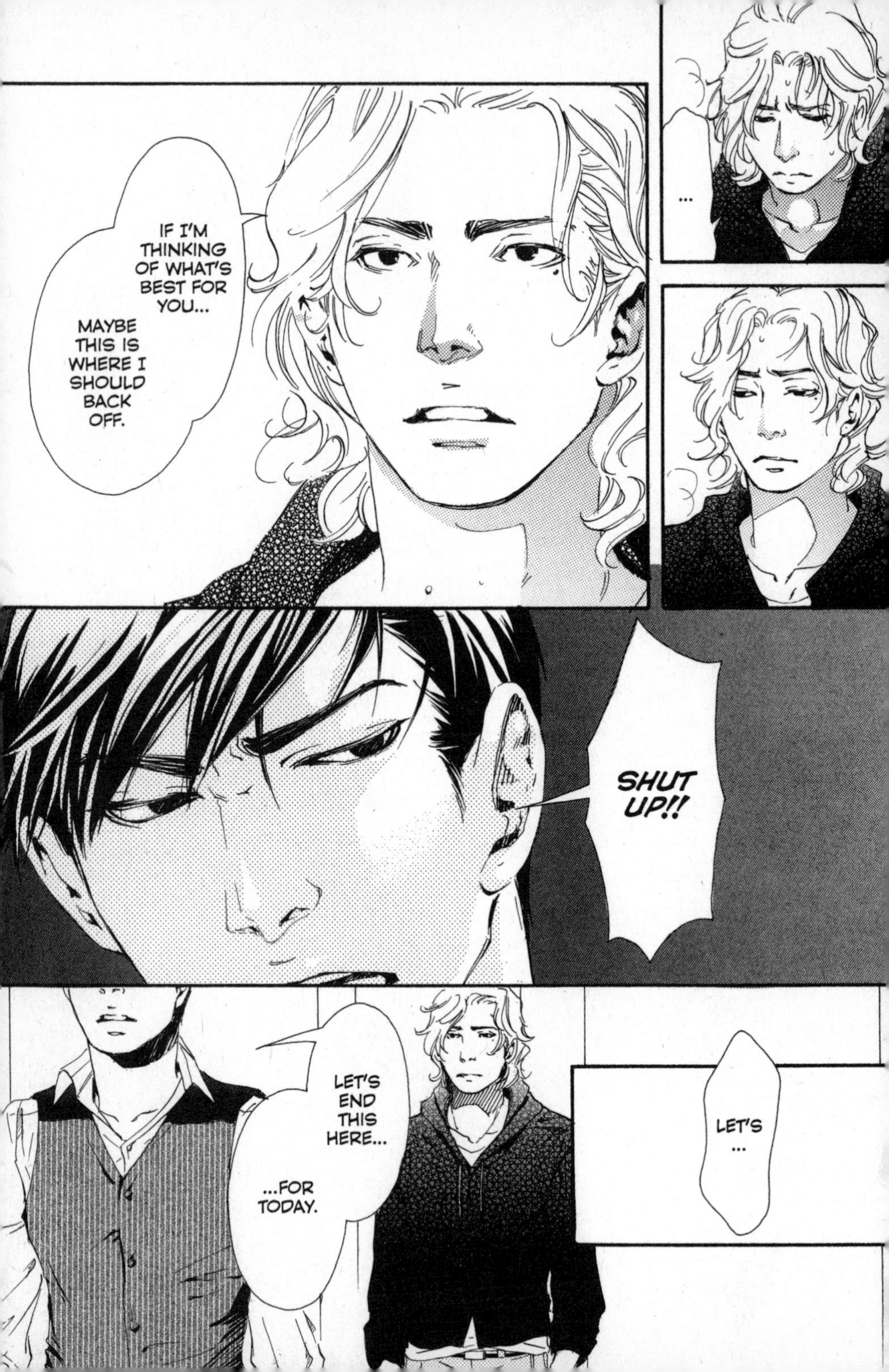
...
IF I'M THINKING OF WHAT'S BEST FOR YOU...
MAYBE THIS IS WHERE I SHOULD BACK OFF.
SHUT UP!!
LET'S ...
LET'S END THIS HERE...
...FOR TODAY.

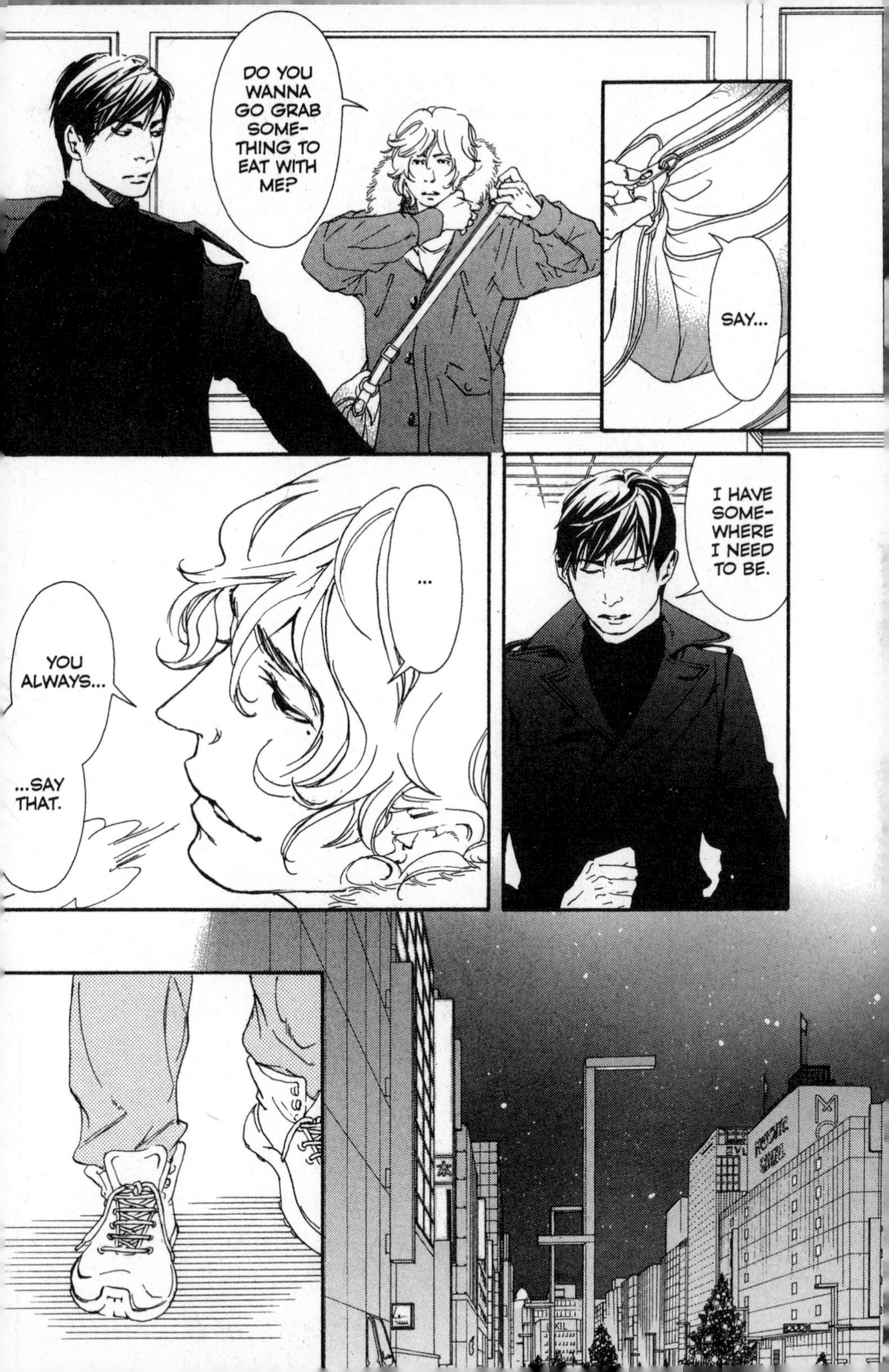
SAY...
DO YOU WANNA GO GRAB SOME-THING TO EAT WITH ME?
I HAVE SOME-WHERE I NEED TO BE.
...
YOU ALWAYS...
...SAY THAT.

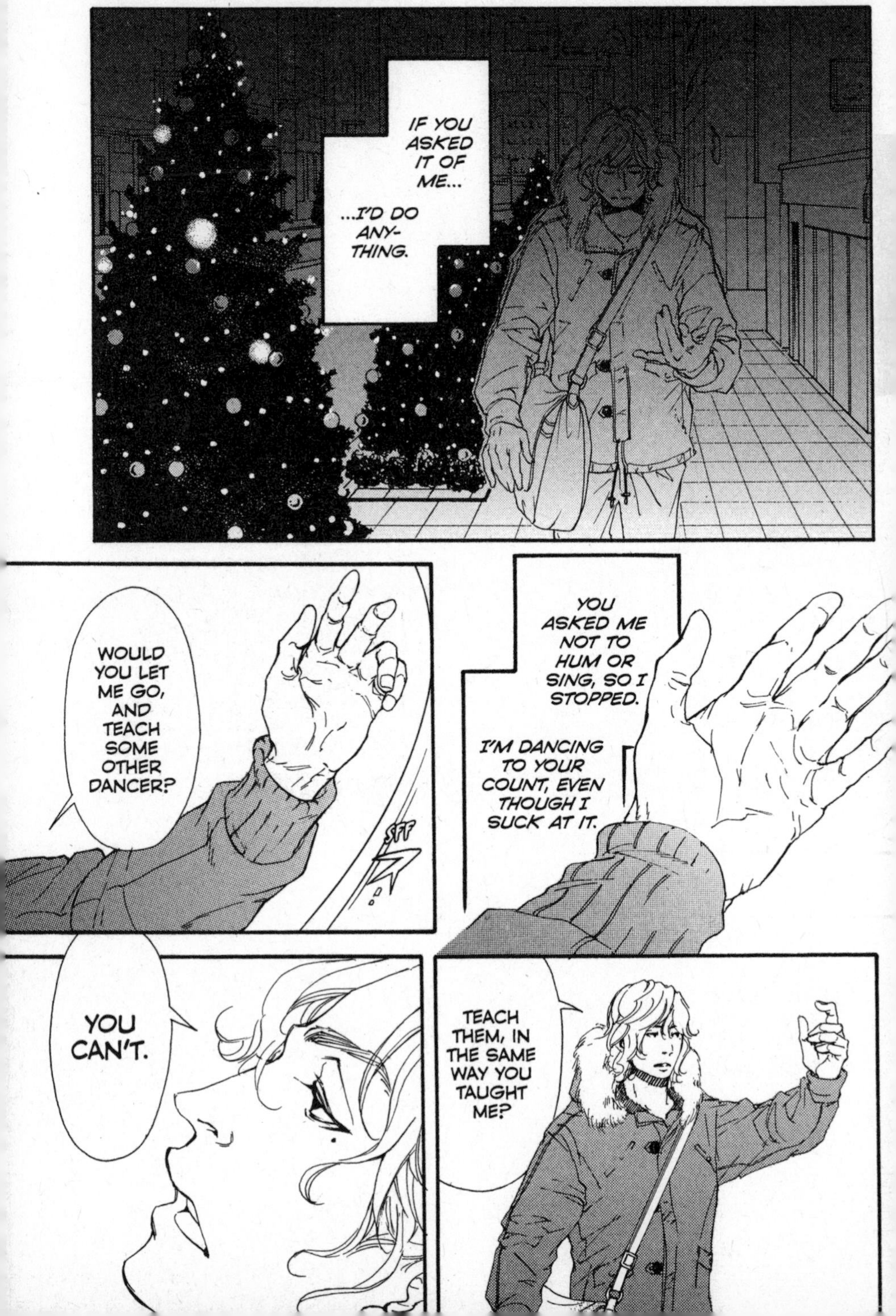
IF YOU ASKED IT OF ME...
...I'D DO ANY-THING.
YOU ASKED ME NOT TO HUM OR SING, SO I STOPPED.
I'M DANCING TO YOUR COUNT, EVEN THOUGH I SUCK AT IT.
WOULD YOU LET ME GO, AND TEACH SOME OTHER DANCER?
SFF
TEACH THEM, IN THE SAME WAY YOU TAUGHT ME?
YOU CAN'T.

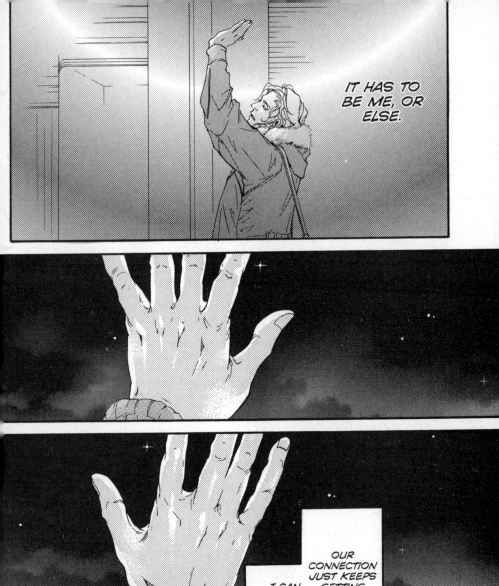

IT HAS TO BE ME, OR ELSE.

OUR CONNECTION JUST KEEPS GETTING MORE INTIMATE.

I CAN FEEL SUZUKI-SENSEI'S ANXIETY AND IMPATIENCE FROM HERE.

PAIN-FULLY SO.

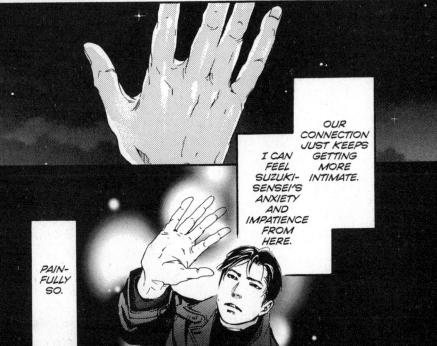

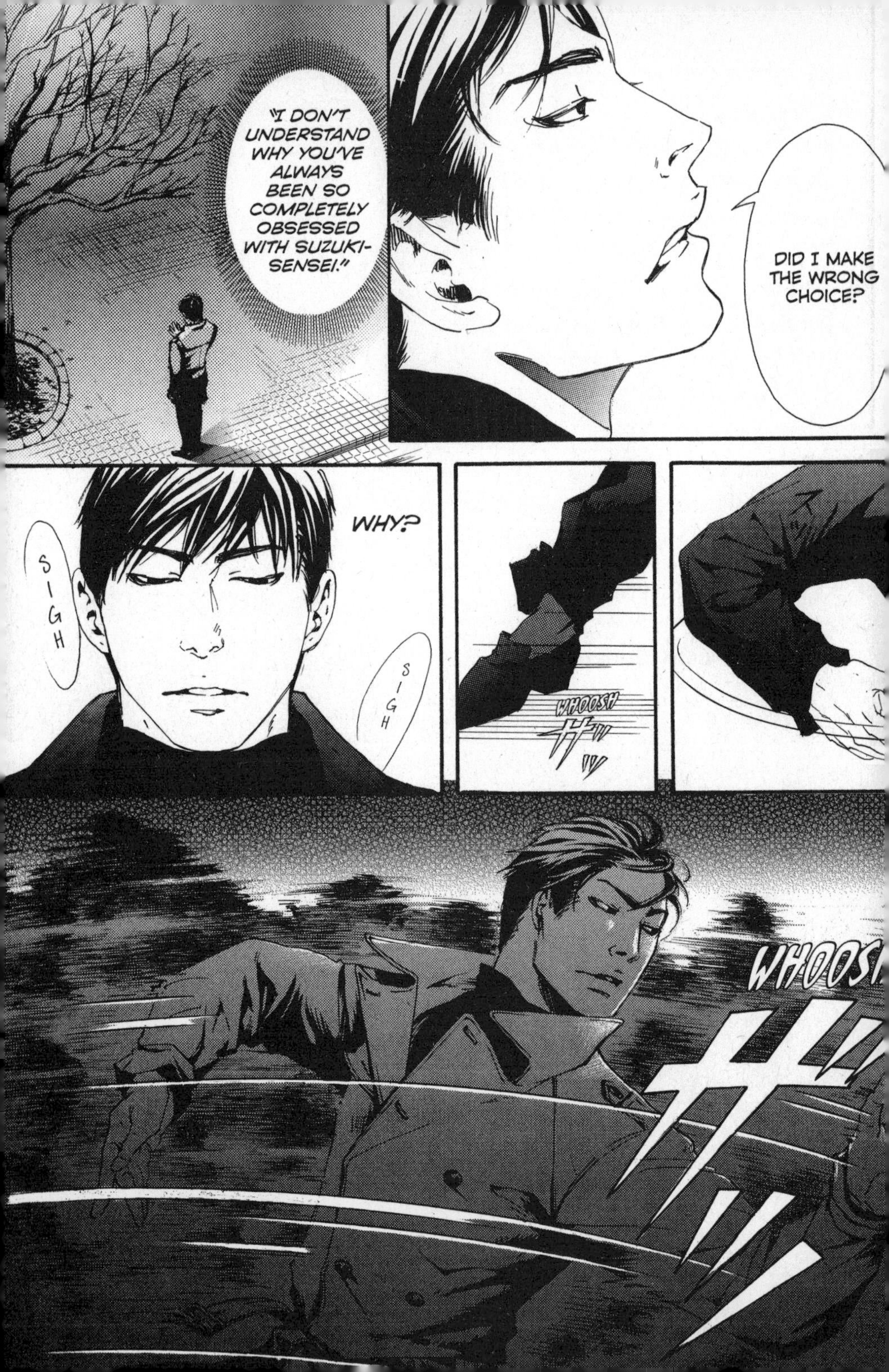
DID I MAKE THE WRONG CHOICE?
"I DON'T UNDERSTAND WHY YOU'VE ALWAYS BEEN SO COMPLETELY OBSESSED WITH SUZUKI-SENSEI."
WHOOSH
ザッ
WHY?
SIGH
SIGH
WHOOS
ザッ

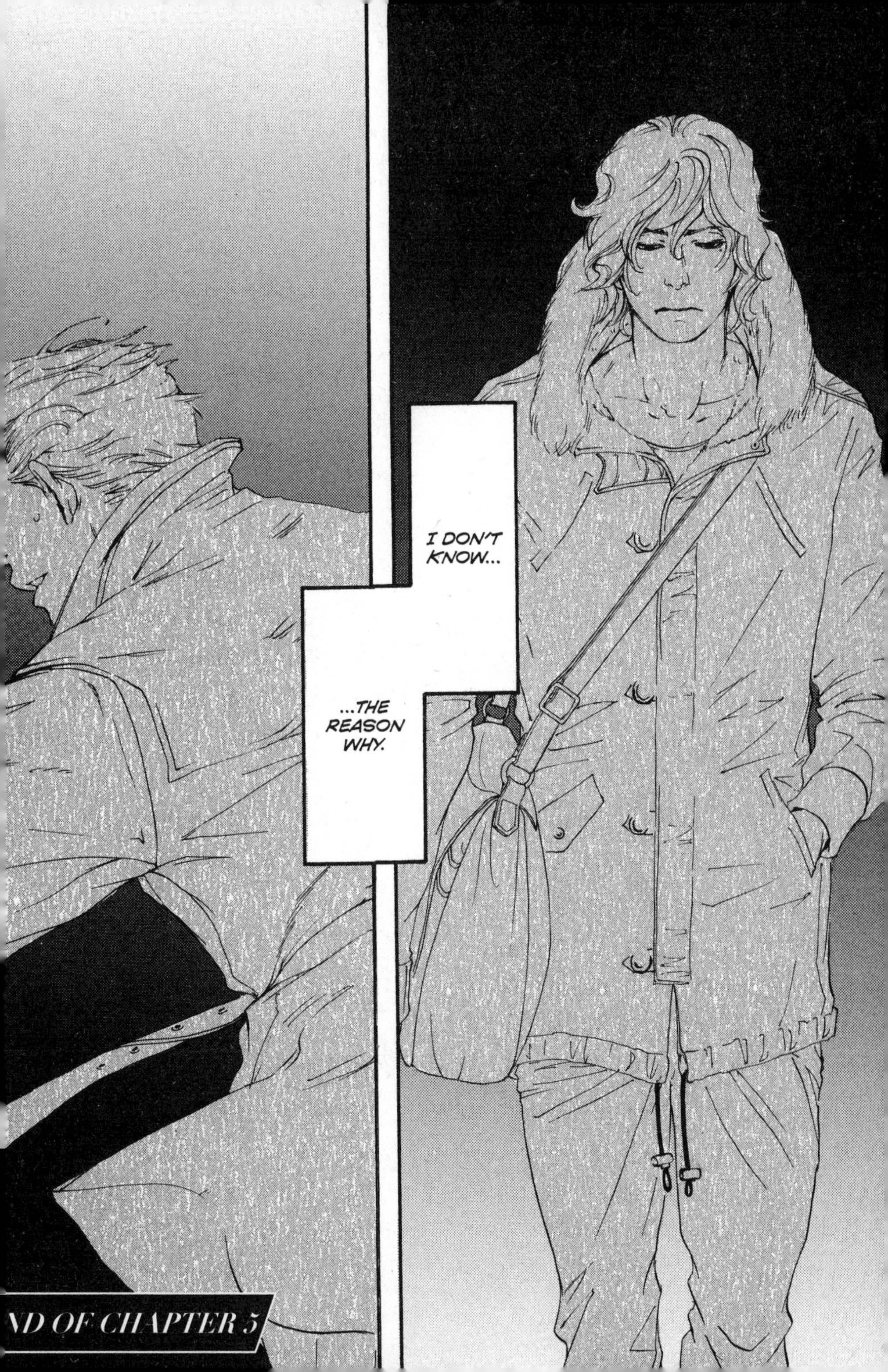
I DON'T KNOW...
...THE REASON WHY.
ND OF CHAPTER 5

SPECIAL CHAPTER

SAMBA DE MEN'S LOVE

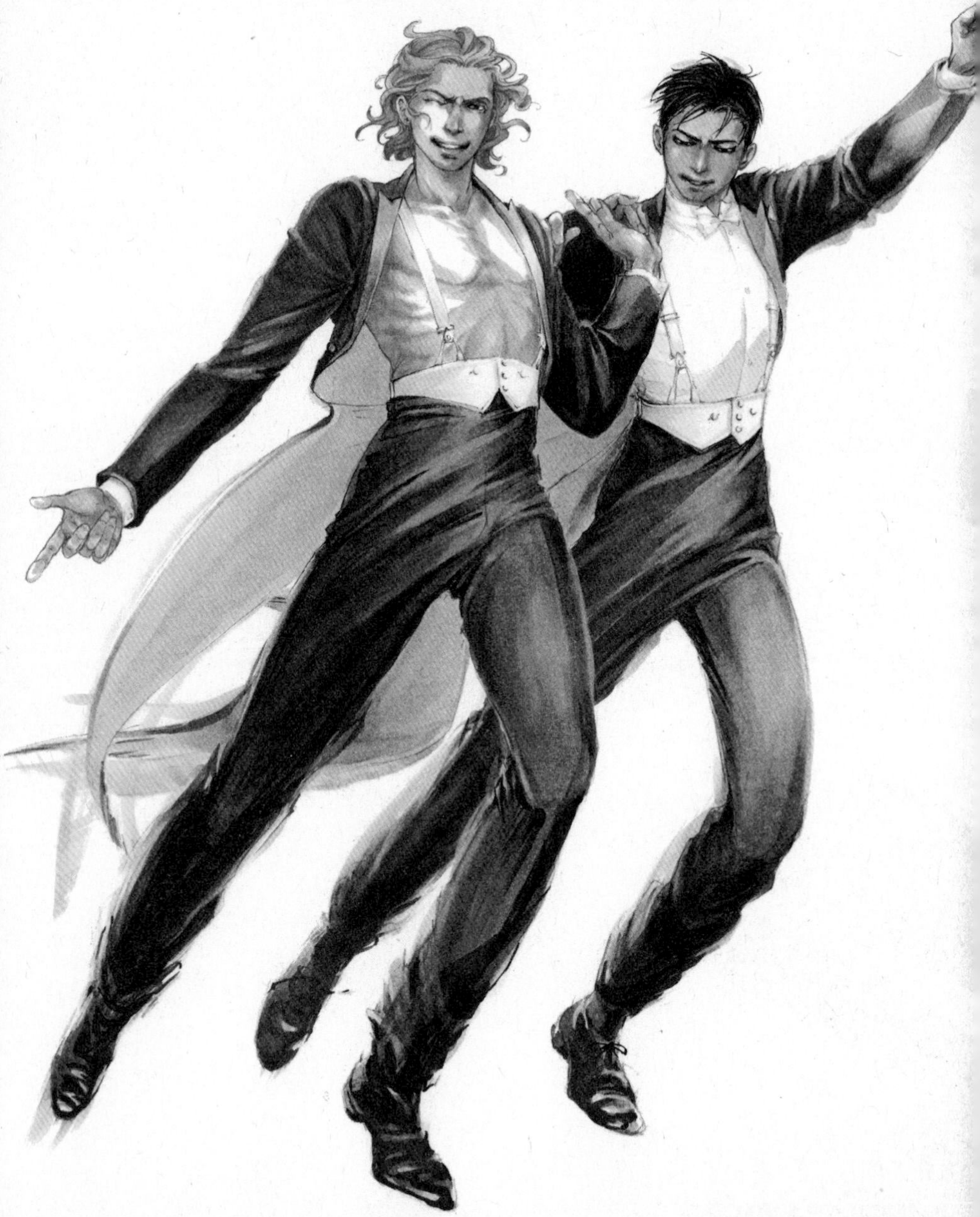

The is the first story I wrote after transferring to *Young Magazine the 3rd*.

The story starts with Mukai-kun, the new recruit in the editorial department who was introduced in Chapter 5. Here he has matured and now works as a writer.

I tried to write it so that even people who'd never read *10 Dance* before could get drawn into the story.

The story, which focuses on our two Shinyas, is set before the international championships in Chapter 7.

I hope you enjoy it.

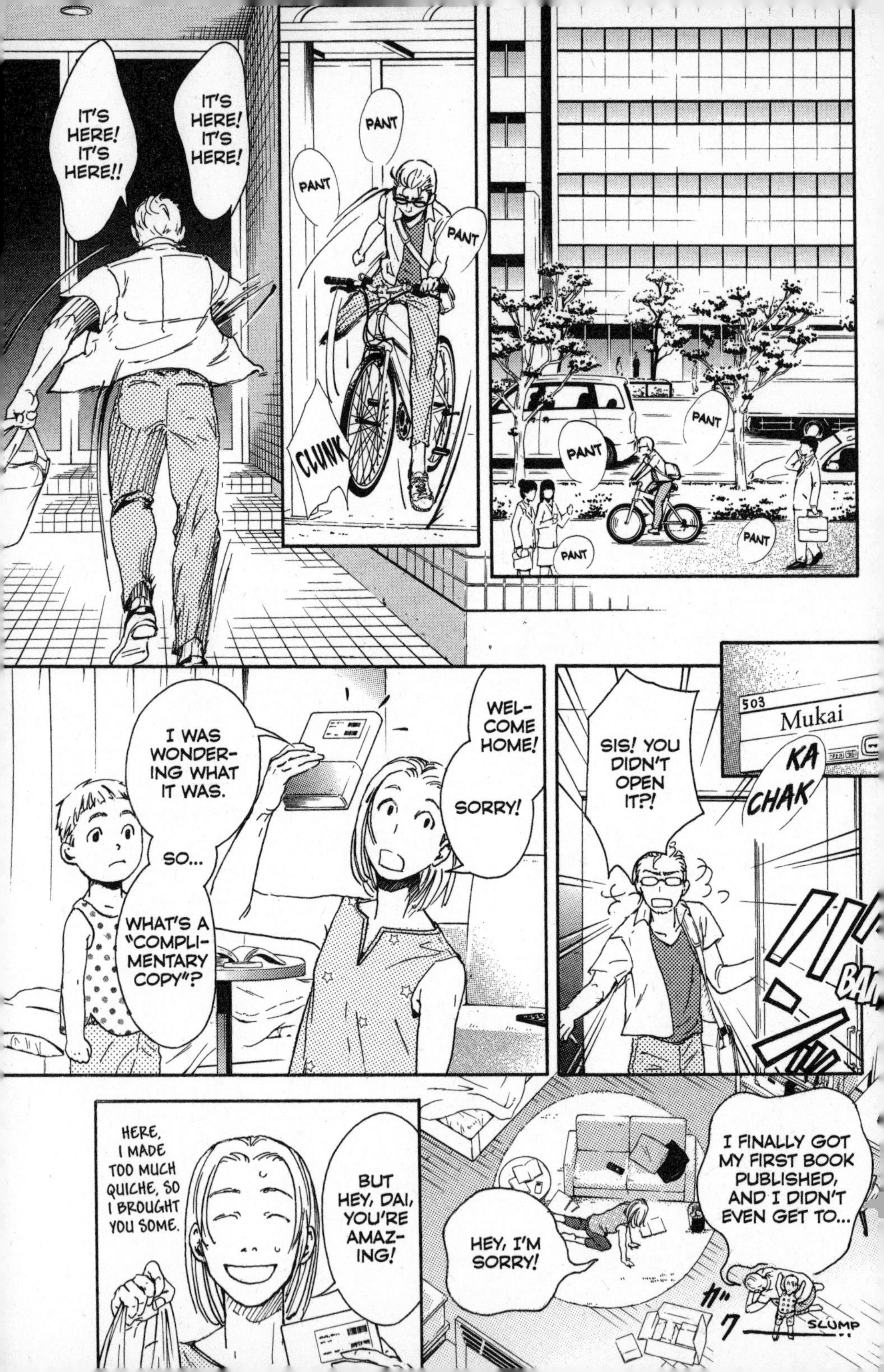
PANT
PANT
PANT
PANT
PANT
PANT
PANT
CLUNK
IT'S HERE! IT'S HERE!
IT'S HERE! IT'S HERE!!
503
Mukai
KA CHAK
SIS! YOU DIDN'T OPEN IT?!
WEL-COME HOME!
SORRY!
I WAS WONDER-ING WHAT IT WAS.
SO...
WHAT'S A "COMPLI-MENTARY COPY"?
I FINALLY GOT MY FIRST BOOK PUBLISHED, AND I DIDN'T EVEN GET TO...
HEY, I'M SORRY!
SLUMP
BUT HEY, DAI, YOU'RE AMAZ-ING!
HERE, I MADE TOO MUCH QUICHE, SO I BROUGHT YOU SOME.

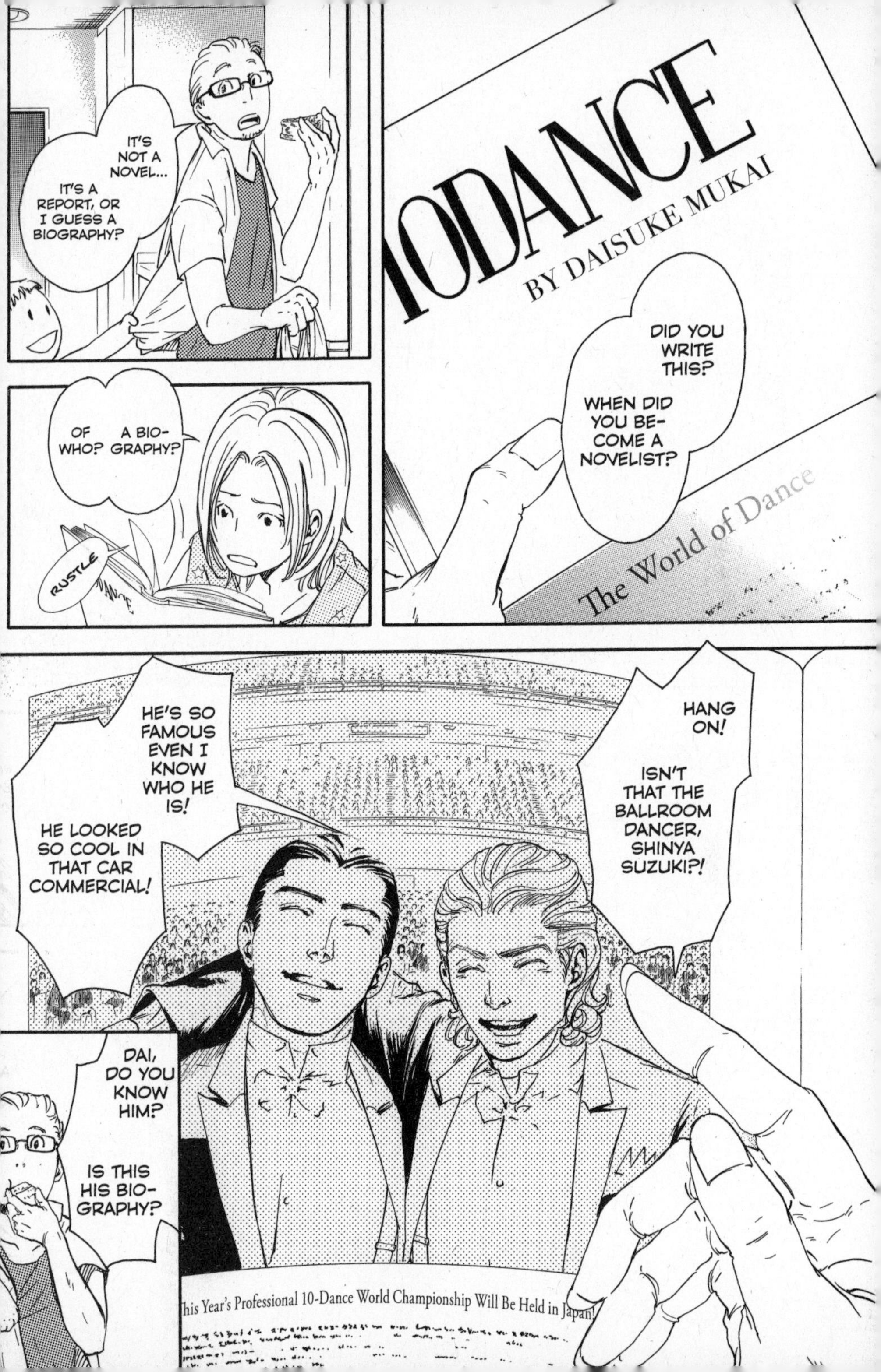
10DANCE
BY DAISUKE MUKAI
DID YOU WRITE THIS?
WHEN DID YOU BECOME A NOVELIST?
The World of Dance
IT'S NOT A NOVEL...
IT'S A REPORT, OR I GUESS A BIOGRAPHY?
A BIOGRAPHY?
OF WHO?
RUSTLE
DANCE
HANG ON!
ISN'T THAT THE BALLROOM DANCER, SHINYA SUZUKI?!
HE'S SO FAMOUS EVEN I KNOW WHO HE IS!
HE LOOKED SO COOL IN THAT CAR COMMERCIAL!
This Year's Professional 10-Dance World Championship Will Be Held in Japan!
DAI, DO YOU KNOW HIM?
IS THIS HIS BIOGRAPHY?

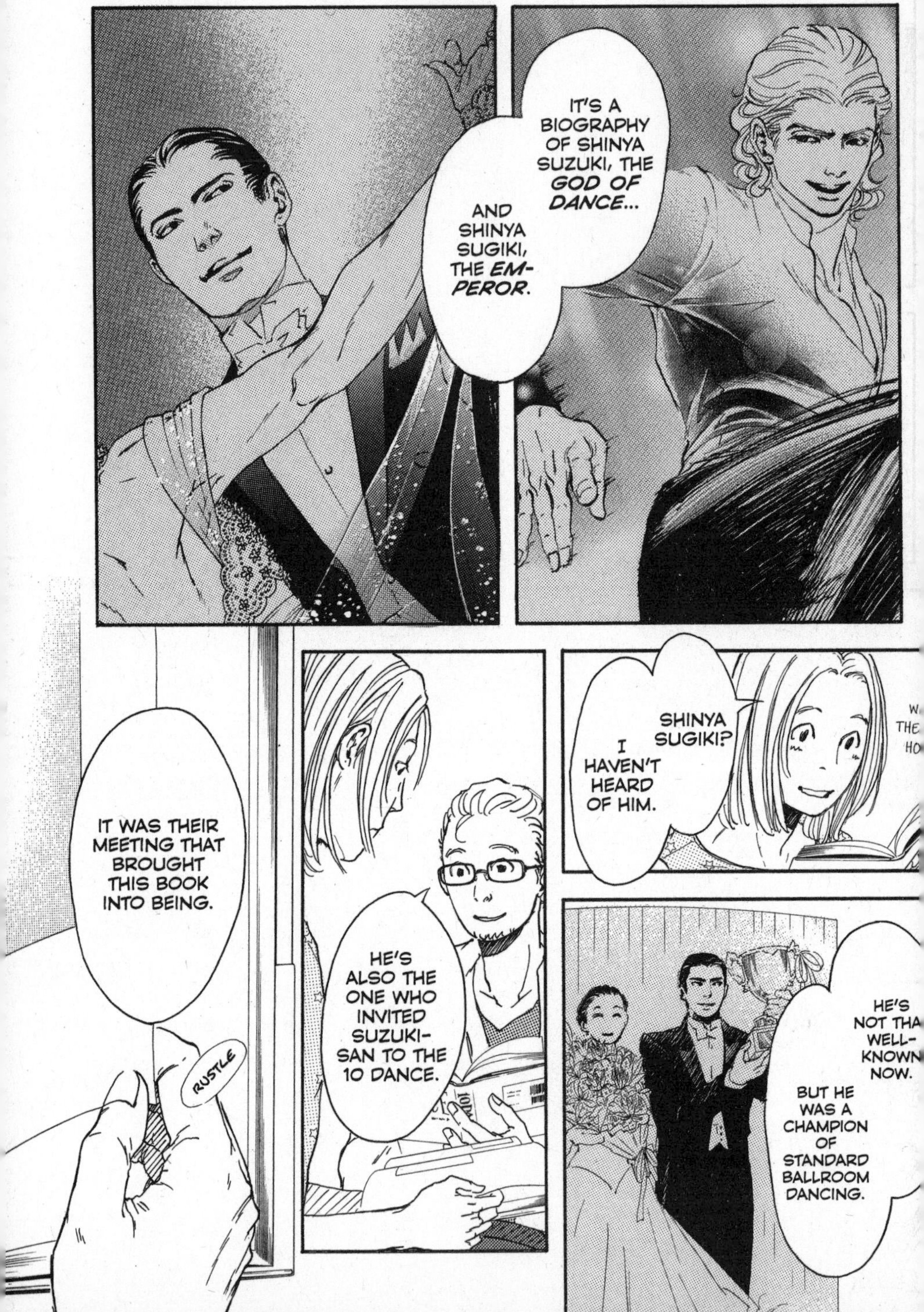
IT'S A BIOGRAPHY OF SHINYA SUZUKI, THE *GOD OF DANCE*...
AND SHINYA SUGIKI, THE *EMPEROR*.
SHINYA SUGIKI? I HAVEN'T HEARD OF HIM.
HE'S NOT THA WELL-KNOWN NOW.
BUT HE WAS A CHAMPION OF STANDARD BALLROOM DANCING.
HE'S ALSO THE ONE WHO INVITED SUZUKI-SAN TO THE 10 DANCE.
IT WAS THEIR MEETING THAT BROUGHT THIS BOOK INTO BEING.
RUSTLE

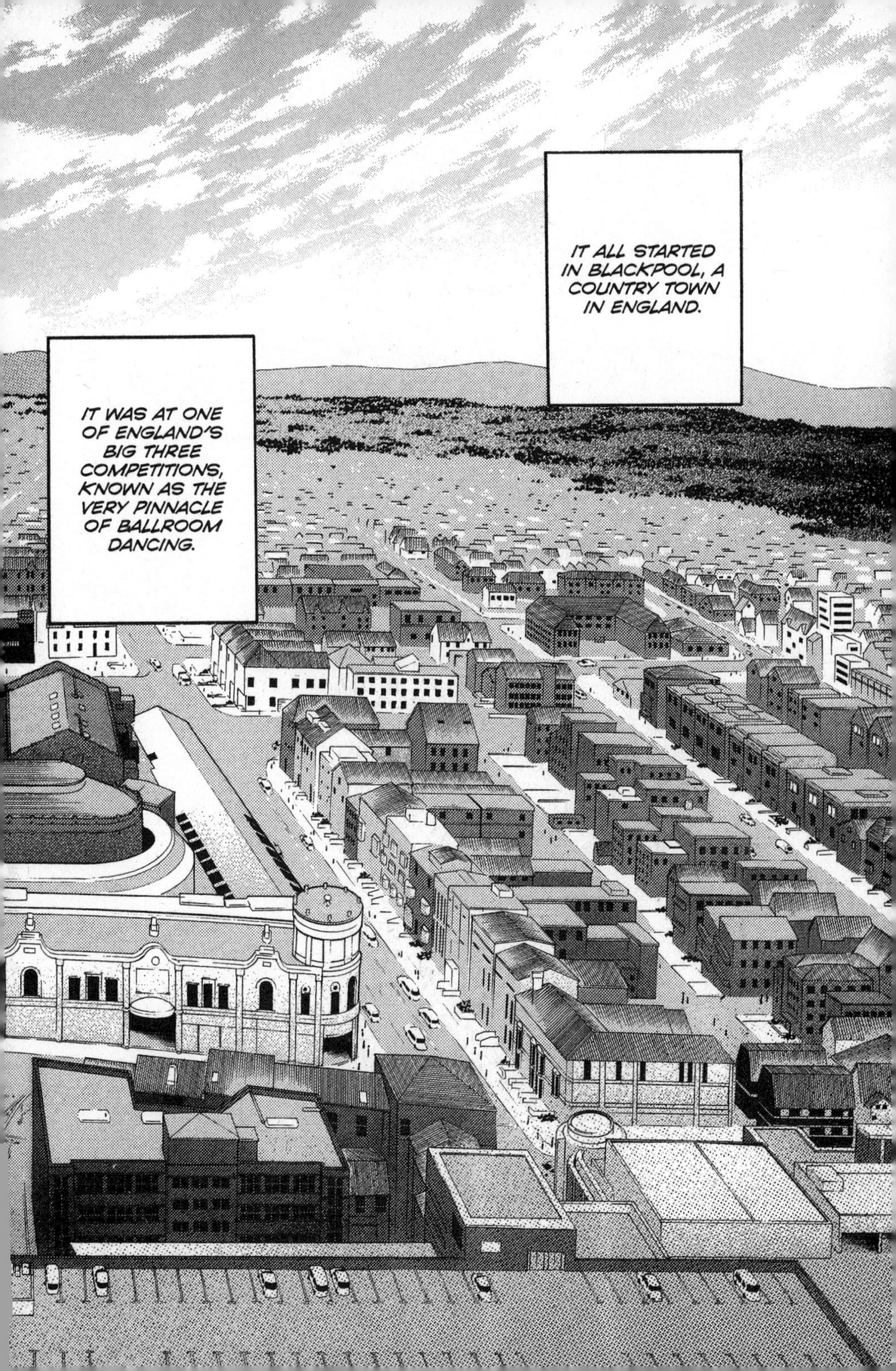
IT ALL STARTED IN BLACKPOOL, A COUNTRY TOWN IN ENGLAND.
IT WAS AT ONE OF ENGLAND'S BIG THREE COMPETITIONS, KNOWN AS THE VERY PINNACLE OF BALLROOM DANCING.

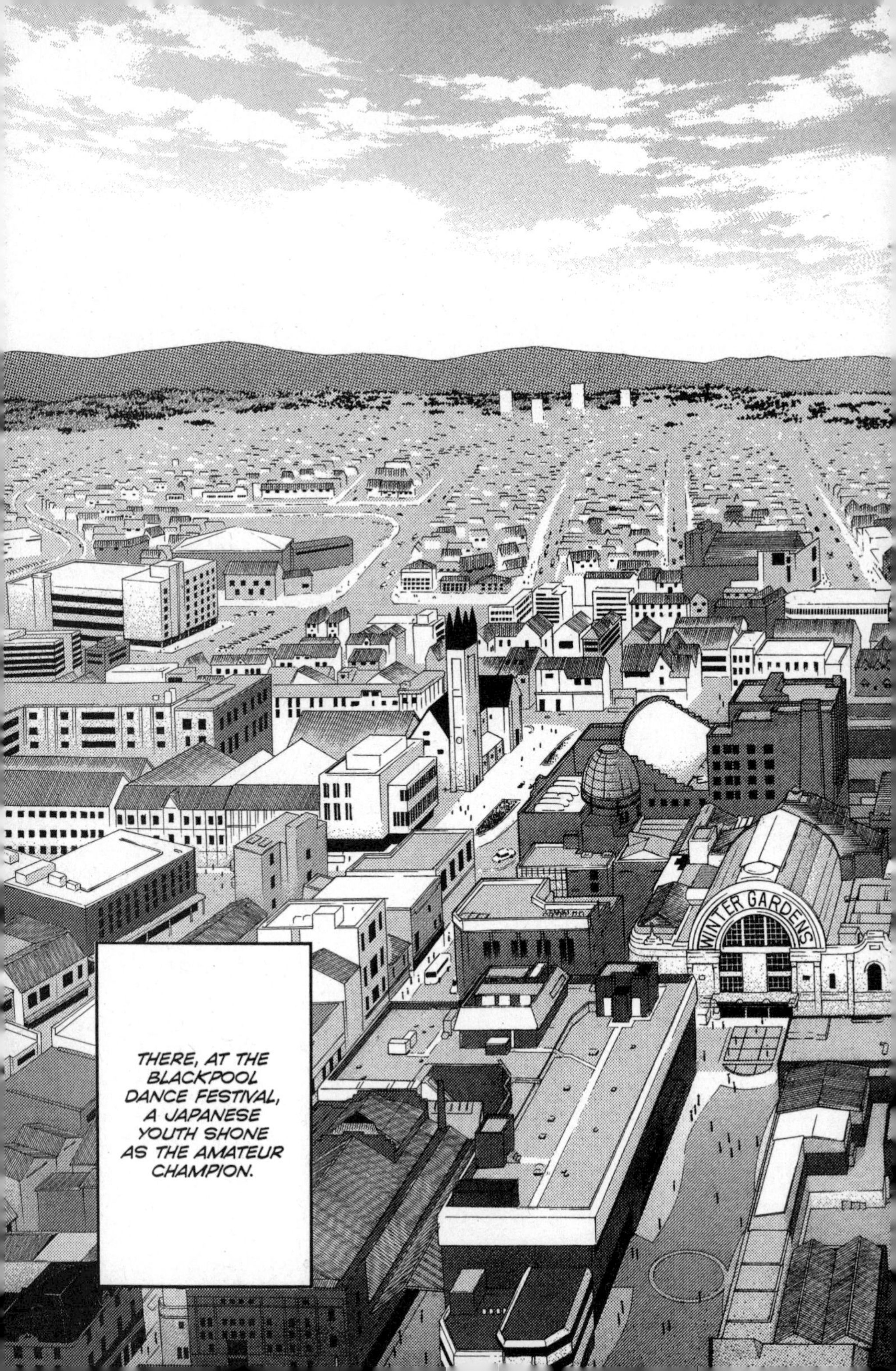
WINTER GARDENS
THERE, AT THE BLACKPOOL DANCE FESTIVAL, A JAPANESE YOUTH SHONE AS THE AMATEUR CHAMPION.

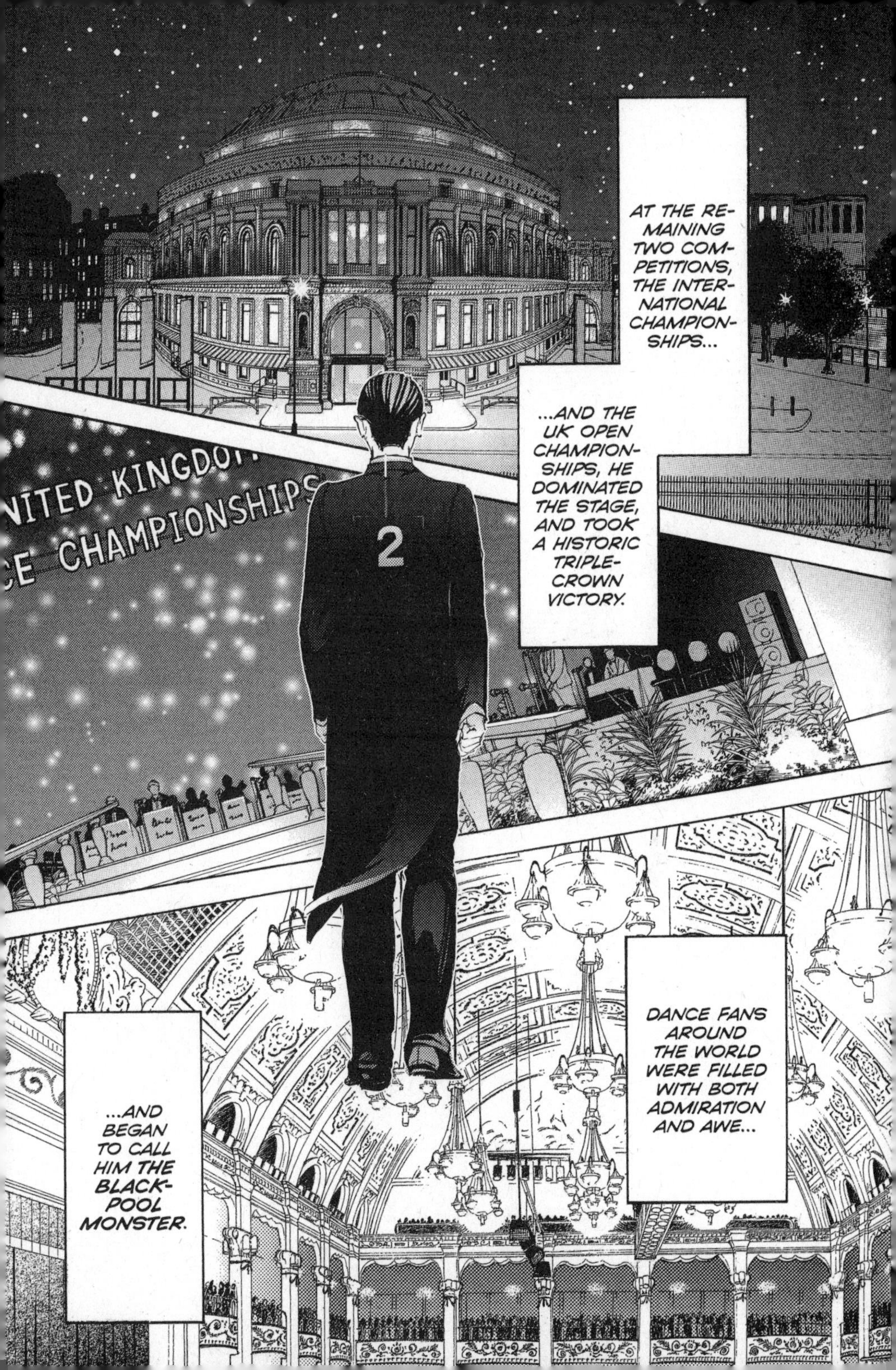
AT THE REMAINING TWO COMPETITIONS, THE INTERNATIONAL CHAMPIONSHIPS...
...AND THE UK OPEN CHAMPIONSHIPS, HE DOMINATED THE STAGE, AND TOOK A HISTORIC TRIPLE-CROWN VICTORY.
NITED KINGDO
CE CHAMPIONSHIPS
2
DANCE FANS AROUND THE WORLD WERE FILLED WITH BOTH ADMIRATION AND AWE...
...AND BEGAN TO CALL HIM THE BLACKPOOL MONSTER.

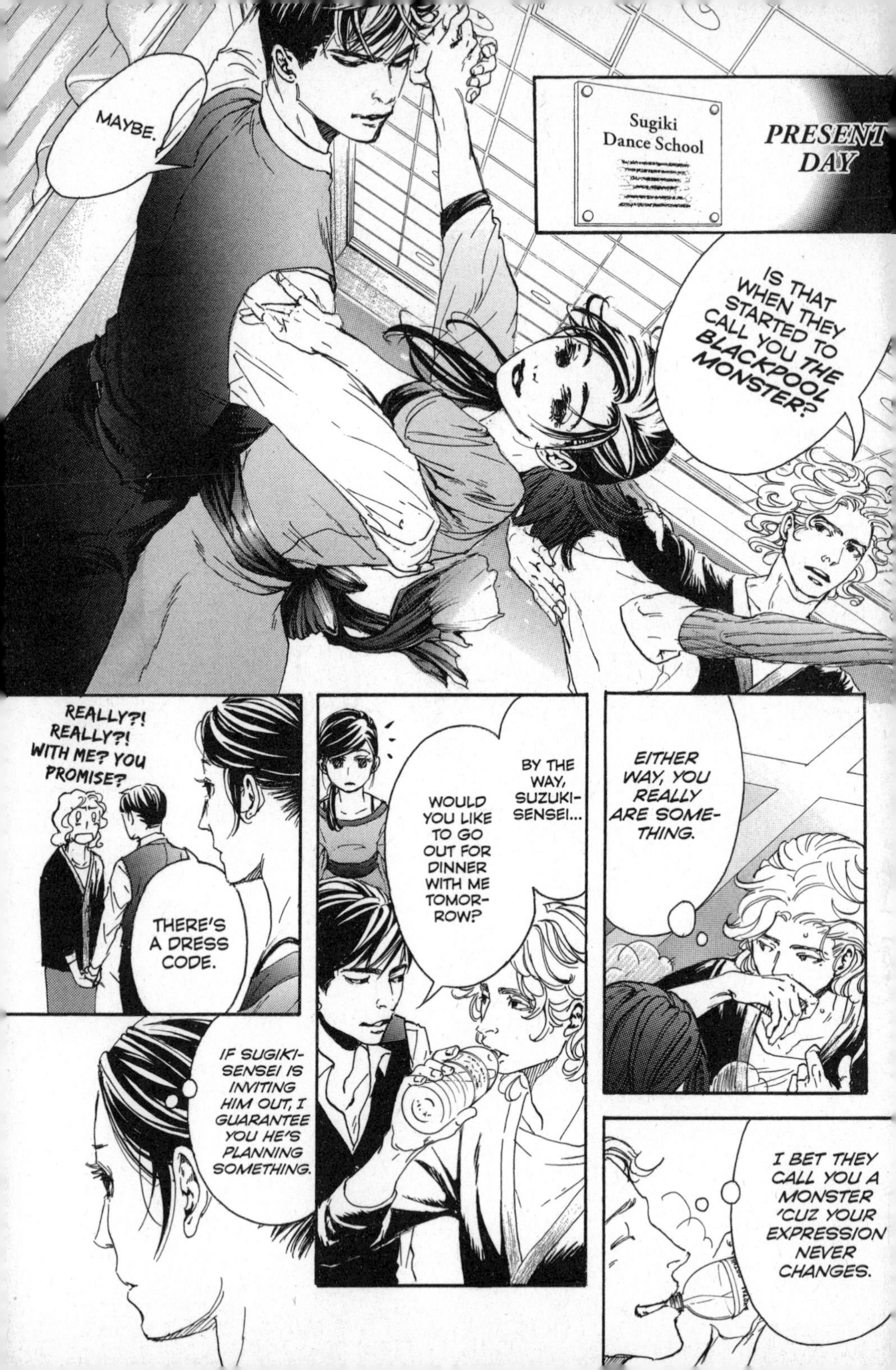

Sugiki Dance School
PRESENT DAY
IS THAT WHEN THEY STARTED TO CALL YOU THE BLACKPOOL MONSTER?
MAYBE.
EITHER WAY, YOU REALLY ARE SOME-THING.
I BET THEY CALL YOU A MONSTER 'CUZ YOUR EXPRESSION NEVER CHANGES.
BY THE WAY, SUZUKI-SENSEI...
WOULD YOU LIKE TO GO OUT FOR DINNER WITH ME TOMOR-ROW?
REALLY?! REALLY?! WITH ME? YOU PROMISE?
THERE'S A DRESS CODE.
IF SUGIKI-SENSEI IS INVITING HIM OUT, I GUARANTEE YOU HE'S PLANNING SOMETHING.

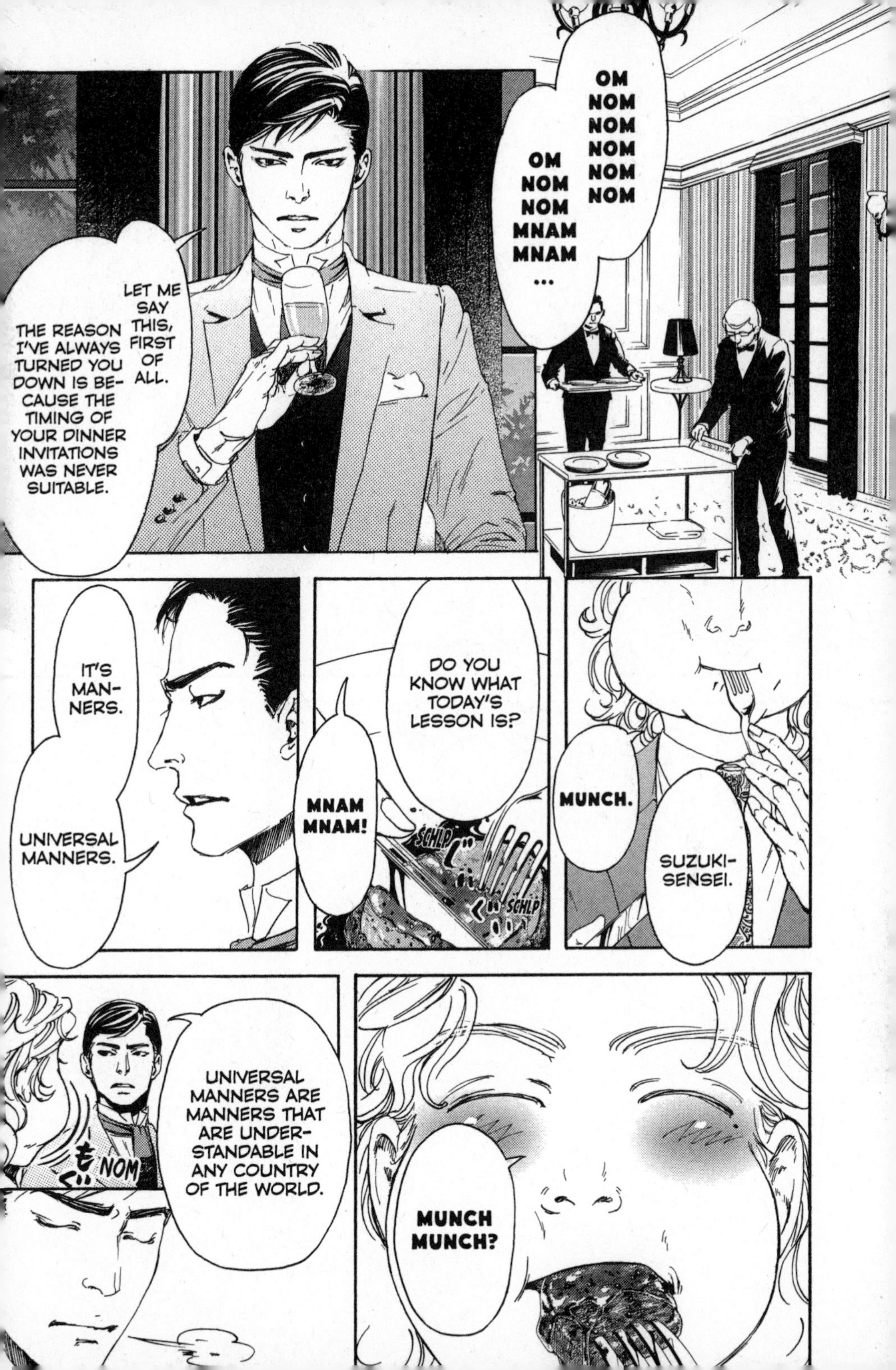
OM NOM NOM NOM NOM NOM
OM NOM NOM MNAM MNAM ...
LET ME SAY THIS, FIRST OF ALL.
THE REASON I'VE ALWAYS TURNED YOU DOWN IS BE-CAUSE THE TIMING OF YOUR DINNER INVITATIONS WAS NEVER SUITABLE.
MUNCH.
SUZUKI-SENSEI.
DO YOU KNOW WHAT TODAY'S LESSON IS?
MNAM MNAM!
SCHLP
SCHLP
IT'S MAN-NERS.
UNIVERSAL MANNERS.
MUNCH MUNCH?
UNIVERSAL MANNERS ARE MANNERS THAT ARE UNDER-STANDABLE IN ANY COUNTRY OF THE WORLD.
NOM

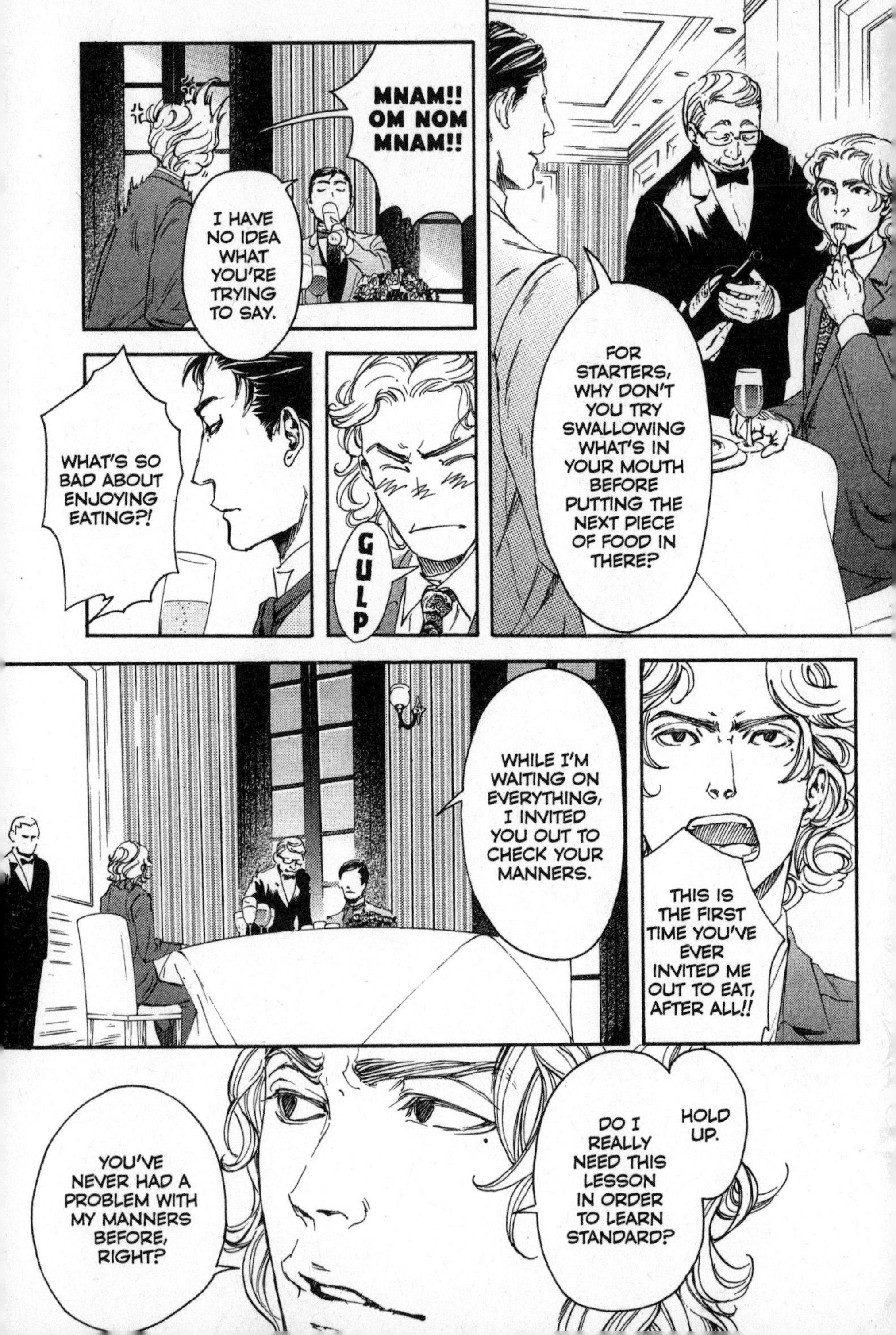
FOR STARTERS, WHY DON'T YOU TRY SWALLOWING WHAT'S IN YOUR MOUTH BEFORE PUTTING THE NEXT PIECE OF FOOD IN THERE?
MNAM!! OM NOM MNAM!!
I HAVE NO IDEA WHAT YOU'RE TRYING TO SAY.
GULP
WHAT'S SO BAD ABOUT ENJOYING EATING?!
THIS IS THE FIRST TIME YOU'VE EVER INVITED ME OUT TO EAT, AFTER ALL!!
WHILE I'M WAITING ON EVERYTHING, I INVITED YOU OUT TO CHECK YOUR MANNERS.
HOLD UP.
DO I REALLY NEED THIS LESSON IN ORDER TO LEARN STANDARD?
YOU'VE NEVER HAD A PROBLEM WITH MY MANNERS BEFORE, RIGHT?

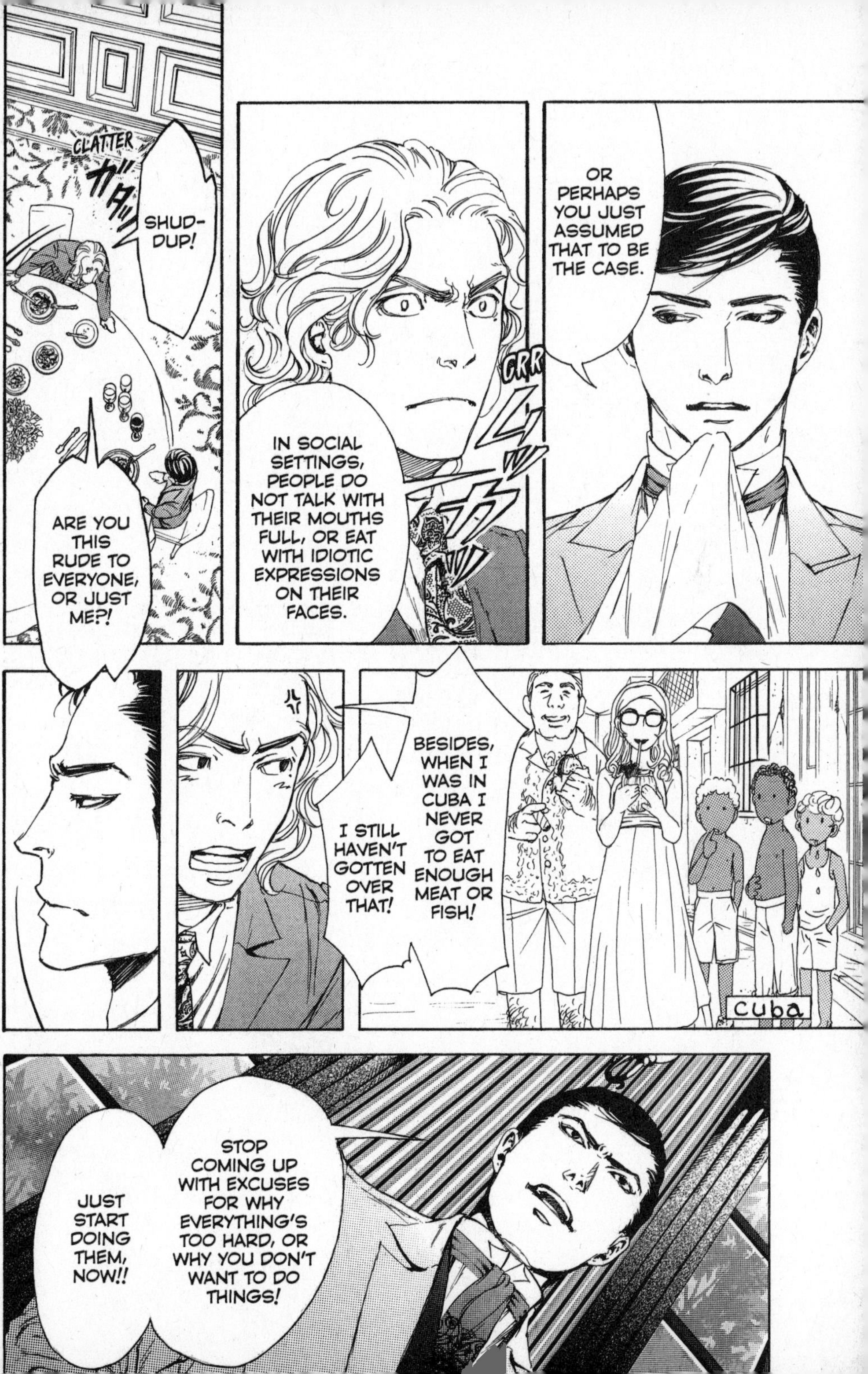
OR PERHAPS YOU JUST ASSUMED THAT TO BE THE CASE.
CRR
IN SOCIAL SETTINGS, PEOPLE DO NOT TALK WITH THEIR MOUTHS FULL, OR EAT WITH IDIOTIC EXPRESSIONS ON THEIR FACES.
CLATTER
SHUD-DUP!
ARE YOU THIS RUDE TO EVERYONE, OR JUST ME?!
BESIDES, WHEN I WAS IN CUBA I NEVER GOT TO EAT ENOUGH MEAT OR FISH!
cuba
I STILL HAVEN'T GOTTEN OVER THAT!
STOP COMING UP WITH EXCUSES FOR WHY EVERYTHING'S TOO HARD, OR WHY YOU DON'T WANT TO DO THINGS!
JUST START DOING THEM, NOW!!

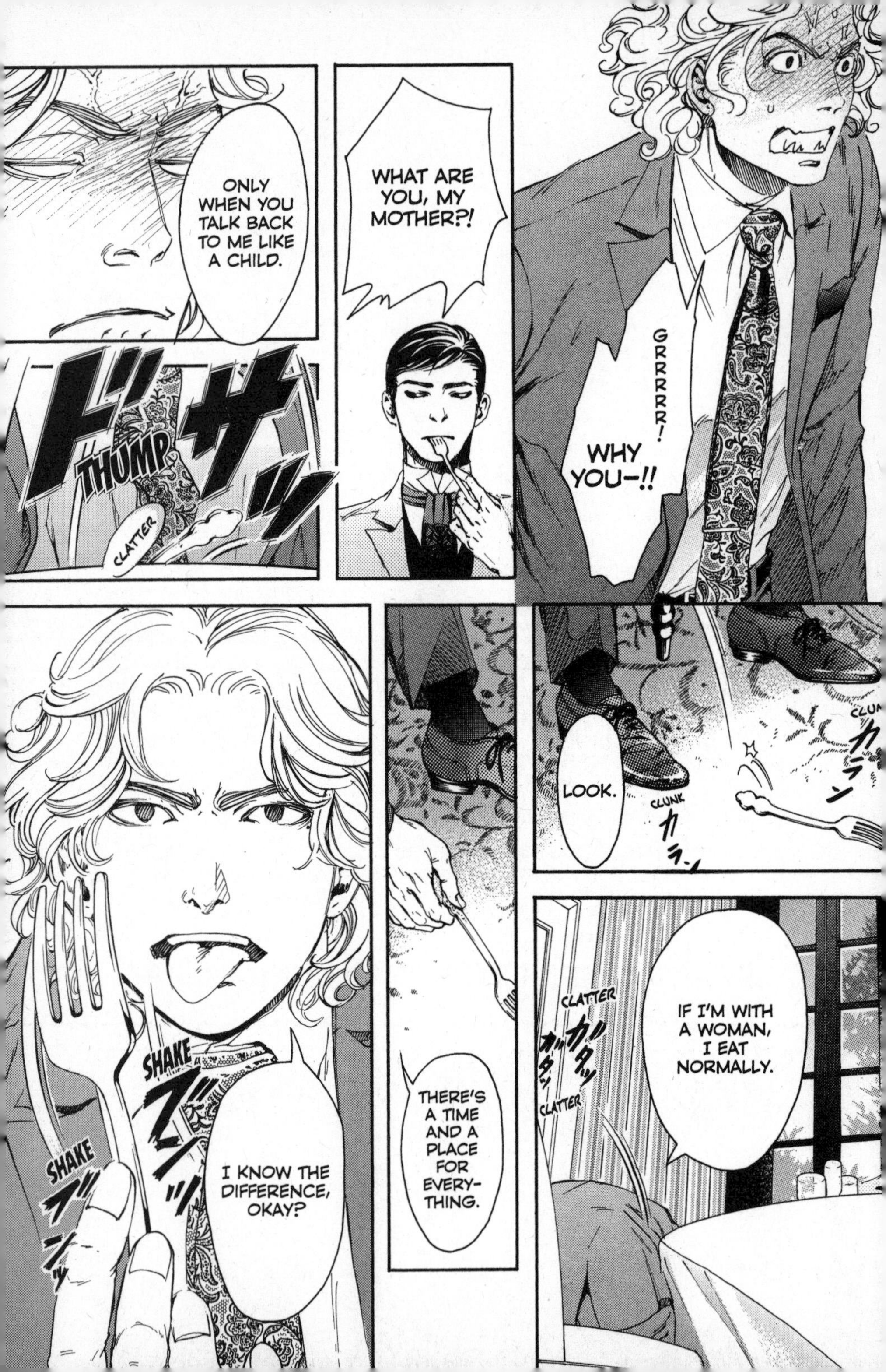
GRRRRR!
WHY YOU-!!
WHAT ARE YOU, MY MOTHER?!
ONLY WHEN YOU TALK BACK TO ME LIKE A CHILD.
THUMP
CLATTER
CLUNK
LOOK.
CLUNK
CLATTER
CLATTER
IF I'M WITH A WOMAN, I EAT NORMALLY.
THERE'S A TIME AND A PLACE FOR EVERY-THING.
SHAKE
SHAKE
I KNOW THE DIFFERENCE, OKAY?

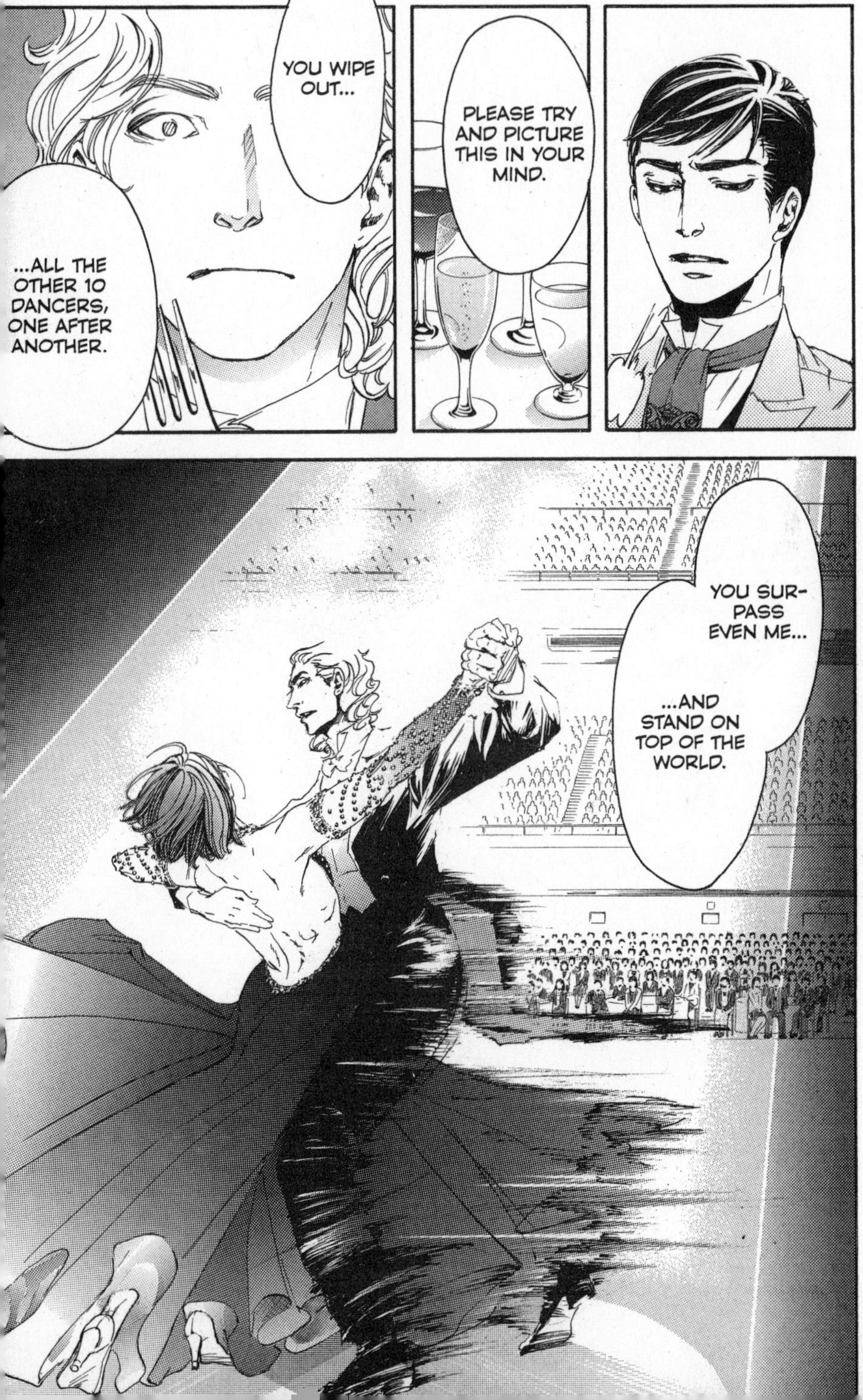
PLEASE TRY AND PICTURE THIS IN YOUR MIND.
YOU WIPE OUT...
...ALL THE OTHER 10 DANCERS, ONE AFTER ANOTHER.
YOU SUR-PASS EVEN ME...
...AND STAND ON TOP OF THE WORLD.

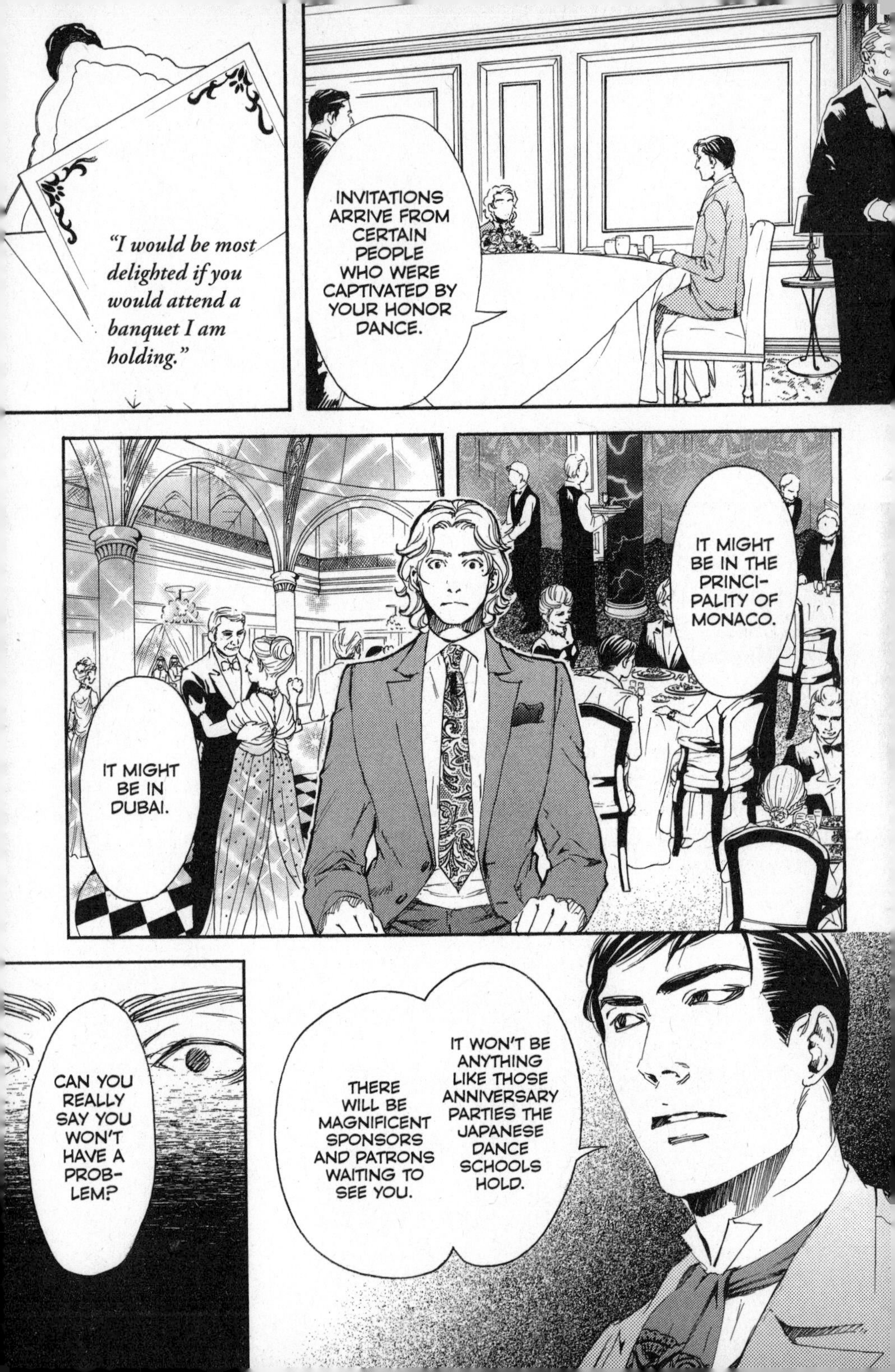
INVITATIONS ARRIVE FROM CERTAIN PEOPLE WHO WERE CAPTIVATED BY YOUR HONOR DANCE.
"I would be most delighted if you would attend a banquet I am holding."
IT MIGHT BE IN THE PRINCIPALITY OF MONACO.
IT MIGHT BE IN DUBAI.
IT WON'T BE ANYTHING LIKE THOSE ANNIVERSARY PARTIES THE JAPANESE DANCE SCHOOLS HOLD.
THERE WILL BE MAGNIFICENT SPONSORS AND PATRONS WAITING TO SEE YOU.
CAN YOU REALLY SAY YOU WON'T HAVE A PROBLEM?

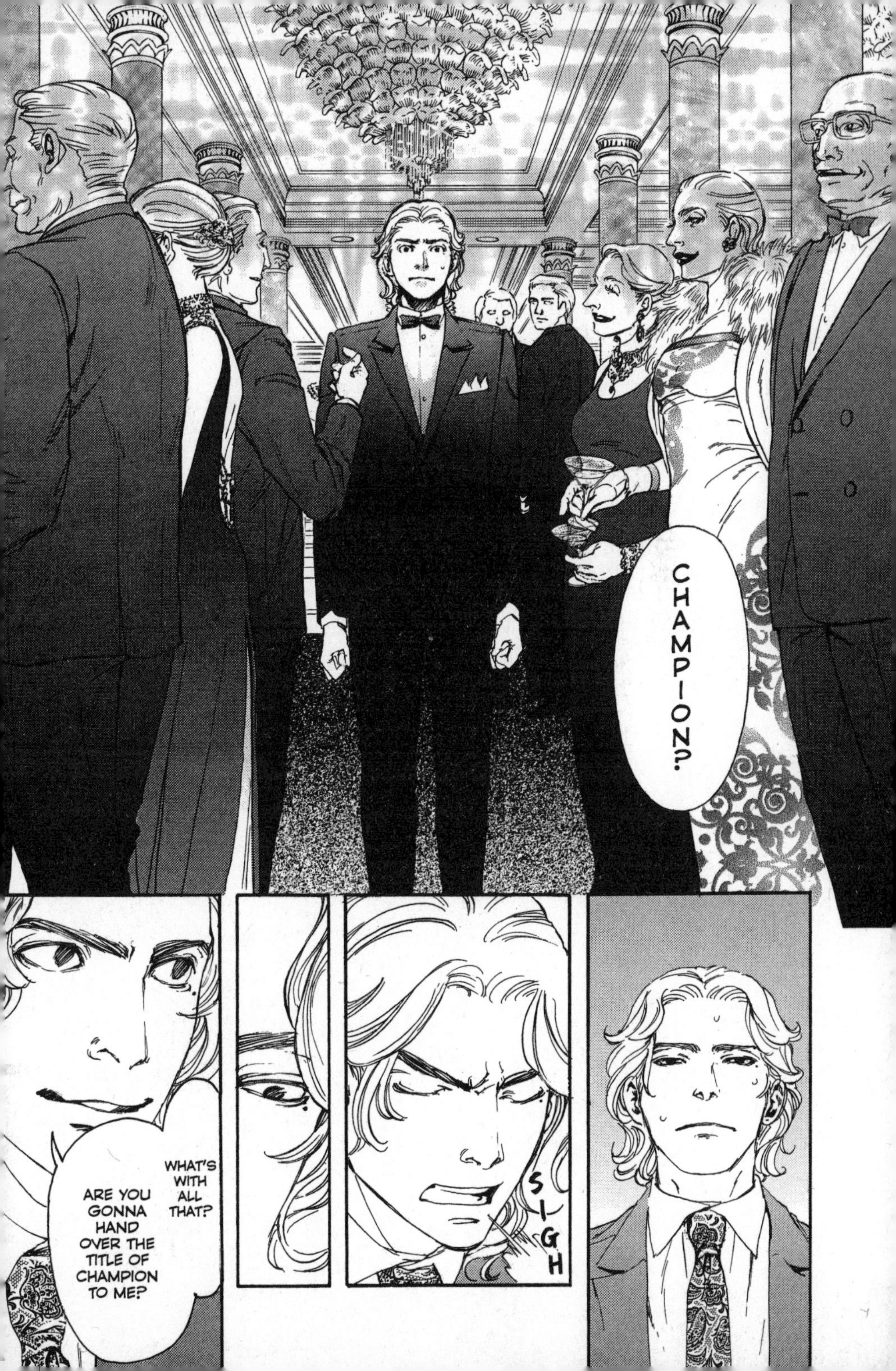
CHAMPION?
SIGH
WHAT'S WITH ALL THAT?
ARE YOU GONNA HAND OVER THE TITLE OF CHAMPION TO ME?

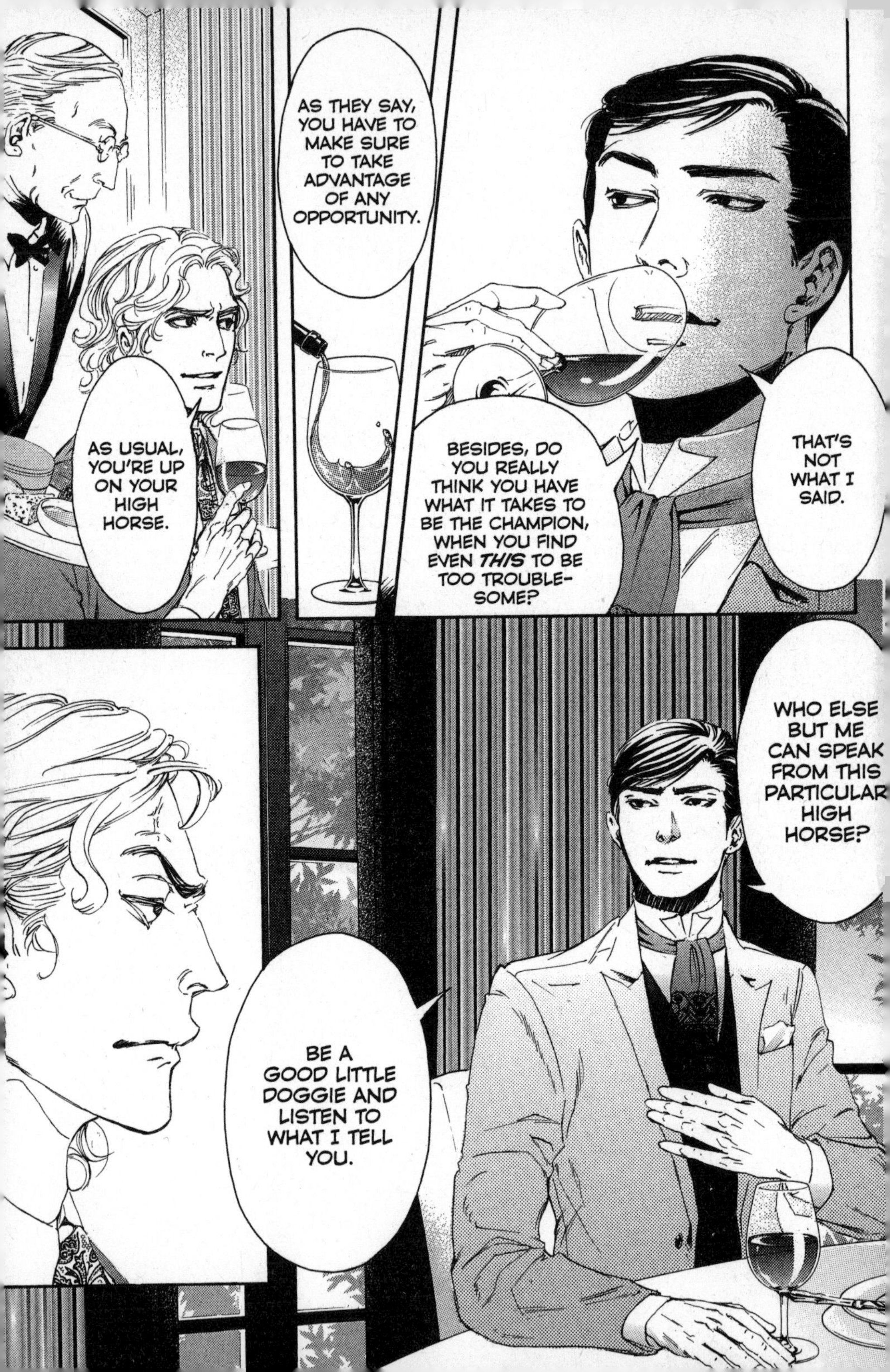
THAT'S NOT WHAT I SAID.
BESIDES, DO YOU REALLY THINK YOU HAVE WHAT IT TAKES TO BE THE CHAMPION, WHEN YOU FIND EVEN *THIS* TO BE TOO TROUBLE-SOME?
AS THEY SAY, YOU HAVE TO MAKE SURE TO TAKE ADVANTAGE OF ANY OPPORTUNITY.
AS USUAL, YOU'RE UP ON YOUR HIGH HORSE.
WHO ELSE BUT ME CAN SPEAK FROM THIS PARTICULAR HIGH HORSE?
BE A GOOD LITTLE DOGGIE AND LISTEN TO WHAT I TELL YOU.

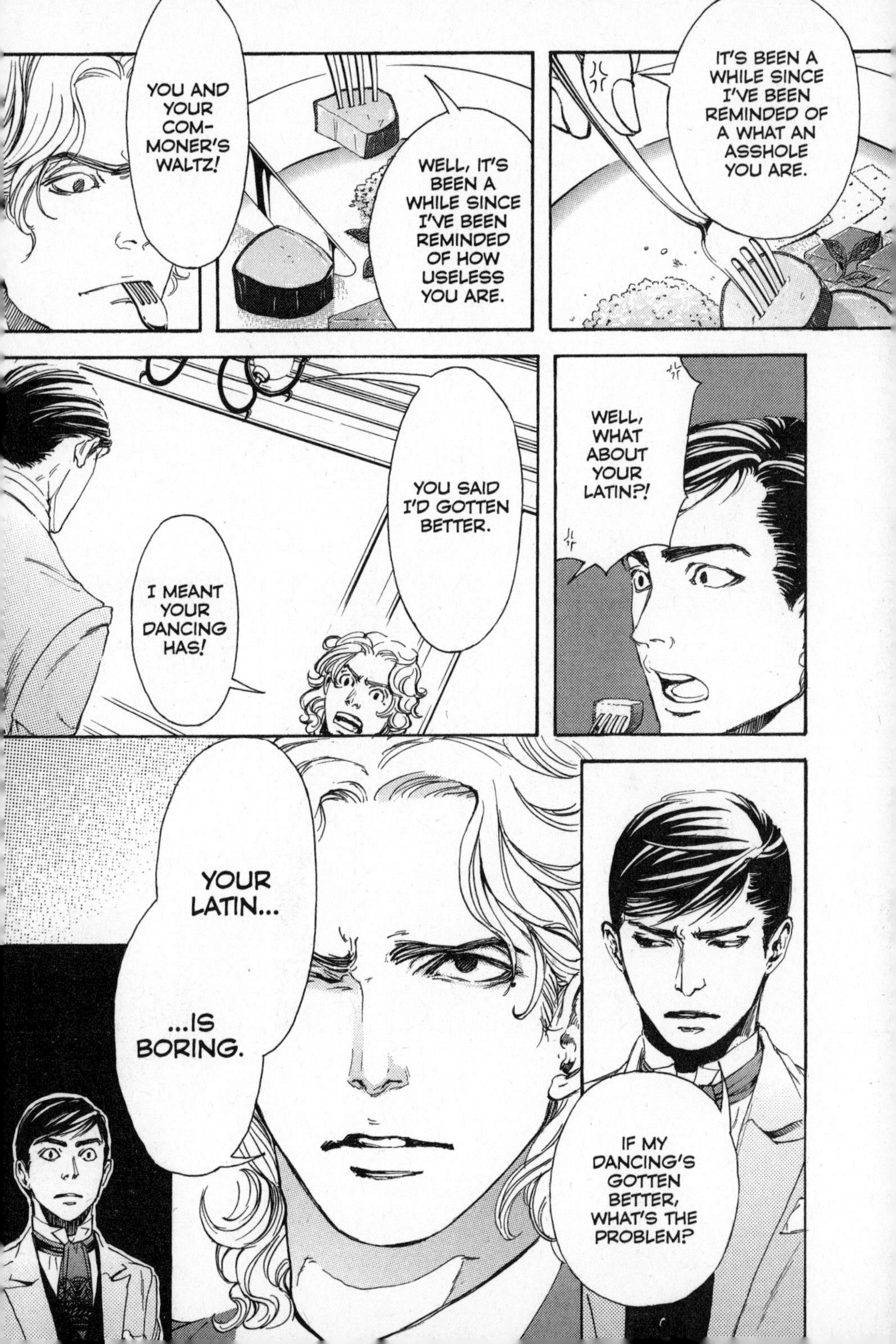
IT'S BEEN A WHILE SINCE I'VE BEEN REMINDED OF A WHAT AN ASSHOLE YOU ARE.
WELL, IT'S BEEN A WHILE SINCE I'VE BEEN REMINDED OF HOW USELESS YOU ARE.
YOU AND YOUR COM-MONER'S WALTZ!
WELL, WHAT ABOUT YOUR LATIN?!
YOU SAID I'D GOTTEN BETTER.
I MEANT YOUR DANCING HAS!
IF MY DANCING'S GOTTEN BETTER, WHAT'S THE PROBLEM?
YOUR LATIN...
...IS BORING.

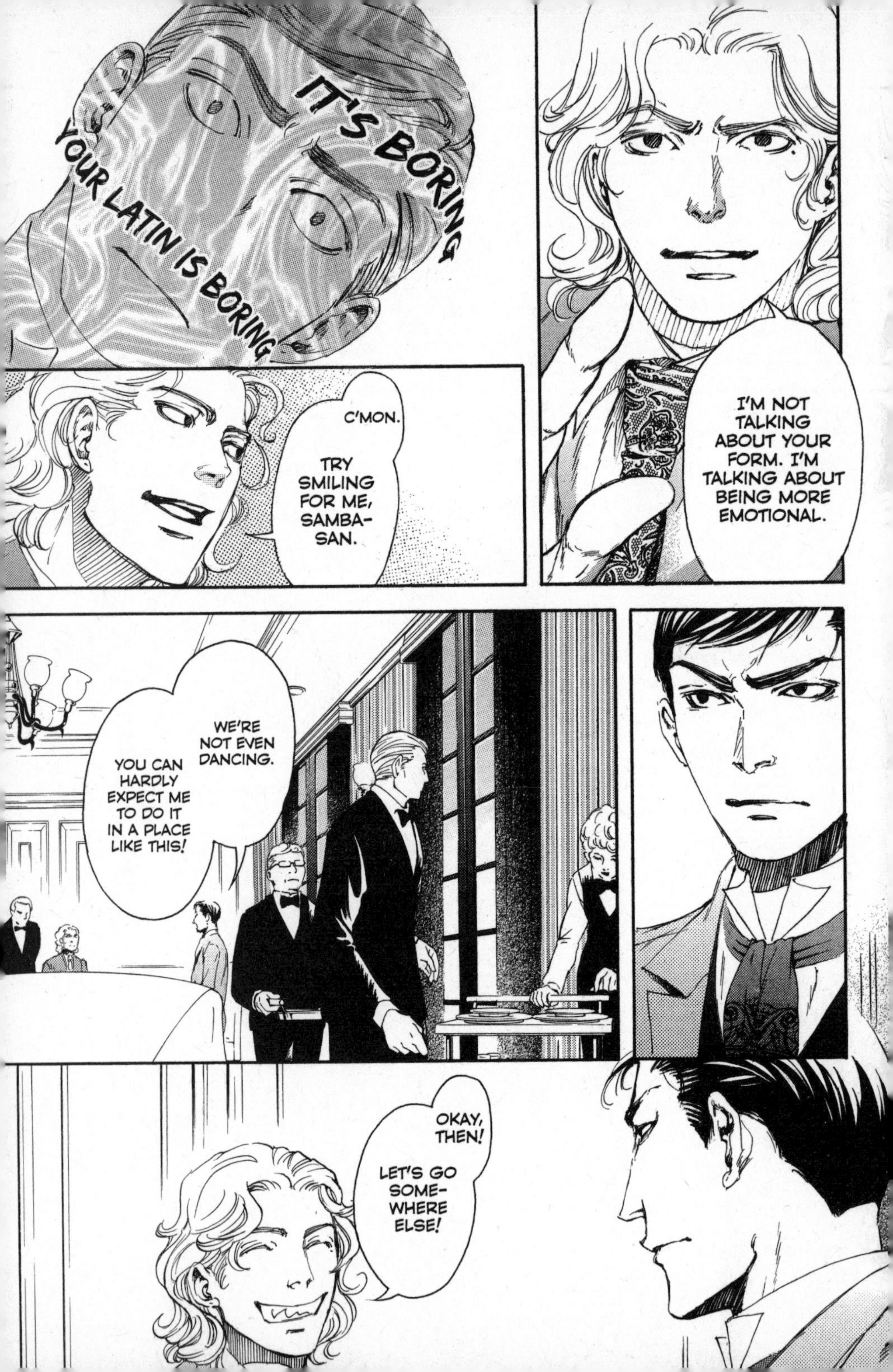
I'M NOT TALKING ABOUT YOUR FORM. I'M TALKING ABOUT BEING MORE EMOTIONAL.
IT'S BORING
YOUR LATIN IS BORING
C'MON.
TRY SMILING FOR ME, SAMBA-SAN.
WE'RE NOT EVEN DANCING.
YOU CAN HARDLY EXPECT ME TO DO IT IN A PLACE LIKE THIS!
OKAY, THEN!
LET'S GO SOME-WHERE ELSE!

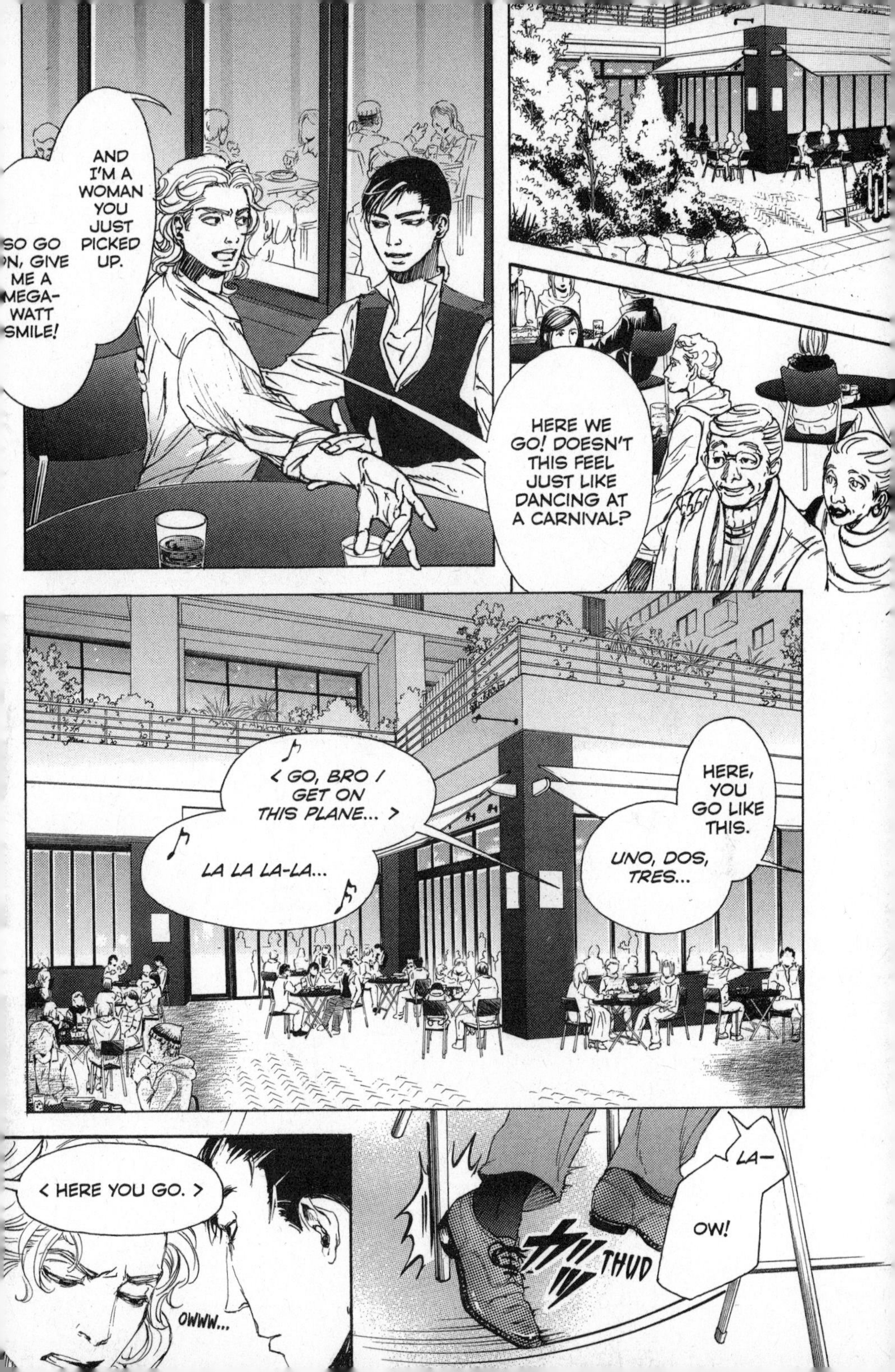
HERE WE GO! DOESN'T THIS FEEL JUST LIKE DANCING AT A CARNIVAL?
AND I'M A WOMAN YOU JUST PICKED UP.
SO GO ON, GIVE ME A MEGA-WATT SMILE!
HERE, YOU GO LIKE THIS.
UNO, DOS, TRES...
< GO, BRO / GET ON THIS PLANE... >
LA LA LA-LA...
LA—
OW!
THUD
< HERE YOU GO. >
OWWW...

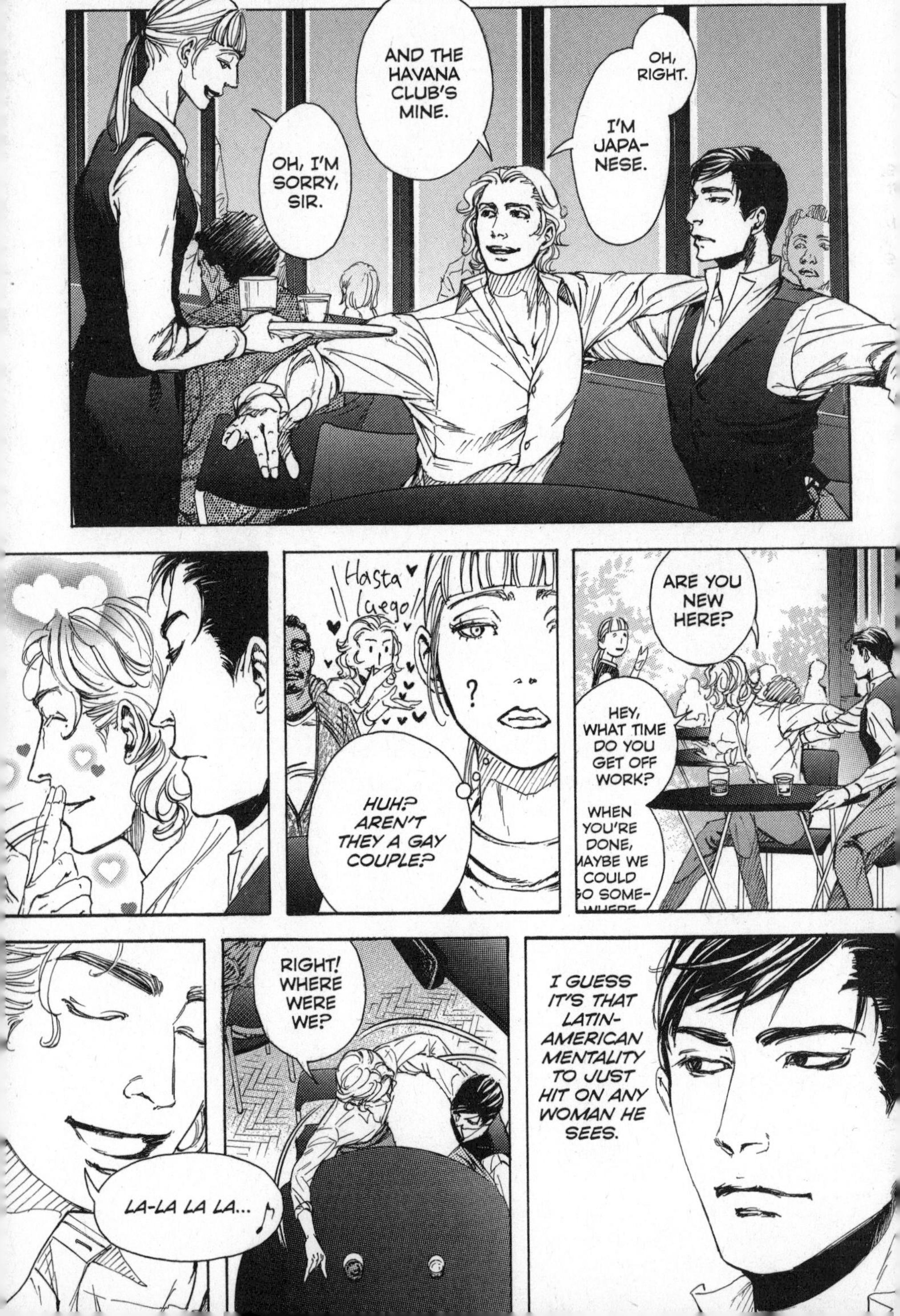
OH, RIGHT. I'M JAPANESE.
AND THE HAVANA CLUB'S MINE.
OH, I'M SORRY, SIR.
ARE YOU NEW HERE?
HEY, WHAT TIME DO YOU GET OFF WORK?
WHEN YOU'RE DONE, MAYBE WE COULD GO SOME-
Hasta luego
?
HUH? AREN'T THEY A GAY COUPLE?
I GUESS IT'S THAT LATIN-AMERICAN MENTALITY TO JUST HIT ON ANY WOMAN HE SEES.
RIGHT! WHERE WERE WE?
LA-LA LA LA...

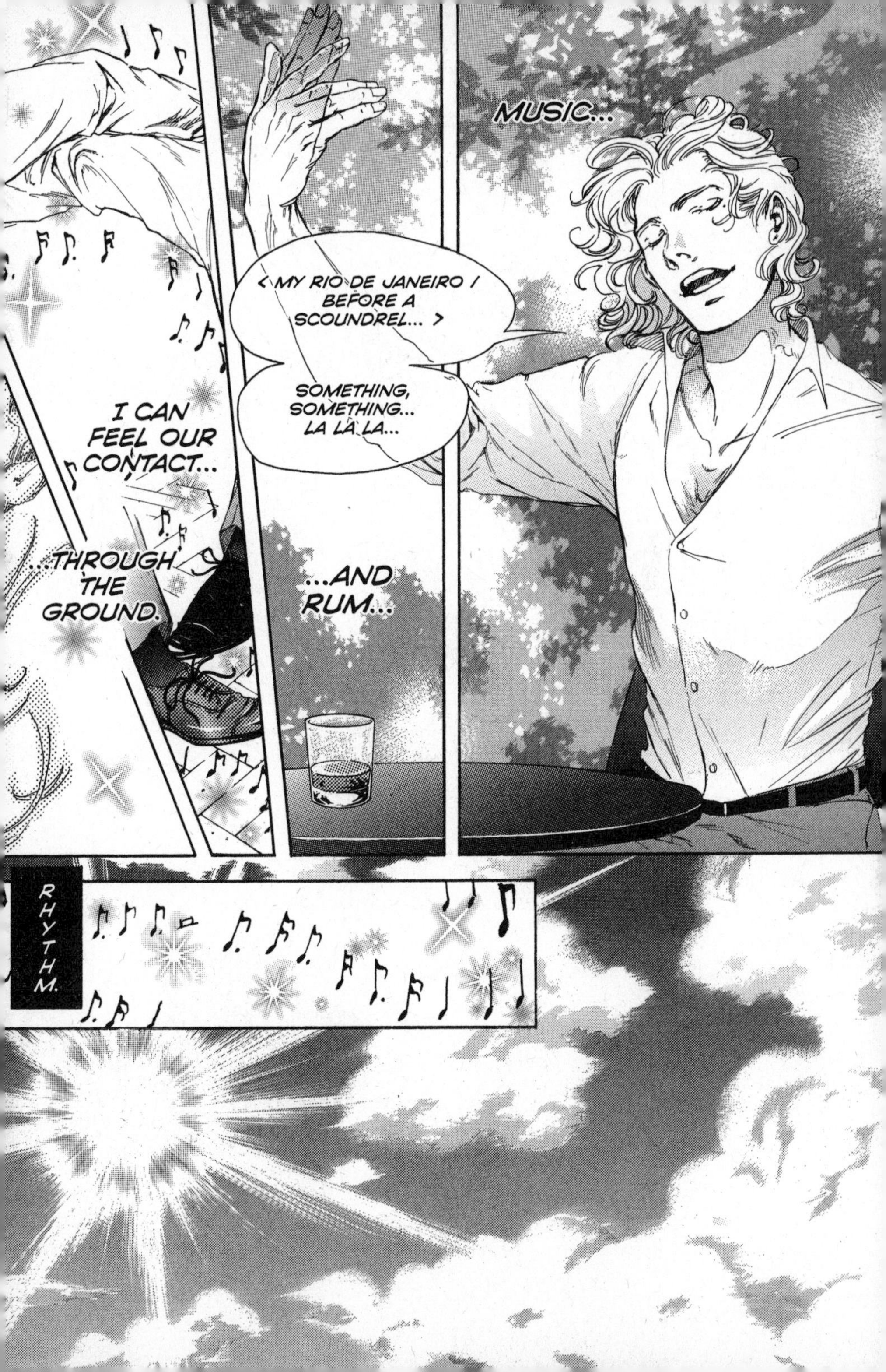
MUSIC...
< MY RIO DE JANEIRO / BEFORE A SCOUNDREL... >
SOMETHING, SOMETHING... LA LA LA...
...AND RUM...
I CAN FEEL OUR CONTACT...
...THROUGH THE GROUND.
RHYTHM.

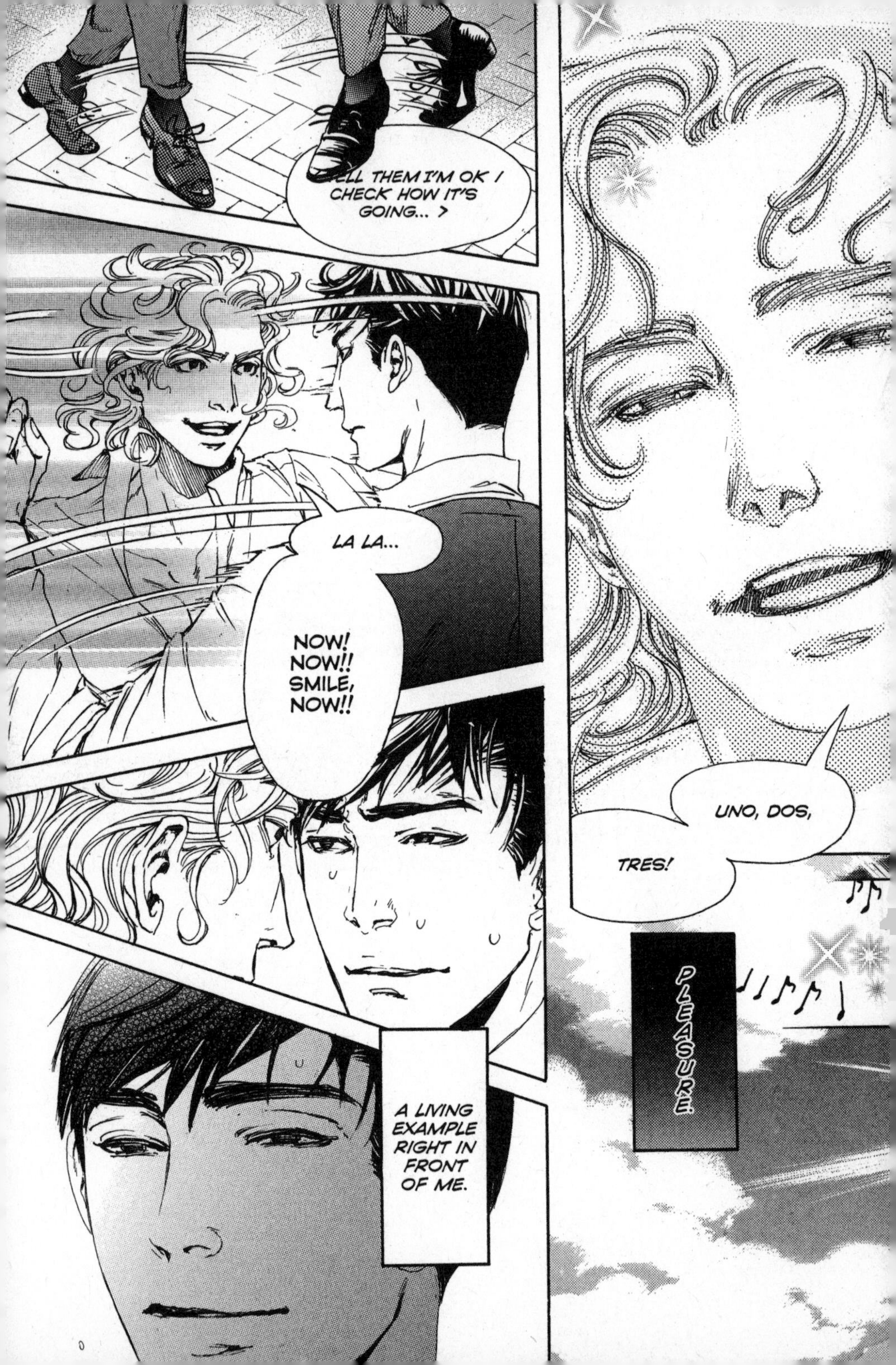
UNO, DOS, TRES!
PLEASURE.
ELL THEM I'M OK / CHECK HOW IT'S GOING... >
LA LA...
NOW! NOW!! SMILE, NOW!!
A LIVING EXAMPLE RIGHT IN FRONT OF ME.

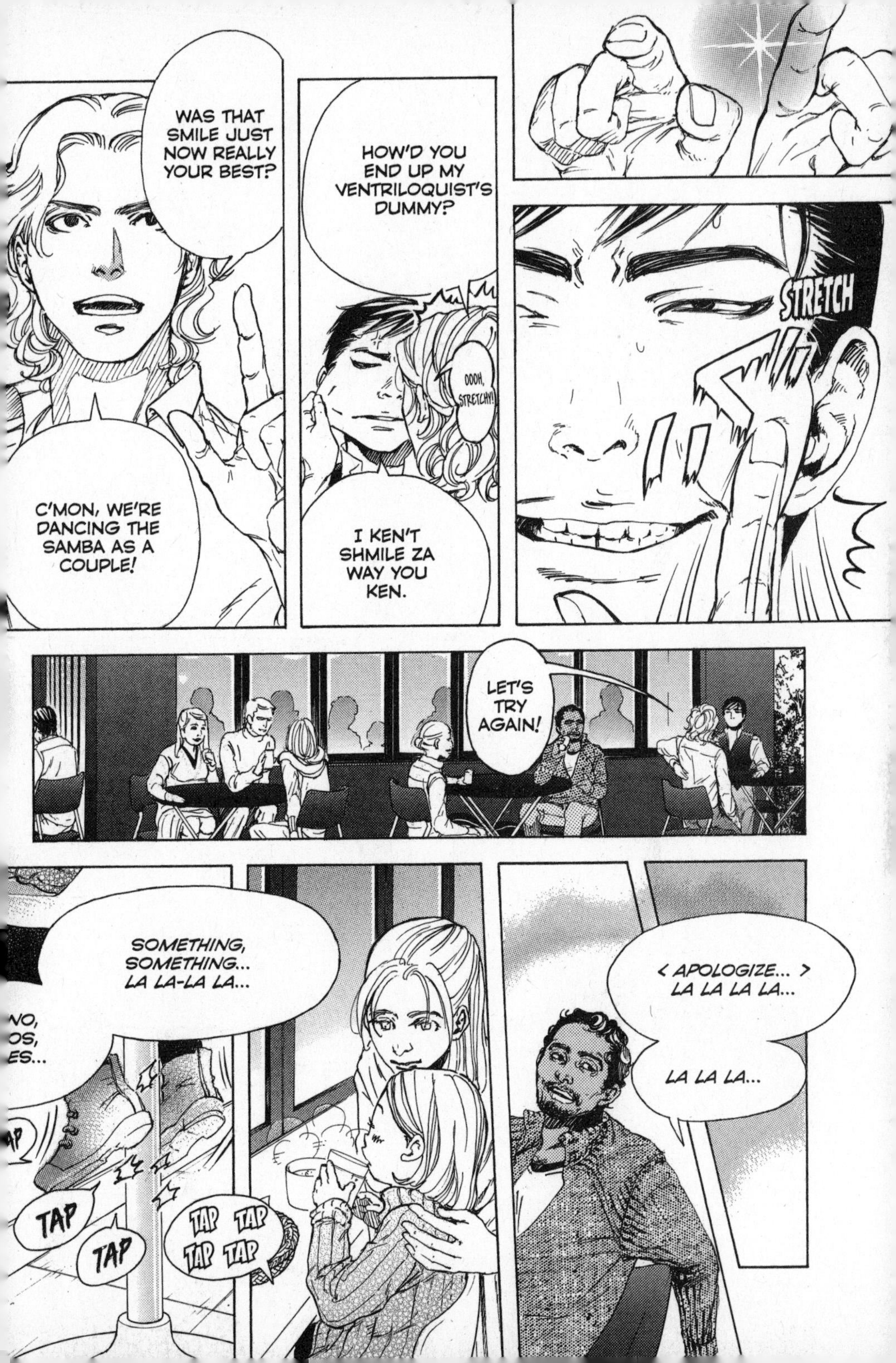
STRETCH
HOW'D YOU END UP MY VENTRILOQUIST'S DUMMY?
OOOH, STRETCHY!
I KEN'T SHMILE ZA WAY YOU KEN.
WAS THAT SMILE JUST NOW REALLY YOUR BEST?
C'MON, WE'RE DANCING THE SAMBA AS A COUPLE!
LET'S TRY AGAIN!
< APOLOGIZE... > LA LA LA LA...
LA LA LA...
SOMETHING, SOMETHING... LA LA-LA LA...
TAP TAP TAP TAP
TAP
TAP

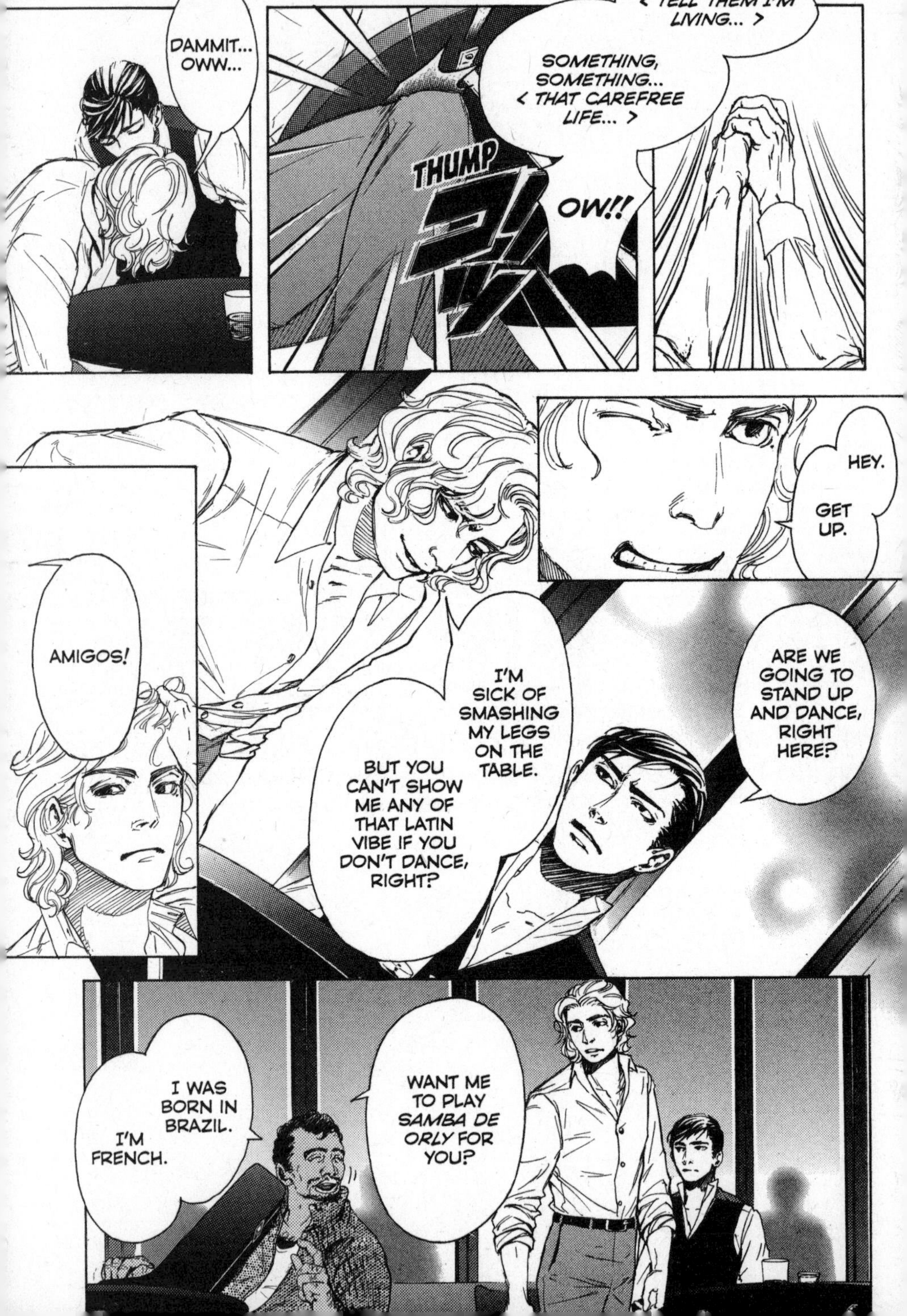
< TELL THEM I'M LIVING... >
SOMETHING, SOMETHING... < THAT CAREFREE LIFE... >
THUMP
OW!!
DAMMIT... OWW...
HEY.
GET UP.
ARE WE GOING TO STAND UP AND DANCE, RIGHT HERE?
I'M SICK OF SMASHING MY LEGS ON THE TABLE.
BUT YOU CAN'T SHOW ME ANY OF THAT LATIN VIBE IF YOU DON'T DANCE, RIGHT?
AMIGOS!
WANT ME TO PLAY *SAMBA DE ORLY* FOR YOU?
I WAS BORN IN BRAZIL.
I'M FRENCH.

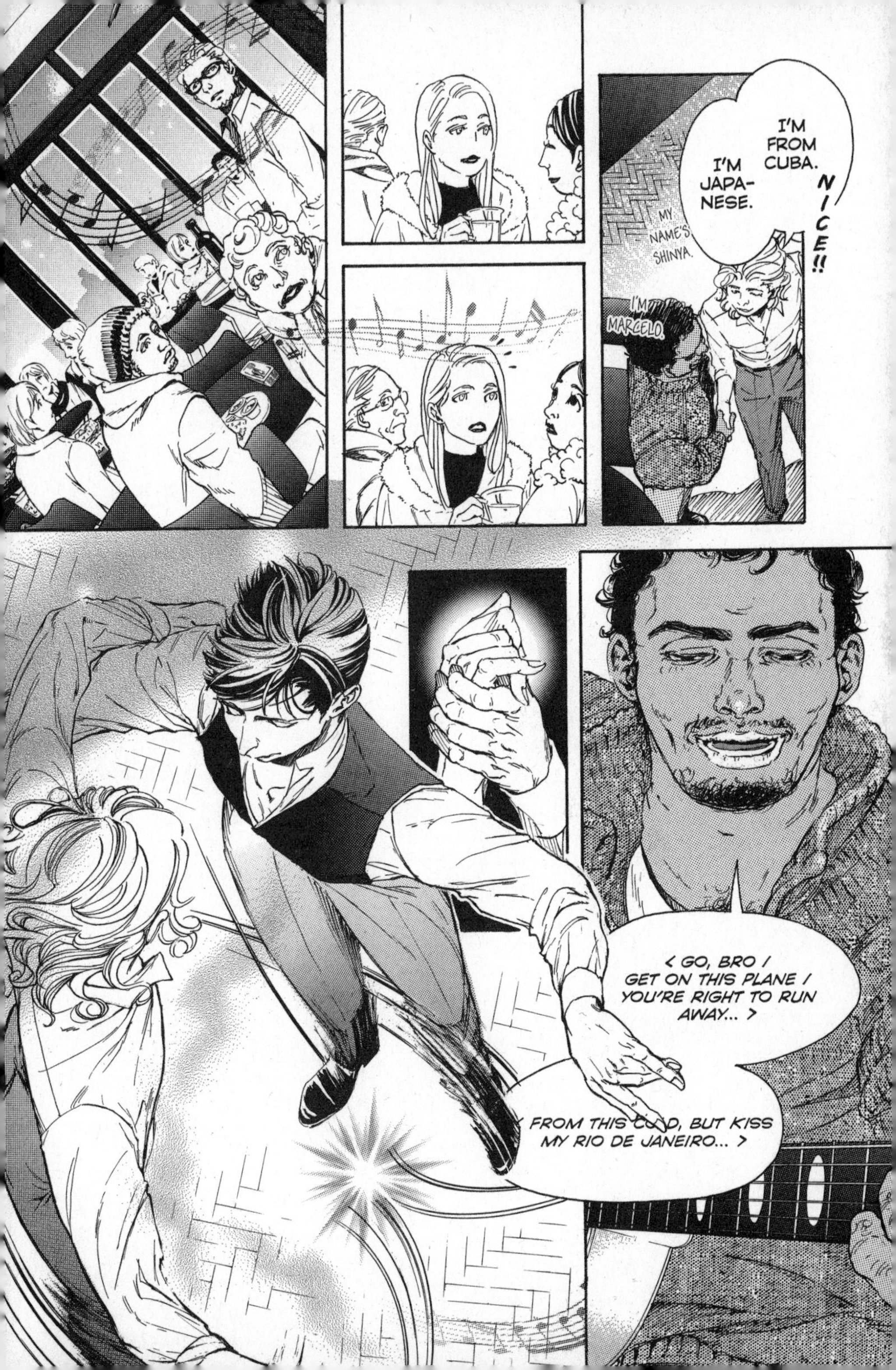
I'M FROM CUBA.
I'M JAPA-NESE.
NICE!!
MY NAME'S SHINYA.
I'M MARCELO.
< GO, BRO / GET ON THIS PLANE / YOU'RE RIGHT TO RUN AWAY... >
< FROM THIS COLD, BUT KISS MY RIO DE JANEIRO... >

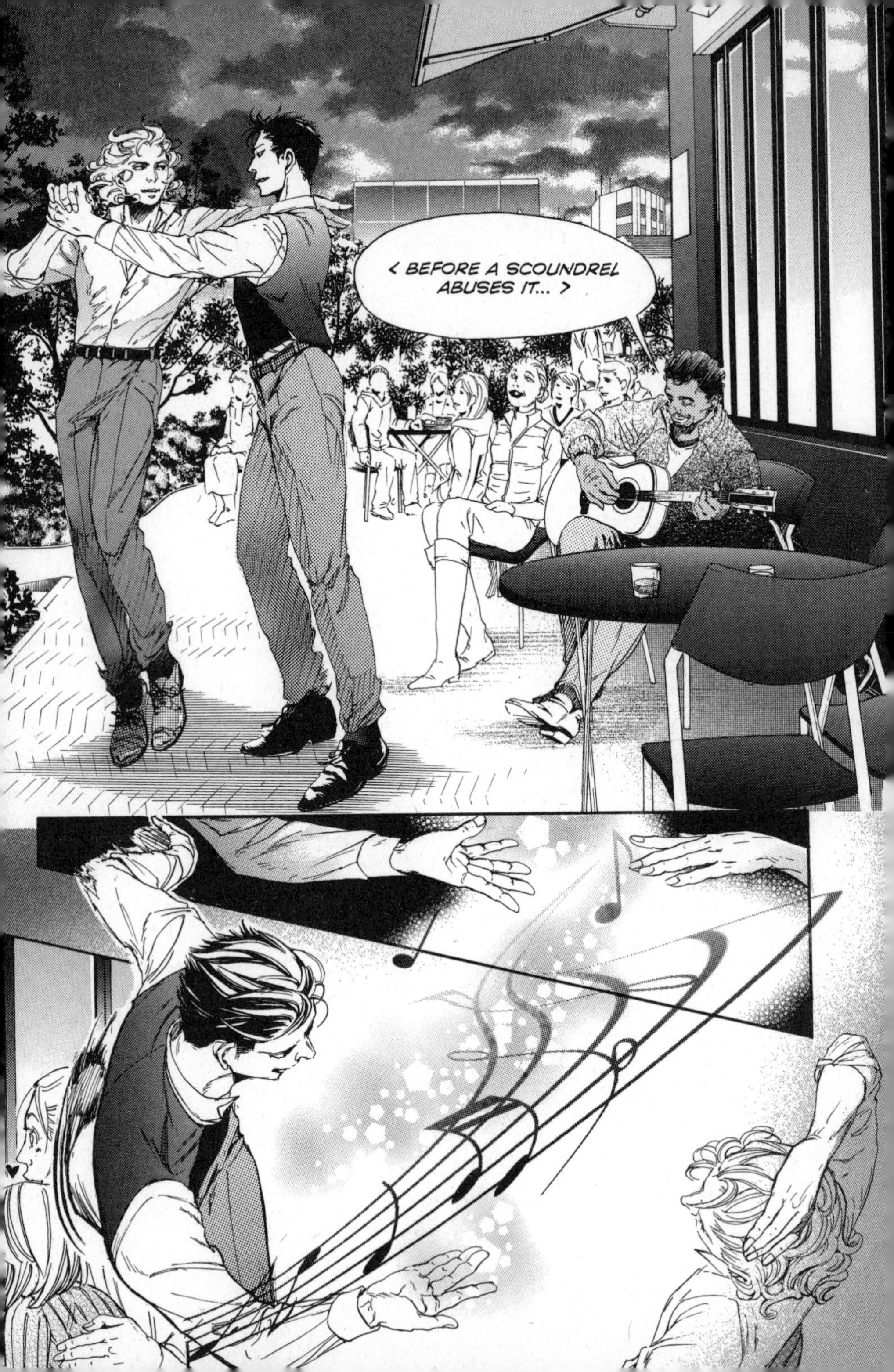
< BEFORE A SCOUNDREL ABUSES IT... >

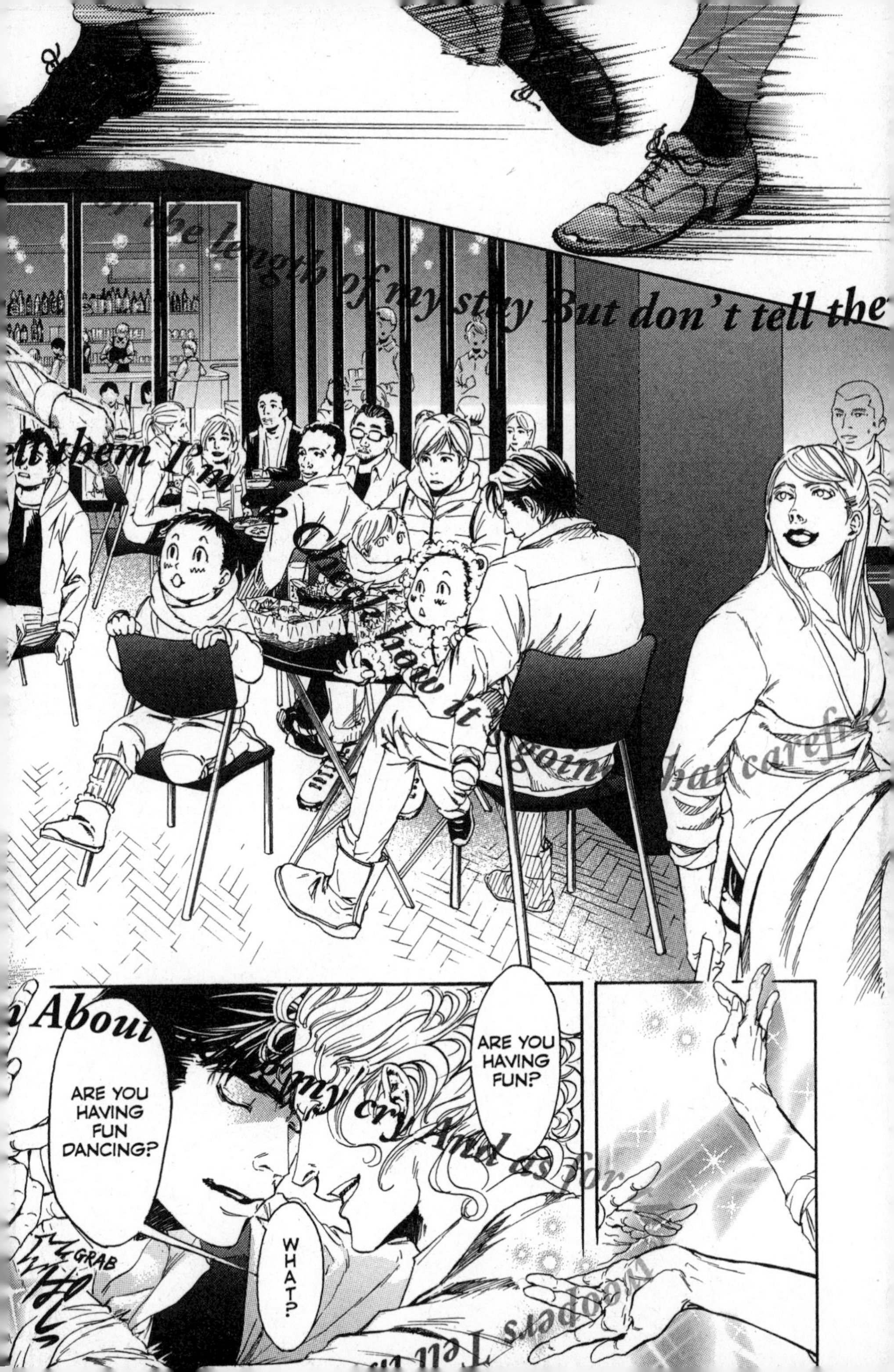

the length of my stay But don't tell the
them I'm
Check how it's going
that carefre
ARE YOU HAVING FUN?
ARE YOU HAVING FUN DANCING?
WHAT?
GRAB
About
my cry And as for
Woodpeckers Tell

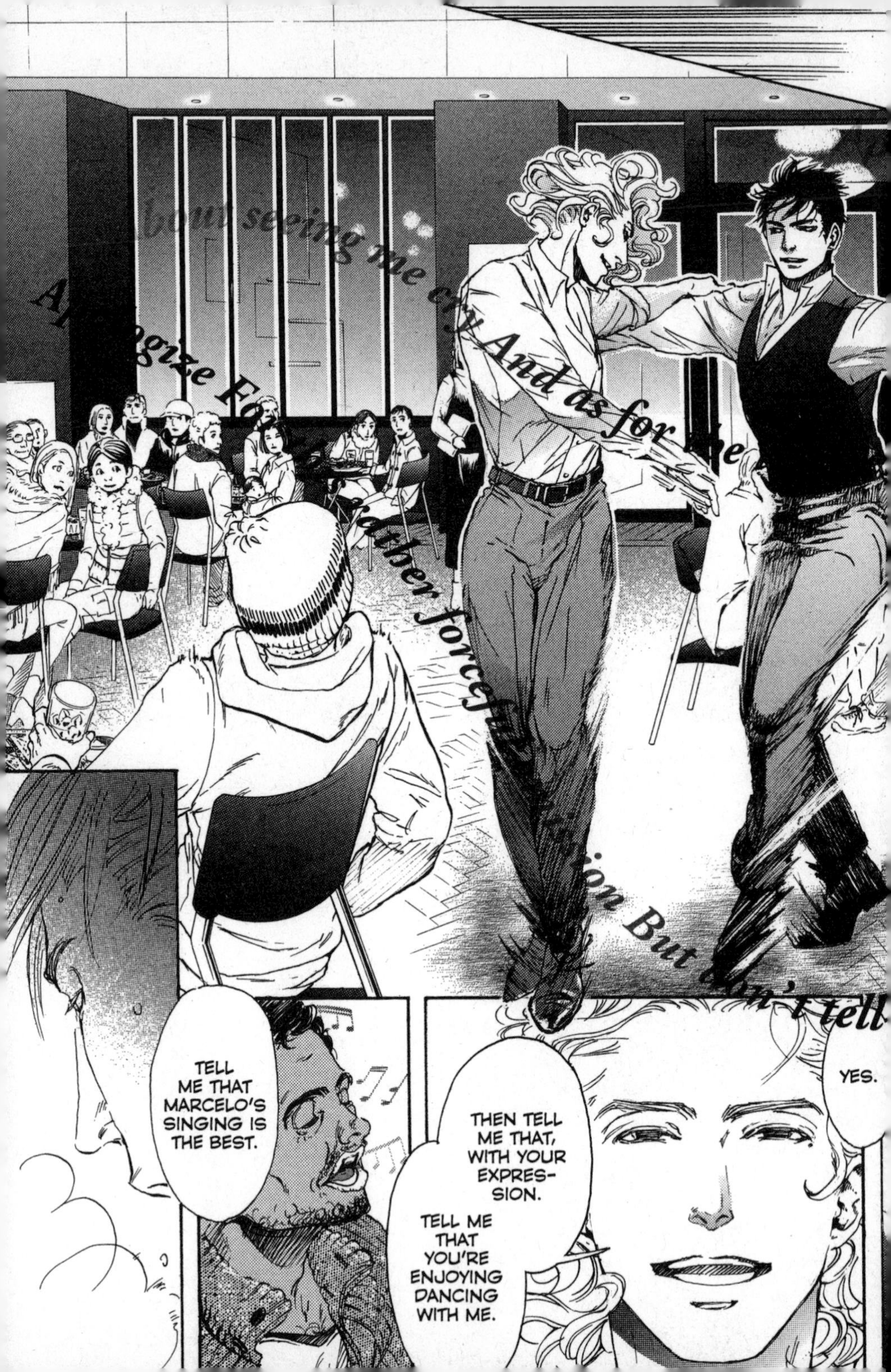
seeing me cry And as for the
But
YES.
THEN TELL ME THAT, WITH YOUR EXPRES-SION.
TELL ME THAT YOU'RE ENJOYING DANCING WITH ME.
TELL ME THAT MARCELO'S SINGING IS THE BEST.

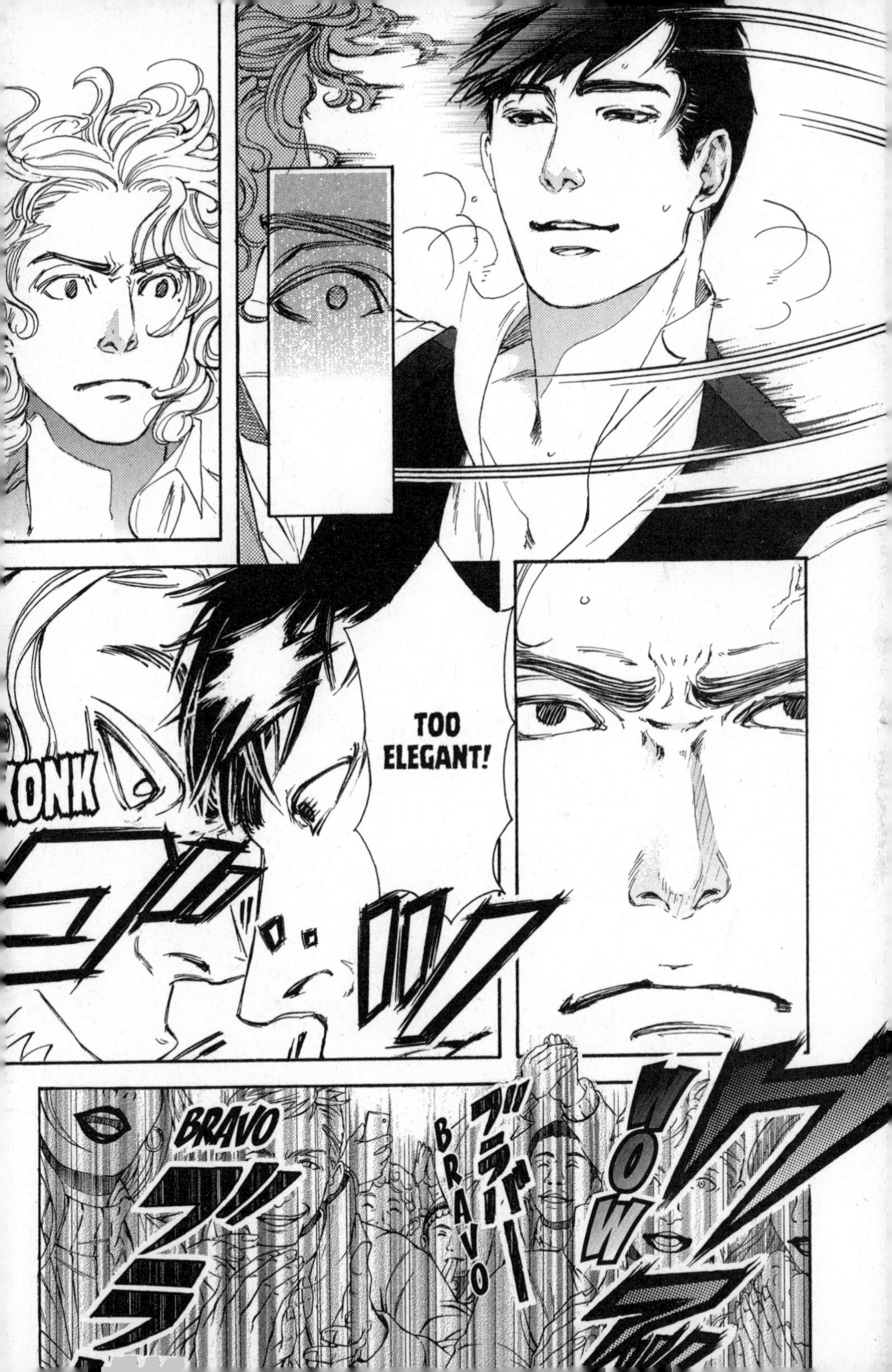
TOO ELEGANT!
KONK
WOW
BRAVO
BRAVO

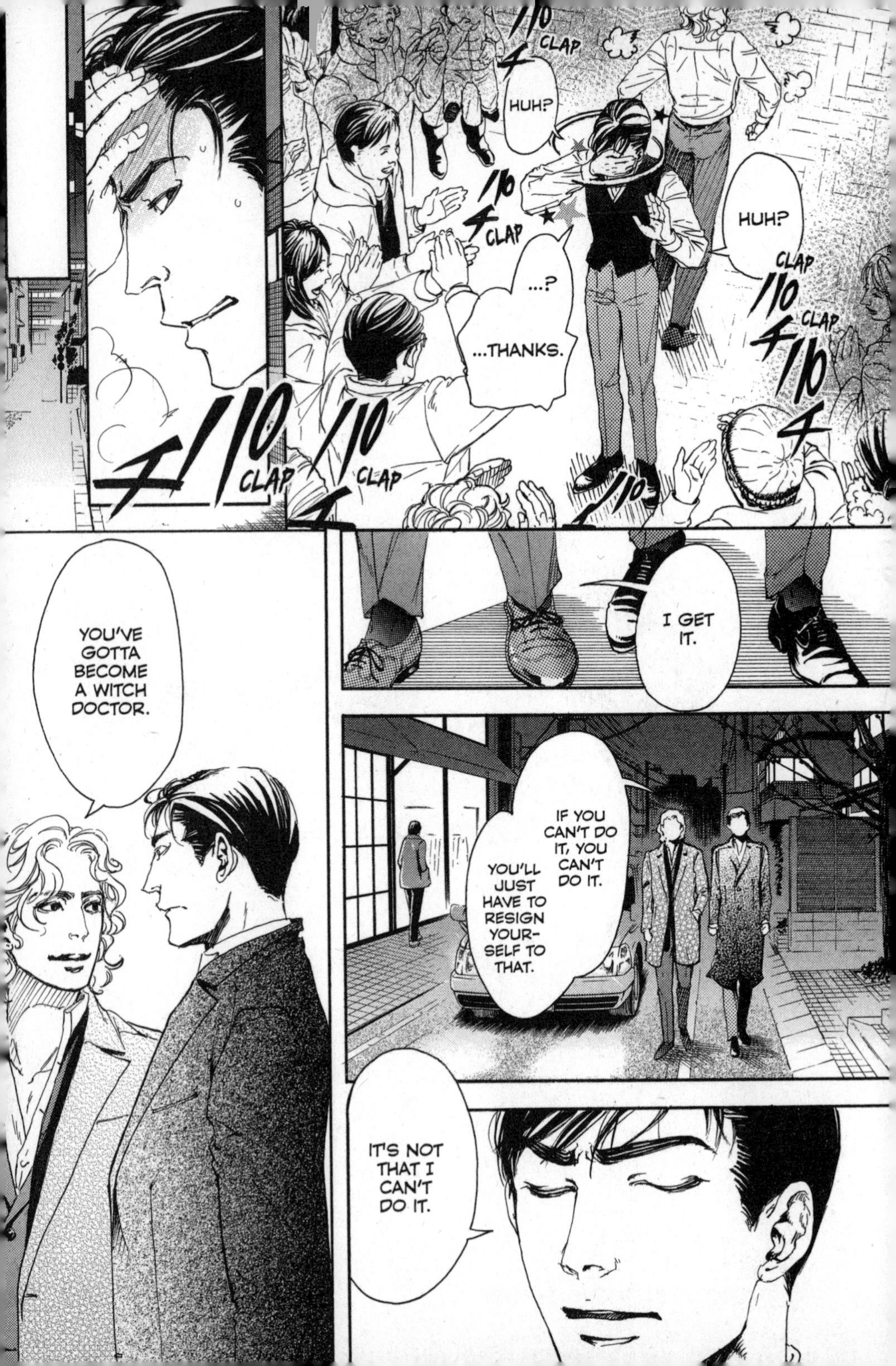
CLAP
HUH?
HUH?
CLAP
CLAP
CLAP
...?
...THANKS.
CLAP
CLAP
CLAP
I GET IT.
IF YOU CAN'T DO IT, YOU CAN'T DO IT.
YOU'LL JUST HAVE TO RESIGN YOUR-SELF TO THAT.
IT'S NOT THAT I CAN'T DO IT.
YOU'VE GOTTA BECOME A WITCH DOCTOR.

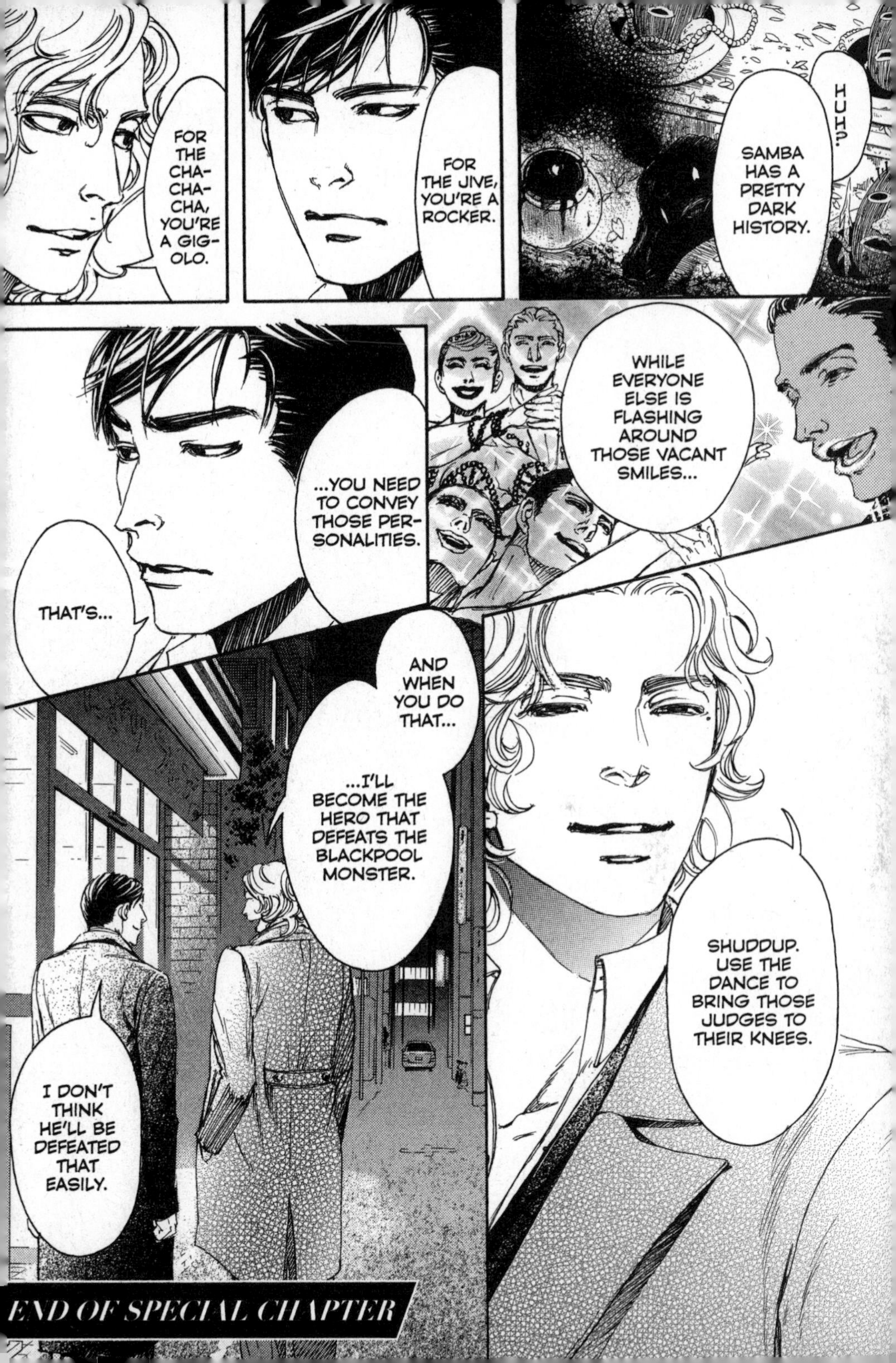
HUH?
SAMBA HAS A PRETTY DARK HISTORY.
FOR THE JIVE, YOU'RE A ROCKER.
FOR THE CHA-CHA-CHA, YOU'RE A GIGOLO.
WHILE EVERYONE ELSE IS FLASHING AROUND THOSE VACANT SMILES...
...YOU NEED TO CONVEY THOSE PERSONALITIES.
THAT'S...
SHUDDUP. USE THE DANCE TO BRING THOSE JUDGES TO THEIR KNEES.
AND WHEN YOU DO THAT...
...I'LL BECOME THE HERO THAT DEFEATS THE BLACKPOOL MONSTER.
I DON'T THINK HE'LL BE DEFEATED THAT EASILY.
END OF SPECIAL CHAPTER

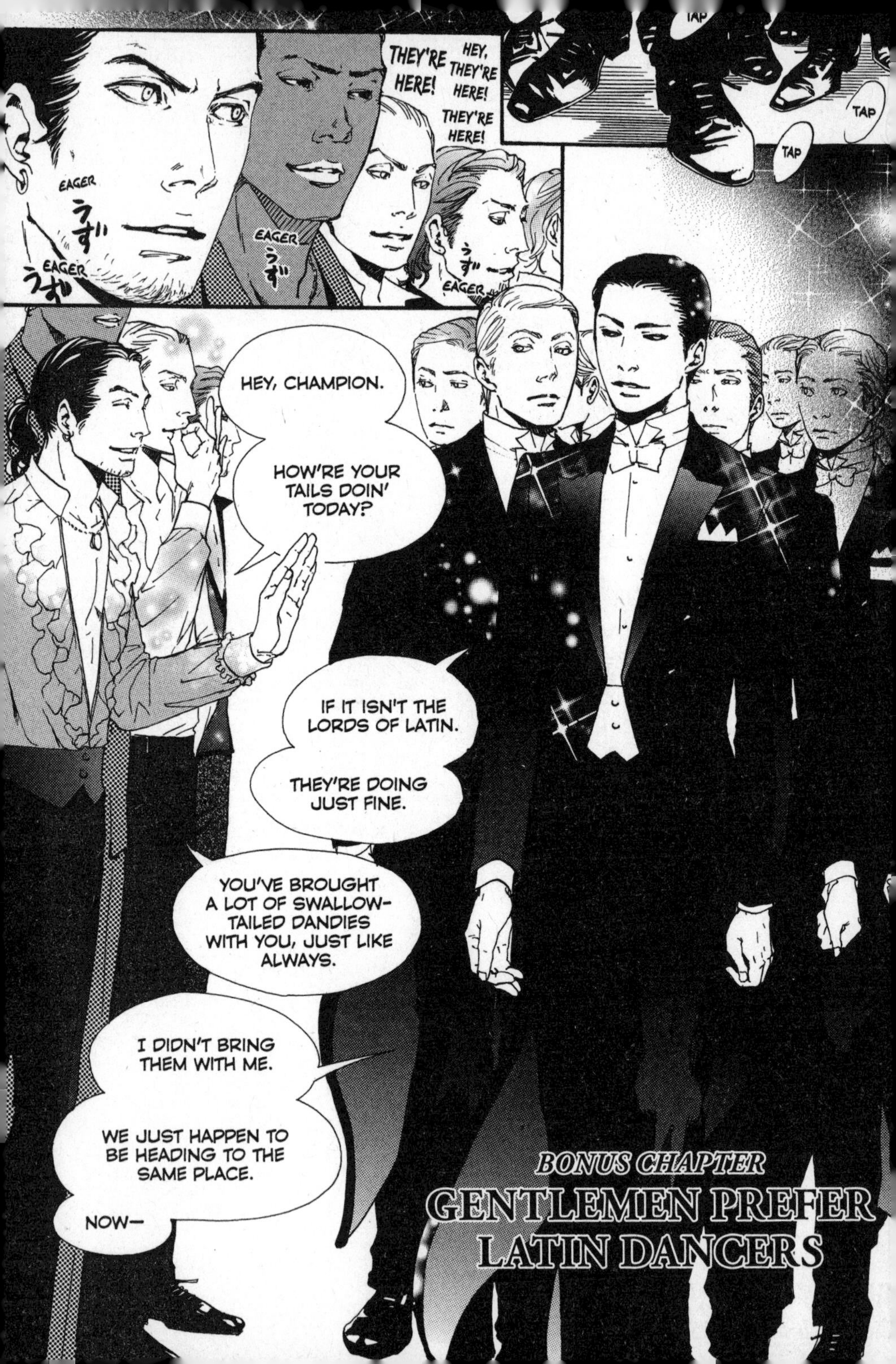
TAP
TAP
TAP
HEY, THEY'RE HERE!
THEY'RE HERE!
THEY'RE HERE!
EAGER うず
EAGER うず
EAGER うず
EAGER うず
HEY, CHAMPION.
HOW'RE YOUR TAILS DOIN' TODAY?
IF IT ISN'T THE LORDS OF LATIN.
THEY'RE DOING JUST FINE.
YOU'VE BROUGHT A LOT OF SWALLOW-TAILED DANDIES WITH YOU, JUST LIKE ALWAYS.
I DIDN'T BRING THEM WITH ME.
WE JUST HAPPEN TO BE HEADING TO THE SAME PLACE.
NOW—
BONUS CHAPTER
GENTLEMEN PREFER LATIN DANCERS

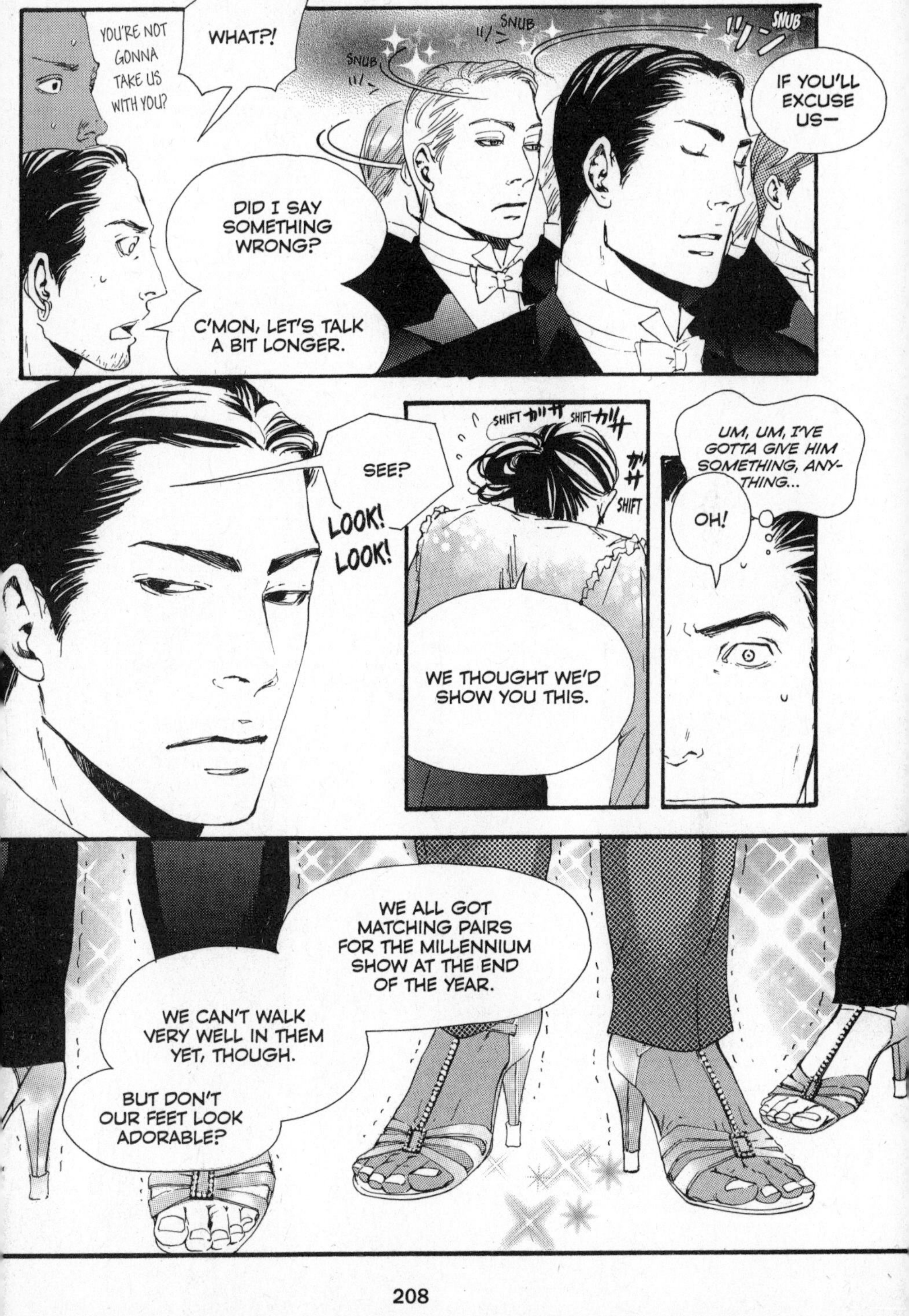
SNUB
IF YOU'LL EXCUSE US—
SNUB
SNUB
WHAT?!
YOU'RE NOT GONNA TAKE US WITH YOU?
DID I SAY SOMETHING WRONG?
C'MON, LET'S TALK A BIT LONGER.
UM, UM, I'VE GOTTA GIVE HIM SOMETHING, ANYTHING...
OH!
SHIFT
SHIFT
SHIFT
WE THOUGHT WE'D SHOW YOU THIS.
SEE?
LOOK! LOOK!
WE ALL GOT MATCHING PAIRS FOR THE MILLENNIUM SHOW AT THE END OF THE YEAR.
WE CAN'T WALK VERY WELL IN THEM YET, THOUGH.
BUT DON'T OUR FEET LOOK ADORABLE?

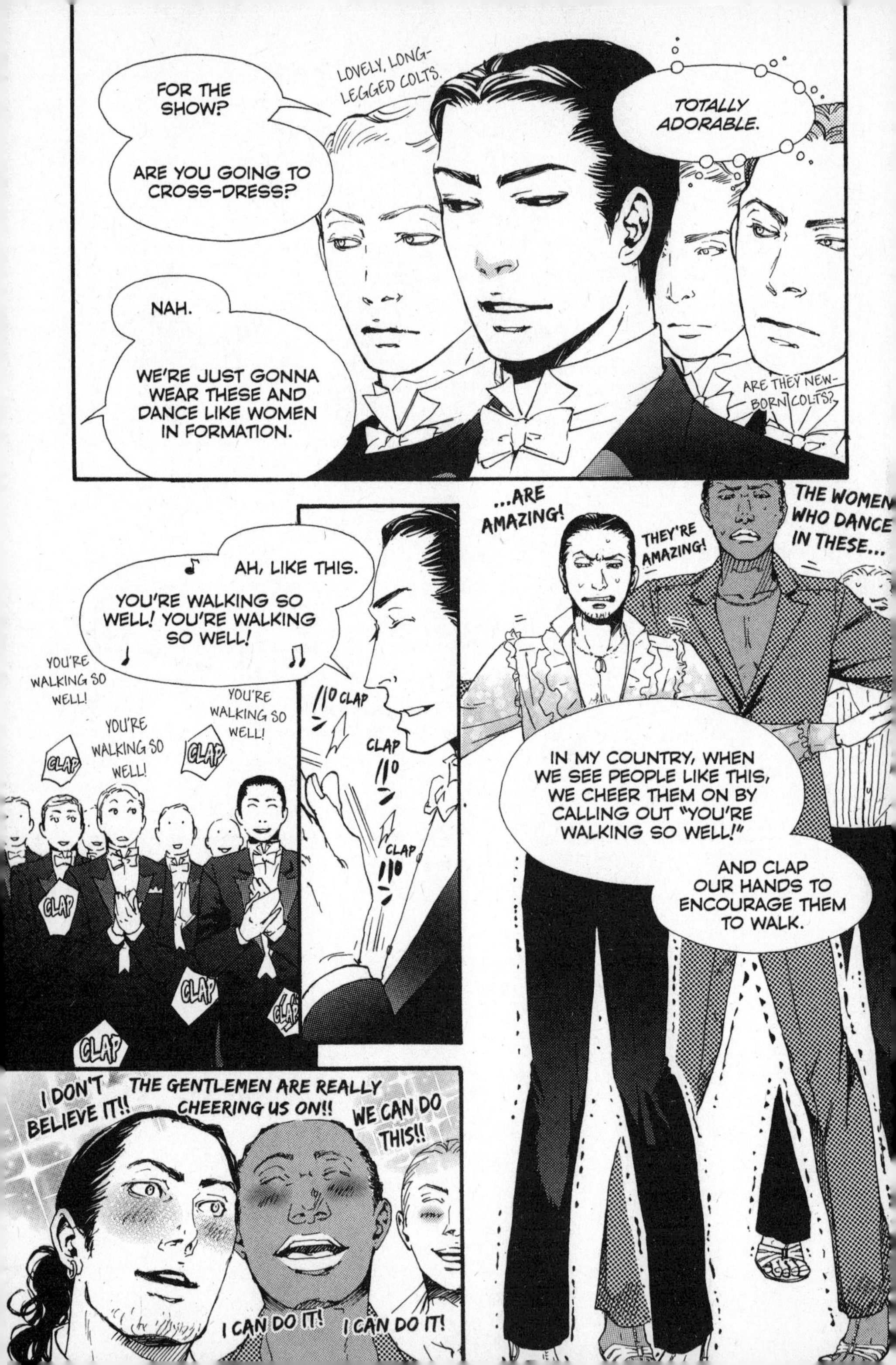

TOTALLY ADORABLE.
LOVELY, LONG-LEGGED COLTS.
FOR THE SHOW?
ARE YOU GOING TO CROSS-DRESS?
ARE THEY NEW-BORN COLTS?
NAH.
WE'RE JUST GONNA WEAR THESE AND DANCE LIKE WOMEN IN FORMATION.
THE WOMEN WHO DANCE IN THESE...
THEY'RE AMAZING!
...ARE AMAZING!
IN MY COUNTRY, WHEN WE SEE PEOPLE LIKE THIS, WE CHEER THEM ON BY CALLING OUT "YOU'RE WALKING SO WELL!"
AND CLAP OUR HANDS TO ENCOURAGE THEM TO WALK.
AH, LIKE THIS.
YOU'RE WALKING SO WELL! YOU'RE WALKING SO WELL!
CLAP
CLAP
CLAP
YOU'RE WALKING SO WELL!
YOU'RE WALKING SO WELL!
YOU'RE WALKING SO WELL!
CLAP
CLAP
CLAP
CLAP
CLAP
CLAP
WE CAN DO THIS!!
THE GENTLEMEN ARE REALLY CHEERING US ON!!
I DON'T BELIEVE IT!!
I CAN DO IT!
I CAN DO IT!

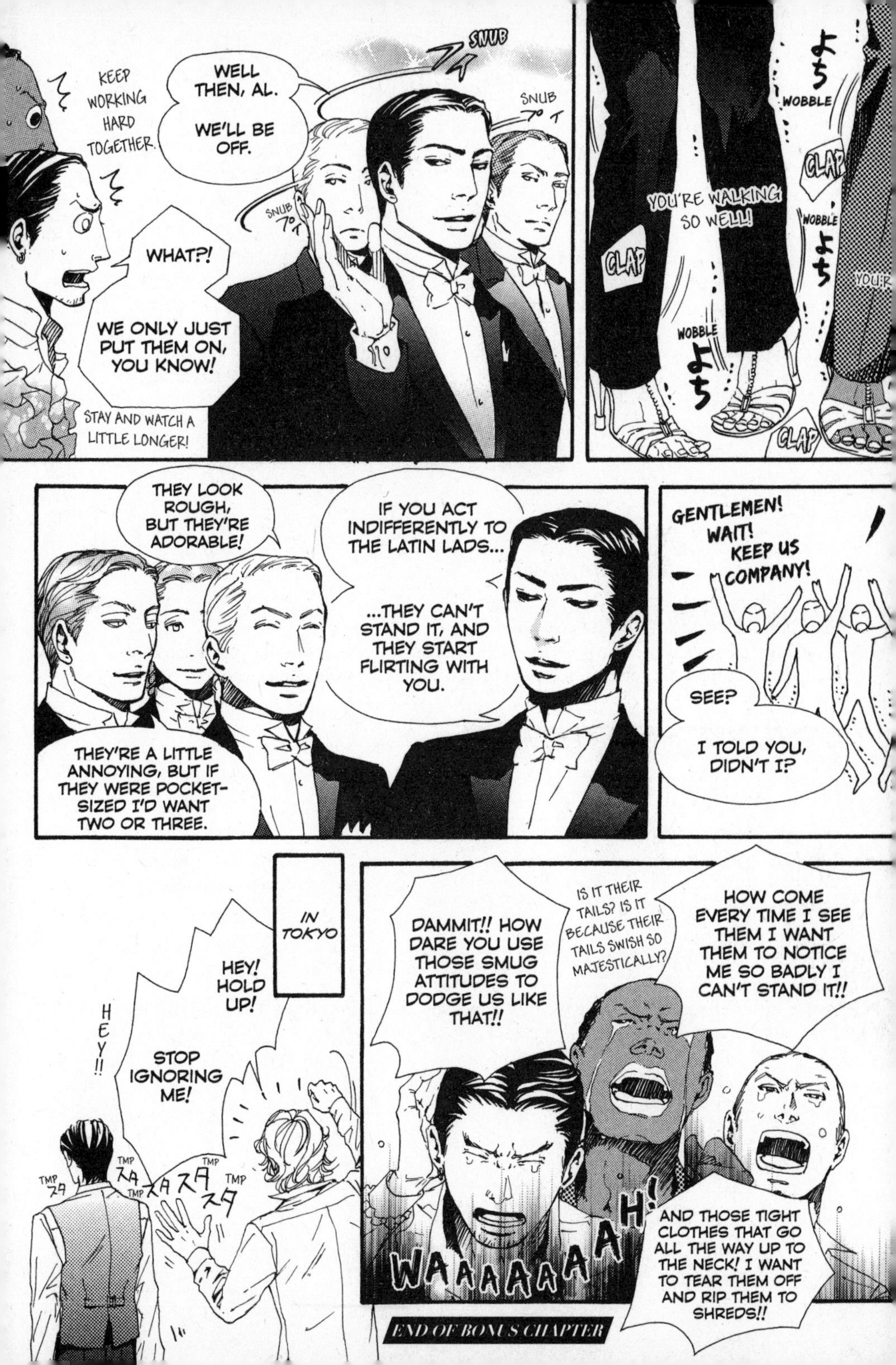
よち
WOBBLE
CLAP
YOU'RE WALKING SO WELL!
CLAP
WOBBLE
よち
YOU'R
WOBBLE
よち
CLAP
SNUB
フイ
WELL THEN, AL.
WE'LL BE OFF.
SNUB
プイ
KEEP WORKING HARD TOGETHER.
SNUB
プイ
WHAT?!
WE ONLY JUST PUT THEM ON, YOU KNOW!
STAY AND WATCH A LITTLE LONGER!
GENTLEMEN! WAIT! KEEP US COMPANY!
SEE?
I TOLD YOU, DIDN'T I?
IF YOU ACT INDIFFERENTLY TO THE LATIN LADS...
...THEY CAN'T STAND IT, AND THEY START FLIRTING WITH YOU.
THEY LOOK ROUGH, BUT THEY'RE ADORABLE!
THEY'RE A LITTLE ANNOYING, BUT IF THEY WERE POCKET-SIZED I'D WANT TWO OR THREE.
HOW COME EVERY TIME I SEE THEM I WANT THEM TO NOTICE ME SO BADLY I CAN'T STAND IT!!
IS IT THEIR TAILS? IS IT BECAUSE THEIR TAILS SWISH SO MAJESTICALLY?
DAMMIT!! HOW DARE YOU USE THOSE SMUG ATTITUDES TO DODGE US LIKE THAT!!
WAAAAAAAH!
AND THOSE TIGHT CLOTHES THAT GO ALL THE WAY UP TO THE NECK! I WANT TO TEAR THEM OFF AND RIP THEM TO SHREDS!!
IN TOKYO
HEY! HOLD UP!
HEY!!
STOP IGNORING ME!
TMP
スタ
TMP
スタ
TMP
スタ
TMP
スタ
TMP
スタ

END OF BONUS CHAPTER

Afterword

Hello, this is Inouesatoh.

This is my first *10 Dance* comic since my transfer. I'm sure some of my original readers were worried, but I was able to publish it without any problems. I am thankful and grateful every day to all my readers, to everyone at my publisher, and to all the people who've assisted me.

This manga is a reworked version of a story that was released in the October 2003 edition of a BL magazine from the publisher Takeshobo. It was a story I brought to them soon after debuting. It was far too long, so they told me to write something shorter first, and I shelved it at the time. It's been several years since then, and I've been writing for Takeshobo, but I'm scheduled to move to Kodansha's *Young Magazine the 3rd* and be published there. I myself am not all that knowledgeable about ballroom dancing, so for *10 Dance* I wanted to avoid using technical terms as much as possible. There are also a few things I changed to work better from a manga perspective, so I hope that people who aren't familiar with ballroom dancing will still be able to enjoy reading it.

Chapter 1: 10 Dance

The title page shows Suzuki not understanding anything and making a mess of his hold as he drags Sugiki around, but to think the day would come when his colorful clothes would emit such bright white sparkles...

Chapter 2: *Moliendo Café* is a Samba

When my teacher saw the title page, they told me their very clear, specific impression, which was "he looks like one of the main characters from a battle anime, who uses attacks that use fire (but he's not the protagonist)." They're not wrong.

Chapter 3: A Clear Blue River Somewhere

I mistook the month that the International Championships are held by one month, so they are dressed rather warmly for October.

Chapter 4: Someday My King Will Come

My editor put in all the text for *Dance With* for me. It ended up looking quite realistic, which made me very happy.

Chapter 5: *Estrellita*

I've heard *Estrellita* played on a guitarra before, and it was poignant, so I used it as a chapter title here. It's meant to to be a mellow rumba. Suzuki's and Aki's hair has grown a bit compared to chapter 1.

...Special Thank Yous...

Ariga-sama, Kobato Uchida-sama, Minoru Chiaki-sama, Michi Aze-sama, Yoko Sano-sama, Yoko Tadano-sama, everyone in the *Young Magazine* Editorial Department, designer Fukumura-sama, Ota-sama, my teacher Inoue, my own U-chan, Yuki Uewaki-sama, Ran Shimoda-sama, Koichi Nishio-sama, Yumi Kojima-sama, my boss who waited patiently for me, and all my dear readers.

Inouesatoh

Translation Notes

Moliendo Café, page 4

The song *Moliendo Café* is known as *Coffee Rumba* in Japan, so this title is a play on the fact that a song called a rumba is, in fact, a samba.

Mr. Cha-cha-cha, page 19

In the Japanese, Sugiki calls Suzuki "Latino," here meaning "one who dances Latin Ballroom." As the meaning of and connotations are very different in the United States, the many uses of the word "Latino" have been adjusted to capture the spirit of the use in the Japanese.

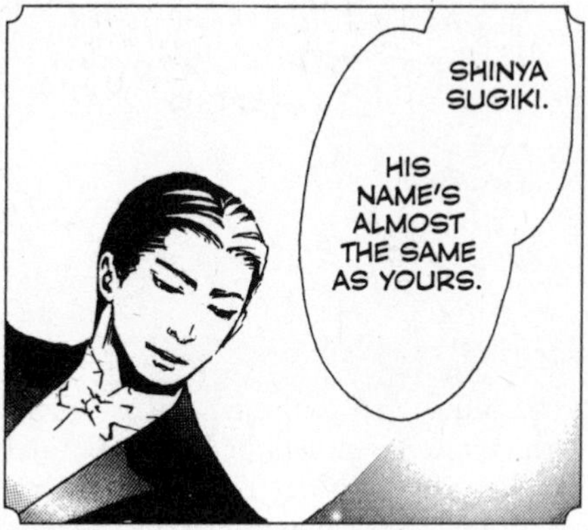
SHINYA SUGIKI.
HIS NAME'S ALMOST THE SAME AS YOURS.

Names, page 21

Both Shinyas have the same two kanji characters for their first names, and for the *ki* in their surnames. Only the *Sugi* and the *Suzu* kanji in their surnames are different.

Shadow dancing, page 57

Shadow dancing is practicing the dance steps by yourself, but as if you were dancing with a partner.

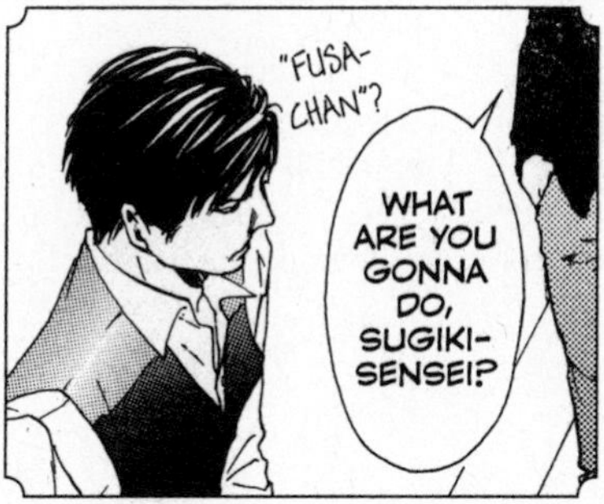
WHAT ARE YOU GONNA DO, SUGIKI-SENSEI?
"FUSA-CHAN"?

Fusa-chan, page 64

The Japanese language has a number of different suffixes for names, which are chosen and used based on the relationship between the speakers. The most common and polite suffix is *-san,* which is equivalent to "Mr./Ms./Mrs." in the U.S. Here, Suzuki uses the suffix *-chan* for Fusako, which is often used between female friends, or to refer to a woman or children with whom the speaker is close, as a cutesy term of endearment. By using *-chan* along with her first name, Suzuki is deliberately bending the social rules to create an easy feeling of closeness and familiarity, almost like using a nickname (thus Sugiki's surprise). Suffixes are only omitted in extreme cases of rudeness, or when the speakers are close enough to have foregone them (as in the case of Shinya and Aki, who refer to each other by their first names alone).

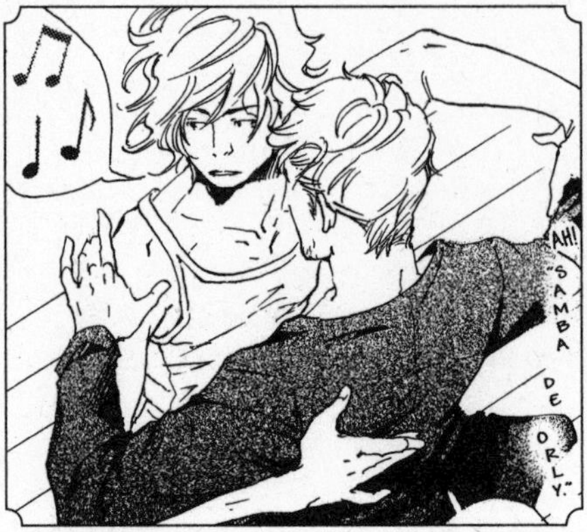
AH!
"SAMBA DE ORLY."

Samba de Orly, pages 81, 199

Samba de Orly is a samba by Chico Buarque, with the lyrics here in translation from the original Brazilian Portuguese. It is titled for Orly Airport in Paris, where many exiled Brazilian musicians and artists first arrived as they escaped the military dictatorship in their country in the 1960s.

PP, page 97

PP is short for promenade position, a specific position used in ballroom dancing.

Senshu, page 140

Urashima refers to the dancers as *-senshu*, which means "player," or "athlete." It's a polite term he's using to reference their position in the competitive dance world.

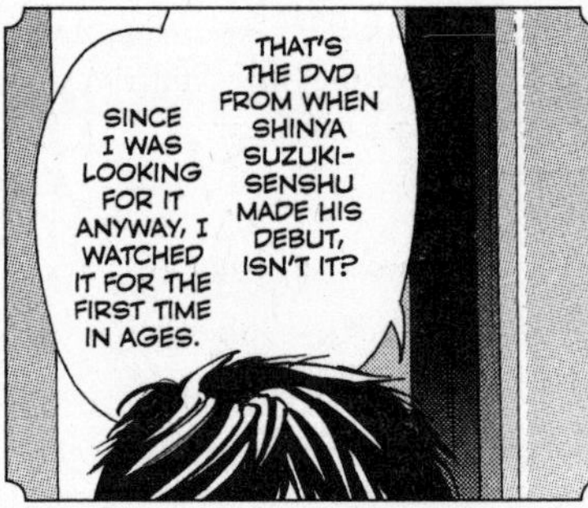
THAT'S THE DVD FROM WHEN SHINYA SUZUKI-SENSHU MADE HIS DEBUT, ISN'T IT?
SINCE I WAS LOOKING FOR IT ANYWAY, I WATCHED IT FOR THE FIRST TIME IN AGES.

Cover Flap Comic, page 215

The *ma-something-ko* word that Suzuki is actually trying to teach Sugiki is *manko*, a crass Japanese slang word that refers to a woman's genitals. However, for reasons known only to her, Yagami decides to tell Sugiki that the word is "*matsuko*" instead, a word which has no particular meaning of its own, and then has her own fun making up increasingly ridiculous sentences in which to use the word. This could refer to Matsuko Deluxe, who is a prominent cross-dressing entertainer in Japan.

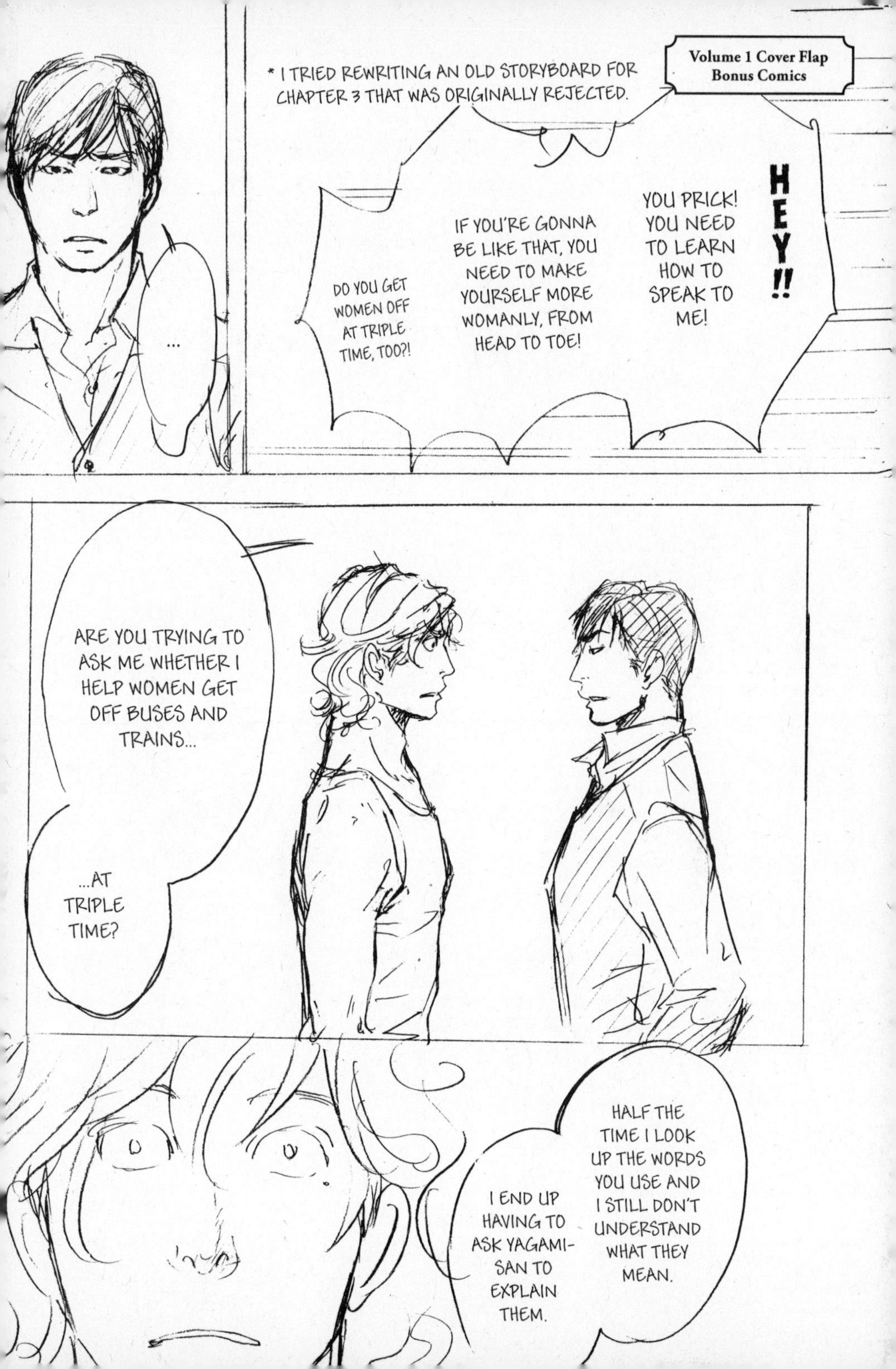
Volume 1 Cover Flap Bonus Comics
* I TRIED REWRITING AN OLD STORYBOARD FOR CHAPTER 3 THAT WAS ORIGINALLY REJECTED.
HEY!!
YOU PRICK! YOU NEED TO LEARN HOW TO SPEAK TO ME!
IF YOU'RE GONNA BE LIKE THAT, YOU NEED TO MAKE YOURSELF MORE WOMANLY, FROM HEAD TO TOE!
DO YOU GET WOMEN OFF AT TRIPLE TIME, TOO?!
...
ARE YOU TRYING TO ASK ME WHETHER I HELP WOMEN GET OFF BUSES AND TRAINS...
...AT TRIPLE TIME?
HALF THE TIME I LOOK UP THE WORDS YOU USE AND I STILL DON'T UNDERSTAND WHAT THEY MEAN.
I END UP HAVING TO ASK YAGAMI-SAN TO EXPLAIN THEM.

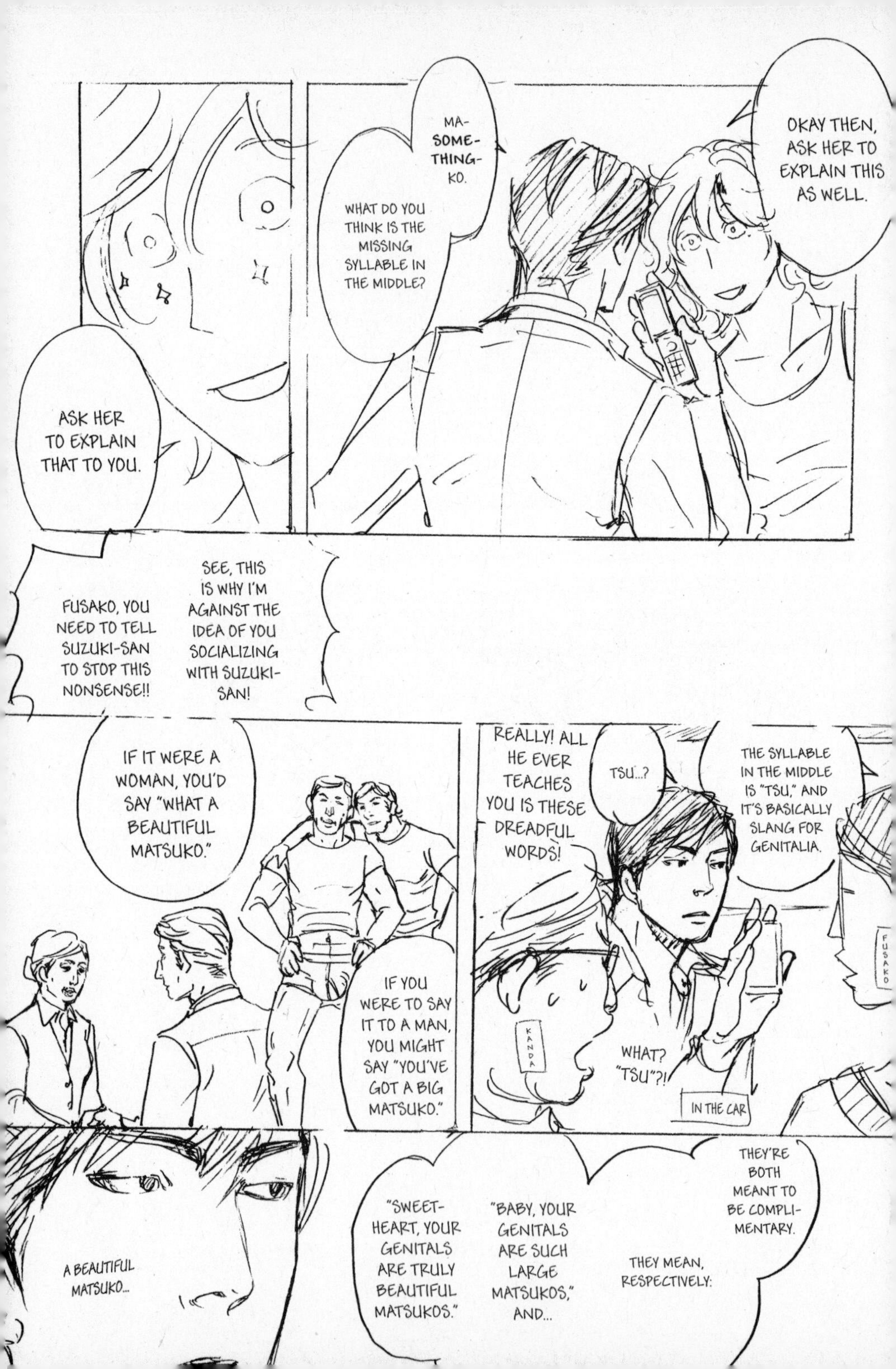
OKAY THEN, ASK HER TO EXPLAIN THIS AS WELL.
MA-SOMETHING-KO.
WHAT DO YOU THINK IS THE MISSING SYLLABLE IN THE MIDDLE?
ASK HER TO EXPLAIN THAT TO YOU.
SEE, THIS IS WHY I'M AGAINST THE IDEA OF YOU SOCIALIZING WITH SUZUKI-SAN!
FUSAKO, YOU NEED TO TELL SUZUKI-SAN TO STOP THIS NONSENSE!!
THE SYLLABLE IN THE MIDDLE IS "TSU," AND IT'S BASICALLY SLANG FOR GENITALIA.
TSU...?
REALLY! ALL HE EVER TEACHES YOU IS THESE DREADFUL WORDS!
FUSAKO
KANDA
WHAT? "TSU"?!
IN THE CAR
IF IT WERE A WOMAN, YOU'D SAY "WHAT A BEAUTIFUL MATSUKO."
IF YOU WERE TO SAY IT TO A MAN, YOU MIGHT SAY "YOU'VE GOT A BIG MATSUKO."
THEY'RE BOTH MEANT TO BE COMPLIMENTARY.
THEY MEAN, RESPECTIVELY:
"BABY, YOUR GENITALS ARE SUCH LARGE MATSUKOS," AND...
"SWEETHEART, YOUR GENITALS ARE TRULY BEAUTIFUL MATSUKOS."
A BEAUTIFUL MATSUKO...

"I'm pleasantly surprised to find modern shojo using cross-dressing as a dramatic device to deliver social commentary... Recommended."

-Otaku USA Magazine

The prince in his dark days

By **Hico Yamanaka**

A drunkard for a father, a household of poverty... For 17-year-old Atsuko, misfortune is all she knows and believes in. Until one day, a chance encounter with Itaru–the wealthy heir of a huge corporation–changes everything. The two look identical, uncannily so. When Itaru curiously goes missing, Atsuko is roped into being his stand-in. There, in his shoes, Atsuko must parade like a prince in a palace. She encounters many new experiences, but at what cost…?

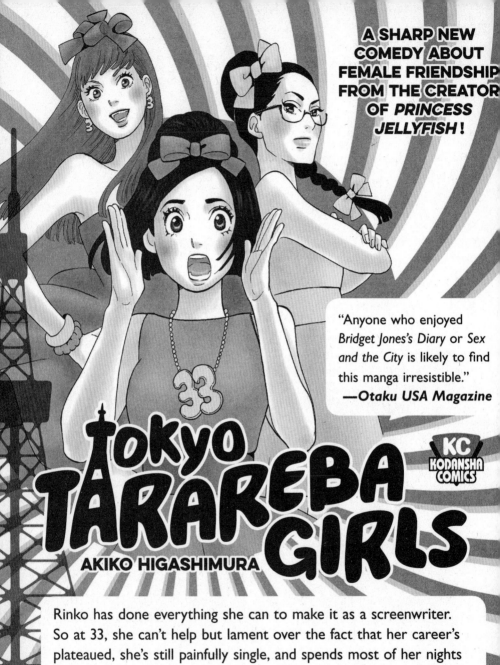

A SHARP NEW COMEDY ABOUT FEMALE FRIENDSHIP FROM THE CREATOR OF *PRINCESS JELLYFISH*!

"Anyone who enjoyed *Bridget Jones's Diary* or *Sex and the City* is likely to find this manga irresistible."
—Otaku USA Magazine

KC KODANSHA COMICS

Tokyo TARAREBA GIRLS

AKIKO HIGASHIMURA

Rinko has done everything she can to make it as a screenwriter. So at 33, she can't help but lament over the fact that her career's plateaued, she's still painfully single, and spends most of her nights drinking with her two best friends. One night, drunk and delusional, Rinko swears to get married by the time the Tokyo Olympics roll around in 2020. But finding a man—or love—may be a cutthroat, dirty job for a romantic at heart!

Princess Jellyfish

Akiko Higashimura

ALSO AN ANIME!

"One of the best manga for beginners!"
—*Kotaku*

Tsukimi Kurashita is fascinated with jellyfish. She's loved them from a young age and has carried that love with her to her new life in the big city of Tokyo. There, she resides in Amamizukan, a safe-haven for geek girls where no boys are allowed. One day, Tsukimi crosses paths with a beautiful and fashionable woman, but there's much more to this woman than her trendy clothes...!

KC KODANSHA COMICS

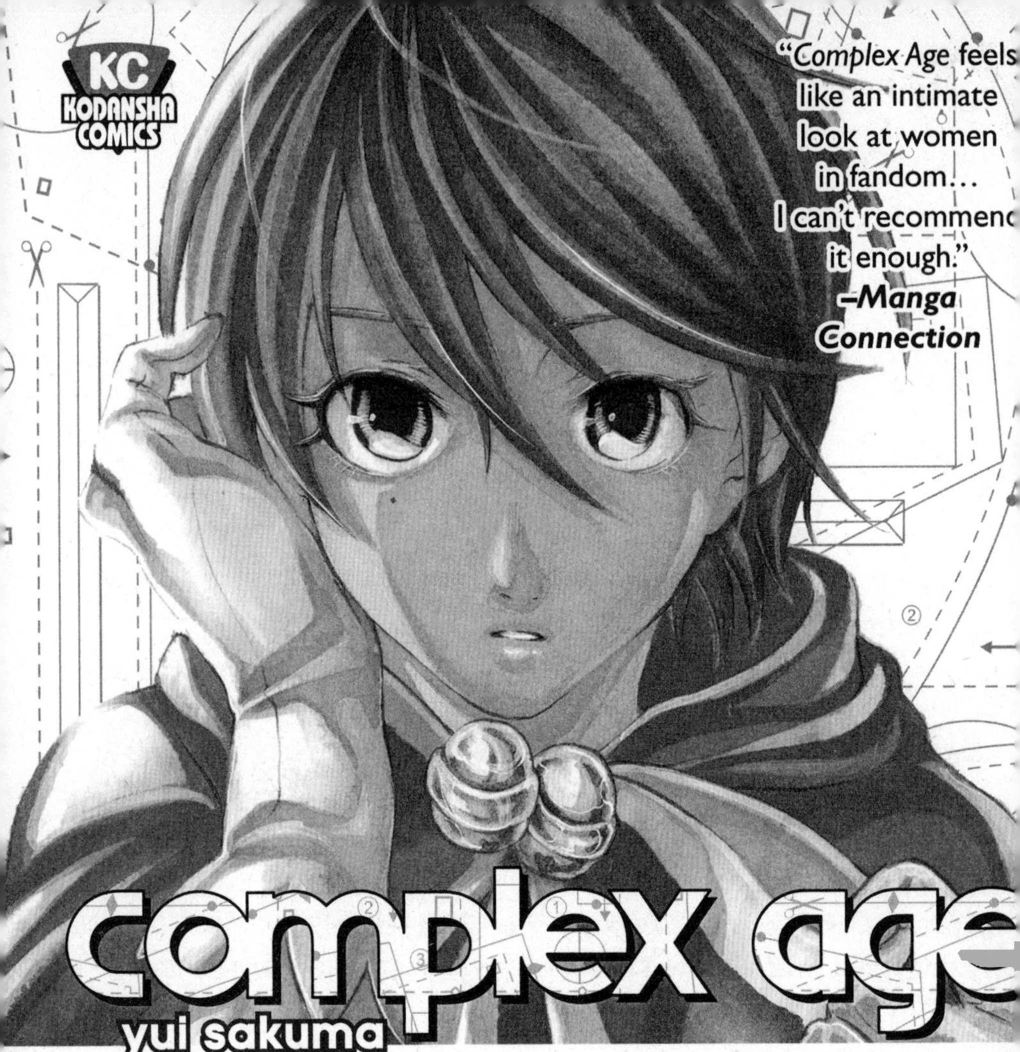
KC
KODANSHA COMICS
"Complex Age feels like an intimate look at women in fandom... I can't recommend it enough."
–Manga Connection
complex age
yui sakuma

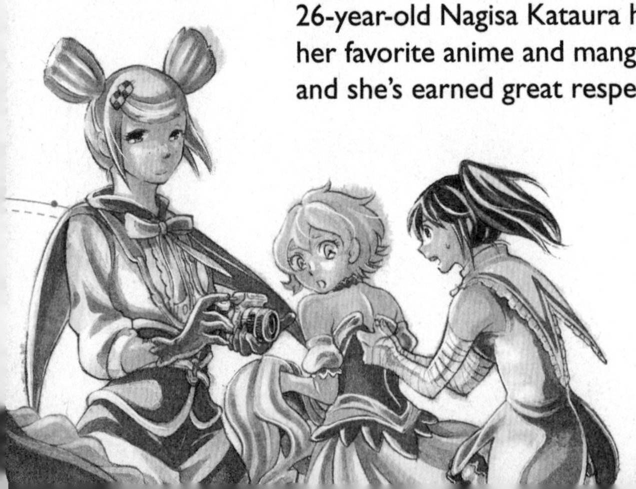

26-year-old Nagisa Kataura has a secret. Transforming into her favorite anime and manga characters is her passion in life and she's earned great respect amongst her fellow cospayers. But to the rest of society, her hobby is a silly fantasy. As demands from both her office job and cosplaying begin to increase, she may one day have to make a tough choice—what's more important to her: cosplay or being "normal"?

In love, there are no save points.

NOW AN ANIME!

ヲ
タ
ク
に
恋
は
難
し
い

WOTAKOI:
LOVE IS HARD FOR OTAKU
by FUJITA

Narumi has had it rough: Every boyfriend she's had dumped her once they found out she was an otaku, so she's gone to great lengths to hide it. At her new job, she bumps into Hirotaka, her childhood friend and fellow otaku. When Hirotaka almost gets her secret outed at work, she comes up with a plan to keep him quiet. But he comes up with a counter-proposal: Why doesn't she just date him instead?

WELCOME TO THE BALLROOM

By Tomo Takeuchi

Feckless high school student Tatara Fujita wants to be good at something—anything. Unfortunately, he's about as average as a slouchy teen can be. The local bullies know this, and make it a habit to hit him up for cash, but all that changes when the debonair Kaname Sengoku sends them packing. Sengoku's not the neighborhood watch, though. He's a professional ballroom dancer. And once Tatara Fujita gets pulled into the world of ballroom, his life will never be the same.

KC
KODANSHA COMICS

Again!!

Kinichiro Imamura isn't a bad guy, really, but on the first day of high school his narrow eyes and bleached blonde hair made him look so shifty that his classmates assumed the worst. Three years later, without any friends or fond memories, he isn't exactly feeling bittersweet about graduation. But after an accidental fall down a flight of stairs, Kinichiro wakes up three years in the past... on the first day of high school! School's starting again—but it's gonna be different this time around!

Vol. 1-3 now available in **PRINT** and **DIGITAL!**
Vol. 4 coming August 2018!

Find out **MORE** by visiting:
kodanshacomics.com/MitsurouKubo

ABOUT **MITSUROU KUBO**

Mitsurou Kubo is a manga artist born in Nagasaki prefecture. Her series *3.3.7 Byoshi!!* (2001-2003), *Tokkyu!!* (2004-2008), and *Again!!* (2011-2014) were published in *Weekly Shonen Magazine*, and *Moteki* (2008-2010) was published in the seinen comics magazine *Evening*. After the publication of *Again!!* concluded, she met Sayo Yamamoto, director of the global smash-hit anime *Yuri!!! on ICE*. Working with Yamamoto, Kubo contributed the original concept, original character designs, and initial script for *Yuri!!! on ICE*. *Again!!* is her first manga to be published in English.

Kodansha COMICS

Having lost his wife, high school teacher Kōhei Inuzuka is doing his best to raise his young daughter Tsumugi as a single father. He's pretty bad at cooking and doesn't have a huge appetite to begin with, but chance brings his little family together with one of his students, the lonely Kotori. The three of them are anything but comfortable in the kitchen, but the healing power of home cooking might just work on their grieving hearts.

"This season's number-one feel-good anime!" —Anime News Network

"A beautifully-drawn story about comfort food and family and grief. Recommended." —Otaku USA Magazine

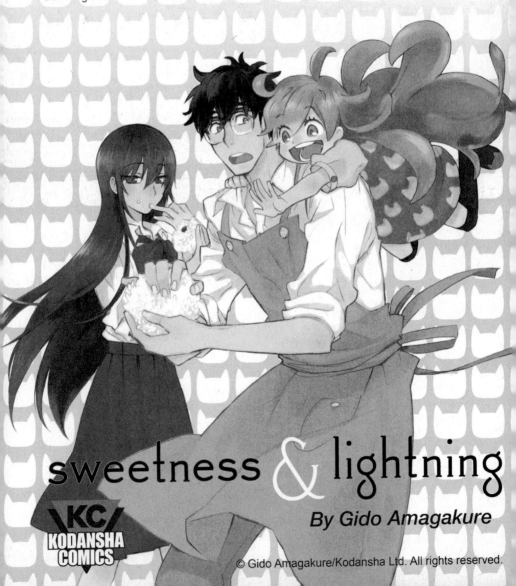

sweetness & lightning

By Gido Amagakure

KC
KODANSHA
COMICS

Japan's most powerful spirit medium delves into the ghost world's greatest mysteries!

Story by Kyo Shirodaira, famed author of mystery fiction and creator of *Spiral*, *Blast of Tempest*, and *The Record of a Fallen Vampire*.

Both touched by spirits called yôkai, Kotoko and Kurô have gained unique superhuman powers. But to gain her powers Kotoko has given up an eye and a leg, and Kurô's personal life is in shambles. So when Kotoko suggests they team up to deal with renegades from the spirit world, Kurô doesn't have many other choices, but Kotoko might just have a few ulterior motives...

IN/SPECTRE

STORY BY KYO SHIRODAIRA
ART BY CHASHIBA KATASE

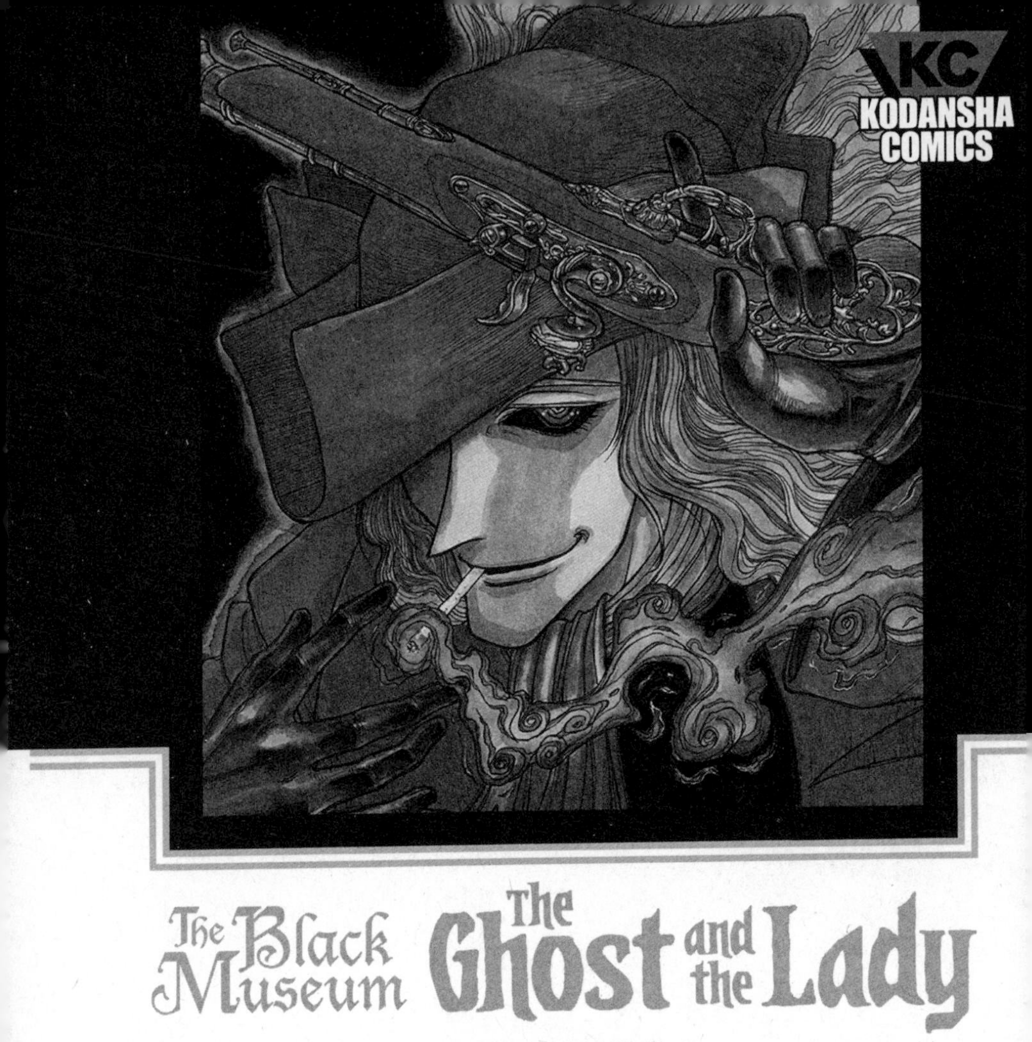
KC
KODANSHA
COMICS

The Black Museum The Ghost and the Lady

By Kazuhiro Fujita

Deep in Scotland Yard in London sits an evidence room dedicated to the greatest mysteries of British history. In this "Black Museum" sits a misshapen hunk of lead—two bullets fused together—the key to a wartime encounter between Florence Nightingale, the mother of modern nursing, and a supernatural Man in Grey. This story is unknown to most scholars of history, but a special guest of the museum will tell the tale of The Ghost and the Lady...

Praise for Kazuhiro Fujita's *Ushio and Tora*

"A charming revival that combines a classic look with modern depth and pacing... **Essential viewing both for curmudgeons and new fans alike.**" — Anime News Network

"**GREAT!** The first episode of Ushio and Tora captures the essence of '90s anime." — IGN

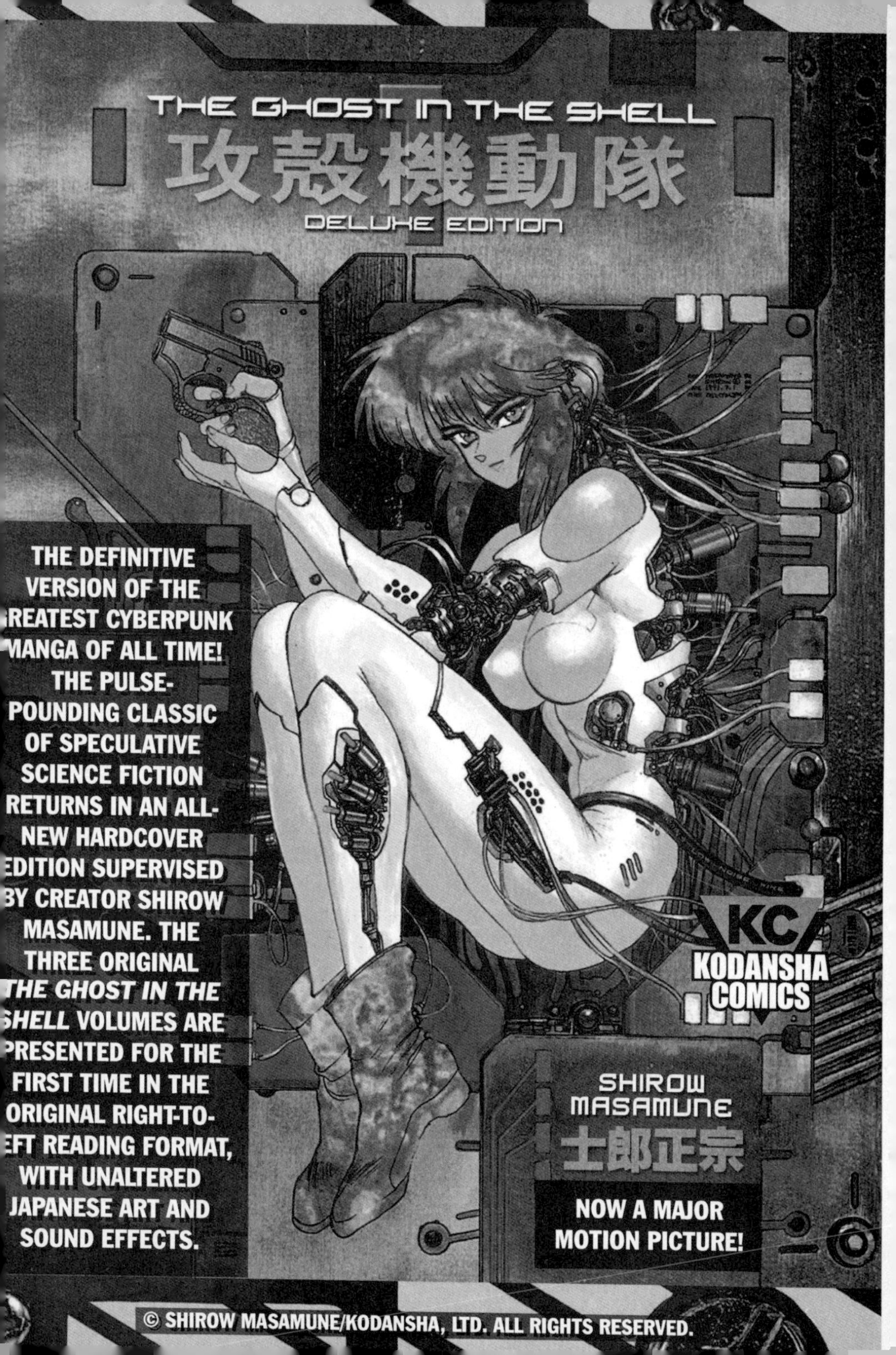
THE GHOST IN THE SHELL
攻殻機動隊
DELUXE EDITION
THE DEFINITIVE VERSION OF THE GREATEST CYBERPUNK MANGA OF ALL TIME! THE PULSE-POUNDING CLASSIC OF SPECULATIVE SCIENCE FICTION RETURNS IN AN ALL-NEW HARDCOVER EDITION SUPERVISED BY CREATOR SHIROW MASAMUNE. THE THREE ORIGINAL *THE GHOST IN THE SHELL* VOLUMES ARE PRESENTED FOR THE FIRST TIME IN THE ORIGINAL RIGHT-TO-LEFT READING FORMAT, WITH UNALTERED JAPANESE ART AND SOUND EFFECTS.
KC
KODANSHA COMICS
SHIROW MASAMUNE
士郎正宗
NOW A MAJOR MOTION PICTURE!
© SHIROW MASAMUNE/KODANSHA, LTD. ALL RIGHTS RESERVED.

KODANSHA COMICS

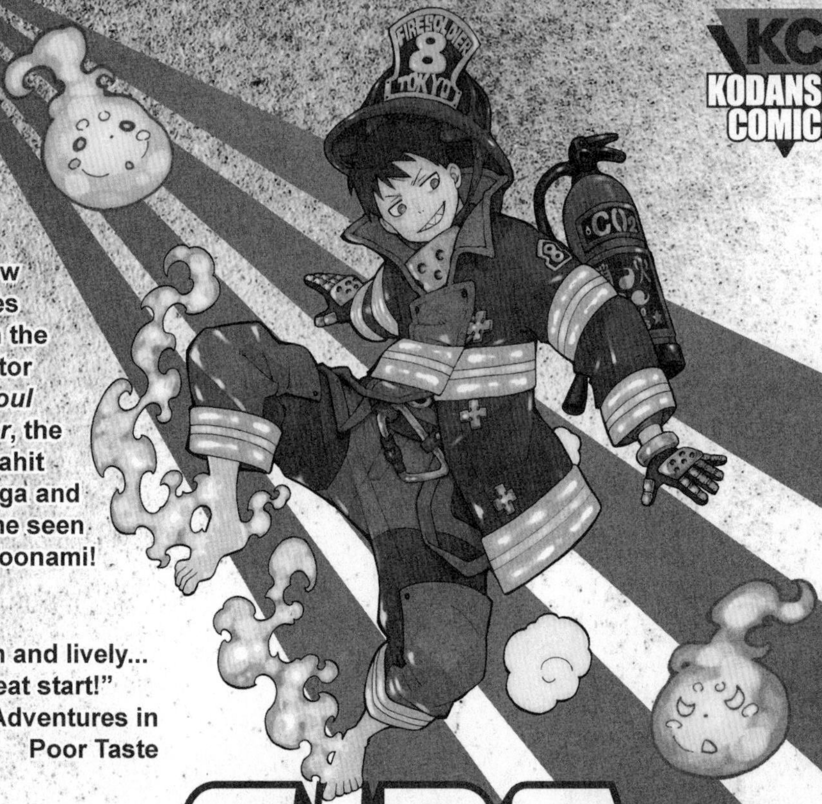
FIRE SOLDIER
8
TOKYO
CO_2

A new series from the creator of *Soul Eater*, the megahit manga and anime seen on Toonami!

"Fun and lively... a great start!"
-Adventures in Poor Taste

FIRE FORCE

By Atsushi Ohkubo

The city of Tokyo is plagued by a deadly phenomenon: spontaneous human combustion! Luckily, a special team is there to quench the inferno: The Fire Force! The fire soldiers at Special Fire Cathedral 8 are about to get a unique addition. Enter Shinra, a boy who possesses the power to run at the speed of a rocket, leaving behind the famous "devil's footprints" (and destroying his shoes in the process). Can Shinra and his colleagues discover the source of this strange epidemic before the city burns to ashes?

10 Dance volume 1 is a work of fiction. Names, characters, places, and incidents are the products of the author's imagination or are used fictitiously. Any resemblance to actual events, locales, or persons, living or dead, is entirely coincidental.

A Kodansha Comics Trade Paperback Original.

Published in the United States by Kodansha Comics, an imprint of Kodansha USA Publishing, LLC, New York.

Publication rights for this English edition arranged through Kodansha Ltd., Tokyo.

First published in Japan in 2017 by Kodansha Ltd., Tokyo.

ISBN 978-1-63236-765-5

Printed in the United States of America.

www.kodanshacomics.com

9 8 7 6 5 4 3

Translation: Karhys
Lettering: Brndn Blakeslee
Editing: Lauren Scanlan
Kodansha Comics Edition Cover Design: Phil Balsman